ian Film Directors Great Canadian Film Directors Great Canadian Film Directors Great Canadia

The University of Alberta Press

Great Canad

Great Canadian Film D

Edited by George Melnyk

Great Canadian Film Direct

Great Canadian Film Directors

Published by
The University of Alberta Press
Ring House 2
Edmonton, Alberta, Canada T6G 2E1

Copyright © The University of Alberta Press 2007

LIBRARY AND ARCHIVES CANADA CATALOGUING IN PUBLICATION

Great Canadian film directors / editor: George Melnyk.

Includes bibliographical references and index.
ISBN-13: 978-0-88864-479-4
ISBN-10: 0-88864-479-5

1. Motion picture producers and directors—Canada—Biography.
I. Melnyk, George

PN1998.2.G735 2007   791.4302'330922   C2006-906918-2

The University of Alberta Press is committed to protecting our natural environment. As part of our efforts, this book is printed on Enviro Paper: it contains 100% post-consumer recycled fibres and is acid- and chlorine-free.

The University of Alberta Press gratefully acknowledges the support received for its publishing program from The Canada Council for the Arts. The University of Alberta Press also gratefully acknowledges the financial support of the Government of Canada through the Book Publishing Industry Development Program (BPIDP) and from the Alberta Foundation for the Arts for its publishing activities.

This book has been published with the help of a grant from the Canadian Federation for the Humanities and Social Sciences, through the Aid to Scholarly Publications Programme.

Canada Council   Conseil des Arts
for the Arts   du Canada

Canadä

Contents

CONTEMPORARY GREATS

Introduction
Canadian Cinema and the Film Director

GEORGE MELNYK

UNLIKE HOLLYWOOD OR BOLLYWOOD with their star systems, Canadian cinema is director-driven like French and Italian cinema in their heyday and many other non-Hollywood cinemas. The reasons for this are rooted in Canada's cultural history as a colony, as well as its tradition of state support for cinema that ends up emphasizing directorial accomplishment. However, coming to a clear understanding of why Canadian directors are so crucial to the development of a distinct cinematic identity, both thematically and aesthetically, is the raison d'être of this book. By analyzing both the trajectory and the substance of a director's career and body of work, we come to a better understanding of the Canadian cultural psyche and its various paradigms based on nationality, race, gender, ethnicity, and class.

The Canadian feature film industry began slowly in the 1960s, mushroomed out of control in the 1970s, settled back in the 1980s, and since 1990 has become a small but powerful presence on Canadian screens, both theatrical and televised.[1] Current Canadian cinema is an integral part of

Canadian culture, but it has a relatively short history compared to other national cinemas. Today's multi-billion dollar industry is divided between location shooting for American films and indigenous product. Centred in Toronto, Vancouver, and Montreal, with smaller centres in Halifax, Winnipeg, and Calgary, the Canadian film industry long ago put aside its government-sponsored, National Film Board legacy of animation and documentaries. Even so, the feature film industry continues to be dependent on state support, now more than ever because of the limited audience for Canadian product. The main audience for Canadian cinema in English Canada is the art house cinema circuit, which involves only several dozen screens across the country. Occasionally an English-Canadian film is promoted through the mainstream theatres, but such a film is the exception that proves the rule. This is not the case in Quebec, especially since 2000 when Quebec French-language films started becoming a significant part of the film theatre experience. In recent years these films have occupied close to 25 per cent of screen time in Quebec, a figure that many national cinemas in the world never achieve.

This is the context in which the Canadian film director has risen as a cultural icon. The auteur director has been integral to the Canadian cinematic imagination and has served as its prime foundation. To present the Canadian director in such a fundamental role may seem strange to those for whom the director is simply a part of a larger, multi-person, creative mechanism, but in the Canadian context it is the surest way to understand how Canadian feature films have come to present distinctly English-Canadian and Quebeçois cultural grammars, resulting in Canada having two established national cinemas.[2] This claim does not diminish the work of talented actors, original screenwriters, award-winning cinematographers, perceptive producers, and risk-taking distributors in bringing a film to completion. However, this claim finds its foundation in the literary metaphor of the writer on whom the whole book industry rests. So, too, Canadian directors, because of the strong auteur tradition, have defined English Canada and Quebec because they speak out of their experience of the country and its peoples.

The adjective "great" carries a certain connotation that may not register with everyone when used to describe Canadian film directors. What is so great about these directors? Why are these directors considered great and others not? Both are valid questions. The concept of greatness when applied to the directors discussed in this book implies two things—first, that these directors are figures of artistic achievement comparable to those considered great in other national cinemas, and second, that these directors have made Canadian cinema something great in general cultural terms to a global audience. Of course, both claims are debatable. The argument for individual greatness and the argument for collective greatness do meld since they reflect each other. Without great films there is not great cinema and without great directors there are no great films. The directors in this book have all made one or more great films. This means that a particular film measures up to the criteria that are applied in general to films that are considered a contribution to the Canadian cinematic canon. It also means that Canada's now tri-lingual national cinema collectively represents a contribution to global cinema. Since 2000, Inuit language cinema is part of the cultural map. Because Zacharias Kunuk's Inuktituk-spoken *Atanarjuat: The Fast Runner* won the Cannes' Palme D'Or in 2001 and Denys Arcand's French-language *Barbarian Invasions* won an Oscar for Best Foreign Film in 2004, one can rightly claim that Canadian cinema has come of global age. The international celebrity status of such Canadian directors as David Cronenberg and Atom Egoyan only strengthens the argument. Canada does have great directors and so it has a great cinema, equal to other national cinemas that themselves have come of age in the past forty years. Canada's is now a cinema with a serious canon.

■ From Film to Text

WHEN THE AVANT-GARDE FRENCH FILM DIRECTOR Jean-Luc Godard exclaimed that "texts are death, images are life," he privileged the visual over the literary when it came to impact on the popular imagination.[3] He placed the human eye at the centre of our "reading" of both the verbal and the visual, and he made a single still from a moving picture worth a thousand words. The scholar and the critic do not create visual imagery; they only write words and create text, which Godard claimed was "death." In a way he is right. Most people would prefer to watch a film rather than read about it. Somehow the film seems life-affirming because of its emotional impact, while texts, especially critical as opposed to fictional ones, seem deadly because of their rational argumentation. One has only to compare a film with the text of a screenplay to visualize the difference. The critic always comes second to the artist, but if one is to enter a film more fully, "to see" what was in it that first impressions often miss, one requires analysis and understanding, thought rather than emotion. In the best critical writing the insights presented by the author can be stirring and exciting. This kind of writing can invigorate, surprise, and excite because its insights are revelatory, and revelation is an emotional experience. That is what this book attempts to achieve for the reader. It is meant to augment the viewing of films and bring that viewing to the level of informed reading. For Canadian readers, this volume is also meant to bring out a sense of cultural identity that may be buried or unarticulated in the Canadian collective subconscious, and for non-Canadian students of Canadian film it is meant to reveal the distinct elements of English-Canadian and Quebeçois culture and society, which are clearly their own. Additionally, Inuit feature film, which has developed an international audience, is itself a new cultural manifestation, comparable to such phenomenon as Maori-themed films from New Zealand.

■ The Directors and Their Critics

THIS TEXT CONTAINS essays on twenty Canadian film directors divided into three categories—the Late Greats, who are no longer with us but made an impact on Canadian film; the Contemporary Greats, who have a solid track record and are continuing to create; and the Future Greats, younger filmmakers who have been making films since 1995 and whose directorial careers have been heralded as ones of promise. Of course, the book does not cover every single outstanding feature film director in Canada. For example, two major figures from English-Canada who are not in this collection are Guy Maddin and Deepa Mehta. Nor are Denis Villeneuve and André Turpin from Quebec included in this volume. There are several reasons for this. First, inclusion of all the major figures would have made the book much too large. *Great Canadian Film Directors* is not meant to be comprehensive; it is meant to provide an informed sampling of directorial talent in Canada. Second, working within a one-year time line, contributors could not be found for every director of note, and using a longer time frame would have resulted in dating the material that had been written. The pressure of deadlines exists in scholarly publishing as well as other fields.

There are a variety of ways in which I, as the editor, could have grouped directors—by gender, nationality or region, genre, etc. I have chosen to provide a simple chronological framework (past, present, future) and within that framework place directors in alphabetical order, so that there is no judgement expressed as to which director is more important. Each director has her or his strengths and weaknesses, and it is up to the reader to draw her or his own conclusions. Audiences have their favourites, depending on their own taste and predilections, but this book is not about popularity or a hierarchy of talent or success. It is a book about notable talents of various kinds, working in various periods and in various genres of film.

The contributors to this collection are scholars, who range from those who are well-established and known for their work in Canadian cinema to doctoral students, those who are beginning their careers. This eclectic range of contributors, of whom 40 per cent are women and 60 per cent are men, indicates the disparity between the percentage of women and men directors in Canadian film. A third of this volume deals with female directors. Although males are the majority in the field, female directorial input in Canadian cinema is higher than that of most national cinemas, which increases its diversity. Together the contributors have written over 125,000 words on the work of Canadian film directors, highlighting the extent of material available for analysis and commentary and producing a major text in Canadian film studies, including helpful filmographies and selected bibliographies for further reading. While mainstream Canadian audiences find Canadian cinema *terra incognito*, this volume proves that the breadth and depth of Canadian cinema is outstanding. Its richness is a direct result of how and why feature films are made in Canada and of the fundamental role of directors in giving it a high artistic quality.

■ What is Argued

THIS TEXT DOES NOT PROVIDE a unified analytical critical discourse because it represents the diverse scholarly approaches of various academics. While there are certain conceptual frameworks provided by different schools of critical thinking that may be found in the essays, there is no overriding discourse that is privileged. Each and every approach has its critical validity and the text welcomes that fundamental diversity. It is for the reader and the critic to find both validity and issues with each contribution. That is what scholarly debate is all about.

Kay Armatage, in "Wieland's *The Far Shore* and Shipman's *Back to God's Country,*" highlights the contributions of early Canadian filmmaker Nell Shipman, who produced, directed, and acted in the silent era, and compares her accomplishments with the Ontario multimedia artist Joyce Wieland, who also directed a feature film, *The Far Shore*, in the 1970s. She concludes that the work of both filmmakers reflect a feminist perspective grounded in the periods they were working in.

David Clandfield, in "The Fatal Leap: Accessing the films of Claude Jutra through History and Symbol," writes about the entry points into the memorable and tragic career of the founding saint of modern Quebec cinema. Claude Jutra's *Mon Oncle Antoine* (1971) has often been voted as the best Canadian film of all time. Clandfield views Jutra's films as "parables of liberation."

Jim Leach's "'It Takes Monsters to do Things Like That': The films of Jean-Claude Lauzon" deals with another tragic Quebec filmmaker who made only two feature films before an early death. He approvingly considers Lauzon's two films—*Un Zoo la nuit* and *Léolo*—as "monstrous creations" that bring the fantasies of the subconscious to the screen in a profound and provocative way.

The first of the remarkable contemporary directors is discussed by Pierre Véronneau, who provides an astute overview of the work of Quebec's best-known director in "Denys Arcand: A Moralist in Search of his Audience." He argues that Arcand through his long career has created an audience for the Quebec story by fictionally documenting the evolving history of that national identity.

Arcand's equivalent in English-Canada is David Cronenberg, whose long, varied, and highly successful career is surveyed in my own "David Cronenberg: Mapping the Monstrous Male." I argue that Cronenberg should be viewed as a liberator of the Canadian consciousness, and a man who has fought a winning guerrilla war against the omnipotence of American cinematic culture through the curious tactic of embracing it in order to overcome its generic strictures.

William Beard's "Atom Egoyan: Unnatural Relations" is a study of English Canada's second most famous director (after Cronenberg). By exploring the "unique angle of vision" that he associates with this ethnic immigrant directors, Beard highlights Egoyan's contribution to art cinema.

In contrast to a mainstream figure like Egoyan, Christopher Gittings's "Activism and Aesthetics: The Work of John Greyson" deals with a lesser-known figure, whose "queer aesthetic shocks us out of the society of normalization" and broadens our perspective on Canadian cinema.

If Greyson represents the margins of Canadian feature filmmaking, then Norman Jewison represents its Hollywoodized side. In a revisionist treatment of Jewison's forty-plus years as a film director, Bart Testa rethinks Jewison as a "Canadian" filmmaker. "Norman Jewison, Homecoming for a 'Canadian Pinko'" finds the un-American elements in a career spent in mainstream Hollywood-style cinema.

Peter Dickinson, in "Double Take: Adpatation, Remediation, and Doubleness in the Films of Robert Lepage," finds Lepage to be "a master of the double take," who has created "a complex poetics of adaptation" that gives Quebec cinema a highly personal edge.

The English-Canadian version of Lepage may be Bruce McDonald, the "bad boy" of Canadian cinema, who is best known for his rock 'n roll road movie trilogy. With an edginess that matches that of Lepage, McDonald's roller-coaster career is analyzed by Aaron Taylor in "Straight Outta' Hogtown: Sex, Drugs, and Bruce McDonald."

Jennifer Gauthier's "Living In/Between: The Cinema of Léa Pool" studies another immigrant filmmaker who made Quebec her home after emigrating from Switzerland. Gauthier focuses on the transition from directing French language films to more recent ones in English.

Another important woman filmmaker in Canada is Patricia Rozema. Brenda Austin-Smith follows her progress in "Woman with a Movie Camera: Patricia Rozema's Revisionist Eye" in which she discusses the "artist-figure" motif as central to her work.

Continuing the discussion of distinguished female directors is Jacqueline Levitin's "Mina Shum: the 'Chinese' Films and Identities," which takes an in-depth look at the films of this Vancouver-based director of Chinese origin. She concludes that in Shum's films "identity is presented as performed identity" in which ethnicity is seen as a response responding to the constructs of a dominant, non-ethnic environment.

Patricia Gruben's "A Problem with Rules: Gary Burns" deals with another non-central Canadian director, Gary Burns of Calgary. According to Gruben, Burns "shares a broad aesthetic...with other filmmakers of his generation" who grew up in suburban North America, which allows him to speak to a North American youth audience.

Another Calgarian filmmaker is Michael Dowse, whose two feature films are dissected by Bart Beaty in "Coward, Bully and Clown: The Dream-Life of Michael Dowse." Beaty confirms Gruben's argument about Burns by stating that fellow Calgarian, Michael Dowse, "highlights the growing realization that nationalist conceptions of cinema are outmoded and insufficient." This mirrors Gruben's view that a globalized and continentalized consciousness has rooted itself in the Calgary psyche.

Moving across the country to the Maritimes, Sally Chivers and Nicole Markotić combine their efforts in "The Problem Body in Thom Fitzgerald's Films." These authors show how this American immigrant to Nova Scotia has been able to "push against the edges of social propriety when depicting physical difference," while dealing with Maritime characters and culture.

A breakthrough in Canadian cinema occurred in 2001 with the release of the first Inuit-language feature film in cinema history—*Atanarjuat: The Fast Runner*. "Zach Kunuk and Inuit Filmmaking" by Jerry White provides insights into the role of video in liberating non-Anglo and non-French filmmakers to tell their stories in their own languages.

The volume concludes with two young filmmakers—one from Toronto and the other from Vancouver. Paul Salmon's "Don McKellar: Artistic

Polymath" deals not only with the two films he directed, but also his lengthy career as an actor and screenwriter. Of the same generation is Lynne Stopkewich, originally from allophone Montreal, who has also made two feature films, including the striking debut about necrophilia titled *Kissed*. "Lynne Stopkewich: Abject Sexualities" by Kalli Paakspuu provides valuable details about the process that young filmmakers in Canada endure in order to make films.

■ What Remains

IT IS CLEAR from the range of filmmakers discussed here that diversity is the key element in Canadian cinema. First, there is the grand division into English and French filmmaking that has endured for over forty years, and which has resulted in the evolution of two national cinemas employing different basic metaphors, symbolic grammars, and themes. Second, there is the division that separates male and female directors and their thematic approaches, which has given Canadian cinema complementary but differing views of the human condition. The strength of female directorial talent means that female characterization has been vibrant, informed with feminist perspectives, and uncompromising. Third, the decentralized nature of the Canadian industry (and the federal government's Telefilm funding mandate) has allowed a diversity of regional voices to augment the pull of central Canadian production. Fourth, there has been a welcome mix of multicultural and minority consciousness in Canadian cinema that has allowed a diversity of voices in narrative cinema that somewhat captures the national mosaic. Fifth, and most important, is the creation of a directorial tradition in Canadian cinema. The success of previous generations of Canadian directors in making names for themselves in the industry since the 1960s has meant that there are always new people coming along to direct Canadian films, in spite of the major obstacles that exist.

We are now into the third generation of Canadian filmmakers. The first wave is represented by names like Claude Jutra; the second wave is represented by names like Patricia Rozema; and the latest wave is the generation of Michael Dowse. Canadian cinema may not have much of a star system, but its directors are important role models for upcoming players in an enterprise where creative talent, business acumen, and dogged perseverance are required.

NOTES

1. English-Canadian films occupy less than two per cent of theatrical release screen time. Quebec films in the past 15 years have varied from 5 to 25 per cent of the Quebec screens.
2. Since 2000, an Inuit language (Inuktitut)-based feature film industry has emerged (Kunuk's *Atanarjuat: The Fast Runner* [2001]) giving Canada a third national cinema.
3. *Libération*, 2 May 1980. Quoted in David Sterrit, ed. *Jean-Luc Godard: Interviews* (Jackson: Mississippi University Press, 1998) 14.

Late Greats

1

Wieland's Far Shore and Shipman's God's Country

KAY ARMATAGE

ALTHOUGH THEIR PERIODS OF PRODUCTION were separated by more than a half century and the industrial conditions under which the film-makers worked show marked differences, *Back to God's Country* (Nell Shipman, 1919) and *The Far Shore* (Joyce Wieland, 1976) have been compared regularly.[1] Barbara Martineau was the first of many to mention Nell Shipman in relation to Joyce Wieland.[2] Why? What do these films have in common? What are the elements that have so insistently instantiated their comparison? Briefly, both films are considered works by Canadian women filmmakers; both are set in Canada and in the same period.[3] Central paradigms in comparative analyses include the treatments of landscape and nature, melodrama as a narrative mode, nationality and nation, and the gender analytic in its encounter with women protagonists.

However, it is high time to interrogate those rubrics across both films and to consider particularly *The Far Shore* as a work of great beauty and sagacity.

■ Career Trajectories and Canonical Status

CANADIAN-BORN Nell Shipman (1892–1970) started her career as a touring Vaudeville actor but was soon installed in the burgeoning film industry in California. She wrote her first screenplay in 1912 and directed her first one-reeler in 1914. Although she performed a variety of roles as a Vitagraph contract player, in 1915 she starred in a wilderness adventure film that earned her the sobriquet "the girl from God's country." *Back to God's Country* (1919) was her greatest success, after which she started her own independent company, Nell Shipman Productions, in which she produced, wrote, edited and starred in a series of genre films. In the beginning, they were decently large-budget productions, but eventually she sold "short subjects" to a distributor who specialised in children's films. Her company eventually went bankrupt in 1925.

Unlike Shipman, who began her career in films in the industrial environment of California but eventually turned to an artisanal mode of production for her last films, Joyce Wieland (1931–98)—following a brief stint as an animator—carved out a niche in the structural avant-garde with her kitchen table-top films. After she became known as a director of short films and an experimental feature, *Reason Over Passion* (1968), Wieland wrote and directed *The Far Shore* (1976), a large-budget period drama produced through the industrial apparatus of Canada's incipient commercial film culture. Feature film production had only recently begun in Canada when Wieland wrote and directed *The Far Shore*. It was a rare species in Canada, not only as a dramatic feature by a woman director, but also as a genre film that aimed for a popular audience.

After devastating appraisals and dismal box office receipts for *The Far Shore*, Wieland's next project, a dramatization of the canonical novel, *The Diviners* by Margaret Laurence (1974), never got off the ground.[4] Wieland retreated from filmmaking for nearly a decade, only returning to complete a few of her earlier unfinished experimental films. Like Shipman's, Wieland's aspirations in narrative feature filmmaking came to an end.

The similarities of the career finales of the two filmmakers notwithstanding, the status of Shipman and Wieland in the cinematic canon has been differentially marked particularly by inscriptions of gender.

In her lifetime, Shipman was denied the avails of the Motion Picture Relief Fund, an organization that assisted veterans of the film industry, on the grounds that she had not had a substantial career after 1929. Nevertheless, she has been rescued for posterity by the "women pioneers" scholarship project, which in the past ten years has become a veritable flood of academic publications. Thus Shipman's filmmaking career has been canonized as a model of artisanal independent production, doomed by the industrial machinations of Hollywood in its formative years. She is ensconced now in film history as a heroic figure, producing, writing, editing, and starring in her own independent productions; eking out a living under penurious circumstances; and carrying on with ever more grandiose production dreams until the end of her life. *Back to God's Country* is taught in virtually every Canadian film course and shown regularly in retrospectives of Canadian cinema.

Wieland's legacy has been inscribed quite differently, however, not only in her lifetime but also in the ensuing three decades of Canadian canon formation. In its time, despite a nomination in the "best movie" category of the Canadian Film Awards in the year of its release as well as polite puff pieces in art magazines and local newspapers, *The Far Shore* was cited generally as a disaster: superficial in characterization, too highly romanticised, confusing in its mix of comedy and melodrama, inconsistent mood, "crass screenplay and onerous direction," blatant symbolism, narrative incongruities, uneven performances, and failure to provide narrative tension.[5] "Beautiful but flat" was one review headline; "rather dull," declared another. Even the film's editor publicly criticized *The Far Shore*, saying, "I would have liked to have shortened many of the scenes. For example, the love scene in the water should have been played as an impression rather than an actuality."[6] Wieland rose to defend the film, arguing that, although precise in historical detail, its intention was not "realistic."[7] Citing her admiration for women actors and directors of the silent era, such as Lillian Gish, Wieland said that she hoped the film would play to matinee audiences of ordinary people who would be moved to tears by the vicissitudes of Canada (illustrated by the ill-fated love affair between a Québecoise and an English-speaking Canadian), the ravages of industrialism on the environment, and the tragedy of a great

Canadian artist.[8] The judgment of one critic revealed the unspoken prejudices of most of the reviews: she dismissed the film as "cloyingly feminine."[9]

The Far Shore was doubly damned. Wieland had stepped boldly out of the small-scale artisanal production mode that was indispensable to the avant-garde to direct a period feature in 35mm with sumptuous settings and costumes, vintage automobiles, recognized Canadian actors, multiple locations, and a melodramatic narrative.[10] Her former supporters in the structural avant-garde turned their backs on the film on account of its mainstream ambitions. Neither was the film able to find contemporary acceptance amongst women scholars, for, in the mid-1970s, feminist film theory was firmly in the grip of the thrill of negativity, which vigorously—and, for Wieland, ironically—advocated anti-narrative, anti-realist, avant-garde structuralism as the appropriate cinematic mode for feminist expression. Wieland later recalled that at the avant-garde film event at the 1976 Edinburgh International Film Festival, where The Far Shore was exhibited along with Wieland's and then-husband Michael Snow's experimental works, her former friends and champions couldn't look her in the eye.[11]

There were some latter-day reassessments of The Far Shore, to be sure. Opposing contemporary trends, Lauren Rabinowitz considered the film at length in Women, Power, and Politics in the New York Avant-Garde Cinema, 1943–71 (1991), the publication of her 1982 dissertation on Wieland, Maya Deren, and Shirley Clarke. In the first scholarly examination of The Far Shore, Rabinowitz set the agenda for feminist discussion, situating the film as a family melodrama and emphasizing its integration of experimental techniques and Hollywood genre conventions as offering new expressive possibilities for women filmmakers.[12] A few years later (1984), in a piece on silence as a cinematic strategy, Seth Feldman judged The Far Shore to be the "most innovative" Canadian film as it used silence to subvert both spoken and cinematic language.[13] In the same year, Peter Morris described the film as "unfairly maligned" and asserted, on the contrary, that it is "formal in conception, deliberate in its innocence, flagrant symbolism and portrayal of Canadian myths, and the most complete expression of Joyce Wieland's artistic sensibility."[14] On the occasion of the retrospective of Wieland's work (Art Gallery of Ontario,

1987), Susan Crean argued that the fault lay not with the film but with audiences who could not adequately "read."[15] Writing from London, UK, in 1988, Michael O'Pray suggested that *The Far Shore* not only looked more interesting than it did ten years before but was also prophetic of feminist feature filmmaking.[16]

In 1993 Joan Nicks examined its pictorial representation of death, comparing it to the acclaimed Québecois feature, *J. A. Martin, Photographe* (Jean Beaudin, 1977).[17] With the exception of Nicks, all of these reassessments appeared in the 1980s.

In more recent scholarly literature, *The Far Shore* has languished in obscurity.[18] Most of the publications from the 1990s emphasized Wieland's significance as an avant-garde filmmaker, returning to her earlier short films (especially *Sailboat*, *Water Sark*, *Hand-Tinting*, *Rat Life and Diet in North America*) and to the experimental feature *Reason Over Passion*.[19]

Recent considerations of Canadian cinema have assiduously ignored both Wieland and the film. Katherine Monk's *Weird Sex & Snowshoes* (2001) mentions neither, and, despite a section on melodrama, nor does Christopher Gittings's *Canadian National Cinema* (2002). *A Postmodern Cinema: The Voice of the Other In Canadian Film*, by Mary Alemany-Galway (2002), doesn't include Wieland. And George Melnyk's *One Hundred Years of Canadian Cinema* (2004) refers to *The Far Shore* on one page. In these recent texts, *The Far Shore* doesn't make it into the Canadian canon.

Shipman and Wieland: Modes of Production, Genre, Landscape

As cinematic texts, *Back to God's Country* and *The Far Shore*, at least at the outset, have in common the broad strokes of their loving evocation of the Canadian wilderness landscape, unusual heroines, and particularly their melodramatic structures (although in opposite modes). Their divergences from each other, however, as narratives and cinematic texts, far outweigh their similarities.

Their production exigencies were separated by more than half a century and their directors worked in markedly different industrial conditions. *Back to God's Country* (1919) was financed by a Hollywood studio and private Canadian investors in a period of independent production, whereas the funding of *The Far Shore* (1976) was provided by the Canadian government, allowing Wieland to hire the best of Canadian practitioners in all key positions.[20]

While Shipman's film was an adaptation of a short story by an American (James Oliver Curwood), which buttressed itself on a mythical Canadian wilderness made famous by the best-selling novels of Zane Grey and Jack London, Wieland's was an original script that seized on a Canadian myth, the death of a well-known indigenous artist (Tom Thomson) who mysteriously perished without a trace. The plot pivoted on a love story between Québecois and English-speaking Canadians, an utopian tale of the national imaginary.

While both films are classic melodramas, they operate in opposing dramatic traditions. *Back to God's Country* functions within the comedic mode: adventure and romance, riven with tension-producing vicissitudes, find closure in a happy ending. The film tells the story of a forest lass who falls for Peter Burke, a government cartographer. The narrative introduces Dolores (Shipman), who lives with her father in a log cabin in the forest. In an early "money shot" she is seen frolicking with a large grizzly bear. Enter the villains. After killing her father, they are temporarily forced out of the picture as Dolores escapes their evil designs, marries Peter, and moves to the city. But she always dreams of going back to her "forest home," and finally Dolores and Peter make a return journey.

Here the meat of the story unfolds. As it turns out, the ship on which Dolores and her husband are travelling back to "God's country" is moored for the winter, and the ship's captain is the rapacious villain from the earlier episode. Moreover, the dastardly captain is in league with the manager of the trading post, an owner of a vicious dog. When Peter is accidentally injured and the trading post manager abets the captain to threaten her virtue, Dolores is forced into intrepid-heroine mode to rescue her husband and defeat the villains. She is assisted by the killer dog, which has been miraculously gentled by "the touch of a woman's hand" (intertitles). After a 150-mile dogsled chase and escape, Dolores and her husband arrive at Fort Constance, where Peter returns to health.

Situating itself within the conventions of the serial queen melodramatic adventure film, the narrative produces the female protagonist as heroic rescuer, saving her husband and defeating the villains. After a series of spectacular set-pieces, including the famous nude swimming scene and many hair-raising travails featuring attempted assaults on her virtue and the inevitable chase-and-rescue, the dénouement depicts Dolores's patriarchal bliss in a comfortable log cabin with her husband, the dog, and a new baby, back in the edenic forest where they belong. Happy ending, as befits the genre of melodramatic adventure.

In contrast, *The Far Shore* is a classic melodramatic weepy, a tragic tale of star-crossed lovers. Eulalie, a beauteous Québecoise, settles for marriage with an English-Canadian industrialist who whisks her to his home in Toronto. His Victorian mansion and crass aesthetic sensibility stifle her cultured modernism, but here she meets an as-yet-unappreciated artist (a fictional character based on iconic Canadian artist Tom Thomson), with whom she forms an inevitable bond.

In the summer, Tom goes off to paint the northern wilderness, which Eulalie's churlish husband sees only as a resource to be mined. That same season, vacationing with her husband at a magnificent rustic cottage, Eulalie spots Tom gliding by in his canoe and spontaneously dives into the water to join him. Nevertheless, although consummated in the magnificent lake-country landscape, their love is not to be. After an extended chase by canoe, the lovers, pursued by Eulalie's husband and his friend, the unfortunate lovers end in death. Tragic ending—an altogether different melodramatic mode.

Nation

Although she was born in British Columbia and her first husband was Canadian (Ernest Shipman), Nell Shipman moved with her family to the US when she was twelve. She made her living as an actor, screenwriter, and director in the US. Although Canadian scholars have claimed her as our own, Shipman returned to Canada only briefly on a research expedition, declared the wilderness of Idaho to be "her *ultima thule*,"[21] and lived out both her successes and failures in the US. Although she returned fictionally to "God's Country"—a signifier of Canada in these films—in a sequel (*The Girl from God's Country*, 1922, now lost), her films as writer-director-star were shot in Washington, California, and Idaho.

In *Back to God's Country*, the sole signifier of the protagonist's Canadianism is her stylish coat made from a four-point Hudson's Bay Company blanket. Later, both the Canadian garment and the Alberta location were excised from the Hollywood remake (starring Rock Hudson, 1953), which was set in Alaska but shot on Hollywood back-lots.

Wieland, in contrast, briefly carved out her career as an experimental filmmaker in New York but returned to Canada in 1971 for her greatest artistic achievements. From the *True Patriot Love* exhibition (National Gallery of Canada, 1971) and for many years thereafter, she took Canada as her subject. Wieland's championship of Pierre Elliott Trudeau is legendary, from her *Reason over Passion/La Raison Avant la Passion* quilts, to the Ontario sequence in the film *Reason over Passion* (1967–69). She devoted many of her artworks to Canadian themes, including the knitted flags, delicately embroidered replicas of letters between Woolf and Montcalm, "Sweet Beaver" perfume, and the evocation of Canada as ecological paradise in *Rat Life and Diet in North America* ("No D.D.T"). In *Reason over Passion,* she documented the country from coast to coast, and in her feature drama, *The Far Shore*, she took on a plethora of issues, including Canada as a nation of two cultures, the wealth of its natural resources, the promises of modernity, and a pivotal moment in the history of Canadian art.

Despite their narratives sharing the same period setting, the visions of Canada central to both films could not contrast more markedly. *God's Country*—always a trope for wilderness Canada in Shipman's films, as in the (American) James Oliver Curwood story on which the film is based—features a primitive but cozy cabin in the forest (shot in California) replete with tame wild animals (including—inexplicably—a burro), on the one hand, and the isolated outposts of the Alberta barren lands on the other. This landscape is peopled by pioneers, explorers, Mounties, callow "half-breeds," mendacious fur traders, and rapacious ship captains. Dogsled is the principal travelling vehicle.

Wieland's Canada in *The Far Shore* is far more complex than usually described. It includes Quebec farmlands, the wealthy urban Rosedale neighbourhood of Toronto, and Northern Ontario lake country—terrains that are peopled with modern entrepreneurs and artists and traversed by automobile and canoe. While protagonist Eulalie may stand for French Canada, as a character she diverges significantly from the cliché version of the Québécoise found as often in classic films from French Canada as in those from English Canada. Eulalie's rural roots are suggested in the opening scenes of the film, but, as it turns out, she is not the earthy nurturer of, for example, *La Vraie Nature de Bernadette* (Gilles Carle, 1972), whose protagonist moves to the countryside to consort with radical farmers and make some old men very happy

Eulalie's lover, a thinly fictionalized Tom Thomson, who first exhibited his paintings in 1913, is not only the quintessential Canadian artist, but also the harbinger of the post-colonial period in Canadian art. Although Thomson died before the inception of the Group of Seven as a movement, he is regularly associated with them. They were part of the Canada First movement, which insisted that Canadian artists should break away from the old European styles and paint their country in a novel way. Unlike other previous Canadian artists who had sought instruction in Europe, Thomson was self-taught and, in keeping with the future members of the Group of Seven, he refused to accept European art as superior to Canadian art. Thomson shunned the delicate styles of the dominant art scene of the early twentieth century, preferring instead raw, heavily impasto brush-work to convey the vibrancy of his subjects.

Thus Tom and Eulalie not only come from different linguistic cultures but also from conflicting aesthetic formations. While Tom, an English-Canadian naturalist, significantly diverges from European styles in his paintings, Eulalie is an educated Québécoise and a lover of European modernism from her taste in music to her fashionable orientalist boudoir apparel (the garb of the moment in Paris). Yet she is moved to return to her cultural roots when she teaches Tom a traditional French-Canadian folk tune. With Thomson's ground-breaking experimentalist painting *The Jack Pine* in the background, the scene is imbued, as well, with post-modernist rejections of distinctions between "high" and "low" art. Similarly, Tom and Eulalie's love affair is a utopian denial of cultural difference. That Wieland's vision is idealistic cannot be denied, but it is far from the cliché notions of Canadian federalist unity.

In this way, *The Far Shore* is consistent with the complexity of Wieland's treatment of Canada as a nation and Canadian nationalism in her other work. *Reason over Passion*, for example, was interpreted as sentimentally nationalistic by some, repeatedly offering chauvinistic national totems (the Canadian flag) in a travelogue that is "a veritable pasture of expansive landscape imagery...a clutter of love for Canada, done in the nick of time before it changes completely into a scrubby Buffalo suburb."[22] The "Ontario" section of the film, which substituted images of Pierre Elliot Trudeau for the Upper Canada landscape, has been described as naively celebratory and iconizing. Such readings, however, can surface only at the expense of the symmetricality of the construction of the film, its highly abstracted imagery, and the multitudinous experimental innovations of its exploration of cinematic perception. Ironies and ambiguities abound in *Reason Over Passion*, as in Wieland's work in all media.

Kass Banning's argument on *The Far Shore* suggests the inadequacy of past conceptual frameworks to deal with the issues of nation that Wieland's work consistently poses, specifically the demythologization of identity, naming, and representation. "All of Wieland's texts" Banning contends, "demand a closer reading; they raise problems, directly or indirectly, of all sorts—historiographic, aesthetic and political—which demand revision."[23]

Protagonists, Treatment of Landscape

Neither do the characterizations of the female protagonists bear significant similarities to one other. In *Back to God's Country*, Dolores is an fearless nature girl who cavorts with a giant bear, swims naked in an idyllic pool, drives a dogsled, and wields a gun to rescue the hapless hero. Eulalie, the protagonist of *The Far Shore*, is a delicate beauty who, despite her fabulous wardrobe, moulders in depression playing Debussy at the grand piano in her mansion. She has scant need of Dolores's wilderness acumen, as her sojourn at the lake finds her in a magnificent Muskoka-style heritage "cottage" until, of course, she joins the painter in his tent, where he is the master of life skills for the wilds. She swims, too, but fully clothed.

The cinematic treatments of the landscape also diverge. The representation of the snowfields in *Back to God's Country* constructs a haptic space of flattened wide shots, sufficient in the chase scene to include both dogsleds—pursued and pursuers—which appear as miniscule strings of dots in the bright white frame that offers no distinction between land and sky. Wieland's landscapes, on the other hand, are rendered in low-angle shots that privilege the swaying grasses of Quebec, the magnificent pines of the northern Ontario forest, and the petroglyphs on the lakeside cliffs. In *The Far Shore*, the chase scene by canoe is managed in close-ups and medium shots with conventional cross-cutting. The cinematic modes not only suggest differing aesthetics and conventions, but also diverse responses to the landscape: barren emptiness versus lush monumentality.

■ Modernity and Nation

BOTH FILMS CONCERN THEMSELVES with Canada's entry into modernity. However, although set in almost identical periods—*Back to God's Country* was made in 1919; Tom Thomson died in 1917—the attitudes of the two films toward urbanization, exploration of the wilderness and contemporary technology could not be more diverse.

In *Back to God's Country*, Dolores desires a way of life that is far removed from the incursions of new regimes. Yet—somewhat ironically—her husband's profession as a government cartographer, inevitably mapping areas for resource development, doesn't seem to be a question. Shipman revelled in a Elysian vision of the untouched forest, from which a brief sojourn in the city provoked daydreams of Dolores's log-cabin home and culminated in a narrative in which a courageous woman, with only a ferocious dog as her champion, single-handedly battled and defeated the villains. This is a vision that pines for the golden days of yore, thus uncannily anticipating Fredrick Jameson's theorization of postmodernism, in which history can only be represented through nostalgic images of pop culture that are, ultimately, merely fantasies of the past. The cozy log cabin of the denouement is precisely that: a Hollywood set complete with rustic props, pipe-smoking hubby and burbling baby on the hearth-rug.

In contrast, in *The Far Shore*, the Victorian Rosedale mansion, currently so treasured by the heritage architectural movement, to which Eulalie's husband brings her, complete with a housekeeper reminiscent of Mrs. Danvers, is a mausoleum that confines the female protagonist to the nineteenth century—a period dreaded by modernists.[24] Moving to English Canada, Eulalie adapts quickly to the English language and to urban life, performs appropriately in corporate situations, and reveals a sophisticated understanding of modern art, not only through her appreciation of contemporary paintings, but also through her accomplished musicianship, especially in performances of such modernist composers such as Debussy. Eulalie can't abide her husband Ross's nostalgic return to the popular culture of his straw-hatted and striped-jacketed student vaudeville days. Embracing modernism and eschewing nostalgia, Eulalie is a thoroughly contemporary protagonist, bespeaking Wieland's understanding of the formative period of modernity in Canadian culture.

Eulalie's liberatory moment is instantiated by the modern conveyance, the automobile, which takes her to a confrontation between husband Ross and painter Tom. Later, when Eulalie and Tom meet in the lake district, they are brought together again by modernist industrialist motivations, Ross's investigation of northern natural resources (clearly marked as rapacious to the environment). While these events are occasioned by modern industrialism *manqué*—the breakdown of the auto; capitalism run amuck—nevertheless, the modern technologies are instrumental in the development of the narrative. Acknowledging and yet retorting to the anxieties of modernization, Wieland's conception of Canadian history and technological change is contradictory and complex. While "masculinist technological modernity" may be the villain of the piece, it is also the narrative vehicle for the inscription of the couple as tragic legends of the national imaginary.[25] In narratological function, contemporary technology plays a significant role.

Another example of the performance of modernity at work in the film is Eulalie's hat. Brenda Longfellow finds in the metaphoric representation of Eulalie's death—her hat floating through water lilies—the final assimilation of the woman's body into nature.[26] At the same time, the hat—a machine-made straw boater adorned with blue grosgrain ribbons that trail over the wide brim—is an historically accurate object of fashionable modernist consumer culture. Through the deceptively simple but highly aestheticized final image of the film, Wieland suggests that modernity and nature co-exist sublimely, if tragically.

What, then, do *Back to God's Country* and *The Far Shore* have in common? What are the elements that have so insistently instantiated their comparison? The simple answer is gender and nation. Both films were created by women (although in Shipman's case, she didn't get credit for directing).

And both women were Canadian (although Shipman made her career and lived her life in the US).

■ Gender: *The Far Shore*

A CONSISTENT BEAT in writing about Wieland's work in all visual media has been the imbrication of femininity, eroticism, and the landscape.[27] "Over a ten year period, from *Water Sark* to *The Far Shore*," writes Janine Marchessault, "the category of Woman is progressively imbued with historical specificity, progressively grounded in place—from her own home to her own country."[28] If the feminine is grounded in Canada and the landscape, it needs to be protected from the depredations of technology and "the military-industrial complex," both putatively masculine. Brenda Longfellow cites Wieland's "deep ecological consciousness" as pertinent here:

> On one level at least, imagining Canada as female recapitulates a classic trope in which the affinity between the nation and the woman is their shared victim-ization.... For [Wieland], the feminine is an elemental principle of life, fertility, and eroticism, an embodiment of all that is abjected by masculinist technological modernity. Within her archetypal consciousness, gender is powerfully related to differential attitudes toward nature and landscape.[29]

Longfellow explores this trope in detail, arguing that Eulalie's body "comes to stand not only for Quebec, but for the landscape itself," effecting a parallel between the woman's body and the land while reiterating a common insight of feminist theorizations of space—that the technocratic/imperialist gaze at landscape and the masculine gaze at women share the same gendered logic. She is quick to point out, however, that, through his aestheticism, taste, and gentleness, the figure of the painter (based on Tom Thomson) "upsets any absolute distinctions based on essentialist ascriptions of gender."[30]

Longfellow considers the "gendered spaces of landscape and nation" in *The Far Shore*, emphasizing Wieland's ecological and nationalist passions. From here she explores the representation of public and private space and the conflicting discourses of the technocratic and aesthetic, which "lay claim to the essential meaning of public space or, more specifically, the Canadian landscape."[31]

It is in the love-making scene between Tom and Eulalie in the lake that Longfellow finds a reciprocity between figures and field: "Wieland poses an aesthetic gaze based on proximity and intimacy, where the boundaries between subject(s) and object, human and landscape, are dissolved."[32] At the end, however, in the image of Eulalie's hat floating through a bank of water lilies, the synecdochic representation of her death, "it is the woman's body that remains thoroughly assimilated into the landscape."[33]

This gendered analytic—usually much less finely traced than Longfellow's—emanates significantly from Wieland's own statements about her work. Along with many other writers, Longfellow quotes Wieland's assertion that she thinks of "Canada as female."[34] Wieland repeated this statement in many different contexts, most often in the frequent interviews and biographical articles with which she colluded.[35]

These biographical and intentionalist pieces, Kass Banning asserts, unfortunately reinforce Wieland's persona as familiar yet enigmatically eccentric, defying methodical categorization, and—more damagingly in the art world—as "feminine," possessing assumed female attributes such as spontaneity, naivety, sentimentality, intuition, and child-like charm.[36] Banning argues that such ascriptions of femininity effectively marginalized Wieland throughout her career and obviated the necessity of dealing with the most "troubling" aspects of her work.[37]

Banning's argument is salutary in its iconoclasm, as it challenges not only the principal tropes of the critical literature on Wieland but also what is often seen as the greatest strength of Wieland's work. Wieland celebrated femininity, women's traditional crafts, and especially the woman's body throughout her career, from the quilts, embroidered and knit pieces, works such as O Canada (a lithograph of lipstick impressions mouthing the words of the national anthem), and films such as Water Sark, in which she explores the objects on her kitchen table and her own body through a variety of lenses. She designed The Venus of Scarborough as an earthwork, a growing, blooming garden of flowers (red posies for nipples and pubic hair), and, in watercolour paintings, likened the hills of Israel to the flowing curves of a woman's body. Following Wieland's own emphasis on the qualities of eroticism, sensuality, playfulness, and delicacy in her work—exemplary in this regard are the coloured pencil drawings of 1981, in which goddesses such as "the Spirit of Newfoundland" penetrate the earth, thereby animating it—most of the feminist scholarship has also celebrated "the feminine" as a central analytic for Wieland's aesthetic. As Banning indicates, the critical discourse has ricocheted between idealization and devaluation, fetishization and sublimation of Wieland's femininity.

It's tricky to argue that considerations of gender in relation to women's artistic production have done more harm than good, particularly in the face of the thirty-year feminist revolution in scholarship that massively installed gender, along with race and class, as a critical category. Much of the scholarship on women artists has been driven by the gender project, which, as a contemporary movement, has actualized what Teresa de Lauretis cited long ago as an "epistemological shift."[38] The gender analytic has contributed to research in every discipline, producing complex methodologies, subtle and illuminating readings of texts, and whole new bodies of knowledge.

Banning's stunning intervention makes the contrary point that the "overdetermined contextualisation" of Wieland's work—i.e., an emphasis on biography, femininity, and her own statements of intent to frame the work—has resulted in a doxalogical discourse that has effectively eliminated all other categories of criticism from consideration.[39]

Furthermore, as is the case with so many women artists, biography eclipses artwork both in numbers of publications and in accessibility. In Wieland's case, there are no complete collections of her wall works yet published; where are those sumptuous coffee table books?[40] There are two hefty biographical tomes in print, one slim critical volume on her art, and Kathryn Elder's anthology on the films.[41] The latter provides a list of distribution sources for Wieland's work in cinema, of which the only complete collection is located with the Canadian distributor (Canadian Filmmakers Distribution Cooperative).

Another aspect of the gender project is the effective limitation of comparators to women artists. Yes, both Back to God's Country and The Far Shore were made by women (although in Shipman's case, she didn't get credit for directing). As Banning would say, let's unpack this a bit.

Currently, we understand gender as far from a unitary category. Inflections of race, class, historical period, cultural traditions, performativity, and the other ever-transmuting formations of identitory categories now inform feminist understanding of what being women may entail. Studies of women filmmakers have long given up the quest for specific gender differences as marking attitudes toward violence, sexuality, marriage, equality, narrative genres, or cinematic modes of production. The diachronical tendency to compare women filmmakers with one another, even across centuries, rather than synchronically to the industrial practices and other filmmakers of their time, must surely be vestigial traces of an outmoded discourse. Gender is clearly not sufficient as a rationale for comparing filmmakers or filmmaking modes. Although, paradoxically, there is a lot to say about gender in many contexts, there is little to be said about it here, except that, as a basis of comparison, it is slight indeed.

Having said this, it is now time to revoke the comparison between Shipman and Wieland, to concentrate on the place of The Far Shore in the Canadian cinematic canon.

■ The Far Shore

FOR LONGFELLOW, the contemporary critics weren't so far off the mark: she judges that the film is "schematic in its articulation of philosophical and political concerns."[42] To the contrary, in her 1982 article, Lauren Rabinowitz charts the contrapuntal registers of the film, which, she argues, combines a "radical feminist polemic" with a concatenation of "codified avant-garde style and the Hollywood generic conventions of domestic melodrama."[43] She asserts that "it is exactly those two stylistic categories" that give the film its strength, "placing a value on simultaneous cognition and on disrupting linear narrativity and illusionist spectacle."[44] Nuancing Rabinowitz, Longfellow celebrates the film as a "flamboyant and self-reflexive embrace of melodramatic conventions."[45]

For Rabinowitz, these strategies are what constitute in the film "a feminist discourse." Her analysis of the film plays off these conflicting discursive modes: "The Far Shore engages and critiques both Hollywood and experimental cinematic style in an attempt to create a commercially viable feminist cinema."[46] She cites Thomas Elsaesser on the importance of the *mise en scène* in critiquing familial relationships, revealing its own internal contradictions by introducing a submerged level of discourse that subverts the very values the narrative attempts to uphold. In *The Far Shore*, Wieland makes the internal contradictions of family melodrama an aesthetic issue, Rabinowitz argues: a host of allusions to personal, filmic, and painterly artistic practice intensify colour, expressionistic light, and Baroque painterly illusionism in references to historic art styles (Dutch and Italian old masters such as Wieland's favourite, Giambattista Tiepolo) and the Canadian Group of Seven.

Rabinowitz situates the film, as well, in the context of Wieland's earlier experimental films. By introducing experimental film strategies, the question of tempo—so abjured in contemporary criticisms of the film—is here related to a deconstructionist project concerning cinematic duration and elapsed time, "a creative mix of experimental and narrative techniques that undermine the film's narrative line."[47] She notes Wieland's fondness for the conventions of the silent cinema. Homages to D.W. Griffith's uses of irises and cross-cutting for the chase scene situate "the cinematic method itself as the subject, creating a narrative rupture during the film's most dramatic moment."[48]

Rabinowitz's article, in short, attends carefully to the dominant discourse of feminist film theory of its day. Rehabilitating the film for feminist scholars, it suggests that *The Far Shore* offered exactly what contemporary film theory called for, an emphasis on anti-narrative, anti-realist, deconstructionist techniques wedded to a popular generic form.

■ Representation and the Avant-Garde

In *The Far Shore*, conception and mode of representation can be assimilated neither to clichés of over-romanticised nationalism nor to 1970s avant-garde techniques. In opposition to Rabinowitz, I would argue that there are few signs of experimental cinema in *The Far Shore*. At the time of Rabinowitz's writing, her inscription of techniques "disrupting linear narrativity and illusionist spectacle"[49] were mandatory for feminist scholars. Linearity, illusionism, and closure were the marks of the realist imperative, which came to be situated as the masculinist unconscious—

calamity for feminist representation, which perforce interrogated the mechanisms of the patriarchal imaginary.

Yet the enduring signs of what P. Adams Sitney called the "structural movement"—a cool treatment of the medium, materiality, absence of narrative, abstraction, the static image, and duration—have rarely been features of Wieland's experimental films. She embraced her own subjectivity in *Water Sark* (1964–65), fast repetitive editing in *Hand-Tinting* (1967–68) and *A & B in Ontario* (1967–84), comedic narrative in *Rat Life and Diet in North America* (1968), and, simultaneously, the close-up and the political subject in *Pierre Vallieres* (1972) and *Solidarity* (1973). In many of her films there is also an ardent, nearly raw insistence on the relevance of the specificity of time, as in *1933* (1967–68). Rather than embracing the structural avant-garde, Wieland was severely critiqued at the time for her introduction of comedy, narrative and political subjects in her experimental film.[50]

Nevertheless, a few congruencies between elements of *The Far Shore* and Wieland's practice in her earlier experimental works must be noted here, specifically the uses of the iris and magnifying lens. I intend to demonstrate that they have vastly differing effects in terms of spectatorial address.

Water Sark plays with a variety of distorting and magnifying lenses, which shift in and out of focus in their hand-held movements across the filmed objects. In *Water Sark*, with Wieland's fingers visibly holding the lens that magnifies objects on her kitchen table and her own breasts, intimate spectatorial identification challenges the coolness of the structuralist avant-garde. The scene in *The Far Shore* when Eulalie and Tom mouth secrets to each other holding a magnifying glass to their lips is reminiscent of the earlier device, but the technical differences are extreme, as the image in the feature film is perfect in its *mise-en-scène* and cinematographic technique. Its spectatorial address also counters the effect of the earlier device. In *The Far Shore*, what the lovers say to each other through the visual microphone of the period magnifier prop is not audibly revealed: thus an intimate secret is withheld from the spectator. This is a reworking of the earlier device that holds the spectator apart and bespeaks sophisticated meta-discursive functions.

In a similar artisanal mode, the glowing circle that outlines the images in *Birds at Sunrise* was created by taping a cardboard toilet paper roll to the lens, resulting in a serendipitous light spill that produces a circular surround. The painterly iris in *The Far Shore*, on the other hand, is a technically perfect optical device created in the laboratory that achieves a beautiful plot segue. From a close-up of Eulalie, a gorgeous iris-in rimmed in a halo of red light closes around her before dissolving to a shot of Tom in his canoe perfectly bisecting the circle, which then widens out to fill the frame. The iris melds Eulalie's reverie to Tom's journey through the lake country. Wieland is at her best here, evincing a postmodern troping on the optical effects of the silent era to achieve a narratological function.

Artisanal effects have been evacuated in the feature film. Rather, *The Far Shore* is a polished production constructed by professionals at every technical level. As the signs of the much-vaunted modernist "coolness" of structural cinema and the hands-on low-tech manipulations of Wieland's earlier work disappear in *The Far Shore*, the forces of the devices become more sophisticated, achieving a postmodern quotational meta-discourse of representation.

A sophisticated understanding of the mediations of representation is fundamental to Wieland's art practice. Despite her garrulous and sometimes wilfully simplistic statements about her own work ("I think of Canada as female.")[51] reductionist clichés on any subject find no purchase in Wieland's creative lexicon. Her work takes up the task of specifying the place from which meaning emerges, in an individual, geographical, and aesthetic sense.

Nevertheless, in contemporary reception, notwithstanding the meta-discursive elements of the mise-en-scène, the narrative of *The Far Shore* seems replete with spectatorial plenitude. The film sweeps along in the way any accomplished melodrama does, provoking groans, laughter, or embarrassed tears—a complex response to identificatory processes and visual excess. There is a laugh, as always, when Eulalie dives fully dressed into the lake to join her lover. There is just something about those darling little lace-up boots hitting the water that provokes a chortle. Is it surprise that takes the audience? Excess? Derision? All of the above? In any case, the ensuing canoe chase, with the couple ducking out of sight at the last moment, returns the mood to tense identification, provoking trauma at the sudden finale, when the lovers are shot. Only in that last brilliant image—Eulalie's hat—do the reflexive mediations of representation reassert themselves, from the melodramatic to tranquil—if sorrowful— contemplation.

History and Cinema

The Far Shore operates through conventional modes of tragic melodrama, not only in its narrative form but also in its deployment of the cinematic vocabulary of the silent era. Griffithian cross-cutting in the chase scene, use of off-screen space, and inscription of archetypal characters in the narrative signify the film's observance of filmic practices from the historical period in which the narrative is situated. The use of silent-era dramatic structures and film language demonstrates once again the multifarious and richly heterogeneous arrows in Wieland's creative quiver.

Let's look, once again, at the sublime iris-in on Eulalie daydreaming in her bed that dissolves into a shot of Tom in his canoe. D.W. Griffith used the iris to isolate specific details, for portraiture and telling juxtaposition, and for narrative transitions, closing down completed episodes or opening out new ones. From a gorgeous portrait of Eulalie's face in close-up, Wieland's iris eventually opens out to a wide shot of Tom paddling down the northern lake as the transitional music swells. The optical device simultaneously reveals Eulalie's unspoken desires and effects the necessary narrative transition to Tom's trajectory. In so doing, it condenses many of the traditional functions of the silent-era apparatus.

Wieland adds yet another stratum of meaning. Like the exquisite and profound beauty of The Water Quilt (wall-hanging), in this scene the meanings of the object also reveal themselves in a succession of layers, each in its turn incisively executed and rhetorically consummated while augmenting the accumulated meanings of the layers that came before. By placing the circle exactly in the centre of the film frame, across which Tom paddles in perfect symmetry—bisecting precisely across its diameter the framing circle—and by outlining the iris in a bright red glowing line, the device is rendered as a stand-alone art object of acute elegance. Wieland not only constructs the past through its own cinematic language but also activates herself as a filmmaker of the period, wielding her artistic talents as she might have done at the time.[52]

These modes and techniques constitute something considerably more complex and rigorous than the ubiquitous Jamesonian concept of "postmodernist pastiche" or reflexivity—what Baudrillard called "simulacra," images that have no referents outside mediation—can adequately suggest. Rather than simply eliminating the fourth wall, producing the past as realistically transparent (thus casting the audience as privileged silent witnesses putatively present at the historical events), the audience for *The Far Shore* is invited to "see" the personages and events of the narrative as they would have been represented in the movies at the time. The period is situated as already cinematic. Rather than merely retro or ironic references, Wieland's deployment of these techniques suggests an ambitious historical project. *The Far Shore* revisits the past not only in its meticulously accurate period settings, production design, costume, dialogue, and performance style, but also sets out to represent the period cinematically in the way it might have been executed at the time.[53]

That the critics and audiences in its time were not comfortable with Wieland's project should not diminish our appreciation of the film today. Neither should the omissions of cinema scholarship—derailed at least in part by gender marginalization—continue. Calling into play nationalistic, aesthetic, cinematographic, and historiographical aspirations, *The Far Shore* is an achievement of a gifted cinematic imagination and an acutely sagacious historical construction of great splendour.

NOTES

1.   David L. Hartford is credited as director on *Back to God's Country*. Nell Shipman wrote the screenplay and contributed significantly to direction. For purposes of comparison with Wieland, I will refer to *Back to God's Country* as a Nell Shipman film.

2.   Barbara Martineau, "The Far Shore: A Film about Violence, a Peaceful Film about Violence," *Cinema Canada* 27 (April 1976): 20–23.

3.   *Back to God's Country* is contemporary (1919), while *The Far Shore* (1976) revisits the period (1917–18) retrospectively.

4. Box-office receipts are no measure of the film's success. Most of the great works of Canadian cinema have bombed commercially.

5. Kathryn Elder, "Joyce Wieland: A Bibliographic Guide to the Film Literature" in Kathryn Elder, ed., *The Films of Joyce Wieland* (Toronto: Cinematheque Ontario Monographs, 1999) 213–251.

6. George Appleby, "On Editing *The Far Shore* (and Other Films)," *The Canadian Film Editor* 3, no. 3 (Spring 1977): 34.

7. Christine Langlois, "Joyce Wieland Likes her Movie," *The Guardian* (Brampton, ON), 7 October 1976.

8. Janice Blue, "On Film: a Woman's Vision," *Houston Breakthrough* (October 1978): 9.

9. Katherine Gilday, "The Far Shore: Script and Film," *Books in Canada* 6, no. 2 (Feb 1997): 30–32.

10. Budget of nearly $0.5 million. Although perhaps equivalent to $5.0 million now, it was less than half the amount allotted to the six other Canadian projects that year. See Paul King, "Seven Canadian Films Set: Productions to Cost $11 Million," *The Citizen* (Ottawa, ON),14 December 1974, 77. In this light, the film's achievement in production values alone is astonishing.

11. Personal conversation with Wieland shortly after the event.

12. Lauren Rabinowitz, "*The Far Shore*: Feminist Family Melodrama," *Jump Cut* 32 (1987): 29–31. Reprinted in Elder, *The Films of Joyce Wieland*, 119–128.

13. Seth Feldman, "The Silent Subject in English Canadian Film," *Words and Moving Images*, ed. W.E. Wees and M. Dorland (Montreal: Mediatexte, 1984), 203–12; reprinted in S. Feldman, ed., *Take Two* (Toronto: Irwin, 1984), 48–57.

14. Peter Morris, "*The Far Shore*," *The Film Companion* (Toronto: Irwin, 1984), 105–07.

15. Susan M. Crean, "Forbidden Fruit: The Erotic Nationalism of Joyce Wieland," *This Magazine* 21, no. 4 (August–September 1987): 12–20.

16. Michael O'Pray, "Video: Joyce Wieland: In Search of *The Far Shore*," *Art Monthly* (March 1988).

17. Joan Nicks, "Sex, Lies and Landscape: Meditations on Vertical Tableaux in *The Far Shore* and *J.A. Martin, Photographe*," *Canadian Journal of Film Studies* 2, nos. 2–3 (1993): 81–93.

18. With the exception of Brenda Longfellow's compendium article: Brenda Longfellow, "Gender, Landscape and Colonial Allegories in *The Far Shore*, *Loyalties*, and *Mouvements du désir*," *Gendering the Nation: Canadian Women's Cinema*, ed., K. Armatage, K Banning, B. Longfellow, and J. Marchessault (Toronto: University of Toronto Press, 1999), 165–82.

19. See Kathryn Elder's "Bibliographic Guide to the Film Literature" for many examples.

20. Distinguished artists such as Cinematographer Richard Leiterman, Production Designer Anne Pritchard, veteran Editor George Appleby and Sound Re-recordist Joe Grimaldi. They must have worked at scale.

21. Nell Shipman, *The Silent Screen & My Talking Heart: An Autobiography* (Boise State Univ Bookstore,1987).

22. Manny Farber, "Film," *Artforum* 8, no. 5 (January 1970): 81–82.

23. Kass Banning, "The Mummification of Mommy: Joyce Wieland as the AGO's First Living Other," *C Magazine* 13 (1987): 32–38; reprinted in J. Radley and L. Johnstone, ed., *Sightlines: Reading Contemporary Canadian Art* (Montreal: Artextes, 1994), 153–67; and in Elder, *The Films of Joyce Wieland*, 29–44.

24. Alfred Hitchcock, *Rebecca*, 1940.

25. Brenda Longfellow, "Gender, Landscape and Colonial Allegories in *The Far Shore*, *Loyalties*, and *Mouvements du désir*," in *Gendering the Nation: Canadian Women's Cinema*, ed. K. Armatage, K. Banning, B. Longfellow, and J. Marchessault (Toronto: University of Toronto Press, c.1999), 165–82.

26. Longfellow, "Gender, Landscape and Colonial Allegories," 170.

27. See Kathryn Elder's "Bibliographic Guide to the Film Literature" for many examples.

28. Janine Marchessault, "Feminist Avant-Garde Cinema: From Introspection to Retrospection," *Cineaction*, no. 24–25 (1991): 30–37. Reprinted in K. Armatage et al, ed., *Gendering the Nation: Canadian Women's Cinema*, 137–47.

29. Longfellow, "Gender, Landscape and Colonial Allegories," 167.

30. Ibid., 169. Longfellow also rehabilitates Wieland for contemporary feminism, situating Tom as "a surrogate Native" through his "rustic living quarters, his proficiency in a canoe, and his knowledge of natural ingredients ('Indian bark tea')."

31. Ibid., 168.

32. Ibid, 170.

33. Ibid., 170.

34. Ibid., 167.

35. Including my own early interview, from which the statement originated: "Kay Armatage Interviews Joyce Wieland," *Take One* 3, no. 2 (November–December 1970): 23–25; reprinted with additions in K. Kay and G. Peary, ed., *Women and the Cinema: A Critical Anthology* (New York: Dutton, 1977), 246–71 and Katerine Elder, *The Films of Joyce Wieland*, 154–60.

36. Kass Banning, "The Mummification of Mommy: Joyce Wieland as the AGO's First Living Other," *C Magazine* 13 (1987): 32–38; reprinted in J. Radley and L. Johnstone, ed., *Sightlines: Reading Contemporary Canadian Art* (Montreal: Artextes, 1994), 153–67; and in Elder, *The Films of Joyce Wieland*, 29–44.

37. Ibid., 37.

38. Teresa de Lauretis, *Technologies of Gender* (Palgrave Macmillan, 1989).

39. Kass Banning, "The Mummification of Mommy," 37.

40. Of course I understand the economics of art publication in Canada. Nevertheless, the unavailability of her artwork is astonishing. The *True Patriot Love* exhibition catalogue is no longer available, and the AGO publication of her 1986 retrospective is not only extremely selective but also available only through the gallery—neither can be found on www.amazon.ca.

41. Iris Nowell, *Joyce Wieland: A Life in Art* (Toronto: ECW Press, 2001), .519; Jane Lind, *Joyce Wieland: Artist on Fire* (Toronto: James Lorimer & Co., 2001), 400.; Lucy Lippard, *Joyce Wieland* (Toronto: Key Porter Books, 1987), 214. Elder, *The Films of Joyce Wieland* (Toronto: Cinematheque Ontario Publications, 1999). I can't thank Elder enough for this scrupulously edited text, which has inordinately informed this paper.

42. Longfellow, "Gender, Landscape and Colonial Allegories," 167.

43. Rabinowitz, "The Far Shore: Feminist Family Melodrama" in Elder, *The Films of Joyce Wieland*, 119. Derived from her PhD dissertation on Maya Deren, Shirley Clarke, and Joyce Wieland, subsequently published as *Points of Resistance: Women, Power, & Politics in the New York Avant-Garde Cinema, 1943-71* (University of Illinois Press, 1991). Reprinted in Elder, *The Films of Joyce Wieland*, 119–27.

44. Derived from her PhD dissertation on Maya Deren, Shirley Clarke, and Joyce Wieland, subsequently published as *Points of Resistance: Women, Power, & Politics in the New York Avant-Garde Cinema, 1943-71* (University of Illinois Press, 1991). Reprinted in Elder, *The Films of Joyce Wieland*, 119–27.

45. Longfellow, "Gender, Landscape and Colonial Allegories," 168.

46. Rabinowitz, "Feminist Family Melodrama," 120.

47. Ibid., 124.

48. Ibid., 126.

49. Ibid., 124.

50. See Mike Zryd's excellent article on reception, especially his outline of the "formalist or feminist" appropriations of Wieland's films. Mike Zryd, "'There are Many Joyces': The Critical Reception of the Films of Joyce Wieland," *The Films of Joyce Wieland*, 195–212.

51. "Kay Armatage Interviews Joyce Wieland," *Take One* 3, no. 2 (November–December 1970): 23–25; reprinted with additions in K. Kay and G. Peary, ed., *Women and the Cinema: A Critical Anthology* (New York: Dutton, 1977), 246–71.

52. Okay, so the film is in colour. You can't have everything.

53. A similar approach can be found in *Bram Stoker's Dracula* (Francis Ford Coppola, 1992).

2

The Fatal Leap

Accessing the Films of Claude Jutra Through History and Symbol

DAVID CLANDFIELD

Il y a beaucoup de moi dans tout ce que je fais.
—CLAUDE JUTRA[1]

THE WORKS OF CLAUDE JUTRA (1930–1986) are something of a challenge to the student of cinema. Pierre Jutras, of the Cinémathèque québécoise, has compiled a list of over one hundred film and television productions and scripts in which Jutra took part.[2] They vary in length from thirty-second TV commercial clips to theatrical films as long as 173 minutes.[3] Jutra's involvement in each of these pieces may include all of writing, directing, playing a lead role, and editing, as with *Mon oncle Antoine* (1971), or only one of any of these roles. The films he directed for which he may be considered the auteur include documentaries, docudramas, fictional shorts and features, experimental works, and animated sequences. Among his fictional works are dramas, comedies, melodramas, and musical comedies. They include works from original screenplays and works adapted from such prominent Canadian authors as Anne Hébert, Mordecai Richler,

29

Margaret Atwood, and Margaret Gibson. The range of documentary sub-genres Jutra directed include traditional documentaries shot from a script with pre-production planning and voice-off commentary, compilation films, and the *cinéma direct* style. Complicating this body of work further is the fact that Jutra's filmmaking career, which was predominantly in French, included a five-year period when he worked in English. So how is one to make sense out of such a heterogeneous collection of work?

Any treatment of Jutra's work with a focus on the major works he directed need not be a test of Jutra's eligibility as auteur or of whether those films taken together constitute a coherent, consistent oeuvre. The arguments that emerge from such an exercise are frequently circular and beg more questions than they answer. Rather the goal in such an inquiry should be the identification of access points to these varied works, to see how they speak to each other and how an understanding of them taken together can provide meanings not readily available from viewing a work in isolation. Jutra's status as an artist is not the targeted conclusion for this study; it is, rather, the point of departure.

There are various access points into Jutra's body of work, beginning with what is most generally known about him. This constitutes the schematic level, the simplest point of access but also the most fragmentary. A second level of access to the work is attained by probing the formative years of the artist's life and discovering elements in his earliest work that anticipate later developments. At a third level, the biographical material can be more fully expanded but understood as a legend performing an interpretative guide drawing upon salient or recurrent features of his life, his times, and his work. At this third level patterns will emerge to suggest a synthesis that harmonizes disparate aspects into one unifying vision. The target is not only a documentary record of Jutra's life, not only an account of the films themselves (a short essay allows only a partial account anyway), but also the importance of this work within its social and historical context. The purpose is not to prove the artistic integrity of the individual artist, but the coherence of a body of work in which the artist's imprint and its historical moment are both taken into account.

The Claude Jutra of Canadian encyclopaedias and film guides is a paradoxical presence in the history of Québécois cinema. Any artist who would end his life as Jutra apparently did in 1986, by leaping off a major bridge into the icy waters of the St. Lawrence, would by that act alone be imprinted in our collective memory. The fact that Jutra seemed to allude to this act in several of his films decades earlier means that we view both what we know of his life and his films differently.[4]

Jutra authored what has, in list after list, been recognized as the finest film made in Quebec and Canada (*Mon oncle Antoine*). That he had difficulty finding the money to finance his later films is an extraordinary irony, reminiscent of Orson Welles's career after *Citizen Kane*, and it made his ending all the more poignant. He was a Québécois nationalist who refused the Order of Canada in 1972 and allegedly danced in the streets when the Parti Québécois came to power in 1976. Jutra was obliged to leave home and make films in English Canada for five years, adding political irony to the other ironies. He was not the only filmmaker to suffer a head injury in a motor scooter accident in his thirties, but he also went on to attribute the onset of subsequent bouts of depression and memory lapses to that accident even as he directed significant feature films, before falling victim to Alzheimer's disease and suicide.[5] Jutra's most personal and apparently autobiographical film (*A tout prendre*, 1963) included the apparent revelation of his homosexuality at a time when coming out was still a rare occurrence. Thus schematized, Jutra's life story is made of paradox and dramatic irony. So the viewer, armed with the above thumbnail sketches, inevitably looks for paradox and irony in key sequences of his films at both individual and social levels. The schematic Jutra story becomes a heuristic as well as a basis for analogy and metaphor.

Among Jutra's documentary films, *Félix Leclerc troubadour* (1959) is perhaps the one that foregrounds paradox the most clearly, as it includes Leclerc's own voice-over exposing the trickery of the documentary filmmaking process. The opening sequence shot from a car driving through a snow-covered countryside to Leclerc's residence is not, we hear, the beginning of the filming, which had begun days earlier, even though the diegetic Leclerc who greets the filmmakers behaves as though it is. And the shot showing him going to feed his hens is apparently the third take, meaning that this is their fifth feed of the day. Of course, the viewer has no way of knowing whether the voice-over is telling the truth or whether the truth is that which is conveyed by the people interacting in the film. However, the traditional authority of the voice-over gives its account greater weight than diegetic speech. Its explanatory function is displaced from the profilmic events to the filmmaking act itself. Even as we become aware of the artifice, there is no weakening of the essential beliefs that this is Félix Leclerc, this is where he lives, this is his voice, and these are his songs. The paradox here is that we continue to believe the expository narrative even as the mechanisms that have helped construct it are revealed.

Perhaps the greatest dramatic irony in Jutra's films is reserved for the climactic closing shots of *Mon oncle Antoine*. Having dropped and abandoned the coffin containing Marcel, the eldest son of the Poulin family, on the nighttime sleigh ride back to town from the Poulin farm, the young protagonist Benoît and his uncle return the next morning but cannot find it. They continue to the farmhouse and Benoît approaches a window with mounting fear and anxiety. What he sees is the family grouped round the open coffin silently grieving. The father has only just returned from the lumber camps unaware of these grim events and has evidently picked up the coffin himself and taken it home. The film ends with an ambiguous freeze frame close-up of Benoît's face. This is a dramatic Kuleshov effect, because what we read into that frozen expression depends on what we read into the scene. It is Christmas Day. In Catholic Quebec, that day is iconographically represented by the biblical nativity scene with Mary and Joseph watching over the newborn baby Jesus in a crib. This is the scene earlier seen in Uncle Antoine's store window for the Christmas display. But here the newborn son is replaced by a newly dead son and the crib is replaced by a coffin. The mood is decidedly that of another mother-and-child scene from Christian iconography, the *Pietà*, showing Mary grieving over her grown son Jesus's lifeless body following his crucifixion and descent from the cross. The promise of redemption and resurrection central to Christian faith and celebrated in the nativity is not realized at this point of death, with which Jutra has linked the nativity scene.

Earlier in *Mon oncle Antoine*, Jos Poulin, the father, angrily quit his job at the mine to go work in the camps and bid farewell to Marcel with the promise that next year they would send him to college. Along with this promise the family's hopes for an end to the deadly cycle of work in the asbestos mine are abruptly ended. Marcel has died from a pulmonary complaint brought on by air pollution. There will be no college education, no escape, no redemption, no rebirth.

Benoît has already reacted more than once with rebellious gestures against church hypocrisy and the mine-owner's exploitation. Faced with the dreadful irony of the Christmas Day scene in the Poulin farmhouse, he must now make a choice whether to accept the status quo as fate or challenge it as an agent of change. But while the film ends with the recognition of irony, it also leaves Benoît the choice of an undisclosed future. By 1971, Quebec had experienced a decade of unrest as francophone nationalism took various forms,[6] culminating in the dark ironies of the October Crisis of 1970. A critical point had been reached in Quebec history. If a secular, modern society was the product of the so-called Quiet Revolution, which ended Catholic conservatism, would a majority now go further along the road to sovereignty in the light of the indignities of the War Measures Act visited upon the population in October 1970? Jutra's film does not end with a clear answer about Benoît's "next steps" either.[7]

Of course, paradox and irony are only part of the complexities that Jutra represents in his work. Jutra's early life provides a second access point to the meanings in his work. Claude Jutra was born in 1930 into a liberally minded bourgeois family of Montreal whose name was Jutras. Claude would maintain that spelling until about 1950, dropping the final –s in the credits of films that appeared after that date. Despite the Great Depression, the young Claude enjoyed a comfortable childhood. His father, Albert Jutras, was a physician on the threshold of a brilliant career as a radiologist, while his mother Rachel Gauvreau Jutras, also from a prominent medical family in Quebec, was a certified cosmetologist. Actively interested in music and theatre, the couple both became amateur painters and, after a three-year stay in Paris in the early 1930s, serious collectors of contemporary Canadian art.[8] Their home on rue Sainte-Famille was metres away from the hospital where Albert would be head radiologist. The house was also close to the home of Alfred Pellan, and the family regularly played host to an array of members of Montreal's artistic community: Pellan, Paule-Emile Borduas, Jordi Bonet, and art gallery proprietor Agnès Lefort.[9] During his teenage years, Claude lived at the heart of controversies flaring around the Québécois *automatistes* and surrealists, which

reached their high point with the publication of the incendiary anar-
chist manifesto *Refus Global* (1948).

This complex family environment helped shape the lives of the three
Jutras children. On the one hand, they bore the influence of a scientist
father. Jutra excelled early at the elite Collège Stanislas and became a
physician in his twenty-second year, although he would never practice.
His sister, Mireille, married one of her father's closest collaborators, Dr.
Guy Duckett, in 1955; and the much younger Michel also became a physician. In addition, the children were exposed to an artistic environment
very early: Claude and Mireille were sent to Camille Bernard's "Théâtre
des petits," a school specializing in elocution, music, and theatre for
children from the age of three.[10] Claude took dance classes at the famed
Lacasse-Morenoff School.[11] Later, after completing medical school, he
studied at the École du Théâtre du Nouveau Monde.[12]

Throughout his teenage years, Claude immersed himself in all things
cinematographic. For his sixteenth birthday, he received a triple-turret
16mm Bolex and the seed was sown. Claude became a stalwart of the
Université de Montréal Ciné-club and took regular trips to New York to
see films banned in right-wing Catholic Quebec. He later hosted two TV
series about the cinema and appeared in others.[13]

Armed with a knowledge of these elements of Claude Jutra's early life,
the viewer can take a fresh look at the films made by Jutra. Naturally,
the documentary films command attention because they take the viewer
into the world of science and technology on the one hand and into the
world of music, dance, and the theatre on the other.[14] He knew these
worlds well. However, the graphic arts are lacking as a subject. It is true
that in his last film, *La Dame en couleurs* (1984), Jutra had wanted to be the
one to play the key adult role of the epileptic artist Barbouilleux, a role
given to Gilles Renaud at the producer's request. This artist, an epileptic
patient in a 1940s psychiatric hospital in Quebec, where orphans of the
poor were put to work to earn their keep, embodies the free spirit of the
romantic artist at odds with society, exploited and denigrated at the
same time.

But the world of the surrealists and modernists that Jutra would have
encountered is found more in the sensibility of his films than in direct
representation. The defamiliarization of a chair in the pixillated mime-

drama he made with Norman McLaren, the search for liberators of the imagination whether through a childhood sensibility or through madness, the dream sequences that pepper his films, the portrayal of "amour fou," these are all features explored by surrealist poets and filmmakers, even though Jutra never made a surrealist film.[15]

Perhaps equally important to the formation of Claude's sensibility was his discovery of the Boy Scout movement when he was at Collège Stanislas, where he joined the Guynemer troop and became friends with his future collaborator, Michel Brault. They remained attached to the troop until their late teens, when they were Rovers. In 1948 Jutra's experience with the Boy Scouts provided the framework for Claude's first attempt to make films for a public. The film was *Le Dément du Lac Jean-Jeunes*, a scary campfire tale in which the narrator and central character is a troop leader recalling an incident from his own first summer camp as a scout. A sequence of events leads the narrator to the discovery of a demented man holding a young boy, presumed to be his son, captive in a log cabin in the woods. The scout troop responds by finding and chasing the two of them out of the cabin. In the chase, the father leaps to his death over a cliff into a river, the scouts rescue the boy from the precipice and go on to find a good home for him before breaking camp.

Claude wrote up this filmmaking experience for the benefit of his fellow scouts.[16] The account shows perfectly that combination of enthusiastic wonderment, irreverence, and fun on the one hand and, on the other, of dispassionate, methodical application to the technical organization of the script, the shoot, and the editing, which constituted the young Claude's hallmark, to the chagrin of those looking for a simpler sensibility at work. In the film itself, we find a similar alternation of shots that advance the plot and shots that convey the exuberance of both the filmmaker and the participants shown in the film. A melodramatic plotline proceeds through the use of low-angle shots, partial shots, day-for-night, enhanced by menacing music.[17] Moments of exhilaration, such as the three bathing and splashing sequences, are shot against the light to make the most of the dynamic chiaroscuro effects. The high-contrast dappled light in the woodland and on the lakeshores creates lyrical moments, enhanced in turn by joyous programmatic music.[18]

The qualities of this youthful work have acquired a near legendary status though few may have actually seen it. It is easy to locate in this film the stylistic traits (expressionistic lighting, multiple angled shots), themes (child abuse, madness, youthful mobilization, dreams), and elements of a sensibility (self-conscious, ironic) that would emerge progressively in Jutra's later professional work. The collaboration of Michel Brault has been credited with much of the cinephilia that informs the work. But Brault himself has said that he learned more from his collaboration with Jutra in this first film than the other way around.[19] The proleptic qualities of the film extend to Jutra's future life. This is one of three films in which the climax shows a central character leaping to his death in water, apparently prefiguring Jutra's eventual suicide, as earlier remarked. As well, the film has attracted a reading through the lens of queer theory because of Jutra's sexual orientation.[20]

It would be easy to exaggerate the importance of this piece of juvenilia. More significant is the film that Jutra calls his first real film, *Mouvement perpétuel* (1949), a film with avant-garde ambitions, incorporating elements of dream, dance, and displacement. Shot by Michel Brault again, it figures three nameless individuals—two men and a woman—whose interactions suggest the nightmarish fantasy of an eternal triangle acting within a narrowly confined interior, which is then displaced to the country, on a cliff-face, and on a road crossing a tall bridge. Ottakar Novacek's musical piece of the same name accompanies the action, but is slowed down eerily. The dramatic scaling of a cliff will again strike viewers like a recurrent obsession of Jutra's,[21] as will the moment at which the man in the white shirt falls from the bridge into the river below—a stunt that Jutra himself performed. Jutra cites the influence of Cocteau's *Le sang d'un poète* (1930) for the use of visual symbols rather than verbal ones and for its elements of mystery and poetic formalism. There are reminiscences of *Meshes of the Afternoon* (Maya Deren, 1941) and the surrealistic obsessions of *La Coquille et le clergyman* (Germaine Dulac and Antonin Artaud, 1927) or *Un chien andalou* (Luis Buñuel and Salvador Dali, 1928). The film catapulted Jutra into public view by winning the 1950 Canadian Film Award for best amateur film of the year. This work anticipates the experimental use of filmic effects like jump cuts, diagonal angles, and associative montage in later films (most noticeably in *A tout prendre* and

Wow (1969), the playing with time in *Pour le meilleur et pour le pire* (1975), and the manipulation of music. A third amateur film was filmed much later. *Pierrot des bois* (1956) features Jutra as a clown in a mime-dance sequence in a fall landscape of birch saplings. Reminiscent of Norman McLaren's pixillated *Neighbours* (1952), it seems more childlike than his other early work and enriches the choreography more with varying camera angles and movements (by Michel Brault) than with animation effects.[22]

There are limits to the detection of early formative influences as an interpretive framework for this work. Jim Leach, the author of the first significant monograph on Jutra's work as a filmmaker, has extended biographical references to the whole of his work by considering the various "public pronouncements,...writings, and...dealings with the film industry" as a tool by which it can be inserted into film history.[23] In doing so, Leach has recalled the Russian formalist theory of "biographical legend." The legend Leach has educed comprises three components: "experiences of childhood and adolescence, an ability to combine scientific thinking with an artistic sensibility, and a fascination with film form."[24] But as Leach proceeds to unpack these components, it becomes clear that they do not exhaust the legend in and of themselves. Each is a complex of elements that overflows the designating term. The components to the legend need further development in order to show how an understanding of them can direct and constrain the interpretative process.

Leach connects youth and adolescence not only to the adolescent coming of age dramas scattered through Jutra's work—he cites *Mon oncle Antoine* and *Dreamspeaker* (1976), as the best-known examples—but also to the acknowledgement of identity (especially the "revelation" of his own sexual identity in *A tout prendre*) and Jutra's reputation as a "perpetual child," a term Jutra used of himself. These elements, when considered alongside Leach's discussion of Heinz Weinmann's thesis about the "infantile mentality" of a chronically indecisive Quebec society, can be used as indicators that make the Jutra of legend and his work a synecdochic version of the Québécois people and Quebec society.[25] According to this view, the Quiet Revolution was not only a period of social and economic change, but it can also be recoded as a period of maturation, a process embedded in a linear development. The restructuring of social identity, as older institutions (Catholic, conservative) lost their power and new ones (secular, liberal) took their place, would be understood as the accession to the next stage. The sense that a people (the Québécois people) is "growing up" means that any hesitation it may show about its future, any tendency to look back with nostalgia to its past, is recoded as a childlike refusal to accept the responsibilities associated with maturation. Continuing hesitancy is a sign of arrested development. The biographical legend of Jutra is used as an analogy for contemporary Quebec history. Or vice versa. The analogical relationship, once established, means that efforts to make meaning out of stories about adolescents coming to terms with themselves and the world around them will draw the interpretant into a link with Quebec's social history.

Leach associates the "reconciliation of science and the arts" with Jutra's experience of his early home life, recounted above. Leach juxtaposes with this a tension in that life between "the orientation towards a new technological future" and "a bourgeois atmosphere where the social and cultural standards were from France." Eventually his argument arrives at a tension between progress and tradition. Naturally it would be tempting to view Jutra's enthusiasm for science and technology as progressive and his interest in the arts as representing the pull of tradition as regressive. Doubtless, Jutra's faith in technological progress sprang from his father's pioneering work in teleradiology and the treatment of cancer.[26] But the artistic milieu that his liberal family cultivated was also highly progressive, challenging the traditional values of the academy. So in the heart of the *grande noirceur* of the Duplessis era, Jutra was close to revolutions in science and technology, as well as to radical challenges in the prevailing aesthetic and social order through the arts.

The opposition between progress and tradition (or regression) leads into an opposition between Jutra's "very documentary" and "very subjective" films, a distinction Jutra himself made in 1968, it should be said, before directing his major fictional feature films. But again, there can be no clear correlation between the two oppositions. After all, *Comment savoir* (1966), a "very documentary" film about putting new technologies to use in a progressive classroom, is in the same category as his documentary films that celebrate traditional musicians. However, Jutra's own distinction between his documentary and subjective films does allow

Leach to make the link to the third component of the biographical legend—Jutra's fascination with the medium of film.

Jutra's fascination with film begs the question of the particular influences that weighed upon him as he began making his own films. His work with Norman McLaren at the National Film Board (NFB) in the 1950s and his later collaboration with Jean Rouch in France and Africa are the starting points for Leach's own examination of Jutra's work at the NFB. Yet, his first independent films show the clear influence of an avant-garde he had discovered in New York, through the works of Maya Deren and Kenneth Anger *inter alia*. And Jutra himself, in a 1980 interview with Jean-Daniel Lafond published more than a decade later, identifies Jean Cocteau as his most important formative influence.[27] Indeed, not only had he made the independent short *Anna la bonne* in 1959, working from Cocteau's own text and music, but we find Cocteau's treatment of the body, his mixing of genres, his transgressions of continuity, and the prominence of recurrent symbols, such as snowballs and mirrors, scattered through Jutra's work. And of course, Jutra got to know François Truffaut, who produced *Anna la bonne*, interviewed Jutra on the radio, and made a cameo appearance in *A tout prendre*. Few are the critics who do not recall Truffaut's *Les Quatre cent coups* (1959) and its closing freeze-frame of the young rebel when they comment on the freeze-frame of Benoît that closes *Mon oncle Antoine*. Truffaut's interest in adolescent rebellion, angst, and maturation runs parallel to Jutra's.

As the biographical legend is developed into a set of categories by which Jutra's work can be analyzed, the categories become oppositions or tensions, patterns that give structure to the personal and the artistic, and which may be construed as exhibiting both a universalizing tendency and a loose allegory of contemporary Quebec history. These oppositions may be thematic, such as science and art or progress and tradition. In *Mon oncle Antoine*, science and art have both been assimilated into commercial enterprise, applied science and technology in the mine, and various applied arts in the local store. The asbestos mine represents technology as the bringer of death (Euclide at the beginning of the film and Marcel at the end) while the applied art of fashion (Alexandrine's luxury lingerie) and folk art (present in the little figurines of the crib) are assimilated into spectacle (Alexandrine's dramatic entry into the store and the dramatic unveiling of the shop window); in each case art is associated with eros.

But the erotic undertones of each "art" sequence are distanced and undermined by Benoît's sexual embarrassment. He is caught by Carmen spying on Alexandrine as she tries on her new corset; and as the two youngsters decorate the window for the crib display, Carmen tricks Benoît into touching her breast, from which he recoils. As for progress and tradition, we have already seen that Benoît is left at the end of the film poised on choosing a new future that will affirm life (this is the meaning of his dream in which he emerges from the coffin for the sexual display of his fantasy Alexandrine) or re-affirming a status quo that carries the promise of premature death.

Oppositions developed from the biographical legend may be episte-mological. The pairing of objectivity and subjectivity is an example. Jutra himself allocates one or the other of these terms to each of his films. But their opposition is problematic, for the films are not as unambiguously divisible as the terms might suggest. The documentaries do not hide the filmmaker subject. A fictionalized Jutra appears in many of them.[28] In the homage to French-Canadian vocal performers (*Chantons maintenant*, 1956), Jutra plays the officious production assistant looking for the pre-senter Guy Laroche, returning with him only after the singers have all performed their songs among themselves, so that all he can do is provide the conventional wrap-up. Traditional documentary objectivity of the Griersonian kind yields to the self-conscious, formalizing tendency so typical of films of the French unit at the NFB during this time.[29]

More significant in the legend may be the opposition between per-sonal explanation and the expression of unexplained wonder or delight. For this we may go back to the celebration of bodily pleasure in the bathing sequences of *Le Dément du Lac Jean-Jeunes*, juxtaposed to Claude's didactic account of the making of the film. The celebration of Leclerc's songs in *Félix Leclerc troubadour* alternates with a combination of explana-tions of Leclerc's own world and tongue-in-cheek descriptions of the filmmaking process. Even in the fictional works, certain scenes have an almost didactic quality (a feature they share with French New Wave films). Examples of this quality are Truffaut's demonstration of a scene from *Jules et Jim* (1962) in *A tout prendre* and the scene in *Mon oncle Antoine* when we are shown how the funeral suit is removed from a corpse after the viewing. At the same time, these films also abound in moments of dreamlike wonderment.

There are also structural oppositions, such as the combination of linearity and circularity in Jutra's plot lines. The continuing interaction of the characters in *Pour le meilleur et pour le pire* follows the twenty-four-hour convention of French classical theatre, but, with a Ionesco-like touch of the absurd, the world outside the married couple's apartment goes through a year-long cycle of the seasons, and their daughter grows from infancy into late adolescence. Three incompatible cycles are thus juxtaposed in the film, so that the constant bickering of the couple takes place all day long, all year long, and for a whole parental-generational cycle. In that sense, the film can be seen as repetitive rather than linear. The linear story that takes us out of the film is the background development of Martine, their daughter, who leaves the family home at the end of the film as the carrier of the hopes for a new generation.

Circular structures are also a feature of films as diverse as *Mouvement perpétuel* in which the tearing of photographs in the opening shot returns at the end, or *Kamouraska* (1973), which frames the action of the film within Elisabeth's dozing vigil by the deathbed of her second husband. The Christmas and funeral rituals that punctuate the action in *Mon oncle Antoine* suggest the repetitive liturgical and life cycles drained of meaning for those charged with realizing them; any hopes for linear progress rest with the maturing Benoît.

At a time when Quebec felt that it was experiencing its own revolution, its own modernization, and that this revolution was perhaps stalling even as it began in the eyes of many of the nationalist intellectuals there, it is not surprising that Jutra's films were frequently viewed for signs of optimism or pessimism where sovereignist ambitions were concerned. Jutra experienced a sense of personal rejection in his career as a Québécois filmmaker, and figures of failed artists began to people his films. This frustration carries its correlative in the fluctuating fortunes of the Quebec independence movement, from its successful consolidation in 1969 through FLQ crisis to electoral defeat (1970–1971), then from electoral success (1976) to referendum defeat (1980) and constitutional humiliation (1981). Jutra's films were often chided for not foregrounding the contemporary political realities clearly enough. And yet Jutra's films thematize a sense of local identity (from Félix Leclerc's definition of national and cultural identity through song in *Chantons maintenant* to the denunciations of Duplessis era heartlessness in *Mon oncle Antoine* and *La Dame en couleurs*).

Jutra's films blow hot and cold on the chances of liberation. Many are set in enclosed institutional environments such as schools, hospitals, the church, and prison. Within these settings Jutra can find external models for an eventual liberation (Célestin Freinet's pedagogy in *Comment savoir*, R.D. Laing's anti-psychiatry in *Ada* [1976]). But more frequently, those who express and long for liberation are the children, the mad, the artists, those who imagine and aspire to freedom and who are most in danger of losing it forever. Jutra, the "perpetual child," the sensibility poised on the edge of madness, the artist of wavering fortunes, is one of them. Freedom is the freedom of the imagination and the realization of personal identity, and in Jutra's context its social correlative is the freedom secured by the realization of a national identity through sovereignty.

For Jutra, the leap to freedom, the unrestrained dance of the imagination, the celebrations of life and eros, had been dreams only briefly realized, more frequently frustrated. When realized, the exercise of Jutra's imagination, the rituals of Jutra's dance, his pursuit of life and delight, were mediated through technologies harnessed to support performance by a sharp, organizing mind. But as access to those technologies and to the organizing capacity of that mind began inexorably to elude his grasp, Jutra was driven calmly, but just as inexorably, toward stasis and thanatos. His last leap would lead to that final embrace of moving water, the water that for him had always ironically provided and symbolized both life and death, sun-drenched pleasure and ice-cold reality. Jutra began realizing his own artistic freedom at the same time as Quebec began to sense a new potential for self-realization through the affirmation of a distinct identity. But threaded into the hopes of achieving sovereignty, despite the fluctuating fortunes of the independentist Parti Québécois, were setbacks to these aspirations: the 1970 October Crisis; the 1980 referendum that saw the sovereignty option rejected; and the 1981 débâcle, when Canada repatriated its constitution without Quebec's consent. These moments coincided with the gradual draining of support for Jutra's artistic endeavours and his eventual exile to the world of the Anglophone Canadian other.

The parallel between the individual Jutra and the society of francophone Quebec is only a parallel. Neither of these trajectories caused the other, nor can the parallel be usefully extended to account for everything in Jutra's films or in his biography. But the viewer who comes to Jutra's films with this parallel in mind will find the critical moments of existential choice in them particularly poignant and ironic. Must the urge to leap to freedom, when frustrated or avoided, yield to a sense of delay, a sense of immobility, or a sense of despair? When memory fails and the indifference of others prevails, is there an alternative to the leap to death, and will it be forced or willingly accepted? Perhaps the legends of Jutra's life and the trajectory of his career and work will not always compel comparison with the social and political context within which they occurred. But the interaction between the two in the viewer's mind should not be taken as evidence of Jutra's own dark despair about Quebec. His films suggest that the urge to challenge authority, to break free, to open up the imagination and give full expression to the complexities of desire and life, is recurrent. The return of the repressed is cyclical. When he leapt to his own end, he did not imply that Quebec would leap with him. The power of the imagination and the will to freedom would lead to more of those euphoric moments that pervade his films and punctuated cycles of liberation dreams that sustained the sovereignty movements. But while the wheel may keep on turning, its celebrants will no longer include Claude Jutra.

AUTHOR'S NOTE

The following people have been generous with me in providing their advice and knowledge in the preparation of this essay: Mireille Jutras, Claire Boyer, Denis Pelletier, Yolande Simard Perrault, Pierre Jutras and his staff at the Cinémathèque québécoise, the staff at the archives of the Université du Québec à Montréal, and Michel Brault.

1. "There is a lot of me in everything I do." Remark by Claude Jutra during a radio interview recorded for Radio-Canada (CBC), first aired on 8 February 1985, at http://archives.cbc.ca/IDC-0-72-752-4582/arts_culture/claude_jutra/clp7 (accessed 27 November 2005).

2. Pierre Jutras, "Claude Jutra: filmographie et témoignages," *Copie zero* 33 (September 1987): 4–14.

3. The director's cut of *Kamouraska* (1973). The theatrical version runs just over 123 minutes.

4. The title character in *Le Dément du Lac Jean-Jeunes* (1949) leaps from a cliff-top to his death in a creek. The man in the white shirt in *Mouvement perpétuel* (1949) falls from a bridge into the river; a stunt apparently performed by Jutra himself, see *Jutra*, film directed by Paule Baillargeon (NFB, 2004). In *A tout prendre* (1963), the central character played by Jutra, who appears to be using autobiographical elements in his film, walks off a dock into the St. Lawrence at the end of the film. Related scenes are found in Philippe's dream in *Wow* (1969) in which several authority figures are tossed into the dockland waters of Montreal; in *Surfacing* (1980), the central character's boyfriend experiences a dramatic fall from a cliff, and she finishes by discovering the drowned body of her father underwater at the base of another cliff.

5. Jean-Pierre Gorin (1969); Jean-Luc Godard (1971); Gilles Groulx (1980). Jutra's attribution of his later difficulties to this accident was derived from an interview with Mireille Jutras in the summer of 2005.

6. These forms included the election of the Liberal government of 1960 on a platform of "Maîtres chez nous," the nationalization of Hydro Québec, the split in the Liberal party, and the eventual formation of the sovereignist Parti Québécois bringing several parties with a similar ambition together. All of this took place alongside the establishment of the direct action of the Front de Libération du Québec and their bomb campaign targeting federal symbols and institutions, until the kidnappings of 1970.

7. Although shooting had finished by June, the film was being edited at the time of the FLQ crisis. The ups and downs in the feelings of the independentist community at that time are well described in Michel Julien and Alain Julien, *Le Dictionnaire du cinéma québécois* (Montréal: Fides, 1978), 218–19 in their discussion of Michel Brault's later film *Les ordres* (1974).

8. Albert Jutras, "Why I collect Canadian Painting," *Canadian Art* 3, no. 4 (1946): 141–45. See also http://www.ccca.ca/c/writing/j/jutras/juto01t.html (accessed 12 November 2005).

9. These are the names recalled by Mireille Jutras in a private interview.

10. The impact was long-lasting. Forty years later Jutra would cast Camille Bernard, then in her seventies, as Madame Tassy in his film *Kamouraska*.

11. Adélard Lacasse opened a dance studio in Montreal 1895; in 1931, it was taken over by his son Maurice and daughter-in-law Carmen, who russified their name to Morenoff and who maintained it until 1986. Their most illustrious pupil was Fernand Nault, choreographer emeritus for Les Grands Ballets Canadiens.

12. Le Théâtre du Nouveau Monde was founded in Montreal by Jean Gascon in 1950 and from the beginning incorporated a school in classical theatre. Claude Jutra was a contemporary of Marc Favreau and Georges Dor.

13. *Images en boîte* (1954) and *Cinéma canadien* (1961) were both thirteen-part series hosted by Jutra, the first of thirty minutes each, the second sixty minutes. Jutra was also an important presence in the eleven-part series *Cinéma d'ici* (André Lafrance and Gilles Marsolais, 1971).

14. His science and technology documentaries include *Petit discours de la méthode* (1963) and *Comment savoir* (1966). The documentaries on the arts include *Chantons maintenant* (1956), *Jeunesses musicales* (1956), *Félix Leclerc troubadour* (1959), *Fred Barry comédien* (1959).

15. The film made with McLaren was *Il était une chaise/A Chairy Tale* (NFB, 1957). Films privileging a childhood perspective include *Rouli-roulant* (1966), and *Wow*; madness is significant in *Anna la bonne* (1959) and *Ada* (1976), while the two perspectives come together in *Dreamspeaker* (1976) and *La Dame en couleurs* (1984). Dream sequences abound in *A tout prendre*, *Wow*, *Mon oncle Antoine*, *Surfacing*, *Dreamspeaker*, and *La Dame en couleurs*. "L'amour fou" is best exemplified in *Kamouraska*.

16. Porc-épic (Claude Jutras), « Le Dément du Lac Jean-Jeunes, » *Le scout catholique* (1948): 12–13. "Porc-épic" (Porcupine), Jutra's scouting name, was used in the film credits. Michel Brault is referred to as the "Héron" in both places.

17. Segments of "Mars" from Gustav Holst's *The Planets* (1916).

18. The "Moldau" from Bedrich Smetana's *Ma Vlast* (1874).

19. In an address to film students at York University, October 2005.

20. Tom Waugh, "Je ne le connais pas tant que ça: Claude Jutra," trans. Bruno Comellier, *Nouvelles vues sur le cinéma québécois* 2 (2004). See also http://www. cinema-quebecois.net (accessed 12 November 2005). This is an extract from his forthcoming *The Romance of Transgression in Canada: Sexualities, Nations, Moving Images* (Toronto: University of Toronto Press, 2006), in which the author discusses the sensuality of the bathing scenes.

21. See *Le Dément du Lac Jean-Jeunes* and *Surfacing*.

22. Jutra had met McLaren when he began working on projects for the NFB and made an abstract film called *Trio-Brio* (1953) on his equipment, a film since lost. Jim Leach believes that McLaren played a role in the making of *Pierrot des*

bois (1956), but there is no clear evidence of what that role might have been. See Jim Leach, *Claude Jutra: Filmmaker* (Montreal and Kingston: McGill-Queen's University Press, 1999) 39–40.

23. Ibid., 7–14.

24. Ibid., 9.

25. Heinz Weinmann, *Cinéma de l'imaginaire québécois: De la Petite Aurore à Jésus de Montréal*. (Montreal: L'Hexagone, 1990), discussed in Leach, *Claude Jutra: Filmmaker*, 18–19.

26. A brilliant medical student, he practised in northern Quebec and Montreal before winning a scholarship to study radiology in Paris at about the time that his son Claude was born. After three years in France, the family returned to Montreal, and by 1938 Albert Jutras had become the head of Radiology at the Hôtel-Dieu hospital, added a chair in radiology at l'Université de Montréal by 1951, and continued thus until his retirement in 1965. His pioneering work in teleradiology gained him an international reputation. Showered with international prizes, he was admitted to the Order of Canada in 1976, four years after his elder son Claude had, along with Geneviève Bujold, turned it down publicly as a mark of solidarity with nationalist friends. A lecture series at Hôtel-Dieu carries his name, as well as a prize at l'Université de Montréal, and a syndrome.

27. Jean-Daniel Lafond, "Claude Jutra et les chats de Cocteau," *Lumières* 27 (Summer 1991): 28–31.

28. Two such examples are *Fred Barry comédien* and *Félix Leclerc troubadour*.

29. See my "From the Picturesque to the Familiar: Films of the French Unit at the National Film Board of Canada (1958–1964)," in Seth Feldman, ed., *Take Two* (Toronto: Irwin Publishing, 1984), 112–24.

3

"It takes monsters to do things like that"

The Films of Jean-Claude Lauzon

JIM LEACH

In the opposition between fantasy and reality, the Real is on the side of fantasy.
—SLAVOJ ŽIŽEK[1]

JEAN-CLAUDE LAUZON directed only two feature films, and he virtually disowned one of them. Nevertheless, he became something of a legendary figure in Quebec because of his lurid stories about his delinquent youth (from which he was rescued by André Petrowski of the National Film Board, or NFB); his numerous run-ins with the media; and, finally, his death in 1997, when the small plane he was flying crashed in northern Quebec, killing him and his companion, popular television personality Marie-Soleil Tougas. Lauzon's reputation in Quebec was also complicated by his insistence on referring to himself as a Canadian filmmaker at a time when most critics and filmmakers felt that Quebec cinema had little in common with its English-Canadian counterpart.

Unsurprisingly, perhaps, Lauzon often claimed that his films—*Un Zoo la nuit/Night Zoo* (1987) and *Léolo* (1992)—were better appreciated outside

Quebec, but critics everywhere were divided between those who passionately defended the films and those who complained they were marred by basic flaws of style and narrative. There were also complaints about the violence and the treatment of sexuality in his films, and the films' ideological implications also came under scrutiny, especially in Quebec. Lauzon always insisted that he worked on "pure instinct," as opposed to more cerebral directors like Denys Arcand, who encouraged the young filmmaker and appeared in small roles in both films. [2] He freely admitted that he was "a tyrant, a fascist, a monster" on set (but only because "it takes monsters to do things like that"), and he would have appreciated the obituary notice in which Marcel Jean wrote that "the least that one can say is that Lauzon never did anything by half-measures, which was his main quality and his greatest fault.... He was a wild filmmaker who had not been domesticated by the system."[3]

Despite his provocations, and although he repeatedly asserted that he did not "think politically," Lauzon acknowledged that he was "from a specific culture and...really proud to be a French Canadian."[4] He admired the films of Gilles Carle and Denys Arcand and felt especially close to the surrealist-influenced work of André Forcier, who insisted that "surrealism is an explosion of the real, not an escape from it."[5] Yet it was difficult to situate Lauzon's films within the highly politicized environment of Quebec culture (and cinema) after the defeat of the separatist forces in the 1980 referendum on sovereignty association. Arcand also came under attack for the alleged ideological shortcomings of the films that revived his career at this time—*Le Déclin de l'empire americain* (1986) and *Jésus de Montréal* (1989). Perhaps paradoxically, Lauzon's anti-intellectual approach allowed critics to interpret his films as allegories of the cultural and political situation in Quebec.

Given his status as a "wild filmmaker," critics could argue Lauzon "ends up saying things without consciously intending to."[6] Accordingly, Heinz Weinmann claimed that *Un Zoo la nuit* reflects the "sad, anguished, depressing post-referendum atmosphere," conveying a widespread feeling that "the dream of the future had been crushed."[7] The expansion of an Italian restaurant into Albert's living space next door, like Léo's fantasy of Italian origins in *Léolo*, evokes the growth of the ethnic population in Quebec that threatens the distinct culture on which the argument for an independent future depends. The casting of Anglophone Lorne Brass as a sadistic cop in *Un Zoo* and as the youth who beats up Léo's brother, Fernand, also invited, and received, political interpretation. Critics also found much to say about Lauzon's use of Pierre Bourgault, a political figure long associated with the independence movement, as the old man who encourages Léo to keep dreaming.

Lauzon always rejected such socio-political interpretations. He claimed to "adore Italians," pointed out that the bully was not an Anglophone in the scenario, and insisted that the casting of Bourgault was not politically motivated.[8] There is, of course, no need to accept his account more than any other, but many critics do seem to have sensed that the films, like their maker, resist such readings. An alternative framework for interpreting Lauzon's films was offered by the many autobiographical elements in his works, but it was their appeal to fantasy that disturbed all attempts at rational explanation and that has provoked the most persuasive critical responses.

Christine Ramsay thus suggests that *Léolo* "invites us below the threshold of rational consciousness," and George Toles evokes Lauzon's "propensity towards the dark extremes of human behaviour and...exploration of the sensuous surfaces of the decaying material world."[9] Lauzon encouraged such readings, when, just after completing *Léolo*, he told an interviewer that his "work as a director...is to be able to show our deepest fears," adding that "right now, there are creative people who are afraid to talk about the real thing."[10] The "our" in this sentence is ambiguous: it could refer to the Québécois and their fears of disappearance, but it also points to the basic human fear of, and fascination with, "the real thing."

In Slavoj Žižek's terms, Lauzon's films set out to break down "the barrier separating the real from reality."[11] Although they certainly resonate with their ideological, political, and cinematic contexts, placing them too readily within the interpretive frames of national cinema, or genre, or whatever, runs the risk of effacing their *strangeness*, the pressure of the Real that is felt through the engagement with fantasy.

After making *Léolo*, Lauzon declared that it was his "first real film" and that it grew out of the final sequence of *Un Zoo la nuit*, which was the only part of that film he now acknowledged.[12] He envisaged *Léolo* as a poetic film in which he would not be "obliged to pass through the explanatory side" that restricted him in *Un Zoo la nuit*, "that is to say the dramatic intrigue, the villains, the good guys, the money, the crime story."[13] By disavowing genre conventions, Lauzon was in accord with many film critics of the time who rejected genre as a threat to the personal (or *auteur*) films on which the reputation of Quebec cinema supposedly depends. Yet this critical perspective was already built into *Un Zoo la nuit*, which he claimed, at the time of its release, was made in opposition to the "stereotyped behaviour" he associated with American cinema.[14]

The crime story that dominates the first half of *Un Zoo* encourages us to view it as "a sardonic commentary on corrupt and corrosive elements in modern Quebec society."[15] Marcel (Gilles Maheu) is a drug dealer pursued by corrupt cops out for their share of the proceeds, his girlfriend Julie (Lynne Adams) is a sex worker, and the climactic shoot-out with the cops takes place in a seedy hotel called the Bangkok Paradise. There are other apparent allusions to post-referendum despondency: Marcel offers to take Julie and then his father, Albert, (Roger Le Bel) to Australia, which he calls "the end of the world"; after Albert suffers a heart attack, a television plays "O Canada" while the father of the restaurant owner tells Marcel (in Italian) that everything will be alright. Yet, without denying that many spectators in Quebec would have read the film in the context of the failure of the "Yes" side in the referendum, its tensions derive from what Toles called, with a much broader context in mind, Lauzon's "attempt to keep the possibilities of 'yes' and 'no' equally in play at all times."[16]

As many critics noticed, the film's balancing act involves a radical shift in tone when the crime thriller gives way to the emotional reconciliation of father and son. According to Corbeil, this divided structure, and the renunciation of genre, had an autobiographical explanation. When his father died while Lauzon was writing the script, "he killed off the cops and started to write about his father," with the result that "a stylish and rather superficial thriller flipped into something uniquely moving."[17] Geoff Pevere called the effect "schizophrenic," and some critics felt that the film made "the mistake of trying to be two movies at the same time."[18] Others, including Maurice Elia, were impressed by "the brilliant dissonances" and by a film style in which "no aspect is privileged in relation to the others."[19]

For Michael Dorland, the crime-film narrative prevented the film from becoming "an authentic slice of the Québécois here-and-now," and he dismissed it as a trendy example of postmodern pastiche, stressing "its derivativeness (i.e., complete unoriginality)."[20] As a crime film, *Un Zoo la nuit* reminded critics of the French "cinema of the look," a term used to describe the films of Jean-Jacques Beineix, Luc Besson, and Leos Carax. In films such as *Diva* (Beineix, 1981) and *Subway* (Besson, 1985), the directors applied techniques derived from television commercials to create what David Russell described as "a form of postmodernist cinema deliberately without depth and endlessly allusive."[21] Since Lauzon worked extensively on television commercials, his crime film thus seems to be the height of inauthenticity, a pastiche of a pastiche.

Yet it is precisely the artifice of pastiche and allusion that allows Lauzon to engage with the relations between fantasy and the Real. Rather laconically, he described *Un Zoo la nuit* as a film "with a high contrast," and Corbeil captured its effect when she observed that, between its violent opening, in which Marcel is raped in prison, and intense ending, in which he lies naked beside his father's body, "the in-between is missing."[22] What happens in-between, however, is the collision of two kinds of cinema. The shoot-out occurs about halfway through the film, and the focus then turns to Marcel's attempt to renew relations with his father just before the old man dies.

At the beginning of the film, two sequences establish the "high contrast" aesthetic, at the same time setting the crime-thriller plot in motion. The pre-credits sequence consists of a single shot in which the camera pulls back from a view of the city through a window to reveal a large room where the furniture is covered with sheets. As the shot begins, a telephone rings and activates an answering machine that consists of two large reel-to-reel tape recorders (we later discover Marcel is a musician). After a male voice explains that he is "out of town," the caller promises to send a "present" and apologizes that it will not be Brigitte Bardot. The credits appear over a shot of the city, accompanied by the calls of wild animals, and Marcel then receives the present in the form of a burly inmate who, with the connivance of a guard, rapes him in his prison cell. The brightly lit but uninhabited studio thus gives way to the dark constricted spaces of the prison and the confinement from which Marcel struggles to free himself even after he is released.

Initially, the brief episodes with the father seem like a distraction from the main plot, and the cops indeed assume that Marcel is spending so much time with his father to divert attention from his real goal of escaping with the drug money. The estrangement between father and son is signified by the verbal games in which Marcel refuses to admit that he has been in prison while Albert pretends that he does not know the real reason for his son's absence. After his release, the Italian couple who own the restaurant next door welcome him as if he were their own long lost son, while Albert stands uneasily by. In keeping with its aesthetic of surfaces, the film does not explain Marcel's change of attitude toward his rather pathetic father, but, as soon as the cops have been eliminated, he invites the old man on a fishing trip. They become so close that Marcel strips and tenderly washes the old man on his deathbed and then lies naked beside the dead man.

The story of the reconciliation of father and son may be, as Corbeil suggests, more personal and moving than what precedes it, but it is far from "unique." The lengthy sequence in which they fish on a lake evokes the traditional iconography of rural Quebec to which Lauzon himself felt very close. According to Weinmann, Albert teaches his son "the ancestral secrets of hunting and fishing" that were handed down from the "Amerindians to the *coureurs de bois*" but are now threatened by "galloping urbanization."[23] Yet it becomes clear that Albert's claim to "ancestral" knowledge is rather hollow. The sequence ends when the two men collapse in laughter after Marcel fails to reel in a fish, for which Albert blames his son. However, Albert's fishing advice has been none too clear. Similarly, Albert's claim to have once shot a gigantic moose is suspect, since he has no evidence, unlike the restauranteur Tony (Corrado Mastropasqua), who has mounted the head of his own hunting trophy in his restaurant.

The traditional imagery comes under even greater pressure when, after Albert's heart attack, Marcel smuggles him out of the hospital to fulfill his desire to shoot one final moose. In the middle of the night, they break into a zoo where, since there is no moose, Albert shoots an elephant instead, and Marcel takes a Polaroid photo to prove his father's triumph. As Weinmann acknowledged, this sequence is both grotesque and absurd: "To hunt an animal in a zoo...for an image!"[24] Yet the photographic image that proves the kill is itself called into question by the increasing uncertainty about the reality of the film's images. In particular, the visit of Albert's estranged wife to his bedroom in the middle of the night may be a real event (arranged by Marcel) but it could equally be a product of the dying man's imagination, and Lauzon even suggested in an interview that "we can ask ourselves if Albert and Marcel really went to the zoo."[25]

If the trip to the zoo and the return of Albert's wife are imaginary events, we are left to decide exactly when the narrative lost touch with reality. This slippage from actual events to imaginary ones, and the audience's consequent loss of confidence in the film's narrative, contrasts with the physicality of the final sequences. The ending is the only part of the film that Lauzon later acknowledged as his own, and its effect is enhanced by the "high contrast" with the opening. Physical closeness has replaced distance and absence in an image in which, as Weinmann puts it, "*Eros* only expresses itself on the basis of Thanatos."[26] The ending thus depends on a tension between body and image, but the film has penetrated to a level of fantasy that pushes the film into the domain of the Real. As Lauzon suggested, Marcel "does something for his father that goes beyond fashion, type, religion" and resembles "the behaviour of animal survival."[27]

After the international success of *Un Zoo la nuit*, Lauzon turned down several offers from Hollywood producers to make action films.[28] Rejecting genre constraints, *Léolo* constructs a rich blend of fantasy and reality in which images and sounds from a variety of classical and modern sources collide and flow into each other, creating what Ramsay aptly calls a "stunning palimpsest."[29] As we shall see, there is a constant impression of different levels of narration competing with one another to tell the story of Léo Lozeau (Maxime Collin), who disavows his working-class Montreal family and constructs an elaborate fiction in which he is actually Léolo Lozone, conceived by chance when his mother (Ginette Reno) was impregnated by a tomato contaminated with sperm that remained on it after an Italian agricultural worker had masturbated on it.

Léo's "real" father is an even more abject figure than Albert in *Un Zoo la nuit*, but here the focus is on the relationship with his mother, an ample woman who is the strongest member of the family and the only one who does not spend periods of time in an asylum. In their documentary on Lauzon, *Lauzon/Lauzone* (2001), Louis Bélanger and Isabelle Hébert include interviews with the filmmaker's mother to show how the film is a fantastic reworking of elements from Lauzon's own childhood. They point out that the house outside which the young Léo sits at the beginning of the film is the one in which Lauzon was born, but the world into which the narrator invites us is one that scrambles normal coordinates of space and time.

The narrator seems, in the opening sequences, to be the older Léo looking back on his past, and he describes the working-class neighbourhood as "Mile End, Montreal, Canada." This formulation pointedly does not mention Quebec, and, a few moments later, the masturbating farm worker explains that the tomatoes are going to "America," a destination confirmed by a caption that sets the following sequence "a few days later in America." While the Montreal setting is unmistakable, the refusal to name Quebec implies a symbolic lack that motivates Léo's desire not to belong to his family and his refusal to admit that he is "French Canadian."

The temporal setting is similarly both precise and elusive. Although the tone of the opening narration is apparently nostalgic—in the manner of Federico Fellini's *Amarcord* (1973), with which some critics compared it—the precise date of the story is difficult to pin down. The film draws attention to its vagueness when, as the narration begins, the camera pans down from the date 1909 carved on top of the building to reveal Léo sitting on the steps. Most critics think the film is set in the 1950s, in keeping with its autobiographical origins, which would situate the story before the Quiet Revolution. If, as Corbeil suggests, Léo was, like Lauzon, born in 1953, the scenes involving his six-year-old self are indeed set in the late 1950s, but the crisis that overwhelms his twelve-year-old self would then take place in 1965.[30] However, the novel by Réjean Ducharme that figures prominently in his memories (or fantasies), as we shall see, was published in 1967, and the narrative structure complicates any sense of linear progression. The music also works against a firm sense of historical time, an effect well-captured in the film's English-language press

kit, which declares that, "in Lauzon's remembrance of a Montreal boyhood, Tom Waits and the Rolling Stones exist side by side with music
from Argentina, Arabia, Canada and France."

The complex structure demands that the viewer be alert to how the
images relate to the music and to the different levels of narration. Many
critics refused this challenge and accused Lauzon of not following the
basic cinematic principles that insisted on the primacy of the visual
experience. Marie-Claude Loiselle, for example, complains that the film
"suffers from an invasive voiceover which is almost systematically imposed on the images" and that there is a systematic "recourse to music,
most often dense and invasive, that deprives the image of its resources."[31]

The narration is problematic not just because of its extent but also
because of the uncertainty about who is speaking it. Because the words
spoken by the narrator are taken from Léo's writings (and often from
Lauzon's own then unpublished poetry), the narrator uses the first person.
The voice, therefore, seems to be that of Léo looking back on his childhood. Some critics identify the narration as "the voice of the man whom
Léolo grows up to be,"[32] but this seems unlikely, given the ending in
which the twelve-year-old boy slips into an apparently permanent catatonic state. In any case, Léo writes on scraps of paper that are retrieved
from the garbage by an old man known as the "Worm Tamer," who
carries them down into his archive at the end. However, it is not his
voice we hear, and the narrator seems thus to be "a phantom reader of
Leo's recorded thoughts" or "the synthetic voice of the visualized Léo and
the extra-diegetic Director."[33]

The enigmatic figure of the Worm Tamer adds another level of mystery.
He was often identified with André Petrowski, to whom the film is dedicated, and is played by Bourgault, another of Lauzon's mentors. Referred
to in the English-dubbed version (and by many critics) as the Word Tamer,
the Worm Tamer (*Dompteur des vers*) first appears in the film walking with
Léo along a rain-swept beach at night, illuminated by burning torches.[34]
They are carrying buckets and wearing pit helmets, and the narrator
explains that the Worm Tamer spends his nights "digging in the garbage
cans of the world." He collects letters and photographs and becomes
immersed in the stories he finds there, as if they were his own. Since he
believes that "images and words must mingle with the ashes of worms

to be reborn in the imaginations of men," he and Léo ceremoniously burn letters and photographs, still wearing their pit helmets. He could be yet another figment of Léo's imagination—or vice versa.

The Worm Tamer is associated with the one book in the Lozeau household, Ducharme's *L'Avalée des avalés* (*The Swallower Swallowed*), whose central character is a young woman who invents her own world to escape from her family. The book has underlined passages, which the narrator recites as Léo reads them, and we later learn that it was brought to the house by the Worm Tamer. Although the book seems to be the inspiration that drives the young boy to write, the explanation for its presence in the working-class home is delayed and casts doubt on the usual relationship between cause and effect. After the narrator describes the fear that led Léo's brother, Fernand, to take up bodybuilding, the Worm Tamer finds this description in a garbage can along with a Bell phone bill that reveals where the words come from. *Then* he visits Madame Lozeau's kitchen and uses the book to balance the table.[35]

The narrator repeatedly intones the words, "because I dream, I am not," and we eventually see them written on the title page of the book. In context, this first seems to imply: "I am not French Canadian." However, as Léo describes his crazy family, the meaning of the phrase appears to be: "I am not mad." In Léo's mind, though, there is little difference between these two implications. It is not even certain that Léo is the author of these words, since he could be appropriating a phrase already written in the book, perhaps by the Worm Tamer, whom he describes as a reincarnation of Don Quixote, the archetypal dreamer. It is also possible that the words make a complete sentence, equating dream with the negation of an intolerable reality.

If, as Corbeil suggests, "the boy's survival depends on his ability to split off into fantasy," the key question at the end of the film becomes the terms on which the film envisages survival.[36] For Bert Cardullo, an American critic, the resort to fantasy leads Léo to a failure to cope with reality and to take action to resolve his problems. Assuming that Léo has grown up to become the narrator, Cardullo argues that the adult has not "grown beyond a replaying of his boyish chimeras" and that "because he too dreams, he does not live."[37] Piers Handling, a rather less pragmatic English-Canadian critic, translates this sense of personal failure onto a broader social and cultural level, describing *Léolo* as "a kind of epitaph for Quebec, which has a long tradition of trying to change reality, of refusing to be a colony."[38]

Yet, while the Worm Tamer tries to improve Léo's situation by speaking to his teacher, he encourages him to dream, and Lauzon described the film as "a kind of homage to dream" and "creativity."[39] Léo's dreams of Italy are embodied in Bianca (Giuditta Del Vecchio), an angelic-looking neighbour who represents everything that his family is not, and they evoke his desire to transcend the narrow limits imposed by his environment. Whereas the Lozeau home is dark and ruled by a father obsessed with bowel movements, Bianca is associated with the white light that accompanies Léo's visions and seems to emanate from her. Léo claims that he first saw this light when his grandfather tried to kill him by holding his head under water—the light evokes death as well as love. Like the similar glowing light that is all that can be seen of the perfect painting in *I've Heard the Mermaids Singing* (1987)—the first feature by Patricia Rozema with whom Lauzon posed on the cover of the May 1987 edition of *Cinema Canada*—the light evokes the Real, a dimension of human experience that defies representation within the imaginary and symbolic structures that make up our everyday sense of reality.

However, the film complicates matters by refusing to clearly distinguish between fantasy and reality. As the press kit puts it, "young Léolo's home life is nearly as surreal as the dreams in which he seeks safe harbor." It is as if Léo, like Bérénice in *L'Avalée des avalés*, has swallowed his world in order not to be swallowed by it. If the film is an exaggerated version of events from Lauzon's past, we can never be sure that what we are seeing has not been transformed by the imagination of a child, however filtered through the narrative apparatus. Thus, when Léo spies on his grandfather in the bath with Bianca standing half naked beside him, his voyeurism excites him sexually, but what we see is the old man persuading her to bite his toenails. This revelation inspires Léo to construct an elaborate trap to kill his grandfather when he next takes a bath. The audience is left to wonder whether the oral perversion that desecrates Léo's image of Bianca may not have been a more common one (censored either by the boy's mind or by more adult or institutional inhibitions).

The motif of a child viewing, and judging, the adult world is a familiar one in Quebec cinema, from the abused girl in *La Petite Aurore, l'enfant martyre* (Jean-Yves Bigras, 1952) to the orphan boy in *Mon oncle Antoine* (Claude Jutra, 1971) to the autistic boy in *Mario* (Jean Beaudin, 1984). This motif also figures in two important films by Francis Mankiewicz, *Le Temps d'une chasse* (1972) and *Les Bons Débarras* (1979), the latter with a screenplay by Ducharme. In all these films, there is the sense of an impoverished reality that offers little future to the child—a sense whose political implications in the Quebec context are apparent but usually only implied—and eventually breaks down as a result of the intrusion of the Real, usually in the form of a death. To varying degrees, these children use their imaginations to create an alternative world more in keeping with their desires. *Léolo* takes this motif but uses the child's point-of-view to expose the entanglement of fantasy and reality and, finally, to disturb the viewer's confidence that the distortions are simply a matter of childhood perception. In all these films, the child suffers from a lack of love, a need that is complicated by their emerging sexuality.

Typically, Lauzon provides an excessive representation of the traumatic encounter with sex and mortality in the controversial ending of *Léolo*. After an excruciating sequence in which Léo watches as another boy is dared into having sex with a cat, he has his first sexual experience in the street with a local prostitute. He believes he has betrayed Bianca and runs through the Sicilian countryside calling for her, an idyllic vision cut short by Fernand's discovery that his brother has succumbed to the family sickness.

In keeping with his sense of himself as an instinctive filmmaker, Lauzon claimed that he had "no idea why he wrote those penultimate lines...about how Léolo stopped dreaming because he stopped loving."[40] Yet these lines do provide a relatively straightforward, if extremely bleak, conclusion to a very fragmented film, at least at the plot level. In the final sequence, Léo lies naked in a bath of ice cubes in the asylum, and we see the Italian landscape of his dreams. The Worm Tamer reads his final words, "I no longer dream," and carries Léo's writings down into his museum filled with artifacts of western civilization.

For Corbeil, the image of Léo in the bath of ice is "so strong that it makes the short epilogue of the movie, which attempts to redeem Léolo's suffering by giving his writings a place in the pantheon of art, impossible to take in."[41] Other critics also stress the negativity of the ending. Cardullo feels that Léo's "only recourse is to become a vegetable," and Handling calls it "a film of despair, of closed doors, of the impossibility of any hope of change."[42] Lauzon, however, insisted that this ending is a "liberation" that affirms "the power of the imagination."[43] While it is difficult to deny that *Léolo*, like *Un Zoo la nuit*, depicts a bizarre and unredeemed "reality," its mosaic style works against the linearity of conventional narrative structures and thus undermines the finality of the ending.

Lauzon's monstrous creations take us into an uncomfortable, but provocative, world that exposes the "high contrast" between human desire and bodily limitations and refuses to smooth out the contradictions involved. In this world, fantasy is on the side of the Real, but its expression is inextricably bound to a reality that seems increasingly fantastic. While these tensions continue to resonate in Quebec cinema after Lauzon's death, his impact is perhaps best seen in the work of a group of young filmmakers whose films combine a dazzling visual surface with dislocated narrative structures that tap into the unconscious. These films include *Maelström* (Denis Villeneuve, 2000), *Un Crabe dans la tête* (André Turpin, 2001), and *Les Turbulence des fluides* (Manon Briand, 2002), all of which engage with the fantastic and the Real, although they do not quite emulate the disturbing power of Lauzon's intense and excessive features.

NOTES

1. Slavoj Žižek, *The Fragile Absolute—or, Why is the Christian Legacy Worth Fighting For?* (London: Verso, 2000), 67.

2. Lauzon, quoted in Carole Corbeil, "The Indiscreet Charm of Jean-Claude Lauzon," *Saturday Night* 107 (December 1992): 89.

3. Lauzon, quoted in André Lavoie, "Vie, mort et résurrection de Jean-Claude Lauzon," *Ciné-Bulles* 16, no. 3 (Fall 1997): 2; Marcel Jean, "Jean-Claude-Lauzon," *24 Images* 90 (Winter 1998): 21.

4. Lauzon, quoted in Michel Buruiana, "Jean-Claude Lauzon," *Séquences* 158 (June 1992): 34, and in José Arroyo, "Howls from the Asphalt Jungle," *Cinema Canada* 141 (May 1987): 10.

5. Lauzon, quoted in Arroyo, "Howls," 8; Forcier, quoted in Philippe Gajan and Marie-Claude Loiselle, "Entretien avec André Forcier," *24 Images* 87 (Summer 1997): 10.

6. Corbeil, "The Indiscreet Charm," 90.

7. Heinz Weinmann, *Cinéma de l'imaginaire québécoise: De La Petite Aurore à Jésus de Montréal* (Montreal: L'Hexagone, 1990), 111.

8. Lauzon, quoted in Buruiana, "Jean-Claude Lauzon," 41; and in Claude Racine, "Entretien avec Jean-Claude Lauzon," *24 Images* 61 (Summer 1992): 7.

9. Christine Ramsay, "Léo Who? Questions of Identity and Culture in Jean-Claude Lauzon's *Léolo*," *Post Script* 15, no. 1 (Fall 1995): 25; George Toles, "Drowning for Love: Jean-Claude Lauzon's *Léolo*," in Gene Walz, ed., *Canada's Best Features: Critical Essays on 15 Canadian Films* (Amsterdam: Rodopi, 2002), 275. Toles is the regular screenwriter for Guy Maddin, the English-Canadian filmmaker to whom this description could equally apply, albeit with a very different effect.

10. Lauzon, quoted in Maurie Alioff, "Jean-Claude Lauzon's *Léolo*," *Take One* 1, no. 1 (1992): 18.

11. Slavoj Žižek, *Looking Awry: An Introduction to Jacques Lacan through Popular Culture* (Cambridge, MA: MIT Press, 1991), 20.

12. Lauzon, quoted in Racine, "Entretien," 5; and in Buruiana, "Jean-Claude Lauzon," 34.

13. Lauzon, quoted in Racine, "Entretien," 5.

14. Lauzon, quoted in Léo Bonneville, "Jean-Claude Lauzon," *Séquences* 130 (August 1987): 16.

15. Henry Garrity, "True Lies: Autobiography, Fiction and Politics in Jean-Claude Lauzon's *Léolo*," *Québec Studies* 20 (Spring–Summer 1995): 81.

16. Toles, "Drowning for Love," 280.

17. Corbeil, "The Indiscreet Charm," 87.

18. Geoff Pevere, "In Others' Eyes: Four Canadian Films Come Home from Cannes," *Cineaction* 11 (Winter 1987–88): 23; Bert Cardullo, "Forbidden Games," *Hudson Review* 46, no. 5 (Autumn 1993): 548.

19. Maurice Elia, "*Un Zoo la nuit*," *Séquences* 130 (August 1987): 60.

20. Michael Dorland, "Jean-Claude Lauzon's *Un Zoo la nuit*," *Cinema Canada* 144 (September 1987): 37. The terms that Dorland uses clearly derive from Fredric Jameson's influential account of postmodernism.

21. David Russell, "Two or Three Things We Know About Beineix," *Sight and Sound* 59, no. 1 (Winter 1989–90), 43.

22. Lauzon, quoted in Arroyo, "Howls," 8; and in Corbeil, "The Indiscreet Charm," 87.

23. Weinmann, *Cinéma de l'imaginaire québécoise*, 118.

24. Ibid.

25. Lauzon, quoted in Bonneville, "Jean-Claude Lauzon," 18.

26. Weinmann, *Cinéma de l'imaginaire québécoise*, 116.

27. Lauzon, quoted in Bonneville, "Jean-Claude Lauzon," 19.

28. Lauzon, quoted in Buruiana, "Jean-Claude Lauzon," 33.

29. Ramsay, "Léo Who?," 35.

30. Corbeil, "The Indiscreet Charm," 60.

31. Marie-Claude Loiselle, "Regard fuyant," *24 Images* 62, no. 3 (September–October 1992): 90–91.

32. Corbeil, "The Indiscreet Charm," 90.

33. Toles, "Drowning for Love," 290; Garrity, "True Lies," 82.

34. The name is an untranslatable pun since "vers" can also mean "poetry," but the context suggests—in the film's dream-like logic—that "worms" is the dominant meaning.

35. The narrator has earlier stated that Léo did not know how the book came into the house, and indeed he is not there when the Worm Tamer calls, but this raises questions about whose perspective the audience is seeing.

36. Corbeil, "The Indiscreet Charm," 89.

37. Cardullo, "Forbidden Games," 548.

38. Handling, quoted in Cardullo, "Forbidden Games," 550.

39. Lauzon, quoted in Racine, "Entretien," 6.

40. Corbeil, "The Indiscreet Charm," 60.

41. Ibid.

42. Cardullo, "Forbidden Games," 549; and Handling, quoted in Cardullo, 550.

43. Lauzon, quoted in Racine, "Entretien," 10.

Contemporary Greats

4

Denys Arcand
A Moralist in Search of His Audience[1]

PIERRE VÉRONNEAU

IT WAS 1961. Denys Arcand was a history student at the Université de Montréal. He was doing a two-year diploma. But more importantly at that time, he co-produced his first feature film, *Seul ou avec d'autres*, for the students' association. How did he get there?

Arcand was born in 1941 in Deschambault, a village on the banks of the St. Lawrence not far from Quebec City. In 1950 his family moved to Montreal. When it came to the children's education, there was only one option for him: a classical education in the best possible schools that would lead either to the priesthood or university. According to standards of that time, Arcand was destined to be part of the elite. He studied with the Jesuits and very early on showed a great interest in literature and cinema, without however giving up on the sports that he loved. He was lured into writing and published several articles in a student newspaper, showing a taste for analysis, freedom, sarcasm, cultural eclecticism, and humour. Maurice Duplessis' conservative regime was coming to an end and youth were declaring themselves to be free thinkers. French existentialism inspired them, and they wanted to overthrow the old and the tired. A period of social, political, economic, and cultural turmoil, named the Quiet Revolution, followed, with Arcand a full participant.

In the spring of 1962, the Office National du Film (ONF) asked Arcand to produce a report on the future direction for historical films about the French colonial regime in Quebec. These films were to be included in *The History Makers*, a film series produced by the ONF in honour of Canada's centennial in 1967. Arcand proposed thirteen films, of which three eventually saw the light of day, and he directed them all. In fact, in the summer of 1962, the ONF gave him his first contract to produce a film on Champlain, the founder of Quebec. The script is titled *Champlain: Une réévaluation*. On a historic level, Arcand wanted to turn his back on myth and hagiography, as the title suggests. This attitude would bring him severe criticism from the ONF and the organization moved quickly to edit, if not censor, the film.

On a cinematographic level, Arcand distanced himself from narrator-based films like the earlier productions in the *The History Makers* series and also from the direct cinema technique used by the most innovative filmmakers of the French group, such as Gilles Groulx and Michel Brault. Arcand had a point of view to communicate and he rejected both approaches. He wanted the audience to understand his interpretation and wanted his style to contribute to the clarity of his account. The trials and tribulations associated with *Champlain* forced Arcand to produce his next two historical films in a more conventional and less polemic style, although they are no less strict in their interpretation of history.

Next Arcand was recruited for a film on volleyball commissioned by the Department of Health. The idea was to use a match between the American and Soviet Olympic teams to promote the sport. However, Arcand framed the film (without commentary) with two short animated sequences by Kaj Pindal. This so irritated the clients that they rejected these sequences and asked for a new cut and another commentary. These experiences taught Arcand about the constraints imposed by funders and clients. For example, he wrote a script with Michel Brault for a project that would become *Entre la mer et l'eau douce* (1967) but the ONF did not want to get into features. So it was no surprise that Arcand appeared as one of the authors of the April 1964 issue of *Parti Pris*, a Marxist journal, criticizing the ONF and its role in Quebec cinema. Nor was it surprising that in 1965 he was one of the five founders of an independent production house, les Cinéastes Associés, all "graduates" of the NFB/ONF. Arcand directed only a few films commissioned for the 1967 world EXPO in Montreal. He eventually understood it was easier to freelance for the ONF, and this was how he came to film a tourist documentary on Cape Breton, *Parcs Atlantiques* (1967), and to act in Jacques Leduc's film *Nomininigue...depuis qu'il existe* (1968).

These bread-and-butter jobs allowed him to devote his attention to a more ambitious project: a documentary trilogy on present-day Quebec. The first piece, started in 1967 as a reflection on technocratic realities, evolved into an enquiry into the textile industry. Shooting began in 1968, and *On est au coton* was completed in 1970. Dissatisfied with the image of himself portrayed by Arcand, the owner of one of the textile factories demanded that the sequences he appeared in be edited, and the textile industry even called for banning the film. The ONF dithered, but shortly after the October Crisis in 1970 it decided to stop the film's distribution. *On est au coton* began to circulate under the table, most often in video format. It became a symbol of Canadian government suppression of a work denouncing capitalism and worker exploitation. As a result, Arcand moved to the forefront of political and militant cinema as a champion of free speech. It wasn't until 1976 that the film was back in circulation in its edited form. All the same, Arcand had produced an important work of direct cinema anchored in the reality of contemporary Quebec and interpreted in his own way, however despairing it was. His forceful tone caught the public's attention. Arcand confirmed the belief that his filmmaking was one that reflected society and that the filmmaker must play his role in a way that is uniquely his, whether he has solutions to propose or not—even if he can only identify the problems and the resignation that people feel.

During all the ups and downs surrounding *On est au coton*, Arcand was working on the second part of the trilogy: a documentary on the political conscience of the Québécois. He wanted to show the continuity of Quebec's political life through the fate of the three registered political parties (Liberal, Union Nationale, Parti Québécois). *Québec: Duplessis et après...* (1972) sees the Union Nationale swept out of power, the Liberal Party elected, and the first Parti-Québécois elected members. It is a film on the political discourse of the 1970s that Arcand put into perspective by using the politically conservative and socially reactionary views of the founder of the Union Nationale, Maurice Duplessis, in juxtaposition to excerpts from the Durham Report, published in 1839 after the rebellion of 1837 had left its mark on Lower Canada. This manner of suggesting the continuity between past and present and putting individuals of divergent opinions back-to-back attracted a certain amount of criticism, but Arcand wasn't in favour of hiding his historical perspective, however provocative it might be.

At the beginning of the 1970s, Arcand worked on several films at the same time. That is how he got into directing his first professional narrative film outside the ONF, *La Maudite Galette* (1972). Unlike some of his colleagues, Arcand did not insist on integrating methods of direct cinema into his narrative films. Surprisingly, he was a director who played by the rules of the game, prepared to change them from within. In this film, a family of modest means decides to rob a rich uncle but is betrayed by the uncle's boarder who, in turn, gets killed. Arcand did not exactly follow the conventions of the genre in terms of the style, the identification of the characters, or the pace of the story. Rather, he opted for a certain distancing that softened his acknowledgement of the violence inherent in the story and made the moral misery seem black, humorous, and cynical. Shown at Cannes, the film marked the filmmaker's first international appearance.

Arcand continued work on another feature film, which would become his third narrative film, *Gina* (1975). But first, he shot *Réjeanne Padovani* (1973), which takes place almost entirely in one evening and tells the story of a construction contractor, linked to the mob, who receives the mayor of Montreal and the minister of transportation to celebrate the inauguration of the freeway he just finished. Two events create problems for the three men: first, the return of the contractor's wife, who refuses to let her see their children and orders her elimination; and second, the intervention of left-wing journalists who denounce the construction of the freeway and the collusion between political power and the mafia. Arcand adopted a similar point of view as before by highlighting political and police corruption as well as the hypocrisy of the elite, combining money, sex, violence, and opportunism. Once again Arcand did not propose suggestions for change; rather, he put a lot of effort into the structure of his script and its cinematographic expression. For this film, which is meant to be a tragedy, he followed what were the classical rules for the genre—unity of place, time, and action—giving the film a dramatic intensity and a concentration of events both baffling and fascinating. Once again, the film was honoured at Cannes but didn't win any prizes.

Arcand could then go back to the story of *Gina*: the rape of a club dancer by a gang of snowmobilers. He added a self-referential element by referring to *On est au coton*—the filming of a documentary on the textile industry by filmmakers who stay in a motel near the club—thus allowing the two stories to be intertwined. In this film, Arcand explores new facets of his themes, notably violence and rape as expressions of sexuality.

Once again, two worlds—those of the petit bourgeois and the working-class—encounter one another. Social fragmentation is palpable and makes for dramatic impact. Moreover Arcand adopted a non-distanced approach, shaping the characters carefully and preferring to show rather than suggest. On the one hand violence explodes, blood spurts everywhere. On the other hand, the filmmakers resemble dilettantes full of good intentions but with little hold on reality.

Up until this point, Arcand had had critical success that in no way paralleled the public response. This time the critics' prejudices were clearly expressed: Arcand had lost his aura of being an "auteur" by embracing the conventions of genre films and had turned his back on political engagement with the fragmented social milieu he described. Worse still, he finishes the film by showing the team of filmmakers in the middle of filming a detective film. If it's true that Arcand wondered about the constraints and limits of direct cinema, he did not condemn this practice but wondered about the practice of his profession where funding bodies encourage a certain kind of commercial cinema and make life more difficult for auteur cinema. At the same time, he posed the question about the role of genre cinema, in which he was now accomplished, and its relationship to documentaries and narrative films and their respective audiences. From this point of view, Arcand's films generated a wider questioning of Quebec cinema that jolted some who could not understand the direction it was moving in. Arcand was once again free of his former allegiances and a pragmatic filmmaker.

The period after *Gina* marked the beginning of a dry spell. To earn a living, Arcand accepted all kinds of jobs: a film for the Confederation of National Trade Unions (*La lutte des travailleurs d'hôpitaux*; 1976), scripts for television (the *Duplessis* series, produced by Mark Blandford, 1977), the direction of episodes of the television series *Empire Inc.* (1983), and the film *Le Crime d'Ovide Plouffe* (1984). As a personal project, he adapted Louis Hémon's novel *Maria Chapdelaine*, but his script was rejected. By chance, in the midst of these difficult times, the producer Roger Frappier, then at the ONF, asked him to shoot a film on the Quebec referendum that the Parti Québécois had promised during the election of 1976. He made use of a filmic approach similar to the one he used in *Québec: Duplessis et après....* He followed the "Yes" and "No" camps during the 1980 campaign, tracking the promises, the pandering to public opinion, the oratorical pomposity, the populism, the irrationality or pseudo-rationality of political choices, and the diversions that terms like "nation," "people," "democracy," "liberty," or "money" cause.

It is likely that Arcand personally was for the "Yes" side. But the "No" side won. He decided to interpret this defeat by turning to a montage, built on repetitions and contradictions that punctuate Machiavelli's speeches, interpreted by an actor who declaims passages from *The Prince* that seem to act as an "explanation" for the behaviour of the Québécois and the politicians. *Le confort et l'indifférence*, a political essay on the thwarted destiny of the Quebec people, would earn, on its release in 1981, a new attack, especially from the sovereigntists hurt by the filmmaker's tone. Once again, in an inquiry unique to him, Arcand demonstrated his absence of idealism and a certain pessimism in his take on Quebec's history. Twenty-five years later, the film seems like a lucid documentary on a key moment in this history. One thing is certain, Arcand reached the public with this film because he appealed to it, provoked it, and challenged its imagination.

After the criticisms of *Le confort et l'indifférence*, Arcand treated himself to several forays into the area of advertising. But, like any director, he dreamed up scripts. And then, in 1983 at the ONF, Roger Frappier started Le Groupe de travail cinématographique, which brought together the

ONF filmmakers (Jacques Leduc, Tahani Rached) and independents (Léa Pool, Pierre Falardeau, and Denys Arcand) with the goal of developing collective film projects that would be co-produced by the ONF and the private sector. A year later, Arcand gave birth to the project that would become *Le Déclin de l'empire américain*, a script he would polish for another year.

Arcand had learned to define his purpose well and to sculpt his subjects. If he seemed to speak less directly about society in his later films, it is because it became more and more present in his characters' lines. They took on volume and complexity, and viewers could identify with them. The filmmaker used fictional stories intelligently; he knew how to blend his ideas with a style and form of expression that hooked the viewer. This approach first resulted in *Le Déclin*. The film presents itself as a comedy on love and sex taking place in a university setting. But Arcand speaks of much more than that, moreover of the values at work in western society, of civilizations in decline, of couples breaking up, of trying to make sense of history. And behind all of these great subjects is the theme of death, a heavy, silent death like the snow that envelops the last sequence in the film. This confrontation between the disintegration of a world and its hopes and approaching death generated a profound melancholy, the strongest yet seen in Quebec cinema, a melancholy that relies more than usual on the musical backdrop of the film. Presented at Cannes in 1986, *Le Déclin* was, in spite of the lasting controversy it aroused, an amazing world-wide success, unique in Canadian cinema. Its success began the reconciliation of Quebec cinema with its public and opened the door to new successes and new filmmakers, such as Jean-Claude Lauzon.

Was *Le Déclin*'s success just a bit of luck? Not at all. In the post-referendum context, Arcand, now almost fifty, began to synthesize all the experience he had had as a filmmaker and took stock of those insights. Still, Arcand had put aside an enormous piece of western civilization that he couldn't properly integrate into *Le Déclin*—Christianity. That's why, immediately after finishing *Le Déclin*, he tackled this subject in the Quebec context. Being a filmmaker of questions and not answers, Arcand wanted to develop an equation that would help him to understand how a Catholic society could become so rapidly de-Christianized, how a thrifty society could fall into consumption and hedonism, how society could lose some of its ideals. To get there, what would be better than to situate the action in the heart of Montreal, this city born of a mystical, missionary project, which he had tackled in *Les Montréalistes* (1965).

Jésus de Montréal is a complex, multiple allegory and, in the end, a tragedy. In the film, Montreal is a place where art and morality are distorted, marred, wounded, and bastardized by a commercial culture of which mass media and advertising are the best examples; it is the city of commerce, of ambition, and of exploitation. The main character, Daniel, a modern transformation of Jesus, wants his disciples to break with business and vulgarity and turn toward true art. From his point of view, to choose business and the world of appearances is to opt for death. And in this context, religion is of no help, for the Church has become a hypocritical institution, incapable of confronting historical thought and modern existence.

The film became another triumph for Arcand, beginning with the Jury Prize at Cannes in 1989. It's not surprising that someone thought of him for one of the sketches of *Montréal vu par...*, an idea to celebrate the 350th anniversary of Montreal in 1992, but he got stalled working on the script. At the same time, Arcand became enthusiastic about a play by Brad Fraser and began to produce *Love and Human Remains* (1993) in spite of the obstacles the production was strewn with. He succeeded in integrating his personal ideas, while offering a wink at genre cinema, because it is a story based on a series of murders. The reception for the film was not the most enthusiastic, and critics were divided. Several didn't understand that Arcand preferred stories that appear banal and simple, where everything is played with classical subtlety that leads one to believe in objectivity and removes any appearance of subjectivity. But the filmmaker did not want his style to stand out or use effects to mask the emptiness of ideas or fall into mannerisms. To those who had put down Arcand for ten years or more were then added those who heaped scorn upon him for having filmed in English, for becoming "Canadian," for getting involved in a "producer's film" and even daring to sign an exclusive contract for five years with Toronto producer, Alliance Atlantis.

With this last project taking a long time to complete, Arcand agreed to make a film for television on a script proposed to him. It was *Joyeux calvaire* (1996), which tells the story of two tramps in the streets of Montreal who allow a filmmaker to revisit the city and to portray appealing characters. Even with its low budget, Arcand was able to penetrate to the heart of a universe where he describes despair and tenderness with subtlety.

Arcand returned to his "Toronto" script on feminine beauty and superficiality after *Joyeux calvaire*. *Stardom* was released in 2000, seven years after his last feature film: Arcand paid a high price for his exclusive contract with Alliance Atlantis. His passion for opera is confirmed here as never before, for the film is practically an adaptation of *La Traviata*, where his character is a modern-day representation of Marguerite Gautier, who became a courtesan because of her beauty. In *Stardom* it is television that hunts down and defines beauty, that perverts it, too. The film also touches on the theme of parent-child relationships, which would become a major focus for Arcand in his next work. The production style is disconcerting because it alternates between "real" images and images supposedly taken by a television cameraman. This very subtle construction, relying only on the materiality of the image, distracted some viewers who did not catch the criticism of the media to which Arcand devoted himself and found the film had the aesthetics of a television film. This second film in English was a commercial failure in spite of its $1.3-million budget.

Without allowing himself to feel too beaten down, Arcand set to writing another script. When a rumour circulated that it would be a sequel to *Déclin de l'empire américain*, some saw it as yet another indication of the filmmaker running out of steam. But that didn't stop him, for his new film was much more than that. He wanted to use a theme that occurs in all his narratives—death and the family milieu. At the same time, the cultural, social, religious, and political context is a vital background to the anguish, confusions, and reconciliations of the drama. The title sounds like a *cri de coeur*—ambiguous and striking—*Les Invasions barbares* (2003).

Without saying who the barbarians are and what invasions are threatened, the film puts the viewer on multiple tracks that don't necessarily have any relation to one another. In 2003 the film had a double win at Cannes, a triumph later confirmed by an Oscar. Suddenly, Arcand found himself at the height of his fame, removed from the rest of the crowd, just when he had given the impression of bringing up the rear. Critical approval followed, except from those perpetually contemptuous of Arcand, who accepted neither the style—too classic for their taste—nor the subject—not political enough and too reactionary—nor the commercial success—proof of the filmmaker's co-option. The public, however, overwhelmingly endorsed it, both in Canada and abroad. It saw itself in the multiple subjects that are interwoven with tight editing: the deplorable state of the health system, aging, sickness and death, parent-child relationships, drugs, the values of the younger generation, the turning away from traditional ideologies and religion, friendship, solitude. The public appreciated the use of emotions, the tone somewhere between melodrama and comedy, and the characters seen up close that it either liked or criticized. It let itself be absorbed by the story that the filmmaker developed. It saw that he had no easy solutions to offer; he set the story up so that the viewer had to solve the problems. One other trait stood out in the film: hope and love are present, something new in Arcand's work.

As a filmmaker who is both classic and modern, Arcand doesn't let himself be defined by a single interpretation, a single frame of reference. He confirms and innovates. He also demonstrates ubiquity: *both* in documentary and narrative, *both* in auteur cinema and commercial success, *both* where one expects him and where one doesn't. To those who believe that cinematographic genres cannot be included as a vehicle for cultural and aesthetic nationalism because they are not "native" to Quebec culture, Arcand displays an original way of using filmic devices that demonstrate his adaptive ability. He makes an effort to get the best from his subjects, in the clearest style possible. Except for *Gina*, he doesn't do action films, but rather a cinema of the human condition. For, following the example of Renoir, Buñuel, Kobayashi, or Lang, Arcand considers himself a moralist who, with intelligence and lucidity, favours the human condition in spite of the pessimism and melancholy he feels, the dark zones that he encounters, and the absence of solutions that would satisfy those who want easy answers.

Arcand has given his audience an intelligent body of work, provocative, insolent, melancholic, and tragic, peopled with characters that we remember and stories that are more than anecdotes. His perpetual preoccupation with narrative and his audience have led this modern storyteller to produce works that are a reflection on genre and cinematographic codes. He has found a popular way to approach identifiable, personal themes, giving Quebec cinema something that was often missing in his own history: an audience.

NOTE

1. Translated from the French by Julia Berry Melnyk.

5

David Cronenberg
Mapping the Monstrous Male

GEORGE MELNYK

So MUCH HAS BEEN WRITTEN about the work of David Cronenberg over the past thirty years that it would be fair to ask: what more can be said about Canada's most famous director?

The answer is not simple. While a great deal has been written about Cronenberg's work, his continued productivity and the evolution of cinema criticism and theory means that Cronenberg will continue to be an object of attention and new insights. Now in his sixties, he continues to make award-winning films. His *A History of Violence* (2005) won the Toronto Critics Award for Best Film and resulted in Cronenberg being named "artist of the year" by *The Globe and Mail*.[1] His cinematic imagination has always attracted attention, while his international reputation assures his films are taken seriously. Listing his accomplishments makes for a lengthy chronicle because of his prolific body of work (fourteen features) and the length of time he has been a feature filmmaker (thirty years). Under-standing such a large oeuvre by tracing its basic elements and then creating a rationale for his work is not a simple task. As many critics have observed previously, Cronenberg is fond of crossing genres and mixing them to suit his own purposes.[2] Untangling these elements may undo some of the mystique that his work has collected over the years, but it is the only way to reveal the fundamental metaphors that guide his art.

William Beard, the world's leading authority on Cronenberg's films, confirms the existence of a unified vision that underlies his cinema, when he writes of "the terrific consistency of his thematic concerns..."[3] On a global scale he does not consider Cronenberg "a major artist" but "a powerful minor one."[4] This judgment, dropped in later editions, is highly nuanced and raises questions about the status of Cronenberg's art. If Cronenberg is not a major artist like Kurosawa, Bergman, or...(take your pick), what has prevented him from being considered one—unseemly subject matter, innovative style or lack thereof, the limitations of genre, the barriers of nationality? Could it even be that his thematic consistency is actually a sign of this putative minor status? When examining a large body of work, the level of canonical achievement becomes an issue.

The question of status aside, there can be no disputing Cronenberg's pedigree as an auteur, the foremost factor in acknowledging artistic achievement in cinema. It was his auteur vision that created "disturbing cinematic drama" in the 1970s, when Canadian cinema was finally emerging from its National Film Board (NFB) cocoon.[5] Quite simply, Cronenberg set a new agenda for national cinema in Canada. His films made money, stirred public discussion, and liberated English-Canadian consciousness from the straitjacket of realism. Reni Celeste writes:

> His works cohere stylistically and thematically, and document a private and obsessive interest in the body and its intersection with technology...Cronenberg's works raise an unavoidable question, "What is an auteur today, and what might such a figure offer the field?"[6]

Cronenberg's auteurism is a cornerstone of postmodern Canadian cinema because he has sought to embrace the visualization of the disturbing, the hidden, and the unspoken. He has sought to provoke his audiences by using the grotesque and the frightening to pry open up the darkest corners of the psyche. In discussing Cronenberg's 1991 film *Naked Lunch* and his 2002 film *Spider*, Celeste argues that the metaphors underlying these films—disease, mental illness, and addiction—end up compromising the traditional idea of authorship (i.e. taking a position) because the director effectively blends "screen, author, and spectator."[7] In other words, the postmodernist auteur seeks to deceive through illusion and then reveal the deception so as to unnerve the spectator, who finds himself mirrored by a subconscious self that may be frighteningly close to his own.

■ Sex and Science

CRONENBERG WAS BORN in Toronto in 1943 to a secular Jewish family. He attended the University of Toronto in the 1960s, where he started out studying science but switched to literature (he was a devotee of both Nabokov and Burroughs), graduating in 1967. He made two shorts in 1966 and 1967, while an undergraduate, and then his first feature in 1969, when he had started graduate studies. *Stereo* is a sixty-three minute black and white story set at the Canadian Academy of Erotic Enquiry, using voice-over for sound. The film contains nudity, sexual tension, Freudian innuendo, and a lab-coat aura that evolved into his cinematic trademark of science as psycho-sexual madness. Cronenberg created the film out of his own imagination, which gave him license to innovate his basic approach. He wrote, directed, photographed, edited, and produced the film. In a 1992 interview with Chris Rodley, he stated:

> I realized that what I liked about the classic filmmakers of the 1960s and 1970s, like Bergman and Fellini, was that you entered a world of their own creation when you went to see their films. The world was consistent from film to film.[8]

The emergence of a singular Cronenbergian vision with its telltale consistency became evident in *Crimes of the Future* (1970) in which he performed all roles except that of an actor. The film centres on the creation of a cosmetic that kills and a hero who works in the House of Skin, where sufferers from the cosmetic plague, named Rouge Malady, are incarcerated. Among the focal points of the film are the Institute of Neo-Venereal Disease, the Oceanic Podiatry Group, Metaphysical Import/Export, and the Gynaecological Research Foundation, where all sorts of bizarre activities take place and human beings sprout new organs. The world of the film is populated by males except for a pre-pubescent girl who appears at the end, a reincarnation of the mad scientist inventor of the killer cosmetic.

The film contains the imagery—institutional, individual, and group—that appears over and over again in his later films, of an aberrant sexuality brought on by some sort of malevolent scientific intervention. In Cronenberg's films, the human mind (and especially the male mind) is filled with evil desires. The scientific lust for manipulating nature is Cronenberg's equivalent of the libido's limitless passion. If one were to be biblical about this equation, one might refer to Adam and Eve being driven out of the Garden of Eden when the acquisition of knowledge brought with it sexual shame. Beard terms the presentation of sexual consciousness "a kind of narcissistic sexuality."[9] The problem with this sexuality is that it is "sick"—sick in the sense of being a disease that takes over the person, suppressing what is normal and expressing itself as a physical mutation. "Here is the archetypal Cronenberg 'mind-body' scenario...," writes Beard: the attempt of the human mind to reinvent the body results in tragedy.[10] When the mind blends sex and science, the result is pathological and destructive. The unravelling of the natural order that begins with the hope of altering reality brings forth a world where devastation can be the only result. The cinematic outcome is Cronenberg's famous genre-busting trinity that combines the futuristic essence of science fiction, the titillation of pornography, and the subliminal fears of the horror genre. In the world of scientific experimentation, the individual human figure, whether innocent or guilty, is overwhelmed. In seeking to salvage something from a situation gone awry, the inventor and those around him are destroyed because the price of hubris is pain and death.

After *Crimes of the Future*, Cronenberg spent some time in France and did "fillers" or brief documentaries for Canadian television to earn a living. *Crimes of the Future* had been funded by the Canadian Film Development Corporation (CFDC), which was now the funder of choice for an emerging feature-film industry. Cronenberg turned to the CFDC for his first commercial project, titled *Shivers* (aka *Orgy of the Blood Parasites*, *They Came From*

Within, or *The Parasite Murders*) but without initial success. He had teamed up with Cinepix, a Montreal firm, which was making waves and money with films that later came to be called "Maple Syrup Porn." Cinepix liked Cronenberg's script because its explicit sexual content appealed to their market. While Cronenberg considered *Shivers* a "serious horror film" and a breakthrough for Canadian cinema, the CFDC was taken aback and refused to fund the film for three years because, in Cronenberg's words, the film was "disgusting...horrific, perverse."[11] Its grade-B film approach was simply too radical for a government agency. Cronenberg tried to find interest in the script in Los Angeles, but before he succeeded, Cinepix finally got the funding from CDFC and his commercial career was launched.

■ Commercial Success: The Auteur Years from 1975 to 1982

CRONENBERG MADE AUTEUR FILMS from 1975 to 1982, which established him as a "bankable genre auteur."[12] First there was *Shivers* in 1975, followed by *Rabid* in 1976, *The Brood* in 1979, *Scanners* in 1980, and finally his Canadian masterpiece, *Videodrome* in 1982. These five films, all of which he wrote and directed, form the cornerstone of his identity as a Canadian filmmaker who developed the horror genre in Canadian film. These films were funded by CFDC and the tax-shelter program of the Canadian government, made in Canada, and sold around the world as low-budget, horror flicks. After *Videodrome* Cronenberg moved out of this grade-B category into a series of mainstream Hollywood-style films adapted from the work of other writers or remakes of earlier films.

Shivers has been likened to such sci-fi horror classics as *Invasion of the Body Snatchers* (1956) and *Night of the Living Dead* (1969), but Cronenberg was working inside a Canadian imaginary more so than a Hollywood one.[13] The extent of sexual violence in the film is not typical of Hollywood, where the presentation of sex mania has always been problematic. For example, in one scene a parasite enters a bath being taken by a woman and crawls into her vagina. The creatures are the product of a scientific experiment gone wrong and they create a psycho-sexual plague in which humans lose control of their bodies. While this may seem similar to elements found in the genre, Cronenberg's psyche is distinctly his own.

Working within Cinepix's soft porn culture, he adds an explicit linkage between sexuality and science, both of which he portrays as being beyond our rational control. When the mad scientist realizes what he has wrought, he tries to destroy the parasite by raping, murdering, and then dismembering his lover, where he initially hosted the creature.

The sexual-scientific linkage and metaphoric relationship is specifically Cronenbergian—what the mind has wrought, man cannot tear asunder. This pessimism is rooted in the genre, but it is also rooted in a Canadian pessimism about technology and its uncontrollability. As a nation that ordinarily imports rather than generates technological innovation and scientific experimentation, the sense of being a victim of technology is a normal response. Likewise, there is a powerful sense of male sexual transgression in the film that is part of the mad-scientist character, whose medical experimentation works in an utterly irrational way. The male superego, type-A personality is actually the same as the superego's opposite—the libido—because expression and repression are twin emotions, though they are thought to be opposites. The rational is not idealized in Cronenberg. Instead, rationality becomes monstrous, and since civilization is a patriarchal construct, the end result is the monstrous male, monstrous in what he creates and monstrous in what he destroys.

In the Canadian context, the superego personality, often read as the United States, is viewed as a totally destructive power destined for a fall. The film that denounces scientific hubris ends up being a kind of assault on Hollywood's control of the market, where an unknown auteur with an atypical genre script and a small Canadian company take on the world and succeed. Although the film cost a mere $180,000 to make (about $1 million in current Canadian dollars), it grossed $5 ($25) million worldwide and was distributed in forty countries.[14]

Because of political concerns over CFDC funding of such outlandish material (read: taxpayers dollars for porn), the next film, Rabid, had to receive surreptitious funding from the agency. The film starred Marilyn Chambers, a porn star, and tells the story of a woman who grows a blood-sucking penis from her armpit that eventually effects the destruction of Montreal. The budget was grander—three times that of Shivers—and the income was 50 per cent more.[15] Obviously, here was a successful formula that generated two further films in the same vein—*The Brood* (1979) and *Scanners* (1980).

The Brood is "the most classic horror film" that Cronenberg has done.[16] Again the script came out of his imagination, and he also directed this story of a man undergoing "psychoplasmic" therapy in which his subconscious appears as mutant children that bludgeon people to death. Cronenberg was working with a new film production company called Filmplan and got distribution through an American firm, New World Pictures, which released it on four hundred screens in North America aimed at the teenage horror film audience.[17] Because of its young audience censors cut some of the scenes. The film's "classic" material aimed it at a mainstream genre, a prelude to Cronenberg's emphatic embracing of American genre films in the 1980s.

Scanners was a departure, or some might say a return (to *Stereo*), in which science fiction plays a greater role than horror. Men with telepathic powers blow up people's heads as they struggle with one another for individual and corporate supremacy. When the film was released in the US in 1981, "it was so successful that for a week it was actually the biggest box-office draw in the country."[18] Cronenberg, who only five years earlier was working on a budget of several hundred thousand, now had $4 million to play with.[19] At the age of thirty-seven, Cronenberg now found that the Hollywood market was open to him and with it fame and fortune came calling. But Cronenberg had one more film in mind before completely joining the mainstream with its big-budget special effects and name stars. That film turned out to be his Canadian masterpiece.

Videodrome was produced by Filmplan, which had produced his previous two films, and was the last one to qualify for the Canadian government's tax-shelter scheme that was closed down that year. American star James Woods plays a television executive whose desires lead him to come under the influence of "videodrome." Like Dr. Faustus, the hapless executive makes a deal with the devil (in this case a she-devil) that leads to his ultimate destruction when he chooses the illusory life of television over reality.

Cronenberg acknowledged that with this film he was "breaking some new ground."[20] What he meant was that the film centralized the masculine sensibility like no previous film of his had.[21] The monstrous male was no longer a peripheral, though essential, figure of science pushed aside by the real action of the story. Instead, Max Renn, the television producer and the film's main character, is the personification of male sensibility as viewed by Cronenberg. Beard states it best when he writes:

> Now, that center is at last discovered to be not the sexually transgressive woman, nor the inventor-father, nor the unfeeling and predatory elements of society...but, rather, the self.[22]

In the film, Renn becomes a symbol of transsexuality when he hallucinates the birth of a videotape that he pulls out of his stomach. The Freudian symbolism continues when his hand is transformed into a phallic pistol with which he shoots his media business partners.

The film serves as a metaphor for the pernicious influence of televised imagery and even uses a McLuhanesque character, named Dr. Oblivion, to heighten our concern about the power exuded by the electronic media on the human mind. Cronenberg was able to make these philosophical statements about society using his own fantasies and subconscious.[23] These fantasies included sadomasochism, bondage, and torture. In linking the extremism of the heterosexual male imagination with the hallucinatory powers of electronically conveyed imagery, Cronenberg made a definitive statement about technology from a Canadian perspective. If the human being, specifically the male creator of civilization, is basically a sexually rapacious creature, then whatever emanates from his mind, including science and technology, is fundamentally sexually rapacious. The suicidal nature of the libido blends with the self-destructive nature of socialized technology, which propagates itself by eliminating its previous incarnations.

In *Videodrome* Cronenberg's judgement of the human condition exposes the male psyche (and the society it has spawned) as nothing more than a self-destructive monstrosity. The suicidal ending of the film leaves no room for manoeuvre. It is not surprising that Cronenberg had to escape his own dystopian universe by moving closer to Hollywoodized conventions of the horror genre, if only to save himself from trying to surpass his already excessive vision. He found relief by adapting someone else's imagination to the screen.

■ Making Hay the Hollywood Way

THE DEAD ZONE (1983) is based on a novel by Stephen King, the leading practitioner of contemporary American horror writing. "*Videodrome* was a very heavy experience," Cronenberg relates. "At that point I needed to do something based on somebody else's work, as relief...I couldn't take it much further."[24] An agent introduced him to a studio that needed a director for this Stephen King adaptation. The American star Christopher Walken plays a young man who gains the power to see into the future. He co-stars with Martin Sheen and Brooke Adams, both important actors of the period.

The Dead Zone was followed in 1986 with a remake of the 1958 film *The Fly*, in which he co-authored a new screenplay and directed. Starring Jeff Goldblum and Geena Davis, the film solidified Cronenberg's status as a mainstream director. The film tells the story of another mad scientist who has invented a cloning machine that accidentally turns him into a fly. "It made more money than all my other films combined," Cronenberg reported in 1992.[25] According to Caleum Vatnsdal, "*The Fly* was a legitimate box-office hit, providing Twentieth Century Fox with another big summer science-fiction money maker along with fellow Canadian James Cameron's *Aliens*."[26]

Continuing with his Hollywood connection, Cronenberg co-wrote and directed *Dead Ringers* in 1988, in which Jeremy Irons plays a set of identical-twin gynaecologists who operate on Geneviève Bujold, a woman with multiple wombs who suffers from infertility. Cronenberg adapted various material, including the book titled *Twins*, which was vaguely based on two deceased, identical-twin New York gynaecologists—the Marcus brothers. The film, using the Cronenbergian conceit of bizarre scientific and organic entities, features grotesque surgical instruments, meant to send shudders through the female audience in particular. De Laurentis' DEG initially agreed to produce the film, but after several of their films flopped Cronenberg had to find new backers, which he did. His film was a sensation, though it also roused "accusations of sexual disgust and misogyny."[27]

With *Dead Ringers* a success (budget of $9 million or about $18 million in current dollars), Cronenberg felt empowered to tackle more difficult subject matter, in this case, William S. Burroughs's hallucinatory novel, *Naked Lunch*. If anything exemplifies nightmares it is *Naked Lunch* in its literary form. Transforming the novel into a film was a major challenge and a fitting one for a new decade in Cronenberg's career.

■ Cinema as Roller-coaster: The Decade of the Nineties

CHRIS RODLEY VIEWED THE MAKING of *Naked Lunch* as Cronenberg's "cinematic destiny" because of the influence that Burroughs had on Cronenberg and because both men were "criticized and censored for their extreme imaginings."[28] Burroughs was a Beat icon and an American who spent some time in Tangiers, where, under the influence of drugs, he wrote *Naked Lunch*. Cronenberg claims that writing the script was "very cathartic."[29] Eventually the film garnered a US $17 million budget and was completed in 1991 with more of it realized as a Cronenberg creation than a Burroughs one.

The main action of the film is the imagined writing of the novel *Naked Lunch* with episodes approximating Burroughs's tormented life, augmented by repulsive creatures that become typewriters and a huge centipede with a human face. The film represents the ultimate terror of nightmares, and it conveys the idea that the creations of the imagination, even in the form of art, are dangerous, especially when they conjure up images that the superego describes as vile and repulsive.

Just as occurred a decade earlier, when *Videodrome* was followed by the formulaic *The Dead Zone*, Cronenberg needed to take a break from the rigours of portraying the extremes of the imagination by embarking on a less demanding project. *M. Butterfly*, which came out in 1993, is an adaptation of a 1988 American play about a Chinese transvestite who seduces a French diplomat. Cronenberg simply directed. The film failed critically and financially.

However, his next film, *Crash* (1996), was a much smaller film that pushed hard against the boundaries of public morality and was banned in the UK. *Crash* is based on a science fiction novel by British writer J.G. Ballard that deals with a cult that is sexually aroused by car crashes and injuries. Gerald Pratley in his *A Century of Canadian Cinema* describes the film as "an abomination."[30] But for Cronenberg it was a return to the modestly budgeted, purist film that reflects best his morality-skewering cinematic values. Unlike *M. Butterfly*'s $22 million budget, this one cost less than half that amount.[31] It was shot "in Toronto using minimal hardware, special effects, and auxiliary lighting" and yet retained the "perfectionist-minimalist" visual quality that marks Cronenberg's style.[32] Several critics have commented on how *Crash* harked back to early films such as *Shivers* and *Rabid*.[33] It would seem that after a period of recharging his batteries, Cronenberg felt up to a challenge. He took offensive, cultish material and, using a very controlled, super-cool photographic method, restated the unity of the superego (restraint) and the libido (unrestraint) in this parable on sex and technology. That unity is a kind of rigid, technological, metallic sheen underneath which is a uncontrolled, pulsating, yet basically mechanical body. The film is a presented as a kind of mental suit of armour that is constantly being penetrated from the inside by emotion and then resealed, only to be penetrated and resealed again, and again, and again. The metaphor of the steel and plastic automobile as a "natural" extension of the human skin recreates humanity as a metal robot with feelings where the opposites of sadism and sadomasochism come together in celebrating pain and the inevitable death associated with car wrecks.

Crash is populated with alienated, disconnected, and unhappy souls whose techno-sex seems totally dysfunctional from a social perspective. Their desires are anti-social and ultimately deadly, and Cronenberg addresses them and their acts with a highly artistic shooting style to raise the issue from the prurient to the philosophical. The overt blending of violence, sexuality, and technology is the spirit of *Crash* and earned Cronenberg a Special Jury Prize at Cannes. *Crash* is clearly not a studio picture like *Dead Ringers* or even *M. Butterfly* and so serves to indicate Cronenberg's untameability and ongoing need to push, from time to time, the boundaries of his films.

For Cronenberg, the 1990s ended up being a period of adaptation of and inspiration by others' writings, which seems to suggest that his auteurism had become a blend of imaginations. But he ended the decade with *eXistenZ*, a sci-fi film that did not do well at the box office but was based on his original screenplay. His eleventh feature after *Shivers* in 1975, *eXistenZ* reflected twenty-five years in commercial film. The film has unusual body orifices, parasites, and "mushy-gun imagery."[34] Cronenberg drew on his established bag of images for this film, which shows how video games and reality cross over and become each other. Shot like his other films in Canada, *eXistenZ* cost a hefty $30 million to make with its extensive special effects.[35] That it did not do well against Hollywood films of the day, including hits such as *The Matrix*, suggests that Cronenberg was not as marketable in the mainstream as he once was. It would seem that on the eve of the millennium Cronenberg's vision did not resonate with the video-games generation, whose psyche is so embedded in the Internet. Perhaps Cronenberg's sexually charged, prophetic angst about technology invading the mind and then the body had become passé.

In a very real sense the critical and financial success of his 1980s Hollywood-style films were not repeated in the 1990s because budgets were either too large to recoup (*M. Butterfly*) or the subject matter was too offensive (*Crash*) for the mainstream.[36] Cronenberg's roller-coaster decade evolved into a pattern that saw him alternating between small- and large-budget films. Falling into this schedule allowed him artistic freedom on the one hand and commercial profile on the other. Even when Cronenberg did smaller budget films such as *Crash* he always connected them to a genre. But when a director has achieved as much as Cronenberg had by the end of the 1990s and has developed a persona as a director, it becomes a kind of burden that he must overcome in order to continue looking new.

■ **The Artist in his Sixties**

AWARE OF THE DANGER that he might become passé in the science-fiction genre, Cronenberg decided to embrace serious dramatic material with *Spider* (2002). "You wouldn't see this film and say that I've mellowed," Cronenberg retorted in an interview as he was finishing principal photography in the fall of 2001.[37] The story is adapted from a novel by British author Patrick McGrath, about a character termed "Spider" who is mentally disturbed. The author also wrote the first draft of the screenplay, which Cronenberg discarded in favour of his own version.

When *The Globe and Mail* reviewed *Spider* in 2003, reviewer, Ray Conlogue, commented on how the film "contains nothing whatever of the body grotesque."[38] The tense sombreness of the film earned Cronenberg a Genie for best director that year, beating out Atom Egoyan for *Ararat*. *Maclean's* Brian D. Johnston termed it "a chilly masterpiece of Oedipal dread."[39] The film, heralded a new, more serious, dramatic director. Cronenberg had given himself a remake.

Spider was followed by *A History of Violence* in 2005, which confirmed this new non-genre film path, in which the study of individual pathology is made convincing by the talent of outstanding actors rather than special effects. Both *Spider* and *A History of Violence* are set in the present and deal with the main characters' violent psychology. It is as if the director, now in his sixties, wanted to prove that he was a "major" director of dramatic material. The film was nominated for the Palme d'Or at Cannes.

A History of Violence is based on a literary form that was gaining prominence in the new millennium—a graphic novel of the same title by John Wagner (writer) and Vince Locke (artist) originally published in 1997. The graphic novel's illustrative style and minimal dialogue resembles a cross between movie storyboards and comic books drawn in a noir spirit.[40] The appeal to the new Cronenberg is obvious. The film got mainstream theatre release. It opened on eight screens in Calgary in October 2005, which reflected a hoped-for serious dramatic appeal.[41] Rick Groen of *The Globe and Mail* termed it an "eloquent dissection of violence" in which "the monster within sits politely...quiet now but just waiting to be fed."[42] Jay Stone of the *CanWest Global* chain of Canadian newspapers listed it as number one in his top ten films of 2005, while Katherine Monk of the same chain, listed it as number seven.[43]

Discussing the film, Cronenberg said honestly that *A History of Violence* "has very strong American mythology attached to every aspect of it. Obviously, I embraced it; I wasn't trying to fight it."[44] With its edgy sexuality, its frightening lead character, and its contemporary setting, it had more in common with *Crash* than either *eXistenZ* or *Naked Lunch*. Its

exploration of the dark deception that is human nature and its connection to violence combines dramatic tension and genre elements of the
American Western.

But the film, along with Atom Egoyan's controversial *Where the Truth
Lies*, did nothing to raise Canadian audiences from their deep slumber
when it came to Canadian cinema. In 2005, while Quebec's theatre screens
were showing Quebec cinema 26 per cent of the time, English-Canadian
screens actually dropped from 1.6 per cent in 2004 to 1.2 per cent, meaning
that Canadians outside Quebec spent under $9 million viewing Canadian
features in movie theatres or $0.30 per capita.[45] While Cronenberg was
achieving critical acclaim with his serious investigation of the American
mythology of violence, the Canadian box-office figures for such films
were dropping.

■ Reflections on a Star—Red or White?

CRONENBERG'S THIRTY-YEAR career in commercial cinema has reached
a certain crossroads. If one were to survey the various stages of that career
one could identify four distinct periods since the release of his first commercial horror film, *Shivers*, in 1975. First, there is the "baron of blood"
phase from 1975 to 1982, in which as an auteur director he created a
Canadianized horror cinema for an international audience with great
commercial success. This was done in partnership with the Canadian
Film Development Corporation and the feature-film-promoting tax-shelter
program of the Canadian government. Second, there is the "Hollywood"
phase from 1983 to 1993, which began with *The Dead Zone*, his adaptation
of a Stephen King novel, and ended with his adaptation of an American
play, *M. Butterfly*. In this "Hollywood" phase Cronenberg was not an auteur
as he was primarily adapting previously written material, and he enjoyed
large budgets, the use of big-name American actors, and mainstream
distributors for his films. The third phase was shorter—from 1994 to
2000—and involved two films only, *Crash* (1996) and *eXistenZ* (1999). One
might term it the "transitional" stage, in which Cronenberg moved from
the provocative small film (*Crash*) to another Hollywood entertainment
model (*eXistenZ*). He was vacillating, trying to find himself and his place
at a time when his career was seeking new directions. That new direction,

the more risky, less genre-bound, serious drama phase, was announced by *Spider* in 2002 and was followed by *A History of Violence* in 2005. In this phase Cronenberg has staked out new territory as a director to be reckoned with and taken seriously as a world-class dramatist.[46]

So what is the critical assessment of Cronenberg's achievement? In a piece comparing the lifetime achievement of Atom Egoyan and David Cronenberg, Rick Groen makes it clear that Cronenberg is not "resting on his laurels."[47] He concludes that Cronenberg is a "monarch" who has achieved the status of an artist with his work. The Canadian film magazine *Take One*, in its 2005 celebration of Canadian cinema, claimed that "Cronenberg is the most audacious and challenging narrative director in the English-speaking world."[48] This opinion follows the views of *The Village Voice* critic, J. Hoberman, who is equally fulsome in his assessment.[49] While one might question such male journalistic hyperbole, the more sombre and staid assessments made by academic critics like William Beard suggest that Cronenberg as a powerful minor director may be the best that English Canada has produced in the twentieth century and that he is yet to be surpassed in this one.[50] But this view is not shared by everyone.

Genre directing, with which Cronenberg has been associated in the past, seldom creates the status of a master or major artistic talent. Cronenberg could be said to have added to the problem of status by mixing genres, his innovation in the 1970s, which offered originality, but also uncertainty in terms of assessment. Mixing porn and science fiction to create a conscious Freudian subtext for a film requires acknowledgement, but it also does not necessarily raise one to global artistic status. It is the issue of genre status—of tragedy over comedy.

In *One Hundred Years of Canadian Cinema* I summarized the reaction to Cronenberg as "varied and contradictory" with one school viewing him as a packager of racy material and the other considering him an artistic genius.[51] Bart Testa of the University of Toronto considers Cronenberg's horror films a "Canadian meditation on technology offered by Frye, Grant, McLuhan, Harold Innes and others."[52] Such statements raise Cronenberg to the status of a public intellectual, at least in the Canadian context. In an earlier study of Cronenberg, when only his 1970s films had been produced, William Beard claimed that "Cronenberg's work represents a search for wholeness," meaning that it postulates a broken human spirit that seeks to be made whole again.[53] This attribution of philosophical or psychological depth to Cronenberg's vision. Even the independent critic, Robin Wood, who has attacked Cronenberg's work from the beginning, was able to write in the 1980s that the work had "artistic authenticity... [and] integrity."[54]

Writing more recently, Beard concluded that Cronenberg is "a compelling, embattled investigator of masculine subjectivity...."[55] This emphasis on gender, especially in its heterosexual manifestation, is what unites sexual imagination, libidinal violence, and technological power into a distinct sense of the horrific nature of the human (male) condition. The emphasis on the monstrous male, even with due acknowledgement of the femme fatale, is what rests at the core of Cronenberg. Because Cronenberg has refused to be pigeonholed in his art and has always wanted to push the boundaries of genres, while blending them into his own idiosyncratic statements, he has always remained on the cusp of greatness. While his own auteur imagination may be waning, Cronenberg seems to be embracing the identity of a serious filmmaker with dramatic aspirations, and this may be his final and most acknowledged stage. But there are only two films (*Spider* and *A History of Violence*) to go on at this point. This does not a body of work make. Because the underlying image of the monstrous male exists profoundly in both these films, the film's innate darkness limits the audience. The question of whether Cronenberg has moved beyond genre or is only adapting genre is still open. And the question will remain as long as he continues to produce films like no other.

One can think of Cronenberg as a representative of the English-Canadian imagination as it struggles to express and define itself within an American-dominated universe. The psychological source of evil in Canadian culture comes from within the self and is not posited in the other as the horror and science-fiction genres of American ilk prefer. Working in the continentalist paradigm of contemporary Canada, Cronenberg's statement that the embracing of "harsh reality" is the only way to avoid being "crushed, destroyed or diminished by it" suggests strongly that the Canadian psyche as expressed in the films of David Cronenberg can actually survive American domination and play an original role in the global community.[56] Whether Cronenberg will go down in film history as a great director in the global canon is not all that important for Canadian culture, as such. What is important is that he, more than any other Canadian film director, has given voice to the Canadian subconscious, which has a universal relevance. When the leading American film critic Roger Ebert chose not to include *A History of Violence* in his top ten films of 2005, though it had a decidedly American subject matter and characterization, while the Canadian critic Jay Stone listed it as number one, though it was so overtly American, we were able to see the clash of two distinct cultures that are in fact two solitudes. Thanks to Cronenberg the Canadian imagination has embraced the American one in various genres and come out whole and singular. In this David and Goliath war of cultural understanding and opposing fantasies, Cronenberg has been a victorious guerrilla leader who awaits ultimate triumph. In his portrayal of the battle with the inner beast, Cronenberg will always remain controversial, a situation in which he seems comfortable and which he first fostered four decades ago. That a director continues to challenge means that his claim to a mature vision is valid.

AUTHOR'S NOTE

The earliest academic collection dealing specifically with Cronenberg is *The Shape of Rage: The Films of David Cronenberg* , Piers Handling, ed. (1983). The most extensive treatment of Cronenberg is offered by William Beard, *The Artist as Monster: The Cinema of David Cronenberg* (2001). Not only are there numerous articles on his films, he is also discussed in Canadian works such as George Melnyk, *One Hundred Years of Canadian Cinema* (2004), Katherine Monk, *Weird Sex and Snowshoes and other CanadianFilm Phenomema* (2001), and Caelum Vatnsdal, *They Came From Within: A History of Canadian Horror Cinema* (2004). A personal account of his career may be found in Chris Rodley ed., *Cronenberg on Cronenberg* (1992).

NOTES

1. Liam Lacey, "Artist of the Year," *The Globe and Mail*, 31 December 2005, R1.
2. *A History of Violence* is read as a remake of the Western theme of the stranger comes to town.

3. William Beard, *The Artist as Monster: The Cinema of David Cronenberg* (Toronto: University of Toronto Press, 2001), xi.

4. Ibid.

5. George Melnyk, *One Hundred Years of Canadian Cinema* (Toronto: University of Toronto Press, 2004), 148.

6. Reni Celeste, "In the Web with David Cronenberg," *Cineaction* 65 (2004): 2.

7. Ibid., 5.

8. Chris Rodley, ed., *Cronenberg on Cronenberg* (Toronto: Knopf, 1992), 19.

9. Beard, *The Artist as Monster*, 22.

10. Ibid., 24.

11. Rodley, *Cronenberg on Cronenberg*, 39.

12. Wyndham Wise, *Take One's 1001 Greatest Canadian Films & Filmmakers of All Time* (Special Limited Edition of *Take One* magazine, 2005), 41.

13. Beard, *The Artist as Monster*, 28.

14. Rodley, *Cronenberg on Cronenberg*, 52.

15. Ibid., 57.

16. Ibid., 78.

17. Caelum Vatnsdal, *They Came From Within: A History of Canadian Horror Cinema* (Winnipeg: Arbeiter Ring, 2004), 124.

18. Beard, *The Artist as Monster*, 119.

19. Rodley, *Cronenberg on Cronenberg*, 86.

20. Ibid., 96.

21. Beard, *The Artist as Monster*, 121.

22. Ibid.

23. Rodley, *Cronenberg on Cronenberg*, 98.

24. Ibid., 109.

25. Ibid., 134.

26. Vatnsdal, *They Came From Within*, 184.

27. Rodley, *Cronenberg on Cronenberg*, 151.

28. Ibid., 157.

29. Ibid., 162.

30. Gerald Pratley, *A Century of Canadian Cinema: Gerald Pratley's Feature Film Guide 1900 to the Present* (Toronto: Lynx Images, 2003), 50.

31. Beard, *The Artist as Monster*, 379.

32. Ibid.

33. Ibid., 383.

34. Doug Saunders, "Cronenberg ready to shock us again," *The Globe and Mail*, 16 February 1999, A16.

35. Alan Freeman, "*eXistenZ* draws crowds in Berlin," *The Globe and Mail*, 17 February 1999, D1.

36. As Cronenberg himself said of *Crash*: "We knew it had a limited audience, that it wasn't going to play in malls in Iowa," Ibid.

37. Brenda Bouw, "Baron of blood meets Beckett," *The Globe and Mail*, 29 September 2001, R8.

38. Ray Conlogue, "Insider Cronenberg's web," *The Globe and Mail*, 27 February 2003, R1.

39. Brian D. Johnston, "An Exquisite Madness," *Maclean's* (3 March 2003): 42.

40. The publisher of *A History of Violence* is Vertigo, an imprint of DC Comics. The book is 286 pages.

41. *Calgary Herald*, Theatre Listings, 17 October 2005, D4.

42. Rick Groen, "Dissecting the monster within," *The Globe and Mail*, 25 September 2005, R2.

43. *Calgary Herald*, 30 December 2005, C1–2.

44. Maurie Alioff, "Double Identity: David Cronenberg's *A History of Violence*," *Take One* 14, no. 51 (September–December 2005): 9.

45. Kate Taylor, "Quebec's up. English Canada? Never mind," *The Globe and Mail*, 30 December 2005, R3.

46. Interestingly, Roger Ebert in his list of top ten films of 2005 does not mention Cronenberg's *A History of Violence*, which suggests that Cronenberg has not yet touched the core of American cinematic imagination.

47. Rick Groen, "Two kinds, but only one ruler," *The Globe and Mail*, 5 September 2005, R5.

48. Wise, *Take One's 1001 Greatest Films and Filmmakers*, 41.

49. Liam Lacey, "Artist of the Year," *The Globe and Mail*, 31 December 2005, R1.

50. Canada's most prominent female film reviewer, Vancouver-based Katherine Monk in her *Weird Sex and Snowshoes and other Canadian Film Phenomena* (Vancouver: Raincoast, 2001) calls Cronenberg a dichotomous "thinker and sensationalist" (234).

51. George Melnyk, *One Hundred Years of Canadian Cinema*, 155.

52. Bart Testa, "Technology's Body: Cronenberg, Genre and the Canadian Ethos," <www.utoronto.ca/cinema/testa1.htm> (accessed 16 Mar. 2005) .

53. William Beard, "The Visceral Mind: The Major Films of David Cronenberg," in Piers Handling, ed., *The Shape of Rage: The Films of David Cronenberg* (Toronto: General Publishing, 1983), 78.

54. Robin Wood, "Cronenberg: A Dissenting View," in Handling ed., *The Shape of Rage*, 125.

55. Beard, *The Artist as Monster*, xii.

56. David Cronenberg, *Crash* (London: Faber and Faber, 1996), xix.

6

Atom Egoyan
Unnatural Relations
WILLIAM BEARD

ATOM EGOYAN (b.1960) is, along with David Cronenberg, English Canada's best-known filmmaker. His work has been heaped with international awards, and has inspired a mountain of writing. Since 1984 he has written and directed ten feature films, as well as having a prodigious output in a variety of forms.[1] Egoyan's films bear as clear a personal fingerprint as those of any filmmaker in the world, and there has never been any doubt about the originality and consistency of his artistic vision, even if, inevitably, not all viewers have responded to it with equal enthusiasm. His cinema is rich and complex but returns obsessively to the same formal strategies and thematic materials. This is especially the case in the films of his first decade as a feature filmmaker (1984–1994, that is, from *Next of Kin* to *Exotica*). Here the individual movies have such a strong family resemblance to each other that they seem like shufflings of the same pack of cards, or—to invoke one of the musical metaphors that have so often been applied to Egoyan's work—a set of variations on a theme.

After *Exotica*, Egoyan struck off in new directions, seeking fresh stimuli for his artistic imagination. Probably he needed to get away, at least for a while, from the cycling chamber-piece repetitions of his own foundational imaginings and practices. The movies of his second decade have arisen from the literary work of others (*The Sweet Hereafter* by Russell Banks, *Felicia's Journey* by William Trevor), or engaged with vast, world-historical themes (the Armenian genocide in *Ararat*), or simply moved in directions completely different. His most recent film, *Where the Truth Lies*, is an investigative mystery reportedly in the manner of a *film noir à clef* about a Hollywood entertainment duo not entirely dissimilar from Martin and Lewis. And yet throughout these films, too, Egoyan's unique angle of vision has been unmistakable.

■ Formal Practices

THE FORMAL STRUCTURES of Egoyan's films are unusually present and visible. When Egoyan's cinema is seen against the general background of movies featuring classically realist, character-based stories, their difference is obvious. His narratives are powered by a principle of rigorous thematic organization rather than an engine of problem-setting and -solving. The events of the films unfold in contrapuntal juxtaposition, always commenting on and illuminating each other under the skilful direction of the designer's hand. They constantly proclaim a pattern, an abstract schema. Their characters often seem to function more as representations of positions or points of view with respect to that thematic core than as figures of psychological depth and roundness or even as exercises in recognizable observation. But, in spite of their chess-piece qualities, they are not unconvincing in their own terms, and they are capable of engaging the viewer and even inspiring sympathy. Still, their placement within a patterned grid and their subordination to that grid gives an effect of coolness or detachment in their presentation.

There are never single protagonists in an Egoyan movie—almost always there are several disparate central characters.[2] The whole narrative stance of these films creates that impression: of detachment, of manipulation, of a laboratory experiment whose analytical investigation finds meaning at a structural or molecular level rather than on the surface. As one looks at an Egoyan film, it begins to resemble one of those visualizations of fractals where the more penetrating and magnified the gaze, the more the same disposition appears. One feels that at the end of *Speaking Parts* or *Exotica* Egoyan can hold up a carefully constructed, complex, three-dimensional molecular model, with characters attached to each other and circling around a thematic nucleus in obedience to the laws of human proclivity. This sense is strongest in the films at the core of Egoyan's first decade, but it can be found to a greater or lesser extent in all his films. It is evident even in *Calendar* or *Felicia's Journey*, films with essentially only two or three characters, and it certainly returns loud and clear in *Ararat*.

The distanciation created by these formalized structures is augmented by a parallel drive in the films: a drive toward self-reflexivity that often reveals itself as a conscious and overt emphasis on the materials of image-making and the cinematic apparatus. The most obvious manifestations of this tendency are Egoyan's constant thematization of video technology, his repeated working of video recording into his narratives, and, most radically, his regular interference in normal practices of diegetic operation to destabilize the narration of the films, point of view, narrative enunciation, and even the "objective" existence of whole sequences. The ubiquitous presence of video footage not only denaturalizes itself and the movies' surrounding film footage but also acts out the constructedness and artificiality of all filmmaking, including that of the works themselves. All of Egoyan's features are fundamentally story- and character-films rather than radically avant-garde or purely abstract works. But, as with their schematic narrative patterns, the films' foregrounding of cinematic activity and problematization of the codes of narrative draws them decisively away from dominant-model movies, and classifies them clearly as "art cinema."

Speaking Parts (1989)

Perhaps Egoyan's purest formal exercise is *Speaking Parts*, a film in which the characters are not only schematically related to each other by occupation and habitation but are also costumed and coiffed in such a way as to emphasize their resemblance to each other. This stylization of appearance hovers just on the edge of overtness. As with many other equally stylized areas of the film, the characters' physical similarity to one another is just containable within the confines of a "realist" fiction—at least until the end of the film, where fundamental boundaries between reality and fiction, fact and imagination, begin to break down radically. The action has very restricted venues, taking place mainly in a large hotel (divided into customer spaces and "backstage" areas) where two of the central characters, Lance and Lisa, work as maids and dress identically in all-black pyjama-uniforms. Lance wants to be a movie actor. Lisa is desperately but unrequitedly in love with him and constantly watches his wretched bit-parts in rented videos of his movies. The third character, Clara, is a guest at the hotel, has written a script now being produced that is based on tragic events in her own life, and picks up Lance to cast in a major role in it because he reminds her of the person the part is based on. It is certainly no exaggeration to describe the behaviour of all three central characters as neurotic: the bizarrely grieving Clara, the romantically zombified Lisa, and the narcissistic Lance. The film circles around issues of representation, with all three central characters involved in one way or another in the production of images to solve some set of personal problems. All three of them end up inside video images at some point (another important character is the icily powerful Producer, who almost always appears as a video image). In the end the laws of representation collapse, the film's diegesis is engulfed in impossible psycho-images, and *Speaking Parts* becomes virtually an avant-garde work. But the sense of formal counterpoint and virtuoso manipulation of character positions and themes is like that of a meticulous, delicate, and beautiful piece of machinery.

■ A Really Postmodern Filmmaker

IN ITS ABSTRACT FORMALIST PURITY and its often anguished philosophical inquiries, Egoyan's cinema is modernist, even high modernist. But in its insistence on multiple and divergent views, scattering and de-verifying of identity and memory, and dissolution of the ground of any possible stable "truth," it is postmodern. Egoyan's relativist and subjectivist view of history, memory, psychology, and human relations is so profound that he cannot get away from postmodernism, even in *Ararat*, a film ostensibly devoted to expounding the actual historical horrors of the Armenian genocide. Even horror and suffering are uncertainly grounded.

All that is solid melts into representation and subjectivity, a condition that actually invades the narrative stances of *Family Viewing* and *Speaking Parts*. Although, as a good postmodern, Egoyan takes all this epistemological chaos as given and in fact appears to be giving lessons in it (a trait much appreciated by cultural-theory commentators), there are signs throughout his cinema that such a position is not entirely a comfortable one for him. The omnipresent technologies of representation are almost always accompanied by an emphasis on their alienating instrumentality and general emotional pathology. The Photographer in *Calendar* needs to be saved from his camera and restored to something more authentic, and a range of characters in *Family Viewing* and *The Adjuster* are seen as suffering from a similar cold and instrumentalizing syndrome.

Egoyan's most extreme "postmodern" film, *Speaking Parts*, is in the end so tortured by its explosion of video phantasmagoria that it crawls back to the simplest and most primitive forms of human contact as to a life raft. The implication of all this is that postmodern ungroundedness is less likely to be liberating (as in *Next of Kin*) than it is to be agonizing (as in *Speaking Parts*, *The Adjuster*, and *Calendar*). And to the considerable degree that truth and certainty are absent in *Ararat*, that is a source of distress for both the characters and the filmmaker. There is also the haunted sense, in a number of Egoyan films which depict Armenian culture, that for a pre-postmodern, and pre-modern, identity such as the one Egoyan imagines Armenianism to be, there *is* truth and groundedness—but it is a place that Egoyan can only imagine, not actually experience.

In paradigmatic postmodern fashion, the place of vanished stable truths and natural laws in Egoyan's world is taken by phenomena of less gravity and substance. Egoyan expresses the fundamental climate of uncertainty in the quasi-paranoia of video-control, surveillance, surreptitious voyeurism, the many scenes of smuggling and scarifying customs inspection, and the general fearful mistrust of institutions. Meanwhile, he reinstalls ordered structure—emphatically so—but, instead of that structure existing as a fundamental human law, it exists only in the detached and weightless form of games-playing, pattern-making, and abstract schemata. In the environment of epistemological disbelief, the narrative instances of human suffering that in a more grounded environment would be felt as tragic are now more aptly described as neurotic, panicked,

pathos-laden but scrambled and free-floating. Egoyan's famous (and sometimes criticized) detachment is quite unavoidable in a world where there
is nothing stable or substantial enough to attach *to*. And from here, too,
the artist's choice of themes seems perfectly logical.

■ Themes

Mediation

In the contemporary western world, says Egoyan, almost nothing reaches
us in pure form; almost everything is filtered through representation. In
turn, our efforts to understand and categorize experience, to express or
defer feeling, to fix and define memory and history and identity, draw
us logically to the devices of technological representation—cameras and
microphones. Meaning may or may not "truly" be found in images and
sounds recorded and replayed, but many of Egoyan's characters turn obsessively to this realm. For this media-obsessed sensibility, nothing has
objective existence until it is captured on film or video. The process of
reifying people and events into their visual records acts as a form of reas-
surance to these individuals, who are distressed by the uncontrollability
of the world and the amorphousness of subjective perception and feeling.
In a broader sense, such an attitude is a symbol of male-dominated ratio-
nalist modernism, which has responded to the historical disappearance
of human existential confidence by displacing everything into science
and addressing every problem by methods of quantification and technological manipulation. The recorded moving picture, with its fabulous
power of capturing the images and sounds of real time and space, is in
this context a tool of magnetic attraction because it promises to render
life objective, knowable, and manipulable. The temptation to use this
tool to resolve the most painful, difficult, and volatile personal problems
is irresistible.

Characters in *Next of Kin*, *Speaking Parts*, *The Adjuster*, and especially *Family
Viewing* and *Calendar*, repeatedly try to remove personal problems from the
internal and emotional sphere and transfer them to the objective-record
sphere, where they can then be fixed like a malfunctioning refrigerator
or at least be metamorphosed into fetish objects like any commodity.
Meanwhile, the films themselves, even as they present such behaviour

as "inhuman," pathological, and psychically dysfunctional, are in one dimension complicit with it, and are in fact practising a form of it themselves. It can even be said that Egoyan uses film and video in rather the same way that his image-obsessed characters do. To be sure, it is also evident that his films are self-conscious and self-critical about this fact. But, in turn, such reflexive self-doubt merely adds another enriching level to the intricate formal mechanism of the films' patterned narratives, one more instance of doubling back and re-examining, whose very existence demonstrates the control of the artist.

Family Viewing (1987)

Family Viewing is Egoyan's most extensive experiment constituting a movie from the dual cinematic levels of film and video. It was in this film that Egoyan really grasped how he could use one creative itch—his fascination with the ease and ubiquity of video recording and the ways people could use it as a psychic and emotional shortcut as well—to scratch another, namely his wish to access the rich and suggestive catalogue of our quasi-Pavlovian responses to the different visual stimuli of video and film. The washed-out graininess of video (especially in 1987); the portability, disposability, erasability of video; what one might call the capitalist-democracy of video, which puts a powerful tool of representation into the amateur hands of a broad but typically male, techno-enthusiast and materially well-off constituency—these are all elements of a medium that Egoyan can use to embody a situation of cultural alienation.

Correspondingly, film, with its richer, denser textures and colours, its "heavier" and more complex apparatus, and its status as the established, traditional moving-picture medium, can embody a more rooted, authentic, substantial cultural heritage and experience of the world. This is wonderful for Egoyan because it allows him to pursue formal and content projects simultaneously with the same device. The two visual worlds (video and film) can be associated with the two thematic worlds of the narrative (WASP and ethnic), which in turn correspond to the two forces pulling at the protagonist Van (his videotaping, pornography-addicted Anglo father on the one hand and his Armenian absent mother and institutionalized grandmother, and his own almost forgotten childhood memories on the other). In effect, this dichotomous alignment also means that the movie ends up representing film as good and video as bad, though this may not have been exactly Egoyan's intention. Technically speaking the director brings off the whole operation triumphantly. If at times the exercise of polarization seems distortive (the film's schematic father-hatred and mother-love can look rather cartoonish), and if the dizzying array of issues springing from culture and representation and memory and psychic strategy is finally somewhat indigestible, *Family Viewing* demonstrates Egoyan's cinematic originality and formal virtuosity beyond any disagreement.

Ritual and Substitution

Commentators, including Egoyan himself, have emphasized the presence in his cinema of ritual. Ritual is another tool his characters can use to deal with mental suffering, akin in some ways to their use of video images to bring chaotic feelings under control. In its most vivid form ritual is an instrument of mourning for the most devastated of these characters.[3] The scriptwriter, Clara, in *Speaking Parts* endlessly consuming a home movie of her dead brother at a video-mausoleum, the abandoned photographer-husband interviewing female escorts to remind him of his lost wife in *Calendar*, and, strangest of all, the grieving father, Francis, in *Exotica*, who comes again and again to a club to watch a stripper (Christina) dressed in a schoolgirl's uniform do lap-dances for him—these characters are rather spectacularly devoted to self-made rituals that minister to their emotional needs but that strike the viewer as grotesque. Like all rituals, these have qualities of repetition, formalization, and abstraction—qualities that *ipso facto* link them to the map-like abstract patterning of the films' narrative structures. So Egoyan replicates the same mechanism at different strata of his films, adding to the sense of their density and intricate craftedness.

As with the use of video to reify and capture experience, rituals of this kind have the function of transferring unmanageable emotional trouble into a form whose "objectivity" allows characters to handle it. Each ritual involves a principle of *substitution*, where a messy and unresolvable problem is replaced with a procedure that can be contained and controlled. Sometimes it is a case of characters slotting actual substitute people into voids in their lives. A few examples among many: In *Speaking Parts* the bereaved sister, Clara, picks up a hotel employee (Lance) and casts him as her dead brother both in her autobiographical script and in her life, where she can now safely act out incestuous desires toward him; in *Exotica* there is a double person-substitution going on, with Francis "casting" Christina as his dead daughter while Christina in turn "casts" him as the kind of father she never had. In other cases the substitution is more transformational: In *Family Viewing*, the white patriarchal male has substituted everything in his life—his history, his family, his desires—with the video of it; and similarly in *Calendar*, the Photographer, though undergoing severe doubt and jealousy, just keeps on taking pictures of his wife's gradual disaffection from him instead of actually doing anything about it. In *The Adjuster*, the very function of the title character, Noah, is to transform the destructive losses suffered by his clients into monetary terms, while the film's "second" couple, Bubba and Mimi, progress through life via elaborate theatrical impostures that act out their perverse desires. *Exotica* is a symphony of substitutions ranging well beyond the ones already mentioned. Even in *The Sweet Hereafter* and *Felicia's Journey*, Egoyan has brought out similar patterns of substitution from narratives originally created by others. In *The Sweet Hereafter*, for example, the lawyer, Mitchell, replaces his helpless impotence as the father of a drug-damaged daughter with his messianic role of a class-action advocate to transform the grief of a devastated community that has lost its children into vengeful action and cash. In this way, he forges some kind of agency out of personal catastrophe in the substitute sphere when he cannot in his private life. And in *Felicia's Journey*, the strangely calm and gentle serial killer, Hilditch, substitutes a whole variety of mean-ingful-narrative activities (watching his mother's old cooking shows on TV as he prepares and consumes opulent meals, refashioning his role as a factory catering manager into mini-skits of kindness and warmth, and developing caring, quasi-parental relationships with a succession of street girls before killing them) for the hideous emptiness of his actual emotional life.

Next of Kin (1984)

In some ways the most breathtaking act of substitution in Egoyan's feature-length cinema is the first, the one that forms the basis of *Next of*

Kin. Peter, the young protagonist, discovers by seeing some private tapes of the video-family-therapist his own family is visiting that another family, the Deryans, had given up their baby son Bedros for adoption and had never entirely been reconciled to it. Peter decides simply to show up at the Deryans' house and claim to be their long-lost son. He hopes to kill three birds with this stone: to escape from his empty and featureless Anglo-Canadian family, to find something more thick and sustaining in an Armenian-Canadian family, and to act as a healer of the generational problems between the Deryan patriarch and his daughter, Azah. It is an act of jaw-dropping presumption, carried out with a blind confidence that is so unconscious of its own transgression that it can be called innocent (or mad). The fact that this astonishing masquerade actually succeeds in all three of its aims is an index of the bouncing optimism of Egoyan's outlook at this point. Something of this same optimism survives in the next film, *Family Viewing*, where Van's stratagem—bundling the corpse of a suicide ward-mate into his grandmother's nursing-home bed, falsifying the death certificate and holding a false funeral, getting the deceased woman's daughter Aline to check *his* grandmother out under *her* mother's name and help stash her in an empty hotel wing—is equally presuming and equally successful. But in *Family Viewing* the picture is already growing darker, and in later films this kind of substitutive play-acting becomes more and more questionable. *Next of Kin* also demonstrates, with the same kind of innocent unconscious directness, how utterly constructed identities are. Peter can leave his Anglo family identity and enter an Armenian family and identity with an effortless, dreamlike ease that also displays how ungrounded and arbitrary his fundamental self is. Early on, he tells us in voice-over that "there are two of me: an observer and an actor." So both of his selves are detached, analytical, and fabricating. There is no "natural" ethnic identity and no "natural" sense of self, at least not for Peter—and, we can guess, not for Egoyan either, at this point in his life. This kind of identitylessness without tears is an eloquent testimony to Egoyan's foundational postmodernism.

Exchange

Substitution also manifests itself in the realm of exchange: how characters find tangible equivalents for behaviour that can be traded or used as payment. Noah, in *The Adjuster*, dedicates his whole life to this activity as a simple matter of professional duty, though his somewhat pathological way of doing his job shows him continually trying to shovel things in both directions across the line separating the spiritual and the material, emotions and cash. Mitchell, in *The Sweet Hereafter*, is of course engaged in a similar transformation. *Exotica* again offers a particularly juicy range of these activities. Thomas, the gay pet-store owner, buys pairs of scalped ballet tickets and then gives one of them away to single likely-looking guys at the performance, saying that he has gotten them for free and wouldn't feel comfortable taking money for them. Via this circuitous route, he transforms cash into a human relationship that serves an emotional need. The virtuoso exchange-artist, Francis, does the same thing when he pays his niece to come to his house and babysit a child who, being dead, isn't there. Later on, in his day-job capacity of tax inspector, Francis offers to overlook Thomas's tax frauds in return for Thomas's help in surreptitiously taping a conversation with Christina and, later, aiding his plan to kill her ex-boyfriend, Eric. "You do this favour for me, I'll do that favour for you," he says with perfect sincerity, transforming blackmail and criminal exchange into the terms of friendship and compassion.

The characters who engage in these activities of substitution and exchange very often have to cross a line that should not be crossed—or at least not with the kind of heedless tunnel-vision displayed by the characters who cross them. It is the boundary between feelings arising from experience, memory, and history—love, for example, or grief—and that land of substituted quanta whose grounding is always in the secondary desire to make the primary condition go away or get better. In the enactment of this strategy, the characters adopting it perform some bizarre and very artificial-looking actions. When your young daughter is the victim of a sex-murder (as with *Exotica*'s Francis), your emotional devastation is not artificial or constructed; but if you then attempt to fend off the pain through the truly "exotic" range of substitutions that Francis develops, your behaviour begins to appear hermetically distorted and unhealthy. Viewers are struck by the strangeness and apparent inappropriateness of the behaviour of characters like Francis, but never the characters themselves, who act with a kind of blithe audacity that shows not the least consciousness they are doing anything out of the ordinary.

Does Egoyan himself think of his characters as behaving pathologically? Perhaps not: at some point in virtually all of his valuable (and voluble) DVD commentaries he simply points out, often rather admiringly, the amazing inventiveness of people in ministering to their emotional problems and confesses his fascination with this trait.

"Opera"

Because Egoyan's films repeatedly present multiple viewpoints, feature abstract and patterned narrative schemata, and proffer their characters as representations of positions or ideas, he has often been characterized (and criticized) as a "cold" artist. But the cool detachment of his formal methods is always juxtaposed with a narrative content that is, especially in the psychological sphere, highly charged and even lurid. The filmmaker himself suggests that in fact they are "operatic" in their emotional fervour.[4] The ground of every one of Egoyan's films is loss, sometimes terrible loss, and they are often suffused in pathos. From *Next of Kin*, which, although a cheerful film for Egoyan, is based on a family's loss of a child, to *Ararat*, which wrestles with the dreadful trauma of the Armenian genocide, Egoyan returns again and again to situations of damage and impossible yearning. His characters often have a limited self-understanding, even to the point of repression. Indeed, one of the pleasures of Egoyan's cinema is to watch the complex weave of, on the one hand, the game of concealment and partial revelation that he is playing with facts about characters and their pasts, with, on the other hand, the sense we have that we can see the oddness or compulsiveness of characters' behaviours much more clearly than they can themselves. With repression comes an oddness or perversity in its release, a climate of neurosis. "Neurotic," in fact, seems too mild a word to describe the twisted actions and feelings of characters like Lisa and Clara in *Speaking Parts*, the title character of *The Adjuster*, the Photographer in *Calendar*, or almost anybody in *Exotica*, not to mention a real monster like Hilditch in *Felicia's Journey*. "Unhinged" would be just as near. The distance between cool surface and boiling depths, what people are doing and what they think they are doing, is very great; and one can say that Egoyan's cinema in general is powered by the muffled tension of this distance and contrast.

One example will perhaps serve to illustrate the situation. "Family" is another word that is featured prominently in the list of Egoyan's central themes. And it is true that families—their constitution, their identity, their role in forming individual subjectivity—are continually at centre stage, most notably in *Next of Kin*, *Family Viewing*, *The Adjuster*, *The Sweet Hereafter*, and *Ararat*, but importantly present in almost every one of Egoyan's films. All the pieties of "family values"—life-giving rootedness and warmth and strength, the massive bedrock of origins, feelings that are absolutely fundamental—are present here. One sees them in Van's resurrection of his matriarchal ethnic identity in *Family Viewing*, in the silent bond between the sisters and the child in *The Adjuster*, in the opening and often-recurring overhead shot of an ideal nuclear family in *The Sweet Hereafter*, and the passionate family attachments of *Ararat*. But what is at least as characteristic of Egoyan's family relations is their hidden sickness and taintedness. Leaving aside the way family bedrock is destabilized in the dumbfounding fictionalities of *Next of Kin* or the maddeningly obscured or heavily disputed narratives of family history in *Exotica*, *The Adjuster*, or *Ararat*, or the heavy hand of oppressive family tradition in *Felicia's Journey* and *Ararat*, too, the most glaring crack in the foundation of Egoyan's family relations is the alarming incidence of incest, actual or suggested.

Incest is a feature that seems to burrow into Egoyan's cinema by virtue of its strategic place between the realm of family and the equally important realm of sexuality that is a major locus of the volatility and disorder burbling underneath the surface of formal abstraction and control. He is drawn to it repeatedly, and the catalogue of incest-sightings in his cinema is very extensive. Right from the beginning, in *Next of Kin*, there is the suggestion (though not the fact) of brother-sister incest;[5] in *Family Viewing* there is the suggestion of mother-son incest (and the fact of father-son oedipal rivalry) in the relationship between Van and his father's live-in girlfriend Sandra; *Speaking Parts* features a more overt sexual attraction on the part of Clara for her actual dead brother; *Exotica* presents a pattern of suggested and actual father-daughter incest that is one of the structuring beams of the film; *The Sweet Hereafter* features as a crucial element the actual incestuous relationship between Sam and his daughter Nicole; Hilditch, after surviving the rather effulgent embraces of his flamboyantly "seductive" mother as a boy, is the very fatherly killer of multiple young girls in *Felicia's Journey*; and *Ararat* again has a sexual relationship between a brother and a sister (Raffi and Celia) who are not quite a brother and a sister but definitely close enough to produce the incestuous odour.

Other than being the worm in the bud of family, incest also functions as another—the most prominent—iteration of sexuality in all its Egoyan hothouse strangeness. As with his compatriot David Cronenberg (an admired figure and something of a role model), you have to look very hard to find a "normal" sexual relationship anywhere in Egoyan's cinema, even if the "abnormalities" of Egoyan's imagined sexualities pale almost into invisibility next to Cronenberg's. Indeed, with both filmmakers one wants to invoke a stereotype of gray English-Canadian repression that covers every sort of throbbing mutation, in the fashion described by Margaret Atwood in *Survival* and *Second Words*.[6] In his many interviews and commentaries, Egoyan does seem (rather like Cronenberg) stereotypically Canadian: nice, well-spoken, considerate, sensitive, careful, politically correct, verbally very forthcoming but in other ways creating a somewhat recessive impression. The filmmaker's public personality, as seen for instance in his many interviews and commentaries, forms quite a contrast with the sexual transgression going on in his films. *Family Viewing* has video-home-porno, telephone sex, and prostitution. *Speaking Parts* takes place in a hotel that pimps one of its employees (Lance) to guests of both sexes and also presents an ultra-Egoyanesque scene of teleconference-mutual-masturbation. Numerous scenes in *The Adjuster* take place at the censor board where Noah's wife, Hera, works, with transgressive sexuality everywhere in the background; meanwhile Noah goes to bed with clients of both sexes, and Bubba and Mimi act out a series of shocking erotic skits. Even the relatively chaste *Calendar* finds its hero exhausting the resources of an escort service to find multicultural stand-ins for his wife.

Exotica (1994)

Exotica is Egoyan's masterpiece to date. (*The Sweet Hereafter*, which would perhaps be the consensus choice, seems to me a bit of an "Egoyan movie for people who don't like Egoyan movies.")[7] *Exotica* is the jewel in the crown of Egoyan's first-decade filmmaking mode, and in it he has balanced an exquisite formalism in narrative design with a realization of character more vivid and touching than he had hitherto achieved. Electrically enlivening everything is the most extensive deployment of sexual transgression in Egoyan's cinema. The most extreme example is the sex-murder of Francis's little daughter. But there is a whole range of accompanying phenomena stretching from the scandalous tale of Francis's brother having an affair with his wife and possibly fathering his child to the comprehensive smorgasbord of acts that might in some context be characterized as sexually transgressive, including male and female homosexuality, interracial sex, impregnation-by-contract, and of course stripping, lap-dancing, and the strip-club deejay Eric's lubricious discourse of desire. It is true that much of this is presented in a curiously bodiless way, usually *somewhere else* (in the past, narrated, off-screen—as in the case of the murder), often mediated or voyeurized; but it still has an edge that can cut. The most central and structural of these transgressions is incest, which, although nowhere directly visible, ultimately emerges as the hidden link that elucidates the strange stripping ritual of Christina and Francis and, in turn, the whole film in a wonderful exit-line way that leaves viewers still watching things fall into place in their minds even as they go out of the theatre. (Egoyan has said that he "wanted to structure the film like a striptease,"[8] and the final scene is Salomé's seventh veil.) Even more pervasive is the poisoned apple of paedophilic desire: Christina's statutory-rape striptease, the ecstatic yearning of Eric's accompanying rap: "What is it that gives a schoolgirl her special innocence? Her sweet fragrance—fresh flowers, light as spring rain—oh my god! my god!? Or is it her firm young flesh inviting your every caress? Inviting you to explore her deepest and most private secrets?" These moments, undenounced by the film even as it proffers them in the context of child sex-murder and incestuous child abuse, go all the way past "operatic" to "sensational." And yet so strong is the sense of the film's chessboard formalism, so cool is Egoyan's ravishing visual touch, and so sweet the climate of redemptive understanding at the end, that everything is held in superb, elegant suspension.

Pathos and Redemption

Transgressive sexuality in all these forms is complemented by an extensive series of spectacles of emotional suffering. The pathos of such tormented characters as Lisa and Clara in *Speaking Parts*, Bubba in *The Adjuster*, Francis and Eric in *Exotica*, Mitchell and all the grieving people in *The Sweet Hereafter*, and the helpless heroine in *Felicia's Journey* verges on melodrama. Then we can add those embodiments of cold institutional and patriarchal power (often taken by actor David Hemblen) who constantly recur in Egoyan's cinema, and whose steely impassiveness seems frighteningly inhuman. Death, incest, sexual crime, intense suffering, bizarre displacements, cold power, abject vulnerability: these emotionally violent elements are positively gaudy if you look at them divorced from the patterned detachment of their cinematic narration. Add then the already-touched-upon habit of Egoyan's central characters to perform astonishing actings-out and gross imaginative leaps without the slightest self-consciousness or inhibition—seen most clearly in those activities of role-playing, ritualizing, and substitution.

Pain and pathology fill Egoyan's films. There is so much damage and loss in films like *Speaking Parts*, *Calendar*, *Exotica*, *The Sweet Hereafter*, *Felicia's Journey*, and *Ararat* that it is tempting to describe this cinema as tragic in its outlook. Certainly Egoyan has a great sensitivity to the impossible aspects of the human situation. But there is nothing of Cronenberg's implacable grimness of outlook. Rather, Egoyan's work has shown the ability, and the willingness, to turn in the midst of hurt to a prospect of consolation and healing, and so "tragic" is not the right word for them after all. Both *Next of Kin* and *Family Viewing* are resolutely, even unreasonably, optimistic films, given their premises. *Speaking Parts* works its way to something not unlike a happy ending through seas of hallucinatory suffering. The lives of three of *Exotica*'s four central characters (Francis, Eric, Christina) are landscapes of devastation (the fourth, Thomas, is merely under investigation for tax fraud and threatened by the disintegration of his world), but the film shows its will to uplift in the way it emphasizes the roles of compassion, understanding, and forgiveness in the end as forcefully as it earlier did those of suffering and psychological sickness. How *The Sweet Hereafter* manages to find its way through massive trauma to something, if not positive, then wistfully philosophical, is something of an alchemical creative mystery. And when you tabulate all the contradictions, blockages, unassuageable anger, and impenetrable unknowableness in *Ararat*, its final posture of all-embracing wisdom seems equally miraculous. A fine little paradigm of this whole transformative phenomenon may be seen in the ending of *Felicia's Journey*, which conjures some kind of epiphany for the damned Hilditch out of the absurd gospel-preaching of a passing evangelist that in turn results in his walking into his house and hanging himself. The film in one stroke whisks itself back from the brink of the abyss (the murder of Felicia) and provides for its male protagonist what one can only call a grotesque redemption. In several of his films, Egoyan seems in this way to work himself into no-exit situations and yet to find some secret trapdoor that allows the narrative to escape into a more soothing and reconciled dénouement than one would ever have believed possible. Nor do these escapes represent (except perhaps once or twice in marginal ways) any kind of bailing out from the difficulties the films so convincingly expound into an unearned happy ending. Rather, they show Egoyan simply adding another, beneficent, perspective to the cruel ones that also exist in the same works and extending the layeredness of his vision to yet another realm.

Armenia, Armenia

Egoyan was born in Cairo of Armenian parents, moved to Victoria, BC, as a three-year-old, and was not especially interested in his Armenian heritage until he went to university in Toronto as a young man. Since then, he has addressed issues of immigrant and diasporic identity in some ways that are familiar but in quite a few more that are not. In consequence, Egoyan's cinema has found an important place in the booming scholarly literature on postcolonialism, national identity, and diasporic culture, just as it has in the discourse on postmodernity by virtue of its themes of mediation and unstable epistemology.[9] This strand in Egoyan's movies has always had (if we can believe the filmmaker's own repeated testimony) an autobiographical element, dramatizing his own exploration and working-out of issues around his ethnic identity.

 Next of Kin has its origin in the conflict of emotional appeals between a WASP-Canadian cultural environment and an Armenian-Canadian one; it stages Egoyan's own dilemma of cultural schizophrenia metaphorically but with breathtaking simplicity. As a child in Victoria, Egoyan thought of himself as just a "regular" kid without ethnic identity, and, despite his Armenian-speaking parents, resisted seeing himself as Armenian. In a brilliant transposition, the hero of *Next of Kin*, Peter, actually is WASP but, alienated by the bland vacuity of that identity, gravitates toward an Armenian family that has given its infant son up for adoption and whose identity the protagonist now simply assumes as easily as putting on a suit of clothes. Somehow, this Old World environment of family relations that Peter has fictionally adopted seems to him more authentic than his actual mother and father (who, by the way, bear the unkind name of "Foster"). In effect Peter, although "actually" WASP, just *decides* to be Armenian. To the extent that the film is autobiographical, such a figuration represents Egoyan's cultural WASPness as something given, and his Armenianness as something consciously and "unnaturally" tried on. Where in later instances Egoyan has been drawn to depict more fully a vision of the darkness and suffering of Armenian history and the seductive pain of being, or else not being able to be, Armenian, in *Next of Kin* the decision to assume this identity has almost the weightlessness of a hairstyle choice.

Family Viewing continues Egoyan's Armenian journey with another staging of a young male's quest to reclaim a lost ethnicity. As with his predecessor in *Next of Kin*, the young protagonist, Van (in a further point of relation actually played by the younger brother of his counterpart, Peter), again reflects in his family origins Egoyan's cultural in-betweenness: he is the offspring of an (absent) warm Armenian mother and a (present) cold WASP father. We feel that the father has driven the mother away, though in typical fashion Egoyan withholds information about what actually happened. Thus, as in *Next of Kin*, WASPness is somehow to blame for the absence of Armenianness. Like Peter, Van solves his problem of identity with amazing theatrical flair. His rescue of his Armenian grandmother from her state of neglect by switching her with another lady who has died is a ploy that removes the grandmother from the baleful father's regime of ethnic erasure and also repeats from *Next of Kin* the trope of identity forgery. (This is only the first of a series of theatrical gestures that culminates in installing the old lady in the "false" home of a closed-down hotel wing.) It is clear that the grandmother represents for Van the embodiment of his own ethnicity, repressed and maltreated like her. In his DVD commentary, Egoyan remarks on the especially autobiographical nature of this film, in particular its refiguring of his relationship with his own grandmother—as good as saying that she had the same function with respect to Egoyan's buried ethnic history that the movie character has for Van. Although in *Family Viewing* Armenian ethnicity has a far greater affective weight and gravitational pull than it has in *Next of Kin*, it is quite significant that in both films its adoption by the character most closely resembling the author is wrapped in layers of deception, identity forgery, theatrical performativity, and existential ethnic self-invention. It is, in short, anything but "natural."

Speaking Parts takes a break from ethnicity, but the topic returns in its successor. *The Adjuster* is a film that again has, as one of its organizing principles, the distinction, or rather chasm, between mainstream Anglo identity and something Middle Eastern. It is a split that exists in the family of the title character, between Noah on the one hand and his wife, her sister, and (probably) the sister's little son on the other, all of them living together in an incredibly strange show home in the middle of nowhere. The two women and the child speak to one other in a language that Noah cannot understand, look at pictures from "our old neighbour-hood" (their Armenian origins are never specified), and in general form a solid, rooted, somehow truly authentic family bond that Noah cannot really penetrate. The contrast between Noah and his family is doubled with the introduction of the film's second married couple, Bubba and Mimi, whose extravagant role-acting and ungrounded fakery mark them as the symbolic epitome of all-white, all-(North-)American culture. In this polarized climate, the film examines issues of cultural authenticity in general and in particular replicates the basic Egoyan cultural split between WASPness and Armenianness already seen in *Next of Kin* and *Family Viewing*.

Calendar (1993)

In *Calendar*, Egoyan for the first time names Armenia prominently, and much of the film is shot on location there. One of the film's two large themes is the question of Armenian and Armenian-diasporic identity (its other is the alienating effects of mediation). When the principal male role of the film is played by Egoyan himself, and this protagonist is once more placed in a kind of opposition to, or at least at a distance from, the bedrock of "authentic" Armenian identity, *Calendar* becomes the most explicit of all of Egoyan's uneasy stagings of his relation to Armenianness. As the Photographer (he isn't given a name) travels around Armenia from one church to another to provide pictures for a calendar to be circulated among the Armenian-Canadian community, his assignment is to create images that will stand for some kind of timeless and idealized Armenian history to be consumed by that diasporic community. Although the Photographer is of Armenian extraction, he doesn't speak the language. But his wife, who is accompanying him, does; and it is she who translates for him the remarks of their Armenian driver. The Driver seems to feel he must do something to explain the weight and depth of Armenian history to these two visitors. The Wife is quite interested in his remarks, but the Photographer just wants to take photographs and video recordings. Egoyan has said that the three characters represent the three basic kinds of Armenian identity: pure (the Driver), diasporic (the Wife/Translator), and assimilated (the Photographer). In the end the Wife decides to end her marriage and stay in a relationship with the Driver, while the Photographer returns to Canada and attempts to animate and articulate his emotional chaos through the further distancing/substituting device of hiring female escorts to have dinner with him and then leave the table to phone up men and have erotic conversations with them in languages that (like Armenian) he can't understand.

There is much to say about the rich portrayal of ethnic identity in *Calendar*, but what is almost perversely most insistent in the foreground is the exclusion of the protagonist (Egoyan himself) from the pageant of national meaning. He also ends up excluded from his own marriage, and the force that he loses his wife to is the same impenetrable vortex of ancient authentic culture with its somehow deeper human values that Noah also cannot enter into with his wife and her family in *The Adjuster*. In both of these films Egoyan presents us with the same configuration: a man whose Anglo-cultural instrumentalizing routines of mediation have cut him off from a less reified and alienated world represented by Old-World ethnicity and incarnated in the female person of his wife (in both cases played by Arsinée Khanjian, Egoyan's own wife). The Photographer, whom Egoyan describes as "the worst nightmare I have of myself," is the embodiment of the filmmaker's anxieties both about mixed cultural identity and also about the dangerous temptations of over-mediation—his two most obsessive themes.[10] Although the self-critique is excoriating, it is also melancholy.

Ararat (2002)

Egoyan took a rest from Armenia, with *Exotica*, *The Sweet Hereafter*, and *Felicia's Journey* all turning to other matters. But in *Ararat* questions of diasporic and national identity came home to roost with a vengeance. As soon as Egoyan entered into an exploration of his Armenian heritage, he of course encountered the elephant in its room, the horrific Armenian genocide of 1915–1923, in which a substantial percentage of the Armenian population died at the hands of the Ottoman and post-Ottoman Turks. Conscious that there was no film dramatizing these traumatic events, Egoyan, as perhaps the world's foremost filmmaker of Armenian extraction, decided at last to tackle the subject.[11] Yet *Ararat* is nothing at all like *Schindler's List* or other historical-atrocity movies. A key element of continuing Armenian anger stems from the failure of the Turkish government to admit that there was an Armenian genocide and its disputing of events and numbers of dead. Since the Turkish government has admitted that "something happened," and talked about complicating factors (the country was desperately fighting the First World War at the time, there was an Armenian insurgency), the problem becomes a quarrel over whose narrative is going to prevail and, in particular, whether a muddying, distracting, prevaricating Turkish narrative is going to be allowed to impede the installation of the simple, true Armenian narrative: namely, that a million or more Armenians were raped, tortured, and murdered by Turks just because they were Armenian. But if the struggle for narrative precedence is the present-day *casus belli*, Egoyan's own narrative is more "Turkish" than "Armenian," because he cannot bear to present this straightforward story either. Well, he does present it in *Ararat*, but only in the heavily cocooned and skepticized form of the Armenian-genocide movie (also called *Ararat*, in a typically Egoyanesque *mise en abyme*) that is being shot inside the film—a middle-of-the-road historical spectacular à la *Dr. Zhivago*, with big, simple events and big, simple feelings. In the context of the Turkish-Armenian Narrative

War, representing the powerful, straightforward narrative of historical trauma in this distantiating way may be worse than not presenting it at all. Egoyan seems quite aware that this might be the case, since he ends his film with an epigraph solemnly stating that "the historical events in this film have been substantiated by holocaust scholars, national archives, and eyewitness accounts." But this statement, too, like the unambiguous movie-epic being shot in the film, seems to exist as a kind of sub-theme or footnote to Egoyan's own *Ararat*, which absolutely cannot escape from its own uncertainties and enigmas.

In the end, *Ararat* seems like the repository not only of all of Egoyan's multifarious feelings about Armenian identity but also of almost everything else he has ever been interested in. Egoyan could not make an uncomplicated passionate film denouncing the Armenian genocide, even though he has confessed that the idea of doing something like the movie-in-the-movie of *Ararat* was seductive.[12] Judging from the clear-and-simple version made by the character Edward Saroyan, a distinguished international filmmaker in the autumn (or perhaps winter) of his career, it would not be a very good movie. As with Clara's autobiographical screenplay in *Speaking Parts*, the deep passion and commitment of Saroyan and his scriptwriter are not enough to guarantee anything of aesthetic value—and indeed on the evidence of *Speaking Parts* and *Ararat*, Egoyan may be saying that too much unexamined feeling and personal closeness to the project is more likely to be a guarantee of aesthetic superficiality (certainly in comparison with Egoyan's fastidious, formally elegant creations). What is Egoyan, of all filmmakers, going to do with something as blatant as the Armenian atrocity-stories passed down through generations with such anger and sorrow? (The answer, it seems, is: Nest them underneath five levels of quotation marks, as with the horror story of the "burning brides," which is narrated by the female German eyewitness narrated by the American doctor Clarence Ussher narrated by the actor Martin playing Ussher narrated by Saroyan's film narrated by Egoyan's film.) *Ararat* is unable to balance the impossible conflicting demands of Armenian cries for recognition of their trauma on the one hand and Egoyan's constitutional need for a multilayered, schematically organized kaleidoscope of themes and viewpoints on the other. Its piling-on of disputed testimonies, conflicting histories, and contested memories, and its amazingly multi-pronged examination of the status of personal belief, the nature of narrative, and the function of art, lead to a spaghetti-junction of a structure too extensive for even Egoyan's fabulous contrapuntal talents to master.

ARARAT raises a question about Egoyan's future. After the adaptations *The Sweet Hereafter* and *Felicia's Journey*, Egoyan was working once again with an original script but now with a subject that had expanded and escaped from the somewhat hermetic enclosure of the films leading up to *Exotica*. Probably Egoyan cannot go back to that early model of the films leading up to *Exotica*, but, on the evidence of *Ararat*, a more ambitious model may prove unwieldy, especially when the artist has not at all gotten away from any of the formal and thematic obsessions for which the earlier model at its best was such exquisite vehicle. It is simply impossible at this point to predict how Egoyan's career will go, or to speculate with any confidence about what the films he will make will be like. But, in his middle forties, Egoyan still counts as a young filmmaker, and his prodigious creative talents will surely take him somewhere interesting. Given the highly distinctive nature of his vision, it is going to be particularly intriguing to see where that could possibly be. Needless to say, his existing films are already enough to assure him a permanent place in the pantheon of Canadian filmmakers.

AUTHOR'S NOTE

For a selected list of Egoyan's films, with major awards and nominations, see the Appendix. Angela Joosse's bibliography for *Image and Territory: Essays on Atom Egoyan*, ed. Monique Tschofen and Jennifer Burwell (Waterloo: Wilfrid Laurier University Press, 2006), 377–402, lists eighty-seven scholarly books, articles, or book chapters, ten unpublished dissertations, sixty-seven essays in non-scholarly journals, 151 newspaper articles, an astonishing sixty interviews, thirty-two print pieces written by Egoyan, and three websites dedicated to him. Of course the volume's listing cannot be complete and does not include its own further contribution of eighteen essays and two interviews.

1. Egoyan has, as of June 2005, written and directed ten short films and three thirty- to sixty-minute films for television, directed without writing an additional six films for television (the most important of which is the 1993 CBC feature *Gross Misconduct*), created twelve gallery installations, and directed four opera productions and another dozen theatre pieces.

2. Peter Harcourt, in "Imaginary Images: An Examination of Atom Egoyan's Films," *Film Quarterly* 48, no. 3 (Spring 1995): 2–14, talks about the three-person nature of Egoyan's narratives (p. 5ff.). This three-person narrative structure is easily seen in *Speaking Parts* and *Calendar*, for example, but one can also find in *The Adjuster* and *Exotica* central casts of four and in *The Sweet Hereafter* and *Ararat* even larger nuclear groups.

3. Paul Coates has specifically referred to the condition of the characters in *Exotica* as manifesting "faulty mourning," "a ritual of mourning which only accentuates and exaggerates the sense of loss." Paul Coates, "Projecting the Exotic: Atom Egoyan and Fantasy," *Canadian Journal of Film Studies* 6, no. 2 (Fall 1997): 21–33, see in particular page 28. Egoyan himself also introduces and elucidates this term in his interview with Mario Falsetto in Falsetto's *Personal Visions: Conversations with Independent Film-makers* (London: Constable, 1999), 145.

4. He said to Geoff Pevere: "To me, the films are almost operatic. They're almost embarrasingly emotional." Geoff Pevere, "Difficult to Say: An interview with Atom Egoyan," in Egoyan's screenplay, *Exotica* (Toronto: Coach House Press, 1995), 60. We can also recall Egoyan's interest in actual opera and the importance of music in his films.

5. In his DVD commentary, Egoyan expresses regret that he did not go further in this direction by having Peter/Bedros and Azah have an actual sexual relationship.

6. In these books, Atwood repeatedly characterizes Canada as a place that is outwardly passive and frozen with repression, but inwardly awash with twisted emotions. See for example this account of Prime Minister Mackenzie King: "Mackenzie King, formerly a symbol of Canada because of his supposed dullness and greyness…, is enjoying new symbolic popularity as a secret madman who communed every night with the picture of his dead mother and believed that his dog was inhabited by her soul. 'Mackenzie King rules Canada because he is himself the embodiment of Canada—cold and cautious on the outside…but inside a mass of intuition and dark intimations,' says one of Robertson Davies' characters in *The Manticore*, speaking for many" (Atwood, *Second Words* [Toronto: Anansi, 1982], 231–32).

7. In 2004 the Toronto International Film Festival conducted its once-a-decade poll of critics, programmers, and industry professionals to name the "Top

10 Canadian Films of All Time." *The Sweet Hereafter* came in at number three and *Calendar* at number sixteen (tied with *Pour la suite du monde* and *Spider*, a Cronenberg movie for people who don't like Cronenberg movies). *Exotica* is not present in the top twenty, although it was Egoyan's most successful film at the box office. Incidentally, the 1993 poll placed *The Adjuster* at number ten. The 2004 poll, written up by Steve Gravestock, may be viewed in detail at http://www.topten.ca/images/TOP_10.pdf (accessed 13 February 2007). As long as we are playing this game, I can list my five favourite Egoyan films, in order, as: 1. *Exotica*, 2. *The Adjuster*, 3. *Calendar*, 4. *The Sweet Hereafter*, and 5. *Speaking Parts*.

8. *Exotica*, presskit. The remark is repeated on the website of Ego Film Arts, Egoyan's production company. The website copy states, "In telling the story of *Exotica*, I wanted to structure the film like a striptease, gradually revealing an emotionally loaded history." See http://www.egofilmarts.com (accessed 13 February 2007).

9. Hamid Naficy is perhaps the most prominent of the scholars in this area whose work has focused on Egoyan. See especially his *An Accented Cinema: Exilic and Diasporic Filmmaking* (Princeton: Princeton University Press, 2001), where Egoyan features strongly, and also his "The Accented Style of the Independent Transnational Cinema: A Conversation with Atom Egoyan," in George E. Marcus, ed., *Cultural Producers in Perilous States* (Chicago: University of Chicago Press, 1997), 179–231.

10. DVD commentary, *Calendar*.

11. Egoyan told Timothy Taylor, "We have *Schindler's List*, *The Garden of the Finzi-Continis*, and *The Pawnbroker*. But nothing similar about the Armenian genocide." Taylor, "Afterword," in Atom Egoyan, *Ararat: The Shooting Script* (New York: Newmarket, 2002), 125.

12. He says this in his *Ararat* DVD commentary.

7

Activism and Aesthetics

The Work of John Greyson

CHRISTOPHER GITTINGS

The queer—the abnormal—is needed to provide the shock to wake us out of the normal, to challenge the society of normalization.
—R. BRUCE BRASSELL[1]

INTRODUCED TO THE WORLD of avant-garde video at H.B. Beale High School in London, Ontario, John Greyson subsequently travelled to Toronto where he joined Charles St. Video and became a part of the developing 1980s Queen Street West art scene.[2] One of the things that distinguished Greyson from his contemporaries was that he simultaneously belonged to LIFT (Liaison of Independent Filmmakers of Toronto) at a time when "the film community and the video community were mutually exclusive."[3] Greyson spent two years in New York where he was involved with the AIDS activist group ACT UP and then a year of volunteering in a Sandinista-governed Nicaragua defending itself against the US-backed, Honduras-based Contras. These proved to be inspirational experiences that would resurface in Greyson's video shorts and feature titles as engagements with the imbrications of AIDS, gender and sexuality, and imperialism. John Greyson's aesthetic continues to develop and be sustained within and between the spaces of avant-garde video-art gallery installation and the cinema, producing an eclectic body of politically activist queer work.

■ Early Video Shorts

EARLY VIDEO SHORTS, such as "The Perils of Pedagogy"(1984) and "The Jungle Book" (1985), foreground pedagogy as a mechanism through which both destructive and deconstructive teachings of imperialism, gender, and sexuality are possible. Greyson's activist aesthetic is marked in these works by the subversive tension of what queer theorist Lee Edelman would term "homographesis," a doubled in-scriptive and de-scriptive signifying practice:

> one serving the ideological purposes of a conservative social order intent on codi-
> fying identities in its labour of disciplinary inscription, and the other resistant to
> that categorization, intent on de-scribing the identities that order has so oppres-
> sively in-scribed.[4]

The ruling heterosexual masculinity taught in homo-social spaces, such as Scouting, the military, boys' schools, and locker rooms, creates spaces that, in Greyson's words, can be "turned inside out," transformed into spaces for the exploration of an "other" deconstructive teaching of gender and sexuality.[5] For example, in the "Perils of Pedagogy" (1984), pederasty becomes the discourse of instruction for adolescent boys. Through a dense collage of intertextual inserts that range from a depiction of pederasty on a classical Greek vase to 1970s gay porn, school doors and locker room, dining hall and flogging scenes from If (1968)—Lindsay Anderson's indict-ment of British boys' schools—Greyson de-scribes, or queers, a dominant and dominating heterosexual masculinity. These collage-like inserts are cross-cut with a camp music-video performance of "To Sir with Love" by a young man who is being directed and eroticized through the camera eye of an older man. In this way, Greyson's short critiques not only the disciplining limitations of a ruling heterosexual masculinity as taught by straight society's institutions but also represents the shortcomings of

the "gay ghetto" as a "downtown campus" that teaches gay boys the stereotypes of "pretty young thing" or "trick."

The 1985 video short "The Jungle Book" continues this pedagogical
aesthetic. Here, scenes from Greyson's central narrative about the suicide
of a man outed in the 1985 St. Catharines' Police surveillance of gay sex
in public washrooms are intercut with scenes from Zoltan Korda's film
of Rudyard Kipling's *The Jungle Book* (1942), inserts of gay porn, a black and
white photograph of Cub Scouts sitting in a circle, and a sexual encounter
structured around the type of boys' imperial adventure stories found in
Kipling, *Chums* (1892–1932) and *Boy's Own Annual* (1879–1967). The lover of
another man caught up in the toilet sex scandal, a man we later see
reading *The Age of Kipling*, initiates sex by claiming he has been bitten by a
snake and that the poison must be sucked out of his thigh. Greyson's ironic
re-contextualizing of Kipling reveals the author's work as a foundational
text in a regulatory homophobia designed to repress homosexuality from
irrupting in the homosocial. Yet Greyson simultaneously (re)reads and
rearticulates Kipling's work as structuring same-sex phantasy and sexual
acts, suggesting that spaces of homosociality are, perhaps always already
queer.[6]

With "Kipling Meets the Cowboys" (1985), Greyson continues to destabilize the sign systems of compulsory male heterosexuality in the queer
convergence of two of the discourse's iconic figures: Kipling and the
American cowboy. Initiating an aesthetic he will later develop in some of
his features—creative anachronism as re-historicization—the establishing
shots of "Kipling Meets the Cowboys" find a queer Kipling writing a love
letter to Baden-Powel, the founder of Scouting, on the eve a 1988 Toronto
tour date celebrating eighty years of the Scouting movement. Kipling's
image is quickly displaced by Greyson's title sequence, which reframes
images of John Wayne and Montgomery Clift from Howard Hawke's *Red
River* (1948) in a pink circle, demarcating the Hollywood Western and its
heterosexual hero as queer territory. Throughout his film Greyson samples
scenes from *Red River* depicting the male-to-male "platonic" love between
Matthew Garth (Montgomery Clift) and Tom Dunson (John Wayne) and
the sexual tension between the two characters that structures their fist
fight at the end of the film. The sexuality of the cowboy figure has always
been ambiguous as the potential for homosexual tension in the homoso-

cial context of the frontier threatens the very ideal of ruling heterosexual masculinity, which facilitates the formation of homosociality. This instability is reflected in the homosexual tension that structures masculinity in many Hollywod Westerns[7] and is especially palpable in Red River, where Cherry Vallens (John Ireland) and Matthew Garth (Montgomery Clift) have their shoot-off, an event precipitated by Jerry's words: "Good looking gun you've got there. Can I see it?" Jerry later says of Matt's "gun": "I've taken a liking to that gun of his."

"Kipling Meets the Cowboys" juxtaposes Howard Hawke's Hollywood cowboys to four randy, lip-synching cowboys engaged in anal and oral sex in a gay Western bar and later has Kipling and a gay First Nations man masturbate each other in a cinema while watching the spectacle of male bonding through violence as enacted by Matt and Tom at the end of Red River. This queer convergence of Kipling and the cowboys effectively subverts the signification of a hegemonic heterosexual masculinity interrupting and informing our understanding of both British and American imperialisms. After all, the heterosexual cowboy is a formation of masculinity that is an agent of US Manifest Destiny. In translating historical figures such as Kipling or cowboys into a late twentieth-century queer present, and stitching in references to the US-backed Contra war on Nicaragua via newspaper headlines and radio broadcasts, Greyson impresses upon his viewers that the vestiges of turn-of-the-century imperialism are still very much a part of our world, actively interpellating our subjectivities, and that the imperial project was/is a masculinist heterosexual one.

Commenting on his de-scriptive aesthetics and the threads of imperialism and pedagogy that run through his work, Greyson says:

> If the culture of colonial imperial masculinity is being imposed we can take those scraps and with no effort at all turn them inside out and reveal their fault lines and subvert them. And that was very much part of a project which I think queer art partook of in the 70s and 80s. Yes, we have this earnest mandate to create new images but we can also take the images we've been suffocated by all our lives and with just a little twist turn them inside out and reveal a whole new way of interpreting them.[8]

Very much a part of the autoreferential postmodern aesthetic of the 1980s and 1990s, Greyson's work is aware of itself as cinema and, as such, self-consciously directs, after Jean François Lyotard, an "incredulity" or skepticism toward tyrannical and culturally constructed metanarratives or master codes, such as imperialism, gender, and sexuality, which attempt to organize our understanding of the world and our place in it.[9]

A writer (*Urinal and Other Stories* [1993]) and editor (*Queer Looks: Perspectives on Lesbian and Gay Film and Video* [1993]) whose production practice is informed by critical theory, Greyson's work is widely recognized as a cinema of ideas.[10] R. Bruce Brassell's thoughtful essay on "The Making of 'Monsters'" (1991) notes the significant influence of Bertold Brecht's and Walter Benjamin's concepts of distanciation on Greyson's aesthetic.[11] For Brassell, Brecht's term *umfunktionierung* (refunctionalization) best describes the transgressive work Greyson's films perform upon their audiences. Roswitha Mueller defines Brecht's refunctionalization as "the structural reorganization of the relationship between the stage, the author, and the audience...in order to bring about a more democratic structure of communication."[12] As Benjamin understands this process, the cultural apparatus, whether it be the theatre stage or the cinema screen, "is better the more consumers it is able to turn into producers—that is, readers or spectators into collaborators."[13]

Brassell's critique addresses "The Making of 'Monsters'" specifically, but it is quite usefully applied to all of Greyson's oeuvre. Greyson's self-reflexive body of work attempts to render a passive cinema audience active by alienating viewers to the point where they become aware that they are a part of the process of making the film signify by interpreting and working with the screen. It is the audience's responsibility to take the assemblage of audio-visual coordinates the filmmaker has given them and produce meaning. And it is this Brechtian distanciation that may have garnered some of the negative reviews of Greyson's films. Reviewing "The Making of 'Monsters,'" Vincent Canby writes: "this is a very elaborate but not especially productive 'distancing' device that would probably not amuse Brecht."[14] Similarly, Tony Rayn's rather peevish review of *Uncut* (1998) suggests that audience members will "likely find that the film's refusal (inability?) to formulate either question or dramatic premises with any staying power makes it [the film] abysmally tedious."[15]

Brassell, however, argues that the technique of refunctionalization in Greysons's "The Making of 'Monsters'" has important ramifications for queerness: "this means queers function as producers. Queer audiences and queer filmmakers collaborate to produce a queer discourse, one which exists not only during the film viewing process but which also circulates outside in the streets of the lesbian and gay community. One of the primary places that functions as a site for the production of this discourse is lesbian and gay film festivals."[16]

■ Greyson and Queer? Canadian? Cinema

LESBIAN AND GAY FESTS have played a role in Greyson's success, with Lilies (1996) winning awards at the Austin Gay and Lesbian International Film Festival, the LA Outfest, and the San Francisco International Lesbian and Gay Film Festival, as well as a GLAAD (Gay and Lesbian Alliance Against Defamation) Media Award for Outstanding Film. Lilies also performed well outside of the gay and lesbian festival circuit, garnering prizes at Lorcano and Montreal, as well as scoring four Genies in Toronto. The Berlin International Film Festival has figured significantly in Greyson's career, awarding him Teddies for both Urinal (1988—Best Gay Feature Film) in 1989 and "The Making of 'Monsters'" (Best short film) in 1991.

Greyson's films are at least as much a part of a queer cinema and international Art House cinema as they are a Canadian national cinema. When asked if the term Canadian national cinema has any resonance for him, Greyson responded:

> I've never really bought into the notion of national cinema per se. I think it is useful in terms of teaching and festivals and it organizes the world but is it useful? Does it feed me aesthetically, politically, intellectually? Not at all. Some of my favorite filmmakers in the world happen to be Robert Lepage, Mike Holbloom, and Atom Egoyan, but does that mean I work overtime trying to fit those three completely different artists into a notion of a Canadian cinema?[17]

Not dissimilarly, Greyson voices a personal resistance to notions of queer nation, stating: "At the end of the day I don't have that huge an investment in the equivalent queer nationalism. I have much more a sense of solidarity with something like *Vaseline* which is just like this very punk, mixed, once-a-month queer night where everybody goes, straights, gays, queers you know, every age."[18] Significantly, when differentiating between American and Canadian films during a *Planet Out* online chat, Greyson speaks of the Canadian industry's facilitation of queer cinema:

> Our industry is like the European film industry, it's state financed, not commercially financed. By definition film is considered an art medium not an entertainment medium. It also makes for the possibility of a queer cinema. There's Hanging Garden [Thom Fitzgerald], Laurie Lynd, Patricia Rozema, Jeremy Podeswa, Midi Onodera. We're given tax dollars to be queer and artsy![19]

Greyson's work contributed to the development of an important theoretical and aesthetic turn, in what has become known internationally as the New Queer Cinema. He is recognized by B. Ruby Rich as one of the innovative filmmakers whose "The Making of 'Monsters'" helped to shape New Queer Cinema as she conceptualizes it in her defining 1992 *Sight and Sound* article, "The New Queer Cinema."[20] Michelle Aaron lists some of the key characteristics of this recent school of queer filmmaking as: giving voice to the marginalized, not only in the gay and lesbian community but in its subgroups as well; the eschewing of positive imagery in films such as Greg Araki's *The Living End* (1991), Todd Haynes' *Poison* (1992) and Tom Kallin's *Swoon* (1992); a defiance toward the sanctity of the past (Derek Jarman's *Edward II* [1991], *Swoon*); and, finally, formal experimentation.[21]

The violence done to the conventions of film form within the context of queer filmmaking is something B. Ruby Rich foregrounds in her pioneering work in the field. While she is quick to point out that the new queer film and video she is writing about don't share "a single aesthetic category, or strategy or concern," she does see a common style that she calls "Homo Pomo" which constitutes appropriation, pastiche, irony as well as a reworking of history with social constructionism very much in mind."[22] Rich's comments would apply to most, if not all of Greyson's work. While identifying with the sensibility of Jarman's *Richard II* [23] and Haynes's *Poison*, Greyson reads Rich's original essay as emphasizing a market penetration argument for a new queer cinematic sensibility "that seemed to have legs in the theatres," an argument that may have become muted in subsequent conceptualizations of NQC over the last thirteen years.[24] Greyson, one of the editors of the ground-breaking collection *Queer Looks* avers that the most interesting cinema to come out of the new queer sensibility of the 1990s was to be found in Independent Cinema:

> *The reason we did* Queer Looks *was to contribute to this debate around 'what is queer cinema?' But to actually stake out a turf and say the most interesting place for queer cinema is that hybrid film: Indy, Video, Activist, Avant Garde, and that's what that book project was about was trying to say 'don't look for the most interesting stuff within the commercial feature.' The most interesting stuff is the Indy stuff that is being made on the margins facilitated in England by Channel 4; it includes the* Poisons *and others but our big excitement is around this post-colonial hybrid activist practice that comes equally out of AIDS activism and queer activism and new notions around race and sexuality.*[25]

■ The Features

Urinal (1988)

Urinal, Greyson's first feature, continues to develop the "homo pomo" queer activist aesthetic of the shorts through creative anachronisms that work to de-scribe hetero-centrist histories revealing and subverting the bigoted influence these narratives impose upon the film's present. In this case, the law of the closet and its attendant homophobia are placed under scrutiny when five queer historical figures—Frida Kahlo, Yukio Mishima, Langston Hughes, Frances Loring, Florence Wyle, and Sergei Eisenstein—are resurrected and given the "mission impossible" (complete with self-destructing message) of investigating a crisis in the gay community: police surveillance and the arrests and public shaming of men engaged in public-washroom sex throughout southern Ontario. Oscar Wilde's Dorian Grey is thrown into the mix here as an undercover gay agent, a mole working inside the police force. Although outed by Greyson's scripting of them as outstanding gay and lesbian artists, all of these individuals are familiar with the closet and many of them are coded as "suspected homosexuals" on the police data base that appears in close-up onscreen, as the social strictures of their times regulated (i.e. closeted their public construction of self). Greyson's Langston Hughes, in particular, appears to be very unhappy about the revelation of his sexuality. Oscar Wilde, manifest here in the presence of Dorian Grey, served time for desiring differently. In much the same way as Wilde's trial and imprisonment were examples of the state's attempt to regulate the sexual subjectivity of individuals, Greyson's film suggests that the oppressive and culturally pervasive discourse of compulsory heterosexuality creates the closeted homosexual subject whose only space for sexual self-expression becomes, ironically, the *public* toilet.

By having these historical characters time-travel into the Ontario of the 1980s, Greyson peels back the veneer of straight respectability that would contain our received history to reveal an always-already-queer past that can inform our present in a more life-affirming way than the death-dealing closet that extends itself into the film's cultural moment. Through interviews of those arrested and charged with acts of gross indecency and close-ups of newspaper headlines, *Urinal* documents the homophobic bigotry of police washroom arrests as producing unemployment, destruction of the family and, for some, suicide. The closeted subject's fear of being read as abject/queer by the dominant heterocentrist culture simultaneously maintains the closet and the "tea room"/public toilet, which is, after all, not only the extension of the closet *par excellence* but also the conflicted space in which the performance of the closet, of socially regulated straightness, is disrupted and revealed/detected. Frida Kahlo's research report on the policing and state regulation of sexuality encapsulates Greyson's activist agenda and the broader applications of the toilet sex cases for society. "Washroom sex," Frida reports, "becomes not a metaphor but a concrete example...of the battle to emancipate us all as sexual subjects." *Urinal*, Greyson's most expensive production to date was produced for a modest CDN $35,000.[26]

Musical Interventions: Singing and Dancing Queer Subjectivities in Zero Patience (1993)

Greyson's second feature, *Zero Patience*, owes its existence to his 1991 short "The Making of 'Monsters,'" produced during Greyson's internship at the Norman Jewison-founded Canadian Film Centre. "Monsters" develops the activist aesthetic of the earlier video tapes and feature by incorporating the documentary form and the musical to denaturalize homophobia as a pedagogically produced pathology that kills. Taking the real-life gay-bashing murder of Kenn Zeller by teenage boys as his starting point, Greyson creates a self-reflexive film-within-a-film narrative structure where Lotte Lenya, a fictional African-Canadian documentary filmmaker, is shooting a documentary around the production of a made-for-television musical entitled "Monsters" that is loosely based on the murder of a gay man in High Park. Greyson's metacinematic emphasis on the process of television and film production foregrounds the cultural production of the categories of queer/abnormal and straight/normal for the viewer.

In a sequence of shots in which he cuts from black and white hockey footage to the testimony of character witnesses at the boys' trial, to black and white footage of a television beer commercial and back to testimony of the boys' normalcy, Greyson establishes a correlation between the production of a hegemonic heterosexual masculinity and the televisual signs of hockey and beer advertising. The male-on-male violence of hockey viewing, a rite of Canadian masculinity, is interrupted by the breweries sponsoring *Hockey Night in Canada* with commercials saturated with the signs of macho masculinity and compulsory heterosexuality. Greyson represents the beer commercial as a montage of hyper-masculine images—motorcycle men, jocks, and cowboys—that eventually cut to blond, pneumatic women. Ironically, these same male images are appropriated and queered by gay culture to signify as icons of gay masculinity. However, in the compulsory heterosexuality organizing male sport and the beer commercial, the presence of the blond women regulates homosociality, repressing male-male desire. In the discursive structure Greyson creates through editing, these images form the dominant ideology of compulsory heterosexuality that hails or recruits male subjects for membership in the "norm." The cross-cutting of court-room testimony that links hockey and the beer commercial correlates normalcy with hockey, beer drinking, heterosexuality, and, ultimately, homophobic attacks. Bare-chested fathers and coaches wearing goalie masks, cyphers of the ruling masculinity, testify to the normalcy of the teenage killers and, by extension, their savage homophobic attack:

He might yell faggot at another player but it didn't mean anything.

...

They were normal teenage boys. Any queer who goes there knows it's dangerous. Somehow this guy must have provoked them.

...

They were normal teenage boys. It was the peer pressure and the beer.

This testimony, which Greyson said he based on the testimony provided by "an inordinate number of hockey coaches" at the trial of the boys involved in the 1985 killing, evidences a naturalizing of heterosexual male violence against gays and suggests that the innocent victim of the attack "asked for it."[27]

Greyson dispatches the possible irruption of homosexuality in a homosocial context through an attack on the homosexual subject. As the female voiceover of Greyson's film notes, there is "a good chance statistically that one of the five boys who killed Maguire is gay." Greyson unveils the homosexual tensions in the homosociality of hockey in a choreographed musical sequence where young men clad in nothing but socks, jocks, and goalie masks engage in the contact sport of "high sticking." "The Making of 'Monsters'" closes with another musical number that refuses victimization, advocating the "bashing" of the ideological sources of patriarchal homophobia:

Bash back baby the street is ours
   Bash the schools
   Bash the churches
   Bash the courts
   Bash the liberal fools

The opening and closing lyrics of Greyson's film advocate an activist intervention into homophobia by making homosexuality visible, by refusing to be a victim of the homophobia that closets and kills.[28]

The experimentation with the musical genre and the documentary in "Monsters," is further developed in *Zero Patience*, a co-production of Channel 4, having a CDN $1.3 million budget. Of his fondness for the musical genre as a narrative device, Greyson says: "musicals by definition build a bridge and invite an audience to meet half way both in terms of form and in terms of content."[29] Not unlike, the time-travelling characters of *Urinal*, Victorian sexologist and explorer Sir Richard Francis Burton and Gaetan Dugas, the French Canadian airline steward who achieved infamy as Patient Zero, are both resurrected to assist with the pedagogical project of *Zero Patience*: deconstructing the myths of homosexuality and AIDS.

The discursive construction of Dugas as Patient Zero, who is alleged to have brought AIDS to North America, via documentary forms is communicated to the viewer of Greyson's film in its opening shots: the still, digitized, black and white image of Zero, intercut with the classroom shots of the student reading from Burton's translation of *Arabian Nights*. Credits are superimposed on these shots of Zero, mimicking the media's projection of what Cagle calls a "vampiric spectre" onto Dugas.[30] The black and white, digitized quality of the image draws attention to its artifice and its inability to signify, its failure to refer back to a referent existing in material reality. The signifier, Patient Zero, does not refer back to Gaetan Dugas, but only to itself as a media-generated and "documentary" aberration.

This opening sequence brings Burton, Zero, and the documentary forms together, framing the film ideologically. The *mise-en-scène* of the classroom structures our reception of what is to follow. The classroom is located in an ideological, state-education apparatus that attempts to discipline people's thinking in pre-scribed, state-sanctioned ways, a space in which Burton's translation of *Arabian Nights*, with its infamous and pejorative "documentary" essay on homosexual practices, is consumed by young minds. An imperial text, Burton's "Terminal Essay" shaped, and in the context of the genealogy of homophobic texts drawn by Greyson's narrative, continues to shape cultural imaginings of homosexuality as perversion, vice, illness. So, we as spectators, then, are going to be taught a lesson. Cultural prejudices against homosexuals are going to be undone or examined in another type of classroom, the cinema, where prejudice can be taught or undone.[31]

Lilies (1996)

With his critically acclaimed and award-winning third feature *Lilies*, Greyson, for the first time, directs someone else's screenplay: Michel Marc Bouchard's adaptation of his play *Les Fleuettes ou la Répétition d'un drame romantique*.[32] Produced with a budget of CDN $2 million, *Lilies* was the last project to be made under the Ontario Film Development Corporation before the Harris Conservatives shut down its feature-film program.[33]

Set in a 1952 Québec prison for men, the film begins with the arrival of Bishop Bilodeau to hear convict Simon Doucet's confession. In short order, Bilodeau is locked into a time-machine-like confessional box from where he is forced to view the prisoners' re-staging of his youthful same-sex desire and his commission of a murder motivated by homophobia and jealousy. We learn that the young Bilodeau framed Simon for the murder of Simon's lover Vallier and that it is the wrongfully incarcerated Simon who has arranged for this prison theatre of the past to confront the bishop with his crimes. The deforming closet and its painful ramifications are taken up once again by Greyson, here in the figure of Bilodeau and his confinement in the confessional box for most of the film. Christine Ramsay reads the symbolic deployment of Bilodeau as queering the Catholic Church and exposing "the prison of masculinity in our culture."[34] As Ramsay observes, Bilodeau is "the closeted homosexual who…loves Simon but, sexually rejected by him, ruins Simon's life and his love for Vallier."[35] The auto-referentiality of the earlier work is present here in the theatre performance that is staged for both Bilodeau and Greyson's camera; for critic Noreen Golfman this device "constitutes 'the film within a film' of this inventive drama."[36]

Every bit as visually striking as *Zero Patience*, *Lilies'* production design affects a shift away from Greyson's earlier experimentation with the musical genre in favour of melodrama. Through the prisoners' re-enactment we are swept back some forty years into the past to the domestic spaces and family lives of the small town of Roberval. Ramsay's sensitive and original reading of the film locates it in "'straight' (melo)dramatic feature filmmaking" where "the forms and conventions of the 'women's picture'" are used "to stage a gay love story that questions patriarchal authority by exposing the sexual hypocrisies of the Catholic church in 1950s Québec while simultaneously exploding current homophobic norms of acceptable gender behaviour."[37] Part of this subversion of gender behaviour is achieved by the emotionally rich and affecting drag performances of the male prisoners who play all of the women of Roberval. Reviewing the film for *Sight and Sound*, Rob White, while acknowledging that some of the men's naturalistic performances of women "are very good," argues "the overall effect is unproductively disorienting in such an intellectually self-aware film."[38] Ramsay, however, produces an insightful and cogent reading of drag's signification in the film as "bringing the emotional experience of women and gay men under patriarchy together in solidarity."[39]

Uncut (1996)

Shot on digital video for a budget of CDN $100,000, Uncut, Greyson's 1996 feature, developed from the filmmaker's negative experience with copyright law during the release of "The Making of 'Monsters,'" a situation that effectively censored the film.[40] A hybrid of copyright concerns, documentary, performance, and opera, Uncut combines interviews with author Tom Waugh, video artist John Oswald, and playwright/actor Linda Griffiths with the fictive narrative of three Ottawa men named Peter, one of whom has a crush on Pierre Trudeau (long rumoured to be bisexual) and an obsessive interest in circumcision. Greyson talked about the gestation and premise of Uncut to an online chat audience on the eve of the film's American release:

> The script started in 1990 at the height of the Outing debates. I wanted to talk about how gossip was an important factor in the outing debates. Our interest in the private lives of icons. Why do we care about Tom Cruise or John Travolta or Jodie [Foster]? Pierre Trudeau—the only sexy Prime Minister Canada has ever had or ever will have—became a good test case for me. Circumcision was meant to be the counterpoint. With outing you have the in-the-closet/out-of-the-closet debate or the gay/straight debate. And with circumcision you've got cut or uncut.[41]

The development of Uncut is linked in an interesting way to "The Making of 'Monsters.'" Uncut itself was censored early on when Greyson attempted to make it at the Canadian Film Centre, where it was deemed libellous and therefore not approved for production. "The Making of 'Monsters,'" a film later censored by the Kurt Weill estate's withholding of copyright clearance, was Greyson's alternative project for the centre.

The Law of Enclosures (2000)

The Law of Enclosures, adapted by Greyson from a story by Dale Peck based on his novel of the same title, is far removed from the independently produced, low-budget *Uncut*. With a budget of CDN $2.2 million and a cast of fairly well-known actors including Diane Ladd (*Wild at Heart* [David Lynch, 1990] and *Alice Doesn't Live Here Anymore* [Martin Scorsese, 1974]) and perhaps the biggest "star" of English-Canadian cinema, Sarah Polley, Greyson turns toward heterosexual family melodrama in small-town Ontario, where the mundane, yet emotionally devastating, forty-year relationship of Bea and Hank is studied from its romantic beginnings through to its broken hatefulness and rekindling of affection. This being a John Greyson film, things are, of course, not quite as simple as the foregoing description might suggest. Peck's novel is noted for its formal experimentation, something Greyson revels in and was attracted to when looking for material to adapt.[42] Both the novel and film construct a compressed and fluid sense of time; Greyson frequently cross-cuts scenes involving Beatrice and Henry, the younger, romantic versions of Bea and Hank with those of the older, embittered, alienated couple. This cutting, however, does not mark a formal flashback as much as it does a congruence of time as the couples—both younger and older manifestations—are inexplicably stuck in the year they met—1991. Their lives are framed and haunted by continuous news coverage and video footage from the Gulf War. The stasis of 1991 signifies the marital paralysis of the couple; they are stuck with each other in time.

On second glance, the film might not be such a radical departure from the aesthetic of Greyson's earlier work, despite the director's comment that for him *The Law of Enclosures* was an attempt to work with the conventions of narrative-driven film to tell "the most straight-forward story in the most conventional ways. That is as far as I could go, and it wasn't even quite there in realist terms but nevertheless I tried and really hit a wall and realized this wasn't me."[43] Greyson's aesthetic signature, however, is visible in the film, especially in the Brechtian distanciation device of the four actors playing the same couple in the same year for forty years. Initially the audience may be alienated by this device, unsure of the relationship between Henry and Beatrice and Hank and Bea; yet it is this moment of alienation that can work to refunctiontalize, after

Brecht, the audience, making it aware of its role in working with the screen to interpret visual and aural codes, forcing it to actively engage in the process of producing meaning from fractured pieces of narrative unmoored in time.

The signs of a US neo-imperialism present in Greyson's earlier video works resurface here in the film's settings and incorporation of Gulf War footage. The screen adaptation of the novel relocates Bea and Hank from Peck's original Long Island setting to Sarnia, Ontario's Chemical Valley.[44] The relocation to Sarnia affords opportunities for border crossings to and from Michigan and the presence of Beatrice's friend Myra's American soldier boyfriend Stan in Canada, thereby creating a link between US geopolitical ambitions and their affect on Canada and Canadians. Greyson's forty-year Gulf War is depressingly prescient, suggesting that the imperial moment has not and will not pass. As I write this, most of our lives remain framed by Gulf War II, or as the Bush II administration would have us believe: Operation Iraqi Freedom. The stalled lives of Bea and Hank are juxtaposed to the aerial reconnaissance footage of US bombers photographing the "smart bomb" impacts on their targets in the film's establishing shots. The first element in this sequence is a colour long-shot of an oil refinery in Sarnia. Greyson then intercuts this image with grainy black and white shots of Bea and Hank wandering through a field of pumping derricks at the Sarnia museum, site of the world's first big oil gusher in 1862—a sequence we return to toward the end of the film. Here, the editing conveys the interdependence of global economies, Canada's historical and contemporary roles in the oil industry, and its complicity in a destructive global imperial order structuring the lives of people like Bea and Hank, people like you and me.

Proteus (2003) and Cutthroat (2006)

Proteus, Greyson's next feature is a CDN $500,000 co-production with South African director Jack Lewis.[45] Shot on digital beta video and blown up to 35mm, the film has a unique and seductive palate. Greyson's and Lewis's cultural, linguistic, and visual translation of a 1735 sodomy trial transcript marks the director's return to an historical re-visioning of imperial formations of masculinity and sexuality. Their sodomy epic, shot in a staggering eighteen days on Robben Island and in Cape Town, is based on the historically documented sexual relations of Rijkhaart Jacobsz and his Khoi fellow prisoner, Claas Blank, over a ten-year period while they were both inmates of the penal colony. Created for the film, a third character, Scottish botanist Virgil Tyne completes the triangle shaping the film's events. A student of Carl Linneaus, Tyne uses Blank as a Native informant to name the flora of the Cape.[46] While supervising the prisoners in the collection of botanical specimens and the construction of a garden, Tyne, an active participant in what is constructed by the filmmakers to be eighteenth-century Amsterdam's fairly vibrant gay culture, becomes sexually obsessed with Blank. Upon the completion of his work, Tyne returns to Amsterdam only to flee back to the colony ten years later to escape a sodomy scandal in Amsterdam, where his lover and sixty-nine other men were tried and garrotted in the city square. The homosexual panic of the motherland travels back to the colony with Tyne, and shortly after his return, Blank and Jacobsz are arrested on sodomy charges, tried, and executed by drowning in Table Bay. This, despite the fact that their sexual activity had been documented by authorities over a ten-year period with no action taken, suggests that it was the export of homosexual panic from the metropole to the colony that sparked the Dutch Calvinist "need" for sodomitical cleansing.

Greyson's queer practice of temporal translation as a transformational strategy to re-vision imperial histories' constructions of gender, sexuality, and race in the context of present concerns in these areas culminates in *Proteus*. Confronted with the architecture and ghosts of the twentieth-century Apartheid past haunting their reconstruction of the Dutch-colonial eighteenth-century Robben Island, Greyson and Lewis refuse to shoot around them but instead translate these anachronistic traces of dehumanizing racial and sexual oppressions into their film. The three translators we meet early on in the film—costumed as 1960s stenographers—give the audience its first indication of the fluid nature of time in the world of *Proteus*. As they record/translate/produce the transcript of the sodomy trial, the process of translation, of selection, is revealed to the audience. In the film's establishing shots, the word for the same-sex act becomes the subject of a debate amongst the translators, who, in some ways function like a Greek chorus, continually inserting, through the processes of translation and transcription, not only the constructed nature of the story we are watching but, just as significantly, the cultural construction of gender and sexuality through imperial discourse.

South Africa, a country where Greyson has taught film and video production and screened his films, has figured in his work since "A Moffie Called Simon" (1986), a video about the late Simon Nkodi, a Black gay activist and South African student leader who explores the relationships between gay rights and the anti-apartheid movement. Greyson's current feature-film project, *Cutthroat*, which began shooting in September 2005, develops directly out of the series of eight gallery video installations that comprise "Fig Trees," a piece about South African AIDS activist and HIV-positive Nobel Peace Prize nominee Zackie Achmat, who refuses anti-retroviral medication until it is available at an affordable price for everyone in the country.[47] "Fig Trees," a collaboration with composer David Wall, combines Gertrude Stein's and Virgil Thomson's 1928 opera *Four Saints in Three Acts*, with video images to, in Greyson's words, affect a "sculptural immersion" of the audience "in the pieces themselves."[48] Here again, Greyson grapples with a refunctionalizing of the viewer, turning the passive consumer into an active producer through a manipulation of ways of seeing. As Greyson explains:

> the difference between our traditional relationship to opera where we sit and look through a fourth wall to the stage and to the spectacle which might as well be two-dimensional versus in "Fig Trees" the only way you could look into the space of this opera was by being inside it, physically to the point you had to get inside a minivan to hear and see the piece play.[49]

Greyson and Wall believed that if they could get the audience to think about opera in a different way, then perhaps the audience would re-think their investment in the issue of AIDS in Africa.[50]

To get this gallery project out to a larger audience, Greyson and Wall elected to pursue the feature-film route. Greyson imagines *Cutthroat* will reflect the aesthetic of *Uncut*—"fragmented with multi-screens"—but "it will have a much more explicit narrative running through it about AIDS and pharmaceuticals in North America, Canada, AIDS in Africa and additional interview sequences with Zackie."[51] Reflecting on the varying size of budgets he has worked with over his career, Greyson says he favours the smaller budget approach of *Uncut* and *Cutthroat* as it gives him more control as a director. Such are the smaller types of features that he sees himself doing more of in the future.

■ A Passion for Social Justice

JOHN GREYSON'S UNWAVERING PASSION for social justice is visible across the full range of his work. From early avant-garde video installations through to feature-film projects, his formal experimentation has always been in the service of re-visioning a received history that would compromise, demean, and distort our humanity in the present. In this way Greyson is, after Hayden White, very much a cinematic pan-textualist for whom:

> history appears either as a text subject to many different readings (like a novel, poem, or play) or an absent presence the nature of which is perceivable only by way of prior textualizations (documents and historical accounts) that must be read and rewritten in response to present interests, concerns, desires, aspirations, and the like.[52]

Greyson's queer aesthetic shocks us out of the society of normalization that demands compliance with a globalized neo-imperial corporate order. Greyson's work reveals society itself as a process of normalization, of ideological interpellation, and impresses upon us that gender and sexuality are not separable from the matrices of history, culture, and political economy. John Greyson makes it very clear that any understanding of our present positions as sexual subjects is dependent on a radically queer parsing of our disciplining pasts, an interrogation he has enacted so effectively in his films and tapes.

NOTES

1.   See R. Bruce Brassell, "The Making of Monsters: The queer as producer," *Jump Cut* 40 (1996): 47–54; 50.

2. Greyson became a part of the so-called Toronto New Wave of filmmakers that emerged during this period and included Bruce McDonald, Don McKellar, Patricia Rozema, Atom Egoyan, Ron Mann, and Peter Mettler. For a history of this movement, see Cameron Bailey, "Standing in the Kitchen All Night Long: A Secret History of the Toronto New Wave," *Take One* 28 (Summer 2000): 7–11.

3. See Greyson's comments in Cynthia Amsden, "John Greyson's *The Law of Enclosures*," *Take One* 9, no. 29 (Fall 2000): 13–17.

4. See Gittings "*Zero Patience*, Genre, Difference and Ideology: Singing and Dancing Queer Nation," *Cinema Journal* 41, no. 1 (2001): 28–40.

5. Unpublished Interview with the Author, 2005, p.7.

6. See Eve Kosofsky Sedgwick on the maintenance of homosociality in her introduction to *Between Men: English Literature and Male Homosocial Desire* (New York: Columbia University Press, 1985), 1–20.

7. For a discussion of homosociality and homosexual tensions in the Hollywood Western see Vito Russo, *The Celluloid Closet*. Revised Edtion. (New York: Harper and Row, 1987), 81–83.

8. Unpublished Interview with the Author, 2005, p. 7.

9. See Jean François Lyotard, *The Postmodern Condition: A Report on Knowledge*, trans. Geoff Bennington and Brian Massumi (Minneapolis: University of Minnesota, 1984), xxiv.

10. See R. Bruce Brassell "The Making of Monsters: The queer as producer" *Jump Cut* 40 (1996): 47–54; Robert Cagle, "'Tell the story of my life...': The Making of Meaning, 'Monsters,' and Music in John Greyson's *Zero Patience*," *The Velvet Light Trap* 35 (Spring 1995): 69–81; Laura U. Marks, "Nice Gun You Got There: John Greyson's Critique of Masculinity," *Parachute* 66 (1992): 27–32; Christine Ramsay, "Greyson, Grierson, Godard, God: Reflections on the Cinema of John Greyson," in *North of Everything. English-Canadian Cinema Since 1980*. (Edmonton: University of Alberta Press, 2002): 192–205.

11. See R. Bruce Brassell, "The Making of Monsters: The queer as producer," 47–54; 50.

12. Quoted in Brassell, "The Making of Monsters," 50. See also Roswitha Mueller, *Bertold Brecht and the Theory of Media* (Lincoln: University of Nebraska Press, 1989), 21.

13. Quoted in Brassell, "The Making of Monsters," 50. See also Walter Benjamin, "The Author as Producer" in *Reflections: Essays, Aphorisms, Autobiographical Writings* (New York: Schocken Books, 1978), 220–38.

14. See Vincent Canby, "Avante Garde Visions," review of "The Making of Monsters," by John Greyson, *New York Times Review*, 1 October 1991, C13.

15. See Tony Rayns's review of *Uncut* by John Greyson, *Sight and Sound* 8, no. 10 (1990): 59–60.

16. See Brassell, "The Making of Monsters," 50.

17. Unpublished Interview with the Author, 2005, p.27.

18. Ibid.

19. See John Greyson, "On the Cutting Edge in Canada," *Planet Out Online Interview*, 6 January 1999, http://www.planetout.com/popcornq/movienews/199/1/greyson_chat.html (accessed 14 July 2005).

20. See B. Ruby Rich, "New Queer Cinema" in Michelle Aaron ed., *New Queer Cinema: A Critical Reader* (Edinburgh: University of Edinburgh Press, 2004), 15–22. See also original B. Ruby Rich, "New Queer Cinema," *Sight and Sound* 2, no. 5 (September 1992).

21. See Michelle Aaron, "New Queer Cinema: An Introduction," in New *Queer Cinema: A Critical Reader*, 3–14;, 3–4.

22. B. Ruby Rich, "The New Queer Cinema," 16.

23. Early on in the production of *Lilies*, Greyson considered doing "a sort of Jarman anachnronistic thing like *Edward II*. Sticking Harley Davidsons in the middle of a quaint 19th Century street." His screenwriter Michel Marc Bouchard loathed the idea. See John Greyson, "On the Cutting Edge in Canada."

24. Unpublished Interview with the Author, 2005, p.14.

25. Ibid.

26. See Shlomo Schwartzberg, "With his second feature, *Zero Patience*, director John Greyson seems set to make his mark on the Canadian movie scene," *Performing Arts and Entertainment in Canada*, 28, no. 4 (Spring 1994): 35.

27. Unpublished Interview with the Author, 1998.

28. Greyson's film ends on a disturbing note, signalling to the viewer the need for more activist work in a social unlearning of homophobia. One of Greyson's actors was gay-bashed in a public park in October 1990. The Matthew Sheppard case in the United States served to remind people that there is still a lot of work to be done in this area. In a 1998 article entitled "Queer Fear," *The Globe and Mail*, 24 October 1998, D1 and D3, Eleanor Brown, the managing editor of Canada's gay and lesbian newspaper, *Xtra*, details the alarming rate of violence against gays and lesbians in Canada. A Vancouver police spokesperson Sergeant Rick McKenna says of the city's gay and lesbian community: "without a doubt it's the most highly victimized group in Vancouver" (D3). Brown suggests that this may be due to the establishment of a bashing-information phone line and the possibility that police relations with the gay and lesbian community are on a better footing than they might be with "for example, the city's aboriginals" (D3).

29. See Schwartzberg, "With his second feature," 21.

30. See Robert Cagle, "Tell the story of my life...The Making of Monsters," 71.

31. For a more detailed discussion of *Zero Patience* in the context of genre and ideology see Gittings, *Canadian National Cinema: Ideology, Difference and Representation* (London and New York: Routledge, 2002), 285–93.

32. While stating that Bouchard is the author of the screenplay, Greyson explains that the playwright "let me into the writing process and I came up with a lot of the visual scenes and the visual stuff that informed the script and then with the directing he was there for rehearsal and for a lot of the shoot." See Unpublished Interview with the Author, 2005, 14. The film's credits list Bouchard as the film's sole screenwriter.

33. See Unpublished Interview with the Author, 2005, p.14.

34. See Christine Ramsay, "Greyson, Grierson, Godard, God: Reflections on the Cinema of John Greyson," in *North of Everything. English-Canadian Cinema Since 1980* (Edmonton: University of Alberta Press, 2002), 192–205; 196.

35. Ibid.

36. See Noreen Golfman, "Flowers for Greyson's Queer Cinema," *Canadian Forum* (November 1996): 27–28.

37. See Christine Ramsay, "Greyson, Grierson, Godard, God: Reflections on the Cinema of John Greyson," 196.

38. See Rob White's review of *Lilies* by John Greyson, *Sight and Sound* 8 no. 1 (1998): 49.

39. See Ramsay, "Greyson, Grierson, Godard, God: Reflections on the Cinema of John Greyson," 199.

40. "The Making of Monsters" borrows a great deal of its music from the Kurt Weill songbook, making radical changes to the lyrics of songs like *Mack the Knife*. The advisors to the Weill estate were happy to provide festival copyright clearance for Greyson until they saw the film and discovered the songs' gay content and that the filmmaker portrayed Weill as a gay goldfish. At that point the Weill estate, in Greyson's words, "decided to bury the film" pulling its festival clearances and refusing all other copyright requests. Effectively, the film was pulled from circulation until Well's music came into the public domain; "Monsters" is now available commercially in Canada through the Canadian Film Centre. See Unpublished Interview with the Author, 2005, 22.

41. See John Greyson, "On the Cutting Edge in Canada."

42. See Greyson's comments in Cynthia Amsden, "John Greyson's *The Law of Enclosures*," *Take One* 9, no. 29 (Fall 2000): 13–17.

43. See Unpublished Interview with the Author, 2005, 12.

44. While a second unit shot some footage in Sarnia, the bulk of production took place in a Winnipeg dressed to look like Sarnia. This was due, largely, to the demise of the Ontario Film Development Corporation's Feature Film Program. Similarly, the dunes of Manitoba stand in for the Iraqi desert.

45. Although the film was co-written and co-directed, Lewis is not given co-director credit due to the exigencies of the co-production treaty and Telefilm funding. (Unpublished Interview with the Author, 2005.)

46. Botanist Carl Linneaus set about translating and ordering the world into a Eurocentric scientific signifying system in his classification of all living things—*Systema Naturae*—first published in Amsterdam in 1735.

47. *Fig Trees* was exhibited at the Oakville Galleries in 2003.

48. Unpublished Interview with the Author, 2005, 3.

49. Ibid.

50. Ibid.

51. Ibid

52. See Hayden White, "Historical Pluralism," *Critical Inquiry* 12 (Spring 1986): 480–93; 485.

8

Norman Jewison

Homecoming for a "Canadian Pinko"

BART TESTA

I

NORMAN JEWISON has not been highly regarded or carefully discussed by film critics, Canadian or American. Canadian critics regard him with an ambivalence that often slides into dismissal. American critics of late register his presence only lightly. This may be attributed to his age. Born in 1926, Jewison is now in his late seventies. His Hollywood contemporaries, such as Sydney Pollack, Alan J. Pakula, John Frankenheimer and Sidney Lumet, have not fared much better in the critical attention they now receive. Like Jewison they also came from theatre and early television, shared a left-liberal perspective and had a formative influence on the television dramas in the 1950s.[1] Hollywood studios contracted them straight from TV *as directors.* Over the next three decades, they made Hollywood's most pointed political films. They also made a good deal of generic entertainment and saw their critical reputations rise and fall over time. They would make widely acclaimed films like *Seconds* (John

Frankenheimer, 1966), *Klute* (Alan Pakula, 1971), *Serpico* (Sidney Lumet, 1973), or Jewison's own *In the Heat of the Night* (1967), then recede from critical regard for years. This was the Hollywood group into which Jewison enlisted after an interval as a studio director, in fact as a light-comedy specialist. Recruited by Tony Curtis to direct the *Forty Pounds of Trouble* in 1963, Jewison remained at Universal until 1966, when he went independent and set about making *The Russians Are Coming, The Russians Are Coming* (1966) and then *In the Heat of the Night*.

His films started to draw Oscar nominations immediately with these first independent productions and *In the Heat of the Night* took Best Picture in 1967. Occasional nominations came later, too, and Jewison directed the 1981 Academy ceremony telecast. But Jewison never himself received the Best Director's award and in the mid-1990s, after two slight films, *Only You* (1994) and *Bogus* (1996), it looked late for him to be a serious contender again. Nonetheless, at seventy-three, Jewison marshalled his reserves and made *The Hurricane* (1999). Denzel Washington drew for a Best Actor nomination in 2000 for the title role.

In the same year that he made *The Hurricane*, the Academy distinguished Jewison with the Irving Thalberg Memorial Award. The occasion was likely (though we will never know definitely) the lifetime recognition Oscar that same year for Elia Kazan, director of *On the Waterfront* (1955). Kazan is more venerable than Jewison, but he is also a famous turncoat of the McCarthy period. Jewison's liberal fidelity was contrastingly impeccable. Senior enough to have twice directed Doris Day in her heyday, he also braved *In the Heat of the Night*, a film that, in its time, edged to the limits of American racial representation. When Jewison had laughed off the Cold War with *The Russians Are Coming*, it earned him the label "Canadian Pinko."[2] He later made the classic musical, *Fiddler on the Roof* (1971), at a moment when the beloved genre seemed all but extinguished.[3] He continued now and again and for decades after to wage the liberal good fight with films like *A Soldier's Story* (1984). Jewison's clips montage at the Awards ceremony covering thirty years had the ideal Academy mix of popular movie memories and stirring, socially purposeful art.

The conferral of the Thalberg on Jewison did nothing, however, to warm up Canadian critics' attitudes toward him. To them, Jewison remained prototypical of Canadian entertainers who saw a chance in the US and never looked back.

Jewison was born and raised by WASP shopkeepers in the Beach neighbourhood in Toronto,[4] graduated from Victoria College (University of Toronto), worked at BBC, and then apprenticed as a director at the nascent CBC TV in the 1950s. He moved to New York in 1958 to direct television and went to Hollywood four years later. His return to Canada occurred without fanfare in 1978 when Jewison bought a farm in the Caledon Hills near Toronto. In the 1980s, though, Jewison took a seat on the board of the Toronto Film Festival, set up a generous film scholarship, and paid lavishly for a visiting lecture series at his *alma mater*, Victoria College. Then, in 1988, he cut the ribbon on The Canadian Film Centre, and so closely was his name attached to its establishment that people referred to it, for awhile, as the "Jewison Film School."

The homecoming was not all he hoped for. At the very start of his 2004 autobiography, *This Terrible Business Has Been Good to Me*, Jewison complains, "this book is all Jay Scott's fault. He started it, then he died on me. Now, eleven years later, I'm trying to fulfill a promise to Jay."[5] An American-born writer, Jay Scott blossomed quickly at *The Globe and Mail* to be the sharpest critical stylist in English Canada and, for a Toronto first, a film journalist with a significant international reach.[6] Scott was writing Jewison's biography by the late 1980s, but left it unfinished when he died of AIDS in 1993. Jewison rightly feels robbed of the recognition a Scott biography would have bestowed. No one else suitable stepped forward to continue the project and, eleven years later, Jewison wrote the book himself.

It grates on Jewison when critics persistently question whether he is a Canadian film director at all and always imply that he is not. The facts behind their attitude are salient: Jewison never worked in the Canadian film industry, did not shoot a frame of film in his native land before *Agnes of God* (1985) and only made a Canadian-produced film in 2002, *The Statement*, under the aegis of Robert Lantos.[7] These facts assume ideological weight for Canadian critics and become a critical *accusation*—that Jewison is an American director in everything but the accident of his Toronto birthplace. This accusation takes two narrower specifications.

The first places Jewison aesthetically inside Hollywood's film style, plotting, and story material. The second accusation places him politically inside the compromised ideology of the US entertainment industry. I will examine these accusations in succession and then try to recast the question of a "Canadian Jewison" a bit differently than it often has been.

In his *One Hundred Years of Canadian Cinema*, George Melnyk writes, "Jewison's directorial style...was generally indistinguishable from other well-made mainstream American cinema."[8] It is true that, at first glance, to pull a Jewison film from a Hollywood line-up would be tough. Yet, once a critic considers Jewison's films in historical context—the style and narrative norms of Hollywood during the 1960s—the "mainstream American cinema" looks more mercurial than solid and homogeneous and Jewison's participation looks a bit different too. After his stint as a studio comedy director, Jewison thrust himself into a Hollywood no longer comfortably cosseted by the cinematic codes of Hollywood's "classical style." Jewison chose sides and joined a group experiment already underway among left-liberal American filmmakers.

It did not happen at once. After *Forty Pounds*, Jewison stayed at Universal for three more comedies. The first two are Doris Day vehicles, *The Thrill of It All* (1963) and *Send Me No Flowers* (1964), and the third is *The Art of Love* (1965), a Ross Hunter project written by Carl Reiner. The director then replaced Sam Peckinpah on *The Cincinnati Kid* (1965), his first drama. Finally, after four years and five features, he devised his own project, *The Russians Are Coming*, a soft-hearted satire of Cold War tensions. The film still bears the marks of the comedy specialist. His next film, though, *In the Heat of the Night*, marked a sharp departure of tone and style from studio norms. Jewison's jumps between 1965 and 1966, and then 1967, seem abrupt but they had a context.

His first phase (1963–1967), between *The Thrill of It All* and *In the Heat of the Night*, coincides with a period in American filmmaking that film historians note placed serious stresses on Hollywood's style norms. These stresses are sometimes attributed to the challenges posed by popular European new wave cinema and sometimes to the arrival in Hollywood of directors coming from TV drama. The two developments were not entirely distinct. American television in the 1950s offered literate theatre-like omnibus productions, some becoming very famous, like *Marty* (Delbert Mann, 1953) and *Twelve Angry Men* (Sidney Lumet, 1957). These productions laid claim to critical attention because of their topicality, realism, and maturity. Feature-length adaptations that Hollywood quickly made from them employed their original directors and bid to start closing the gap between American commercial films and prestigious foreign imports. The trend established a new generation of Hollywood directors who did not come up through the studio ranks.

Jewison's television work was in variety, not drama. His first notable success was a Judy Garland special; his second a special for Harry Belafonte that made a breakthrough for Black performers on American TV. When Jewison went to Hollywood to direct comedies, he quickly and eagerly noticed that former television directors around him were opening up Hollywood films to social themes. Jewison was a relatively late joiner in the trend, but he proved an assiduous one once he became an independent. It *is* striking, nonetheless, how smoothly he slipped from the New York's TV studio onto the Hollywood soundstage with *The Thrill of It All*, his second film, co-starring Doris Day and James Garner.[9] Riffing off Garner's frustrated suburban doctor-husband, Jewison propelled the film to an overall antic effect that differs noticeably from the pastel predecessors in the series, *Pillow Talk* (1959) and *Touch of Mink* (1962). Jewison did not energize his second Day vehicle, *Send Me No Flowers* to the same degree, perhaps because a phlegmatic Rock Hudson rejoined the partnership. *The Art of Love* mixed TV-Hollywood-European-import casting into a confused film (Elke Summer, meet Dick Van Dyke! Dick, meet Angie Dickinson!). However, Jewison did manage to carry over the frustrated male hysterics from *The Thrill of It All* into *The Russians Are Coming* and he resolved the problems with mixed casting, stirring into the cross rhythms of the film's chase plot bits of TV sketch comedy, ethnic humour, and light political satire.[10]

It was *In the Heat of the Night* that broke Jewison's career arc as a comedy specialist. He used the film to experiment with style codes, largely through his openness to collaborators Hal Ashby (his editor) and Gordon Wexler (his cinematographer).[11] With *Heat of the Night*, Jewison ceased being a pumped-up television director with an eager-to-antic pacing; he now directed like a well-grounded filmmaker. The style Jewison brought to *Heat of the Night* and to its flashier successor, *The Thomas Crown Affair* (1969), in one sense, could be regarded as "indistinguishable" from other "well-made" American movies. But in fact, few such films were being made. They were not the product of set new conventions. Penn, Pakula, Lumet and Frankenheimer thought of themselves as pursuing literary and political inclinations but these were leading them, film-by-film, into stylistic experiment. Left-liberal directors were casting one eye toward European films for stylistic inspiration but their other eye was still firmly fixed on the Stanley Kramer-Paddy Chayevsky-Elia Kazan lineage of literate American social cinema rooted in the 1950s.[12] Their films, in the end, proved more *centrist* to Hollywood than radical—the terms of such comparisons soon being reset by Dennis Hopper's *Easy Rider* (1969) and Robert Altman's *Brewster McCloud* (1970). The liberals' popular successes, moreover, smoothed what political or aesthetic friction they encountered in the studios. The conservative reaction, from Donald Siegel, Herbert Ross, George Roy Hill and Clint Eastwood, when it came at the start of the 1970s, seemed to be aimed not at them but at the new Hollywood group of directors like Hopper and Altman, Martin Scorsese, Hal Ashby, Bob Rafelson, and Francis Ford Coppola.

The late 1960s was, then, a complex, ambiguous, and mercurial moment in American cinema that saw *In the Heat of the Night* draw Oscar nominations. The group with which Jewison aligned himself, however, soon faced a period of seismic shifts when the centre of American politics lurched to the right with the election of Richard Nixon. Nonetheless, their toughest political films lay ahead: *Klute* (Pakula, 1971), *Serpico* (Lumet, 1973), *The Parallax View* (Pakula, 1974), *Three Days of the Condor* (Pollack, 1975), *Shampoo* (Ashby, 1975), *Dog Day Afternoon* (Lumet, 1975) and, performing their vindication, *All the President's Men* (Pakula, 1976).[13] After *In the Heat of the Night* and *The Thomas Crown Affair*, Jewison might well have continued to work alongside them but, aggrieved by the King and Kennedy assassinations and disgusted by Nixon's election, he left the US for Britain in 1971. At the same time, Jewison retreated into the flamboyantly figured ethnic past of *Fiddler on the Roof*. Given the musical genre's dire condition, it was exactly the right (and brave) strategy to realize a three-hour film from a beloved stage musical, which was really a synthetic Jewish folk opera.[14]

Fiddler had a risible twin, however, in *Jesus Christ Superstar* (1973), the Andrew Lloyd Weber rock opera, an incomprehensible lapse of judgement.[15] At the point he made the film Jewison was forty-seven. At first his angry withdrawal from Nixon's America hardly affected the momentum of his success but it blurred his political instincts: *Jesus Christ Superstar* is as shrink-wrapped a betrayal of the 1960s as was ever made. By contrast, during the same time Jewison spent on it and *Fiddler*, Wexler made *Medium Cool* (1969), Ashby *The Last Detail* (1973), Lumet a powerfully mournful *King: A Filmed Record* (1970) and *Serpico*. When Jewison turned again to political material, first with the dystopian science fiction allegory *Rollerball* (1975) and then with the labour biopic *F.I.S.T.* (1978), all stylistic rigour seemed to desert him. These were not "well-made" films at all but bloated specimens of the ruin into which "mainstream" cinematic style could fall by the mid-1970s.

While Jewison was never an originator, after 1966, he rarely sought safety in "mainstream" filmmaking. Given conceptually sound projects, he enthusiastically assimilated thematic and stylistic experiment. But Jewison severed himself from the American political context at just the wrong moment. It was the toughest time for liberals, and not the time to be going soft with an Andrew Lloyd Weber musical. Another factor at play in Jewison having a very bad 1970s was his indulgent vulgarity, a virtue in making comedies but a faulty instinct in drama. His abilities congealed around *disciplined* vulgarity channelling a hysterical charge into *The Thrill of it All* and *The Russians Are Coming* and Jewison's marriage of discipline and sentimentalism reached its apogee in *Fiddler on the Roof*, a film in which exuberance and bathos achieve ideal balance. Yet, with *Jesus Christ Superstar*, *Rollerball*, and *F.I.S.T.*, the same inclination to vulgarity became merely regressive.

This harsh observation returns us to the main point of this glancing overview: rather than being, as Melnyk claims, "indistinguishable" from other "well-made" Hollywood films of the period, the films Jewison directed between the mid-1960s and early-1970s participated in the challenge left-liberal American directors mounted, and that challenge took stylistic as well as thematic forms.[16] In the 1980s, Jewison gradually recovered his footing by realigning his filmmaking with a chastened cinematic style. After he came home to Canada, his recovery, underway with the still seriously flawed *...And Justice for All* (1979), formed around two theatrical adaptations, *A Soldier's Story* and *Agnes of God*. Jewison's tact with actors and taste in screenplays led him to a new caution that suited him. Capping the set, Jewison's liaison with John Patrick Shanley's whimsical script, *Moonstruck* (1987), also saw his comic timing and his control over the mixed ensemble restored. His *Moonstruck* cast featured theatre actors (Olympia Dukakis, Vincent Gardenia), movie stars (Nicholas Cage), and a singer-television star (Cher). Most of his films since then have held steady to the same virtues with occasional flashes of intensity, as in *Hurricane*, and dips into anonymous dullness, as in *Bogus*.

II

I wish Norman would shut up about American politics. He's known as a Canadian here, an outsider. He is getting better, but all the anti-American statements he made in the 1960s really hurt him in this town.[17]

THE SECOND ACCUSATION against Jewison is ideological: that he inserted himself amidst the compromising Hollywood contradictions of American liberalism. Left-liberal directors leaned toward political ideas but took them to be the same as "realism." They sought to articulate the ideological re-centring of American politics during the mid-1960s but they also held fast to the social contract of entertainment cinema. McCarthyism had faded away and the Kennedy era had shifted the axis of American culture leftward. The liberal filmmakers perceived these new circumstances as a suited to a centrist aspiration to make films tied to social justice—the obvious impulse in Jewison making *In the Heat of the Night*— but still bound to entertainment values.[18]

The Canadian critics are dismissive on all this first of all because they do not take American liberal politics or 1960s left-liberal Hollywood filmmaking seriously. Melnyk says of Jewison's liberalism that it may have "worked in differentiating him in a Hollywood context, not a Canadian one."[19] In a chapter on Jewison in *Mondo Canuck*, Geoff Pevere and Greig Dymond likewise claim that that *any* Canadian *is* a liberal in the US context, but a liberal attitude like the one Jewison represents cannot cut through the compromises that American entertainment requires. A Hollywood filmmaker always, they say, works under "the anticipation and avoidance of conflict."[20] Jewison has always freely admitted his compromises with Hollywood entertainment values and portrays himself as having been cagey doing so. Pevere and Dymond use such admissions to argue that Jewison's belief that he could "entertain and enlighten" sucked him into the heart of American liberal entertainment ideology. Their formulation merits extended quotation:

> Moreover, it's in the apparent contradiction between the image of the politically outspoken Canadian pinko and the staid establishment fixture that the real Canadian essence of Norman Jewison may dwell. For the contradiction between the commitment to politics and the commitment to entertain—between mobilization and amusement, between anger and eagerness to please—and even the belief that the two can happily serve the same master, is a deeply liberal notion. The peculiar trajectory of Norman Jewison's career, from the man who was considered a Canadian threat in the 1960s, to the man who seems to spend as much time making public appearances as movies in the 1990s, must be understood in the context of Jewison's deep-seated liberalism.[21]

Some of the rhetoric here is fanciful—like the reference to a "Canadian threat"—as is the idea of a career trajectory inevitably ending with Jewison's retirement into tuxedoed swanning around as one of the "establishment."

The quotation at the top of this section comes from Jay Scott's 1989 profile of the director in which Jewison's agent, Larry Auerbach, was still complaining about his client's political statements of twenty years before because they damaged Jewison's prospects. We can just imagine: Jewison, that foreigner, "a Canadian, an outsider" speaking out against American injustices and misguided government policies, and he spoke no differently than American liberals, but he was not heard the same way. The irritation Americans felt was typical of American annoyance with any Canadian who presumes to bear a right heart and sense of justice by national birthright.[22] On the other hand, Canadians usually know nothing about Canadian liberalism they have not heard on CBC. Few of them know—or care to know—how to calibrate their Canadian liberal differences against American liberalism. Jewison has often proved canny in emulsifying political themes into American entertainment values. He really did speak the language of an American liberal *centre* when he made films like *The*

Russians Are Coming and *In the Heat of the Night*, and is still doing so in 1999 in making *The Hurricane*. The 1960s left-liberal filmmakers' ascent pushed forward liberals' claims to be representing a core American common sense of social justice. In turning such commonplaces against Jewison, Pevere and Dymond are broadly correct when they write that *In the Heat of the Night* was so resonant in 1967 because it belonged to "the period when Jewison's own liberal sensibilities happened to mesh with the popular zeitgeist when, in other words, it was possible for a message movie to make a buck."[23] But they are mistaken to suggest it was an accident of a single career. The film was a consequence of a principled and forceful wing of popular American filmmaking that unfolded over a decade. . Pevere and Dymond seek to dissolve Jewison's "liberal Canuck" sensibility into the American mainstream and then dismiss both of them in toto. But what sort of politics did distinguish Canadian filmmakers who remained in Canada during the same period? This is a question Canadian critics do not answer with conviction. Jewison would hardly be mistaken if he believed that his politics were fundamentally the same as contemporaneous CBC, or NFB, or CFDC-funded productions.

Beside their dismissal of American liberalism and of Jewison by association Pevere and Dymond draw a nastier caricature of a man in his seventies, who visibly twinkles with pleasure at his success and his reputation. Jewison's kind of wealth and renown are not what Pevere and Dymond have in mind when they imagine a Canadian film director. They find these attributes distasteful. Politically, they are really arguing for excluding Canadians from a long decade of North American debate, activity, and cultural production representing liberals' struggle for the control of the political centre. Canadian popular artists seem, in their account, not to have participated in the continental trials of liberalism at all—nor should they have.[24] Such an exclusion, on the grounds of the inadequacy of liberalism, really covers over a culturally atavistic belief that Canadian artists cannot linger abroad long and still expect to be regarded as Canadian. Directors must stay in the Canadian film industry, suffer its neglect, and succeed in the relatively modest ways David Cronenberg or Atom Egoyan have succeeded. For our critics, then, English-Canadian film will be a cinema of homeland-dwelling artists or not be at all. Jewison is, by these lights, to be regarded an alien returned in our midst.

Such political prescriptions such as Pevere and Dymond entertain also serve aprophylactic aesthetic agenda. The struggle to assert an English-Canadian film style is the *critical* base to argue on behalf of the distinctiveness of Canadian cinema. The recognition of *auteurs*, like Egoyan, differentiates them, practically on stylistic grounds alone. Canadian cinema has shrunk to a critic's game of analyzable stylistic idiosyncrasies. A sizable academic industry has grown up around their exfoliation. So, while the professional histories of Canadian filmmakers who left Canada might well be just as interesting,[25] this speculation cannot just leap over the methodological hurdles that the prescriptive criticism that Pevere and Dymond exemplify, and whose basic stance subtends the critical consensus now wrapped around Canadian film.

Melnyk contrasts Jewison with Cronenberg and Egoyan. Melnyk shares the common view that these directors reshaped the English-Canadian narrative feature film, which was previously bounded by social realism stemming from documentaries. The possibility of an Egoyan, our most highly regarded *auteur* since the later 1980s, was made possible when, in the 1970s, Cronenberg opened the path to a new generation. This chronology, which places Cronenberg as first pioneer, really derived from a critical decision to "grandfather" Cronenberg *after* the rise of Egoyan, and Patricia Rozema, and Jeremy Podeswa. In the hopeful early 1970s afterglow of seminal Canadian features like *Goin' Down the Road* (Don Shebib, 1970) and *Mon Oncle Antoine* (Claude Jutra 1970), Cronenberg's professional debut with *Shivers* (1975) was considered an outrage. It also left him open to charges of America influence. This is because all genre filmmaking seemed American and *Shivers* was a horror film. Cronenberg did not leave Canada to make it nor any of his subsequent films. But he tapped into American cult-horror trends pioneered by the regional (i.e., Pittsburg) director George Romero's *Night of the Living Dead* (1968) and by Toby Hooper's *The Texas Chainsaw Massacre* (1969). At the same time, Cronenberg's genre-movie career was fuelled by Canadian government grants and the film policy of "Hollywood North" (i.e., Canadians getting big tax breaks for investing in Canadian genre films designed for entry into the US market).

Of the many who tried and failed under this policy, Cronenberg's horror films made money, and made him the one English-Canadian director with a consistent career. With the end of the tax-break era and *Videodrome*'s failure in 1983, Cronenberg took contract work with Hollywood producers, making *The Dead Zone* (1983) and remaking *The Fly* (1986) for Dino De Laurentis. Only later, following *Dead Ringers* (1988), was Cronenberg re-branded as the heterodox Canadian *auteur*.[26] The career pattern thereafter nonetheless went unchanged: Cronenberg gaining financial refreshment by making Hollywood-funded projects between his "personal" works, such as *eXistenZ* (2000) and *Spider* (2002).[27]

Cronenberg's career pattern should render his relationship to Canadian cinema embarrassing, but it has not. Living in Canada has preserved Cronenberg's candidacy as the great creative deformer of Canadian film-making. In the repositioning of him as a Canadian auteur, Cronenberg makes the promises of a Canadian mannerist art-film style. It is this pro-mise that Egoyan's (and Guy Maddin's, Podeswa's and Rozema's) films keep in the critical consensus that defines English-Canadian filmmaking.

We have seen that Canadian film critics dismiss Jewison for several layered reasons: he allied himself with Hollywood style; he played at a compromised Hollywood liberal politics; and he did not participate at all in shaping Canadian cinema. At the bottom of these, he lived abroad. The dismissal of Jewison would be more convincing were the interpre-tive accounts of Canadian directors *as Canadian* less thematically flimsy.[28] If there can be a belatedly recognized "Canadian Cronenberg" when the critical arguments advanced for believing in such a thing are inadequate, one wonders why there could be no corresponding "Canadian Jewison."

III

AND PERHAPS THEIR STILL CAN BE. There is little point in trying at this late date, though, to construct a "Canadian Jewison" on the more obvious auteurist premises of directorial style or thematic intention. Even when the characterization of Jewison as a creature of the Hollywood main-stream proves to be crude, one can accept that he belongs to an American period and a Hollywood group style. Jewison offers no precise sense of a Canadian difference in his liberalism that all agree shapes at least his drama films. Instead, I suggest a sort of Canadian "political unconscious" applicable to at least most of Jewison's dramas, and that entails finding a "symptomatic" thread in these films.

Most of Jewison's dramas involve a legally sanctioned investigation. His protagonists are, in one form or another, "officers of the court"— lawyer (...And Justice for All), police detective (In the Heat of the Night), military investigator (Soldier's Story), prosecutor-judge (The Statement), court-assigned doctor (Agnes of God), activists aligned with lawyers in the years-long proceeding to free Rubin Carter (The Hurricane). The prominence of Jewison's legalist protagonists does not, at first glance, provide a prominent distinction between his films and other left-liberal directors in American cinema. The legal process, court dramas, and jurist protagonists are devices that liberal American filmmakers have favoured at least since Lumet's Twelve Angry Men and Robert Mulligan's To Kill a Mockingbird (1962). (Precedents go back to Frank Capra and Fritz Lang in the 1930s.) The legal drama extends themes of social justice dramatically but somewhat neutrally through representations of an "objective" (fact-based) juridical process. The legal-thriller genre, where facts of a case and the "human drama" these entail dominate, is conventionally regarded in American cinema as non-ideological. Plots are organized around proofs, and so they structurally perform as a drama of truth that seems to rise above any ideology.

Liberalism signifies, especially for the generation to which Jewison belongs, commonsense ideas of truth, fairness and right principles of law in the pursuit of progressive social relations. The legalistic drama of truth proves itself a powerful resource for such an attitude in the left-liberal American cinema of the 1960s and 1970s. It should be recalled, however, that in Canada such a confidence in a judicial liberalism of this American type cannot be automatically assumed.

Canadians have long entertained a spectrum of conservative, liberal, socialist, and traditionalist political philosophies. These are fully legitimated in the Canadian ethos. While in the US liberalism pretends to be equivalent to enlightened common sense, Canadian liberalism is manifestly an ideology competing with other political philosophies with claims to justice and truth, and Canada has a long history of accommodating this variety in the practice of politics. A difference between the countries is that, in contrast to Canada, the US has only one tradition of politics:

liberalism, which is divided into a right wing and a left wing. There is no significant surviving historic conservatism or entrenched traditionalism. Americanswhocallthemselves"conservatives"or"neoconservatives" are, in truth, just right-wing liberals.[29] American left-liberal preference for an activist judiciary, especially since the 1950s and the rise of the civil rights movement, expresses the priority of constitutional law over politics expressed in legislatures. The neoconservative reaction takes theoretical form in the "strict constructivism" of the US Constitution. This theory is not a demotion of juridical authority but a restraint on its progressive leadership, or "activism."

For Americans the law lies within the individual (immanent in his/her civil rights) and stands over (transcends) the people regarded as polity. Canadians do not regard law in the same absolute or dualistic way but take law as expressing the political wisdom of the nation's parliaments. The judiciary is, in the Canadian political mind, a state institution among others serving the tasks of maintaining social order. Canadians limit the power of courts as arbiters of the social good and legal right, and they rely on Parliament to shape social justice and progress.[30] Canadians regard law as embodied in institutions, and they sanction the law's power only for those who are institutionally appointed. The law does not, in the Canadian political mind, either hover above the polity or dwell especially within the individual. Law lives in and among the citizenry's institutions. This difference between the US and Canada affects the cultural productions of both countries, though usually in subtle ways when police stories or legal dramas are involved.[31]

My interpretive claim about Jewison's "political unconscious" is that Jewison carries something of the Canadian legal and political ethos into his drama films. The differences between his films and those of his fellow American left-liberal filmmakers are, on this account, still slight but not negligible. It accounts, for example, for why the final narrative force in his films lies with institutions and not a personality and why a restraining legalism reins in private passions.[32] If the Jewison protagonist is typically a delegate of the legal process on the surface no different that a Lumet protagonist, the character's role is different in that the legalistic role not only enables but also restrains him or her. Even while in the midst of acting as protector of justice he or she cannot incarnate the law but only follow its dictates and can only act upon its sanctions. And the latter are limited. The thematic motif of the law's restraints—on the hero of the drama—distinguishes Jewison even when he is most consciously committed to the positive outcomes of liberal justice. It acts as an "unconscious" tug on his films. This marks Jewison not as a "Canadian pinko" (i.e., more naturally leftwing than Americans) but as a director of films inscribed with a restraining *Canadian* legalism despite their American situations, plots and characters.

Let's take *In the Heat of the Night*, the film in which Jewison discovers the kind of drama that he will make repeatedly thereafter. Though it is a detection story, Jewison postpones the crime investigation to elaborate on the slovenly ineptitude of the town's small police force. A dead man is discovered. He is Leslie Colbert, an industrialist planning to build a factory in the town. It will provide new employment for the town, still bound economically to the old feudal, cotton-economy of a backward South. Colbert is, therefore, the film's figure of economic progressivism. Later, Virgil Tibbs (Sidney Poitier) is found waiting in the train station in the middle of the night by a local deputy, Sam Wood (Warren Oates). Wood has been trolling the town to pick up anyone who could be a suspect. Roughly arrested and brought before Police Chief Bill Gillespie (Rod Steiger), Tibbs is suspected of the murder simply because he is an unaccounted-for black man. Tibbs frees himself with a single line of dialogue when questioned about his profession: "I am a policeman." At the request of his superior in Philadelphia whom the chief phones to join the investigation, Tibbs soon proves himself a paragon of forensic science and right police procedure—just the opposite of the local cops. Tibbs only takes the case on because, the Chief explains to him, Colbert represented better jobs for black people, who are seen in an emphatic passage, still picking cotton. The businessman's wife (played by Lee Grant) says that there will be no factory without a quick solution to the murder.

As the plot unfolds, the issue of the crime itself is deflected into questions of how one stands with respect to the law, and with how Gillespie and Tibbs stand with respect to the racially freighted narrative apparatus of investigative thriller. Gillespie is the initially wavering figure, unsure of whether he serves the powers of the town or the law, which are decidedly not the same. Tibbs' oscillation is deeper. At first he believes, quite reasonably after he gets a whiff of local racial politics, that Colbert was killed to prevent the factory's realignment of social power. When he confronts the local cotton baron, the man slaps Tibbs for being impertinent. Tibbs slaps the white-haired grandee right back. Although the scene of a black man slapping a white man became famous, what is less often remembered is that Tibbs later reprimands himself for allowing his desire to bring the man down to get the better of him. His ideological passion distracted his investigation into the truth of the crime. It turns out that the murder had only squalid motivations—sex and robbery— among the scurrilous local poor whites. *Heat of the Night* is a film that supposedly belongs to the civil rights movement, and so this plot solution, it has often been remarked, diffuses its political significance. The join between backward prejudice and the motivation to murder Colbert would have made a satisfying occasion for a black detective both to solve the crime and at the same time to bring down the colluding backward Old South social powers of the town. The film's actual resolution of the crime descends into a condescending melodrama. Nonetheless, the more nuanced character-story of the film is that a self-reprimanding Tibbs recovers himself to the purity of his role as the rational agent of the law. This is a role of wider political significance. In the left-liberal view of civil rights, it is the objectivity of law, embodied in the film by Tibbs's reasoning processes and legal purpose (and in American politics by juridical leadership in ending segregation) and not race and class warfare incarnated in a cop serving behind his badge on the right side of an ideological struggle.

The inclination to compromised plotting and legalistic restraint that characterizes Jewison's films in this case served the wider political significance. Jewison does not articulate this rather subtle difference of theme openly. Tibbs's self-reprimand instead operates as a repressive function: he cannot be an agent of the law and also be a crusader against an unjust social world without contradiction. Jewison's film represses the crusader and preserves the agent of the law. Jewison's narrative solution hangs on a deflection of one obvious political civil rights allegory clothed as an investigative thriller into another allegory, namely the tale of institutional law defining a protagonist. Jewison never allows Tibbs to be the hero who has the law within him as a natural part of his personality and passions. His passions must be infuriated and then he must suppress them. Though he remains the threatened and threatening outsider to the end of the film, Tibbs also remains a rational man of procedure, and the allegory of law as reason and social institution prevails.

The pattern of limited juridical resolution proves consistent across Jewison's subsequent films. The social identity of his protagonists mildly deforms the legal drama's familiar genre plotting. In *A Solder's Story*, it is the black soldier and investigator in a white man's army. In *Agnes of God*, a secular doctor, played by Jane Fonda, enters a religious convent to investigate a likely infanticide. In *The Hurricane*, Canadian middle-class idealist amateurs align with Rubin Carter's imprisoned black ex-boxer and to do so must brave the sinister racial and police currents of Paterson, New Jersey, but they remain essentially legal agents. Jewison's protagonists are usually outsiders who, as its delegates, bring the law with them into a complicated and vexed situation. They seem at first to promise a transformation of society. But the question of the hero and society, though elaborated in personalized ways familiar to Hollywood films, is itself finally subordinate to the characters' institutional roles under juridical law. What finally defines a Jewison protagonist's identity in a successful or unsuccessful plot outcome comes in terms of concrete reason, expertise, and a political truth about the society depicted. But in each of these films the protagonist also decides where he or she stands in relation to the institution of law, which is neither a transcendent nor a private immanent power that arises from within him or her. The law, moreover, is always entangled with political and ambiguous situations at the same time it is also always strictly juridical and procedural. In *A Soldier's Story*, the hero, like Tibbs, does decide for the law, and against a racial solidarity. In *Agnes of God*, one of the least narratively resolved of Jewison's films, the court psychiatrist cannot really decide between science and theology. The play insists on granting religion and law (here its aid, psychiatry) equal say on the deciphering of truth, which means the film ends in ambiguity for the reason that religion and law are both institutions that deal with the truth. Jewison, typical of the Canadian political mind, withholds the law's absolute privilege with respect to deciding truth and gives religion its due. Despite his left-liberal commitments, and his willingness to revise (and soften) other plot points in adapting the play, Jewison is restrained from liberal absolutism about the law, a self-repression notable in that it also sometimes, as with *Agnes of God*, precludes him from a Hollywood-style narrative resolution. Indeed, Jewison rarely resolves his films in the topical resolution with which he always seems to begin them—racism ended, madness cured, etc.—or in a character's vindictive triumph.

From film to film, concerns with resolution (*In the Heat of the Night*) and no resolution (*Agnes of God*) of the plot's adjudication of the story enigma are not allowed entirely to centre on the rightness or force of the protagonist. Jewison never allows the legal resolution to be driven, for example, by a character's personality, however passionate or effective. Even *The Hurricane*, which follows the true story of Rubin Carter's eventual vindication, divides and then subdivides that victory among the characters, diffusing the victory so that it is not just Carter's personal triumph over racism, or just the Canadians' victory over a corrupt American urban police and legal system, though it is all these things. Rather, the climax is a juridical success: in an idiosyncratic turn, the much aged Rod Steiger as the final judge in the case, makes a technical juridical decision that frees Carter. Jewison, in effect, defuses the focus of the film's climax—at the cost of dramatic punch—so that the victory is, in one sense, too widely (one might even say *too fairly*) distributed to have a personal focus. But in another sense, the suddenly exclusive focus on the law arranges the players as a localized polity gathered before the law. Given the film's emotional investment in Carter, and in Denzel Washington's charismatic performance, and Jewison's failure to draw much light or heat from the trio who play the Canadians (Deborah Kara Unger, Live Schreiber and John Hannah)—the overall diffusion of the film's dramatic energies is a serious aesthetic shortcoming but is also a positive sign of the constraining Canadian "political unconscious" at work in Jewison's films.

The dramatic films Jewison has made after his return to Canada have in fact become more stubbornly, if still unconsciously, dedicated to the exploration of the Canadian sense of law while still consciously dedicated to a set of American liberal propositions.[33] This contradiction between his intentions and his Canadian "political unconscious" is often actually disabling in its consequences for Jewison as a dramatic narrative filmmaker, but they likewise make him, in a peculiarly oblique and interesting way, one of the most politically complex of Canadian feature filmmakers.

NOTES

1. The term "left-liberal" differentiates a political posture from "Cold War" liberal, which was the predominant position of many mainstream Democrats and most liberal Republicans in the 1950s and early 1960s. John F. Kennedy was such a liberal when he ran for president in 1958–1959 and so was his brother, Robert F. Kennedy, until he defied Lyndon Johnson and opposed the Vietnam War during his run for the presidency in 1968.

2. Geoff Pevere and Greig Dymond note that the *Hollywood Reporter* used the epithet in connection with *The Russians Are Coming, the Russians Are Coming*. See Geoff Pevere and Greig Dymond, *Mondo Canuk* (Scarborough, ON: Prentice Hall Canada, 1996), 109. Jewison himself puts a variation—"goddamn pinko"—into the mouth of John Wayne as they met for a private dinner party at the same time. See Jewison, *This Terrible Business Has Been Good to Me: An Autobiography* (Toronto: Key Porter Books, 2004), 126.

3. And this was during the worst period for musicals in Hollywood history. See David Cook, *Lost Illusions: American Cinema in the Shadow of Watergate and Vietnam, 1970–1979* (Berkeley: University of California Press, 2000), 209–10.

4. There was always some confusion about that due to his name, which often led people to assume he was Jewish. He offers several amused anecdotes about the confusion in *This Terrible Business*, 11–13.

5. Jewison, *This Terrible Business,* 9.

6. By the early 1980s, Scott could launch a failed French film like *Diva* (1982) into the top of the North American box office, interview Clint Eastwood with a prescient sense of his emerging importance, and pen a strong interpretive essay on Fassbinder. His role in the rise of the Toronto Film Festival as a key international film platform event was inestimable. While writing prolifically at *The Globe and Mail*, Scott demonstrated great promise as a biographer when he wrote a book on Native American painter Helen Hardin, *Changing Woman* (Flagstaff, Arizona: Northland Publishing, 1989) while visiting his hometown, Albuquerque, to look after his ailing mother. Although nothing of the Jewison biography ever appeared, Scott did publish one lengthy profile, "Jewison Then and Now," in *The Globe and Mail*'s insert magazine, *Toronto* (November 1987): 37–39; 50–52.

7. He did, however, act as producer for the younger director Bruce McDonald on the successful feature *Dance Me Outside* and its follow-up TV series *The Rez*.

8. George Melnyk, *One Hundred Years of Canadian Cinema* (Toronto: University of Toronto Press, 2004), 147.

9. Garner was then a TV actor. He originated the title role of *Maverick* as a glib, semi-comic, gambling Western hero.

10. Although one would not know it from the director or his commentators but Jewison was likewise astute in carefully gauging American tolerance for Cold War comedy. *The Russians Are Coming* had an important generic precursor in Stanley Kramer's *It's a Mad, Mad, Mad, Mad World* (1963), a caper-and-chase film with a similarly large ensemble cast composed of TV performers schooled in sketch comedy, like Milton Berle, topped by a few veteran Hollywood hands, like Spencer Tracey. Aside from Eve Marie Saint, Jewison drew most of his *Russians Are Coming* players, like Carl Reiner, and their styles from TV comedy. Alan Arkin, his Russian lead, came directly from the stage. The film solidified the popularity of this large-scaled prototype of the "action-comedy." It was a short-lived but immensely popular innovation in comedy during the mid-1960s yielding a cycle of hits before fading. Steven Spielberg revived the large-scale comedy and used a TV-based mixed cast for *1941* (1979), starring John Belushi. It was Spielberg's most spectacular commercial failure. However, John Landis, the next year, got the mix right with *The Blues Brothers* (1980), working from the advantage of Belushi and Dan Ackroyd's recurring routine from *Saturday Night Live*. After this point, the revived comedy cycle quickly modulated into the contemporary "action comedy."

    It should also be added that Jewison was not alone or early either in treating the Cold War. Two years before him, in 1964, Sidney Lumet's solemn *Fail-Safe*, with Henry Fonda playing the US President, had unsealed the ideological containment around the theme of nuclear war. In the same year, Stanley Kubrick's *Dr. Strangelove* tore its top off when he deployed Peter Sellers in multiple roles to make the bleakest and funniest of the Sixties anti-nuclear war comedies.

11. Ashby and Wexler were soon to be at the forefront of the New Hollywood. In comparing his development from the four classically shot contract films at Universal to *In the Heat of the Night*, we have to note Jewison grasped the style shifts in mid-1960s American cinema only in stages. The close-up montage passages in *The Cincinnati Kid*, executed by Ashby, are a rather embarrassing attempt to incorporate a European new-wave style of editing into a film still classically blocked, framed, lighted, and paced. Jewison was not alone in this sort of clumsiness. Another TV graduate, Arthur Penn, in *Mickey One* (1965), which is the film he made *after* the extraordinary breakthrough of *The Miracle Worker* (1962)—showed a he had yet to control his assertive editing but the film was a crucial step on Penn's way to 1967's *Bonnie and Clyde*, in which new stylistic procedures come under his firm control.

The problem with incorporating a modern European style into American films was met only cautiously by the left-liberal directors of Hollywood in the mid-1960s, but their stylistic impact was at least as great as the New Hollywood filmmakers later. The most famous instance, after *Bonnie and Clyde*, was doubtless Mike Nichols's *The Graduate* (1967). Nichols had already used Haskell Wexler's unadorned hand-held new-wave/vérité-style camera rigorously for *Who's Afraid of Virginia Wolf?* (1966). The TV-trained Lumet successfully incorporated Alain Resnais' elliptical flashback editing style into *The Pawnbroker* (1965). All of these films, awkward or not, successful or not, manifested the serious upset that style standards of the well-made Hollywood film were undergoing.

12. Arthur Hiller, another Canadian Hollywood director of Jewison's generation and similar formation at CBC and American television, also broke away from assigned lighter fare in 1967 to make the revisionist war film *Tobruk* and occasionally belonged with this group of Americans. In 1971 he directed the Chayevsky-scripted *Hospital* and, in 1975, *The Man in the Glass Booth*. Neither Hiller nor any of these directors stopped making ordinary entertainment films, which is why Hiller's name will forever be linked to *Love Story* (1970).

13. The critical discernment of these films' historic coherence and endurance is articulated in Frederic Jameson's "Totality as Conspiracy," in Jameson's *The Geopolitical Aesthetic* (London: BFI Publishing, 1992), 9–67.

14. In *Lost Illusions* (210) David Cook observes, "United Artists' big-budget musical [*Fiddler*] ... went against the early 1970s revisionist grain to become the year's most popular film." However, given the hazardous political situation of Israel, which had just fought two wars with its Arab neighbours, and the consequent rising of a Jewish identity politics (which included a powerful new interest in the Holocaust), *Fiddler on the Roof* could be regarded indirectly as an important political film. Jewison's political identification with Jews, which dates from his youth, likely coloured his choice of the project. While not exactly what *The Godfather* was for Italian Americans, *Fiddler on the Roof* possessed a measure of identity politics, however tame and nostalgic, and this political dimension was implicit, though not obvious, in the course of the film's warm reception.

15. On the other hand, we must note that the English impresario Robert Stigwood was co-producer. Beginning with this film, Stigwood specialized in buying up "rock operas" and hiring interesting directors to film them, often in idiosyncratic fashion. In doing so, Stigwood was successfully revising the musical for the rock generation. Attracted, Jewison says (*This Terrible Business*, 158), by the idea of making a movie from a record album (it was only later staged)—and doubtless by the hippie "youth culture" patina on the project—Jewison's adaptation of Andrew Lloyd Webber's rock opera

began a string of similar Stigwood productions, including *Tommy* (Ken Russell, 1975), *Saturday Night Fever* (John Badham, 1977), *Grease* (Randal Kleiser, 1978), and, later, *Evita* (Alan Parker, 1996).

16. By the mid-1970s, the slate was being swept clean by the second group of New Hollywood directors led by Steven Spielberg and George Lucas. *Jaws* (1975), the *Star Wars* trilogy (1977–83), and the *Indiana Jones* films (1981–84) radically reset the parameters of American Holywood cinema for the next twenty years by raising previously low-regard genres like science fiction and action-adventure into high-concept "blockbuster" filmmaking that redefined what we now mean by "mainstream" cinema.

17. Scott, "Jewison Then and Now," 38.

18. For all its contradictions, the left-liberal posture would see these directors toughing-out the harsher right-wing American climate of the 1970s. The counterculture and the New Left with which New Hollywood filmmakers tried to align themselves would not survive the period so well as liberalism, nor would many of the New Hollywood filmmakers prove as able to hold fast to a political perspective.

19. Melnyk, *One Hundred Years of Canadian Cinema*, 197.

20. Pevere and Diamond, *Mondo Canuck*, 108.

21. Ibid., 108.

22. Examples of Americans' irritated responses to Canadians' political attitudes are abundant and in recent years have become more so. To take a random humorous example from a mainstream publication, Kervin Blount prefaces his review of the DVD release of Paul Haggis's *Crash* (2005) with "Don't you hate Canadians? Take this guy Paul Haggis: He sneaks over the border and takes food out of our mouths by stealing TV writing jobs (*thirty-something, Diff'rent Strokes, Walker, Texas Ranger* ...), and now he's trying to teach us lessons about intolerance in America? I mean, seriously, these people are a problem." *Entertainment Weekly* 838, no. 839 (9 September 2005): 131. Haggis is being cast here as a sort of new Jewison, and *Crash* as the new *In the Heat of the Night*. They share the stereotype of the English Canadian that Jewison himself enthusiastically, and without a hint of self-parody, cultivates in many passages in *This Terrible Business*.

23. Pevere and Diamond, *Mondo Canuck*, 109.

24. This position is deeply mistaken. Canadian rock musicians and folk songwriters were saturated with a continental liberal sense of contemporary politics. In some important ways, The Guess Who, Gordon Lightfoot, Joni Mitchell, Bruce Cockburn, and The Band were closer to Jewison's political stance than were Canadian film directors like Don Shebib, Don Owen, and Paul Almond. Canadian cinema was provincial and politically indifferent compared to Canadian popular music of the same period.

25. Charlie Keil has made a start on such a project with "'American' Cinema in the 1990s and Beyond: Whose Country's Filmaking Is It Anyway?" in *The End of Cinema as We Know It: American Film in the Nineties*, ed. John Lewis (New York: NYU Press, 2001), 53-60.

26. There were precedents but the change in critical attitude toward the director begins in earnest with Pier Handling's anthology of critical essays, *The Shape of Rage: The Films of David Cronenberg* (Toronto: General Publishing, 1983), and especially William Beard's contribution of a lengthy and detailed interpretive essay, "The Visceral Mind," 1-79. The book was published in conjunction with a Toronto film festival retrospective of Cronenberg's films. By then, Egoyan had already made the feature *Next of Kin* (1984) and was about to enter his major phase. A peculiarity of Cronenberg's career is that his critical reputation outside Canada rose consistently, particularly among academics, where several of his films, and especially *Videodrome*, became the exemplary bearers of a significant portion of contemporary film theory. Jameson's "Totality as Conspiracy,"26-35, for instance, includes a considered discussion of the film. However, almost none of the international academic analysis of Cronenberg was included in the Canadian reinterpretation of his films.

27. It should be added that Cronenberg did not originate a single script between *Videodrome* and *eXistenZ* but has made adaptations of American (*Dead Ringers, M. Butterfly, Naked Lunch, A History of Violence*) and British (*Crash, Spider*) works.

28. See Piers Handling's "A Canadian Cronenberg," *The Shape of Rage* (Toronto: General Publishing, 1983): 98-114; and William Beard's "The Canadianness of David Cronenberg," *Mosaic* 27 (June 1994): 113-33. The problem that these and numerous other such essays represent does not lie in poor analyses but in the unconvincing thematic models of Canadian cinema that critics apply to the films. My contribution to this discussion of Cronenberg, "Technology's Body: Cronenberg, Genre, and the Canadian Ethos," *Post/Script* 15, no. 1 (Fall 1995): 38-56, addresses some of the issues of genre and thematic interpretation.

29. This reading of North American political philosophies was provided by the Canadian philosopher George Grant through the course of the 1960s and 1970s. See Barry Cooper, "A imperio ad imperium: The Political Thought of George Grant,"*George Grant in Process*, Larry Schmidt ed. (Toronto: Anansi, 1978), 22-39, and Christopher P. Manfredi, "Constitutional Adjudication and the Crisis of Modern Liberalism," in *George Grant and the Future of Canada*, ed. Yusuf K. Umar (Calgary: University of Calgary Press, 1992), 103-22. Today, if one regrets that Canadian conservatism seems to be a spent force, it is largely because Canadians who now call themselves conservatives, notably those who governed Ontario under Harris and those who now follow

Harper's reformulated national Conservative Party, more and more resemble American right-wing liberals (i.e., neoconservative Republicans) and less and less the rooted Canadian conservatism of William Davis (in Ontario), John Diefenbaker (historically), and Joe Clark (nationally).

30. The proposal Pierre Trudeau made for a Charter of Rights and Freedoms gave rise to considerable debate for the good reason that it challenged the sense of where law ultimately resides in Canada. The law should not stand over the people's legislature and over the state, many Canadians argued against Trudeau's initial proposal. The critics prevailed in the compromise, which consisted of the "notwithstanding clause."

31. See, for example, Robert B. Ray's discussion of law and the two types of American hero in his *A Certain Tendency of the Hollywood Cinema, 1930-1980* (Princeton: Princeton University Press, 1985), especially 70–112. Ray describes both kinds of American attitudes toward law, the transcendent and the immanent, in terms of the two kinds of heroes that appear in Hollywood films.

32. Jewison could never, for these reasons, make a film like *Shane* or *High Noon*, *The French Connection* or *To Live and Die in L.A.*, liberal films in which the hero incarnates justice independently of legal institutions and correct procedures. This also accounts for why his films generally lack the dynamism and violence such films devote to a passion for justice, and why Jewison shows a singular preference for heroes dogged in their devotion to legalistic procedure and restraint.

33. The later films Jewison has made, like *The Hurricane* and *The Statement*, are more obvious in their narrative patterning: Jewison provides a strongly constructed opening movement driven by the film's narrative attachment to its protagonist. After these initial passages, however, Jewison allows the dramatic energy to dissipate as the film's narrative network of subplots, added characters and so on develop. He seems constitutively unable to re-gather the strands of the story into a forceful trajectory again. In the case of *The Hurricane*, Carter's "biography" and then his arrest and first section of his imprisonment are the most energetic and best realized sequences Jewison has directed since the late 1960s, and perhaps ever. But thereafter the film seems diffused. A very similar pattern affects *The Statement*, which opens with a narrative elegance and tension worthy of late Hitchcock, centring on Michael Caine's murder of a pursuing agent, and then cracks up into a checkerboard of badly balanced and awkwardly arranged scenes. I think that these compositional problems with narrative arise from Jewison's progressive refusal in his later films to commit the narrative's force to his protagonist and the familiar tightness of composition of American narrative films eludes him. Jewison seems to be compelled to build a polity

of characters whose relationship to the law must be elaborated and this tends to suspend narrative progression in favour of *thematic* dilations of the plot. Jewison has not found a story form that could carry forward narrative energies suited to his thematic preoccupations. Perhaps this is because Jewison does not—cannot—recognize them. They remain unconscious to him. Filmmakers as different in their thematic concerns as Lumet and Friedkin have preferred, under analogous circumstances, to continue to let their protagonists drive their films. Jewison mistrusts his heroes' inherent authority or rightness to such a degree that he must constrain his narrative force and instead works through the thematic problem of their relations with institutional law. Jewison is always asking how they are enfolded by it, how it uses them and they use it to resolve the plot, rather than asking how the protagonist might push his way toward a solution.

9

Double Take

Adaptation, Remediation, and Doubleness in the Films of Robert Lepage

PETER DICKINSON

▪▪▪▪▪▪▪▪▪▪▪▪▪▪▪▪▪▪▪▪▪▪▪▪▪▪

AS A THEATRE AND FILM DIRECTOR, Robert Lepage is a master of the double take, first arresting spectators with the boldness of his images and then inviting us to look again at the mechanism or medium of their presentation—or *re*-presentation. This sense of doubleness seems to have informed Lepage's life and work from the very start. Born in Quebec City on 12 December 1957, Lepage grew up in a bilingual, blended household, the biological French-speaking son of working class parents who had previously adopted two Anglophone children. Not only has Lepage's bicultural upbringing been incorporated into the complicated family dynamics and sibling rivalries at the core of most of Lepage's films, it arguably also accounts for their inherent translational and transcultural quality. According to Aleksandar Dundjerovic, the memory work on offer in Lepage's cinema is as much a product of the filmmaker's local family upbringing in Quebec City as it is his subsequent global itinerancy as a multidisciplinary artistic nomad. As a result, Lepage's film narratives are at once part of a recognizable "national idiom" *and*, uniquely among

175

Québécois *auteurs* (with the possible exception of Claude Jutra and Denys Arcand, both of whom Dundjerovic rightly identifies as major influences on Lepage), disseminable in ways that are "internationally understood and relevant."[1] To this end, Dundjerovic highlights the linguistic hybridity of Lepage's films, noting that each (including the unilingual *Possible Worlds* [2000]) features at least one scene of miscommunication between characters.

As an adolescent, Lepage's feelings of difference and doubleness were compounded by a growing awareness of his homosexuality and by the psychological alienation from his own body that accompanied his physical diagnosis with alopecia, a skin condition that can result in a complete loss of body hair. Lepage sought solace in drama, and after graduating from high school, he studied at the Conservatoire d'art dramatique de Québec from 1975 to 1978, where he would meet such important future collaborators as Richard Fréchette and Marie Brassard. Lepage then travelled to Paris to study with renowned theatre teacher Alain Knapp, whose technique stresses the multiple creative roles of the stage artist. Returning to Quebec City, Lepage founded Théâtre Hummm...with Fréchette, both men then joining Théâtre Repère—the collective run by Jacques Lessard—in 1982. It was at Repère—and later at Ex Machina, the multidisciplinary production company Lepage founded in 1994 after a stint as artistic director of the National Arts Centre's Théâtre Français in Ottawa from 1989 to 1993—that Lepage began to create and co-create the visually dazzling, technically sophisticated, and award-winning stage shows for which he has become famous. These shows can generally be classified into one of two groups: the large-scale, multicast, epic-length plays collaboratively created, workshopped, and refined over a number of years and at various theatre festivals around the world (*The Dragons' Trilogy*, 1985–87; *Tectonic Plates*, 1988; *The Seven Streams of the River Ota*, 1994–96; *The Geometry of Miracles*, 1998; *Zulu Time*, 1999); and the more intimate (although no less theatrically innovative and imaginatively powerful) solo pieces that Lepage creates, directs, stars in, and tours, before ceding the role to another actor (*Vinci*, 1986; *Needles and Opium*, 1991; *Elsinore*, 1995; *The Far Side of the Moon*, 1999; *The Andersen Project*, 2005).

What all of these stage pieces have in common is a fluid dramaturgical and imagistic style that repeatedly produces moments of both verbal and visual doubleness (a French farce simultaneously translated into English *and* Japanese in *The Seven Streams of the River Ota*; a washing machine door that suddenly becomes a portal into space in *The Far Side of the Moon*). Combined with Lepage's penchant for blurring generic, temporal, and geographic boundaries in his work, these moments provoke spectators to look at familiar objects in new ways, to re-evaluate the cultural and historical contexts in which they are being used, and, in short, to question what it is we think we already know. This doubleness of vision is something that carries over into Lepage's significant work in other disciplines, including opera, concert staging for rock musicians, multimedia installations, and, above all, film.

A focus on doubleness also informs the critical work being done on Lepage's cinema, especially in terms of the functions of time and space in Lepage's representations of memory. Drawing primarily on the work of Gilles Deleuze, and making frequent comparisons to the cinema of Alain Resnais and Alfred Hitchcock, critics like Bill Marshall, Henry A. Garrity, Martin Lefebvre, May Telmissany, and Aleksandar Dundjerovic have elaborated a whole taxonomy of space-time collapses—from parallel montage, flashbacks, and films-within-films—in Lepage's cinema,[2] as when, to cite one of the more famous examples, the space of our extra-diegetic, present-tense viewing of *Le Confessionnal* (1995) starts simultaneously to merge with the pastness of Lepage's fictional spectators' intra-diegetic viewing of Hitchcock's *I Confess* (1953).

However, what such a shot sequence mostly demonstrates, according to Garrity, is that the reconstructed past in Lepage's films is essentially a *de-* or *un*authorized one.[3] That is, it is the result of involuntary memories, on the one hand (in *Le Confessionnal* neither Pierre nor Marc can logically be remembering, in 1989, what they were not alive to witness in 1952–53), or an absence of memory altogether on the other (in *Le Polygraphe* [1997]), François claims that he cannot remember the past, something both the police and Judith end up exploiting). The pasts in both films, in other words, lack an identifiable narrator, an implied author, in the sense that the edits used to evoke them temporally and spatially on screen are the result of Deleuzean "irrational" cuts, which cannot be tied to a diegetic character's actual sensory-motor recognition but only to extra-diegetic, or virtual, representation, what Deleuze calls the "recollection-image."[4]

Neither can these recollection-images be tied to a stable point of view (despite, in the case of *Le Confessionnal*, the voice-over narration of Pierre that frames both the film and the film-within-the-film), other, that is, than that provided by the omniscient camera. Which is another way of saying that if Lepage's films, by virtue of their status as mediated texts, generally, and "adaptations" (however broadly defined) more specifically, lack an author (in the Barthesian sense), they do at least have an *auteur*.

In this essay I propose to survey Lepage's cinematic oeuvre through the lens of adaptation, arguing that this accounts in part for the images and themes of doubleness that pervade his films: from narratives focussed on sibling rivalries and romantic couplings played out across parallel temporalities to the projected screen-within-screen references that proliferate through Lepage's inclusion of "found" film, television, and video footage in most of his movies. It is worth pausing for a moment here over the inherently doubled nature of film as a representational medium. In a recent article evaluating Christian Metz's important psychoanalytic contributions to film theory, Richard Rushton reminds us that Metz's comments in *The Imaginary Signifier* about the "doubled imaginariness of cinema" are explicitly made in the context of distinguishing the spectacle of film from the spectacle of theatre.[5] Specifically, Metz notes that whereas in film both what is being represented (the projected object) and the representation itself (the screen image) are imaginary (because both are absent), in theatre what is being represented is likewise imaginary but, crucially, the representation—and the act of representing—is fully real because it is fully present: we see it happening live before us on stage.[6] Moreover, because of the "realness" of the representation, or the act of representation, in the theatre, what Metz identifies as theatre's built-in capacity to "defictionalize" the spectacle of its own representation (from the audience participation solicited by Italian *commedia* to Shakespearean soliloquies to Brecht's catalogue of alienation effects) is largely taken for granted by its spectators. In contrast, narrative cinema, because of its double fictiveness, where there is no material difference between the object and the image (or what is being represented and the act of representation), paradoxically produces a greater feeling of psychological realism in the viewer, to the point where film can largely only escape the constraints of realistic representation through various stock genre conventions (think of Busby Berkeley-style choreography in a Hollywood musical from the 1940s, or the revenant killer who is a staple of the slasher flick).[7]

To be sure, defictionalization in cinema can also be facilitated by interrupting the perceptual "immediacy" of a film's narrative content by drawing spectators' attention to the "hypermediacy" of its form, self-reflexively foregrounding both the apparatus of the cinema and other technologies of representation it is "remediating."[8] This is where attention to the process of adaptation becomes a crucial element in the analysis of Lepage's cinema, both in terms of accounting for the facility with which he works in and moves across the disciplines of theatre and film and, arguably as crucially, explaining the traces and residual presence of one within the other. For if, as Robert Stam suggests, a filmic adaptation "is less an attempted resuscitation of an originary word than a turn in an ongoing dialogical process...., tissues of anonymous formulae, variations on those formulae, conscious and unconscious quotations, and conflations and inversions of other texts,"[9] then it would appear that the particular "doubleness" that marks Lepage's corpus of films must, at some level, have to do with an ongoing meta-dialogue he is conducting with himself as theatre director and film director. The question of whether—and when—one of those roles trumps the other coalesces especially around the *auteurist* reading of Lepage as filmmaker, which has predominated in the critical literature on his work. That is, as film *auteur*, Lepage is arguably able to control his cinematic narratives more vigilantly than his theatrical ones, most of which were created collaboratively with his Théâtre Repère and Ex Machina troupes or with co-writers like Marie Brassard, and which Lepage has famously argued are never "finished" because they are always evolving and being adapted in the necessarily evanescent and non-repeatable context of the performance moment. However, when it comes to the filmic artifact, a degree of authority and fixity necessarily accrues by virtue of each film's temporal positioning after, and thus definitive recording of, each play's constitutive images. To put this in Metz's terms, what Lepage's films perceptually (and perceptively) stage is precisely their movement from the "virtual reality" of a theatrical past (those once fleeting and now lost moments of dramatic inspiration, rehearsal, and performance) to the "actual reality" of a cinematic present, where they can be ceaselessly and unchangeably replayed in the temporal and spatial moment of apprehension that constitutes each film's projection. It is not the precise nature of narrative changes made in the transposition of Lepage's theatrical source texts to the screen that is intriguing as much as the process of intertextual and intermedial exchange manifesting itself in various self-referential moments of representational (temporal, spatial, corporeal) doubleness.

■ Le Confessionnal (1995)

LEPAGE HAD ALREADY RACKED UP a slew of provincial, national, and international awards and honours for his theatrical work when he decided to turn his attention to film in 1995. In coming up with Le Confessionnal, he could not have made a more auspicious debut. Selected to open the Cannes Film Festival's Director's Fortnight series, the film won the International Critics Prize at the Istanbul Film Festival, Genie Awards for Best Film, Best Director, and Best Cinematography, as well as the Claude Jutra Prize for Best First Feature; it was also chosen as Canada's official entry as Best Foreign Film at both the Golden Globe Awards and the Oscars.

As an adaptation, Le Confessionnal is multiply complex: not only does it contain characters from Lepage's first great theatrical triumph, The Dragons' Trilogy (chief among them the protagonist, Pierre Lamontagne), it also consciously quotes and incorporates scenes from Hitchcock's I Confess, itself an adaptation of a 1902 stage play, Nos deux consciences, by French playwright Paul Anthelme. Moreover, as Dominique Lafon and Michael Vaïs have separately pointed out, Anthelme's play received its own québécisation prior to Hitchcock's film treatment via Québec playwright Julien Daoust's theatrical adaptation, La Conscience d'un prêtre, which premiered in Montreal in 1903. According to Lafon, Hitchcock and his scenarists, George Tambori and William Archibald, must have known about Daoust's play because the script for I Confess contains some striking similarities to Daoust's take on the story, independent of their common source in Anthelme's play.[10] Lafon further argues that Daoust's influence upon Hitchcock's film extends beyond the director's retention of the new Quebec City setting to incorporate, as well, a particularly Québécois inflection to

Anthelme's already melodramatic plot, trace signs of which Lepage exploits and expands upon in *Le Confessionnal*. Finally, *Le Confessionnal* is also an anachronistic and anamorphic sequel to Lepage's next great theatrical project, *The Seven Streams of the River Ota*, which concludes by placing the Eastern-identified "linking character"[11] of Pierre (here renamed Pierre Maltais) in Japan.

Le Confessionnal opens with a Hitchcockian establishing shot of the same Pont de Québec that will appear in the film's closing frames, along with a voice-over by Pierre that gestures toward that ending and that establishes the disjunctive and inherently doubled spatial and temporal poetics that govern the film as a whole: "Dans la ville où je suis né, le passé porte le présent comme un enfant sure ses épaules." Immediately bearing this out, there is a cut to shots of the 1953 premiere of Hitchcock's *I Confess* at Quebec City's grand Capitol cinema described at the outset of this essay, Pierre's voice-over recalling, as the camera focusses first on the flickering images of the Chateau Frontenac emerging on the screen-within-the-screen, then on his aunt, Jeanne d'Arc (Lynda Lepage-Beaulieu, the director's sister), and finally on his mother Françoise's (Marie Gignac) swollen belly, that there were actually three Lamontagnes attending the screening that night. In the next scene, the now-adult Pierre arrives home from China, where he had been studying calligraphy, to attend the funeral of his father, Paul-Émile (François Papineau), who has died after a long battle with diabetes. Thereafter, the film cuts back and forth between the "present" diegesis of 1989 and the "past" diegesis of 1952–53. The 1989 narrative concerns Pierre's attempts to reconnect with his estranged adopted brother Marc (François Goyette), who works as a male prostitute and is trying, unsuccessfully, to shake off the proprietary attentions of one particular client, a cultural attaché named Massicotte (Jean-Louis Millette). The 1952 narrative details the pregnancy and eventual suicide of Marc's unmarried birth mother, Rachel (Suzanne Clément), Françoise's younger sister.

Diplomat Massicotte provides the link between the film's past and present narratives. In flashbacks to 1952, we learn that a much younger Massicotte (Normand Daneau) actually began his working life as a priest, serving the church in Quebec City, where Hitchcock (Ron Burrage) and his crew are preparing to shoot scenes for *I Confess* under the guidance of

Hitchcock's harried assistant (Kristin Scott Thomas) and where Rachel also works as a *femme de ménage*. No longer able to hide her pregnancy, Rachel is dismissed from her job, but not before confessing to the young Massicotte that Paul-Émile is her unborn baby's father. Unable to break the seal of confession, and with Rachel unwilling to confirm otherwise, Massicotte is in turn removed from his post after suspicions are aroused in the congregation that he is Rachel's lover. The two storylines converge in a double denouement that features several cuts between parallel scenes in both time-frames, the closing titles and the final shot of the Chateau Frontenac at the end of the 1953 screening of I *Confess* mirroring Pierre's apprehension of the "truth" about his family in Massicotte's room at the same hotel at the end of *Le Confessionnal*.

If parallel montage and invisible cutting represent the most obvious and ready technical means by which Lepage elaborates the film's central thesis about the coextensiveness of the past within the present, so does the director's fondness for retrieving and remediating other visual economies within his own signal an intuitive understanding of how the cinematic apparatus is uniquely able to depict the doubling of time, or arguably more properly, what Deleuze has referred to as time splitting itself in two.[12] Thus, while Lepage employs in *Le Confessionnal* a skilful series of tracking shots and match cuts (usually along or of material surfaces: wooden church pews, a staircase banister, an apartment wall, a porcelain sink) to move seamlessly back and forth between the two diegetic layers of the film, and to connect those layers *spatially*, it is the screen-within-the-screen that emerges repeatedly as the locus of their *temporal* convergence—and disjunction. For the embedded screen's appearance in different forms in successive scenes at once cues us as to how the on-screen characters' pasts are thoroughly embedded in and intertwined with their presents and to how our own (off-screen) visual memories are almost certainly completely out of sync with the film's projection.

Lepage's interpolation of clips from Hitchcock's I *Confess* within his own film narrative is the most obvious example of the use of the doubled screen. They are inserted at three separate points in *Le Confessionnal* and, taken together, not only highlight the seamlessness with which Lepage uses montage to breach the borders of Hitchcock's *mise-en-scène* and visually incorporate it into his own, but also foreground, in their non-sequential placement throughout the film, the very process of (re)mediation. That is, the aforementioned scene depicting the premiere and initial public projection of *I Confess* can be juxtaposed with a later sequence in which Lepage reconstructs the actual filming of a crucial scene from Hitchcock's movie (the one in which Montgomery Clift, as Father Logan, discovers the murderer Keller hiding at the back of his church), his reconstruction eventually merging, via a canny superimposition of tracking shots, with Hitchcock's finished cut of the same scene. Moreover, in between these two scenes, we also witness Pierre, in 1989, watching a *rebroadcast* of the film on television in the old Lamontagne house.

Television screens are another means by which Lepage connects the two timeframes in his film. For example, classic fifties physique films can be seen flickering on TV monitors in the gay sauna where Pierre goes in search of Marc. And the news footage of the Tiananmen Square massacre that we see Pierre following at various points throughout the present-day narrative of 1989 finds its own portal to the past in a clever scene that has a young Quebec City girl auditioning, in 1952, for a role in *I Confess* morph, thirty-seven years later, into local media personality Renée Hudon, broadcasting the latest update from Beijing.

One final doubling of the screen-within-the-screen in *Le Confessionnal* that connects the film's thematization of the traces of memory with a quasi-Benjaminian take on a new artistic medium's role in the de-autho-rization of the "aura" of an older one comes in the form of the living room wall of the Lamontagne house. When we first see it, soon after Pierre arrives home from China for his father's funeral, the wall is filled with framed family photographs. In subsequent scenes, the photos have been removed and the wall painted a succession of vibrant primary colours, the outline of where the photos used to hang nevertheless seeping through palimpsestically, mocking Pierre's attempts to eliminate or cover up the visible evidence of his past. It's a stunning image in a film saturated with such moments and, when read in the context of Lepage's subsequent work, a reminder that his cinematic oeuvre is all about seeing double.

■ Le Polygraphe (1997)

LEPAGE'S SECOND FILM, *Le Polygraphe*, is based on the play of the same name he co-wrote and co-starred in alongside long-time collaborator Marie Brassard. It premiered in Quebec City in a French-language production directed by Lepage in May 1988. The play was subsequently produced in an English translation in Toronto in February 1990. It is this latter version that Lepage chose to have tour the world, as well as to be published.[13] For the film version, however, Lepage reverted to French dialogue and radically revised the original script.

Both the play and the film focus on the complex interrelationships between three characters. David, renamed Christof in the film version (and played by Peter Stormare), is a criminologist who escaped from East Berlin and now works at a forensics institute in Montreal. He meets Lucie (Marie Brassard), an actress from Quebec City, when they witness a suicide in a Metro station. Lucie has just been cast as the murder victim in a film based on an actual unsolved case, for which François (Patrick Goyette), her neighbour, remains the prime suspect. François maintains that he is innocent and has taken a lie detector test to prove it, but the police assert that the results were inconclusive. In the original stage play, the police's continued harassment of François, together with their failure to find the real murderer, eventually drive him to take his own life (also by jumping in front of a subway train). Meanwhile, the theatre audience learns that David has his own secrets: not only did he leave a former lover behind when he escaped to the West, but, in the play's penultimate scene, it is revealed that he was the one who both administered the polygraph to François *and* planted the seeds of doubt within him about the validity of his testimony.

The all-important polygraph scene, which closes the play, opens the film, a temporal relocation that spatially abstracts the forensic thrust of the action that follows. Specifically, Lepage uses the opening credit sequence to capture, with diagnostic precision, François's head, torso, arms, and fingers being attached with all manner of wires and electrodes, as well as, through time lapse dissolves, the prosthetic record of his responses to the questions put to him by the technician Hans (James Hyndman), whom we later learn is an old friend of Christof. What is significant about how this scene has been adapted for film, apart from who is asking the questions this time around, is that the audience not only witnesses François's self-declaration of innocence at the start of the film's narrative diegesis (rather than at the close of the play's), but in effect has "objective" corroboration of this in the form of the polygraph needle's steady and unwavering movement over the printout being monitored by Hans. Whereas in the play the audience is left to wonder about the "othered" François's innocence or guilt until the very end, Lepage's film works to solicit spectators' identification with the character from its opening frames, thereby transferring the weight of narrative suspense to the question of who other than François is responsible for Marie-Claire's (Marie-Christine Le Huu) murder.

Here, again, Lepage resorts to patterns of doubling familiar from *Le Confessionnal*—including the insertion of a subplot about estranged siblings, the use of parallel montage, and scenes documenting the making, editing, and broadcast of a film-within-a-film (about the very events that constitute Lepage's film)—to at once resolve the plot conspiracy at the heart of his crime drama and, arguably, to construct a further meta-argument about the different hermeneutics of truth on display in theatre and film. Thus, among the changes made in the film version of *Le Polygraphe*, is the addition of a backstory that informs the spectator that not only were François, who is gay in the stage version, and Marie-Claire lovers who had quarrelled the night of her murder, but that while she was seeking comfort from her filmmaker friend, Judith (Josée Deschênes), he was getting drunk in a bar, allowing himself to be picked up by Marie-Claire's sister, Claude (Maria de Medeiros), with whom François had had a previous affair. In scenes of double parallel montage near its conclusion, the film cuts from Judith and François talking about the night of the murder in her Montreal editing studio to Lucie showing Claude François's empty apartment in Quebec City, and from shots of Judith's film's in-the-end *false* intra-diegetic reconstruction of Marie-Claire's murder (she blames the cops) to Claude's flashbacks of what really happened: in a fit of jealousy, she had stabbed her sister and set fire to her apartment.

The actress Lucie plays an important dual role in all of this, serving as Lepage's onscreen amanuensis via her simultaneous casting in Judith's film and as the lead in an open-air, cross-gender production of *Hamlet*.

Whereas Lucie defends the authenticity of her avant-garde stage performance to a bewildered Christof, she challenges Judith about her hopelessly contrived representation of the "facts" of Marie-Claire's case after seeing a rough cut of the film. In other words, in this radical reinterpretation of his own play, Lepage seems to be attempting to extend and elaborate on screen Metz's argument about the "double imaginariness" of film, especially when juxtaposed next to the theatre. That is, film's proximate "realism" and apparent active mastery, through the apparatus of the camera, of the "truth," renders obsolete any distinction between actor and role, story and plot, fiction and fact, thus making it easier for Judith—and, presumably, her viewers—to believe her own performed lie. It's a bold thesis that was mostly lost on Lepage's own audience. As André Loiselle has convincingly argued, "What most critics failed to perceive is that Le polygraphe does not (merely) seek to tell the complicated story of people involved in a crime and the film version of the crime. Rather, the film itself is the crime, as it proceeds very purposefully to kill the original play."[14]

■ Nô (1998)

LEPAGE'S NEXT FILM likewise explores the interplay between theatre and film, this time in service of a remediated narrative that works dually as a romantic comedy and a political allegory. Shot with super-16mm film in seventeen days, Nô is based on Section 5 ("The Words") of The Seven Streams of the River Ota. The play, which in its epic entirety comprises seven parts staged over seven successive hours, was developed collaboratively over a three-year period with the members of Ex Machina and subsequently toured to more than twenty-five different locations around the world. Its plot spans fifty years; moves back and forth in time and space between Japan, the United States, and Europe; incorporates over fifty different speaking roles in four different languages (English, French, Japanese, and German); and employs all manner of meta-representational devices to foreground the processes of spectatorship and cultural mediation. Even more boldly, Seven Streams also attempts to make political and historical sense of such cataclysmic world events as the Holocaust, the bombing of Hiroshima, and AIDS, in terms of a recurring set of aesthetic oppositions: between East and West, life and death, tragedy and comedy, masculine and feminine.

Wisely, Lepage narrowed his scope for the eighty-five-minute *Nô*. In the film, he has chosen to focus on Sophie (Anne-Marie Cadieux), a Québécoise actress starring in a production of a Feydeau farce as part of Canada's cultural program at the 1970 World's Fair in Osaka, Japan. Sophie, with the aid of Hanako (Marie Brassard), a blind Japanese translator attached to the show, has just learned she is pregnant. She is not sure if the father is her co-star, François-Xavier (Éric Bernier), or her boyfriend, Michel (Alexis Martin), a writer who, back in Montreal, has suddenly been thrust into the thick of the October Crisis, thanks to an unexpected visit by radical friends intent on planting a bomb. While Sophie finds herself embroiled in her own bedroom farce, when she drunkenly sleeps with Walter (Richard Fréchette), the Canadian cultural attaché in Tokyo, Michel labours over the wording of the political message that will be attached to his friends' bomb, whose detonator, he soon discovers, has been incorrectly set. The two narratives, whose temporal and spatial distinctiveness had previously been signposted by having the scenes in Montreal filmed in black and white and the scenes in Japan in colour, merge during a key scene, where Sophie, returning from Japan to discover only rubble where her home once stood, is arrested by Agents Bélanger (Tony Conte) and Ménard (Jules Philip), plainclothes detectives who had been keeping her and Michel's apartment under surveillance.

Not only does the shift from black and white to colour that occurs during the middle of this scene chromatically connect the doubled diegeses of Lepage's film on a synchronic, or spatial level, linking Sophie's narrative in Japan with Michel's narrative in Montreal; it also diachronically, or temporally, links both of these narratives from 1970 with the coda set in 1980 that immediately follows, via a familiar insertion on Lepage's part of intra-diegetic media footage. Specifically, the conclusion of *Nô* flashes forward from October 1970 to 20 May 1980, the night of Québec's first referendum on sovereignty-association. As Sophie and a newly yuppified Michel watch dispiritedly the television results confirming a victory for the "No" side, Jean Chrétien appears as a talking head on the screen-within-the-screen, expounding, in his inimitable way, on the virtues of federalism. Formally and politically, this crucially ties the ending of the film to the beginning, where in the opening frames Lepage interweaves documentary footage of Pierre Trudeau being interviewed about introducing the War Measures Act to deal with the FLQ during the October Crisis. Further compounding the film's tongue-in-cheek, although no less teleological, representation of the "Je me souviens" rhetoric that continues to haunt Québécois nationalism, Michel then begins to expound upon his theory that "people with a collective project are always a little disadvantaged next to people who don't have a project.... The idea is that it always takes more energy to change political institutions, social institutions than...to do nothing."[15] To Sophie's response that the "common project" of the "No" side in the referendum must surely be the idea of a unified Canada, Michel scoffs that "It's a bit static as a project, isn't it?"[16] He then suggests that perhaps he and Sophie need a common project, something that looks to "posterity," something like a child. Incredulous, Sophie asks him whether he would have considered that a worthy "common project" ten years earlier, at the start of their relationship. Michel replies that it wouldn't have been the same thing ten years ago: "... we were occupied with changing the world.... Times have changed."[17] The scene ends with Sophie—who clearly intends not to tell Michel about her earlier failed pregnancy—gradually acceding to Michel's increasingly amorous arguments, assenting to the idea of a baby in an escalating series of percentages—she goes from being 40.5 per cent sure, to 49 per cent, to 50 per cent, and then finally 50.5 per cent— that mirror the closeness of the numbers for and against sovereignty in Québec's second referendum.

Indeed, it is impossible not to read this scene in light of the events of 1995. The film's release date of 1998, combined with the strategically chosen footage of Chrétien, ensures that Sophie and Michel's conversation will resonate with both Québécois and English-Canadian audiences. Not least because of the discourse surrounding reproduction that emerged over the course of the 1995 campaign, with sovereigntist leaders like Lucien Bouchard and Jacques Parizeau urging *pure laîne* Québécois to do their bit to reverse the plummeting provincial birthrate in order to offset, among other things, the inevitable anti-nationalist consequences of "les votes ethniques." All of which returns us to the doubly coded chromatic significance of the film's final switch from black and white to colour film stock. The resulting focalization of the spectator's gaze on the blood flowing down Sophie's legs as a result of the miscarriage brought on by her arrest serves as a syntagma that connects the various overlapping discourses of nationalism and sexuality throughout the film. And yet while Lepage's film was mostly met with derision and scorn by Québécois critics, who objected to his treatment of the events of 1970 as farce, it is hard not to read this scene as symptomatic of a de facto sympathy with the *indepentiste* cause. Indeed, in Christopher Gittings' estimation, Lepage's cut "from a low-angle close-up shot of blood running down the inside of Sophie's legs to Sophie and Michel watching television coverage of the May 1980 Referendum" can be seen to constitute the director's "rather heavy-handed point about the failure of Québécois separatists to carry the embryonic Québec nation to full term."[18]

■ *Possible Worlds* (2000)

POSSIBLE WORLDS opens with the camera focussing, from the inside, on a window cleaner (Griffith Brewer) who is busy washing, from the outside, the floor-to-ceiling windows of a trendy condominium loft. As the soap suds are gradually wiped away by the deft strokes of his squeegee, the window cleaner is able to see inside the condo, whereupon he makes a shocking discovery: the dead body of its owner splayed across the sofa. We then cut to the arrival of Detective Berkley (Sean McCann) at the scene, who learns from his partner, Williams (Rick Miller), who the murder victim is—George Barber (Tom McCamus), a successful stockbroker. Berkley also finds out what makes this particular crime so gruesome: the killer has neatly sawn off the top part of his victim's skull and absconded with the brain.

Lepage's fourth film, *Possible Worlds* is his first shot in English. And while the film is based on a previously staged work of drama, it is not, this time, one by Lepage. Instead, he is adapting John Mighton's 1992 play of the same name. However, a brief analysis of the plot and structure of Mighton's play reveals some familiar Lepage themes, including the paralleling and overlapping of different temporal and spatial realms, the mourning of a lost love object, and the unravelling of a mystery whose solution is in some fundamental sense beyond imagination.

In the case of *Possible Worlds*, this mystery concerns not just who stole George's brain, and why, but also the exact nature of his relationship with his wife, Joyce (Tilda Swinton). To summarize, both the play and film, like all of Lepage's films, follow two separate narrative temporalities, flashing back from the opening scene described above to trace George and Joyce's initial meeting, courtship, and, it's briefly suggested, subsequent estrangement. But even here, in the flashback narrative, there are further diegetic layers. In one version of events, George and Joyce meet in the cafeteria of the hospital, where she works as a research biologist, or rather re-meet, as it soon becomes clear that they are from the same small town in Northern Ontario. In another possible scenario that we witness, the couple meet in a crowded downtown bar, with a coquettish Joyce, who now seems to work as a stockbroker in the same office as George, aggressively pursuing a liaison. These scenes, and others documenting further stages in the couple's twin relationships, are repeated throughout the film, dramatizing what George describes to Joyce at one point as the metaphysical romance of human interconnection—that we all exist in an infinite number of doubled and redoubled "possible worlds." This is encoded in the film's image-track through a sequence of shots that, for want of a better term, one might call "double takes," scenes from George's life (and death) that are restaged, in different ways and with different outcomes, throughout the film and that together constitute an interesting elaboration of classic apparatus theory's discussion of the operations of identification and desire in the cinema.

The most memorable of these double takes concerns Lepage's intradiegetic remediation of the opening frames of his own film. There, as Detectives Berkley and Williams circle George's corpse looking for evidence and a motive for the crime, Lepage's camera swoops down from the upper reaches of the loft, lingering almost pornographically over the body of actor Tom McCamus, splayed across the back of the sofa, shirt front open to the waist, a look of sublime pleasure on his face. This opening image of George's body draped provocatively across his sofa is repeated once more in the film; this time, however, George wakes up, to the realization that he is merely suffering from a massive hangover and that he has just slept with Joyce #2, the stockbroker. In both scenes George is made into an object of desire for the viewer—even if only clinical desire—regardless of the viewer's gender. But in both scenes it is the camera, and specifically its overhead angle, that is constructing and mediating that desire. In other words, desire here is scopophilic; it is the desire *to see*. And, as Metz would thus conclude, spectatorial identification in both scenes resides not with the subject on screen, but rather with the camera itself.[19]

Meanwhile, in the present tense of the crime narrative, the film's other couple, Berkley and Williams, who kibbutz, cajole, and generally annoy each other like an old married couple, trace the theft of George's brain to a Doctor Keiber (Gabriel Gascon), a neurologist who has been stockpiling the cerebella of very intelligent and powerful people as a way of extracting, adapting, and, in effect, remediating their unconscious thoughts. As Keiber tries to explain it to Berkley, every moment of cognition, even the most trivial, leaves an affective trace, an emotional or sensory disturbance in the field of perception. The question then becomes, according to Keiber, how to harness and control these disturbances. Once again it seems as though Lepage is gesturing here toward another Metzian meta-thesis on the inherent doubleness of the cinema. Indeed, Keiber's defence of his scientific methods accords remarkably with film theorist Patricia White's notion of "retrospectatorship," whereby the reception of a given film "is transformed by unconscious and conscious past viewing experience." As she puts it, "All spectatorship, insofar as it engages subjective fantasy, revises memory traces and experiences, some of which are memories and experiences of other movies."[20] In the specific context of *Possible Worlds*, this helps explain not only Lepage's penchant for internal repetition at the level of individual scenes and even shot construction, but also his homage, at the level of genre, to the B-movie retro classicism of the police procedural and the sci-fi thriller. White's theory of "retrospectatorship" also allows us to assess the film, as an adaptation of a previously staged play, through a more expansive theoretical framework than that provided by fidelity criticism, which tends to measure the changes made in adapting a text to a different medium within an inherently constricting "deficit" model.

■ La Face cachée de la lune (2003)

WINNER OF THE FIPRESCI International Critics Prize in the Panorama Series at the 2004 Berlin International Film Festival and a Canadian Genie Award for Best Adapted Screenplay, Lepage's fifth film, *La Face cachée de la lune*, is shot in high definition video. An adaptation of his award-winning solo play of the same name, the film is set against the backdrop of the American-Soviet space race and current investigations into extraterrestrial life. Jumping back and forth in time between the 1950s and the present day, the narrative through-line concerns the complicated relationship between two Quebec City brothers, Philippe and André (both played by Lepage), and their different responses to the death of their mother (played in flashbacks by a mute Anne-Marie Cadieux). Not only is *La Face* Lepage's most personally memorial film to date (the impetus for the source play came from the death of his own mother), not only does it mark his debut as an actor in one of his own films, but it also sees Lepage, as director, consciously quoting from and adapting his previous work. This self-reflection relates to the concepts of doubleness and remediation in all of Lepage's films.

The theme of narcissism runs throughout *La Face*. Most prominently, it serves as the theoretical cornerstone of Philippe's twice-rejected Ph.D. thesis in the philosophy of science, which argues that the American and Soviet space programs were fuelled not by the desire to seek out and explore new worlds but rather to claim and remake those worlds in each country's national and ideological image. *La Face* elaborates this thesis self-reflexively by incorporating within its diegesis a lot of classic documentary footage of early space flights by rival American astronauts and Soviet cosmonauts, as well as clips from 1950s sci-fi films like *The Day the Earth Stood Still* (Robert Wise, 1951), about the panicked and xenophobic response of a terrified American citizenry when the alien Klaatu (Michael Rennie) lands his space ship on the mall in Washington, DC, and attempts to deliver a message of peace. Lepage also elaborates a counter-thesis in the form of yet another film-within-a-film, this one a video that Philippe is making for a contest seeking the best explanation of the human worldview to a potential extraterrestrial audience.

As for Philippe's own self-image, it has been shaped by childhood memories and battered by adult failures. Still living in the old family apartment, surrounded by his dead mother's clothes and shoes, he is unkempt and socially inept, reduced to taking on a series of menial and underpaid jobs while he revises his thesis. He even manages to sabotage his one shot at academic stardom. Having been invited to present his research at a conference in Moscow, Phillippe sleeps through his scheduled panel. Meanwhile, younger brother André could not be more different. A self-absorbed and pompous weatherman, he lives in a trendy and well-appointed new condo overlooking the harbour with his equally well-appointed boyfriend, Carl (Marco Poulin). André is the stereotypical embodiment of gay male narcissism, obsessed with surface appearances, his own and others'. However, just when it looks like Lepage is in danger of recycling classic homophobic tropes from Hollywood cinema, he inverts this process by exposing his own body to the minoritizing gaze of the camera.

In a very funny scene midway through the film, Philippe, having put in a desultory workout at a local gym, suddenly finds himself sharing a sauna with Carl. Never having met his brother's boyfriend, Philippe misinterprets Carl's friendly grin and casually provocative legs-splayed pose as a cruise and rapidly rushes to declare his heterosexual credentials. It is only at this point that Carl reveals his own identity, noting that he immediately recognized Philippe as André's brother owing to the family resemblance. Thereafter, the two men fall into a casual conversation about work, with Philippe surprised at Carl's interest in his research. What is most interesting about this scene is how it subtly revises and remediates the epistemology of surveillance that governs the sauna scene in *Le Confessionnal*, where Lepage's all-seeing camera relentlessly seeks to expose the queer male body, as when, for example, the outline of Marc's naked body emerges from the steam to be framed alongside his brother Pierre's towelled one in the doorway to the shower area. Not only is it the straight male who is required to out himself in the sauna scene depicted in *La Face*, but it is his body that is subjected to both Carl's and the camera's voyeuristic gaze. That that body is here framed in medium close-ups and a shot-reverse shot sequence of edits rather than via the overhead tracking shots used in *Le Confessionnal* also forces us to consider exactly who is policing whom in *La Face*. In the sexualized space of the sauna, Philippe's overweight, out-of-shape, and pale straight body, when juxtaposed against Carl's tauter, tanned, tattooed, and pierced queer one, cannot help but be found wanting.

This reading of the male body's doubling in *La Face*'s sauna scene would seem to be confirmed by the scene that immediately follows. Back in the locker room, Philippe examines himself in front of a mirror, his expression clearly indicating that he does not like what he sees. He then takes a daub of shaving cream and traces a faux-goatee of the sort worn by André down his chin. We then cut to André wiping his on-camera make-up off in front of a mirror in the television studio. If we understand the mirror in both of these scenes as a metonym of the movie screen, as so many Lacanian film theorists have famously encouraged us to do, then Lepage's brief representation of himself as a "body double" in this sequence of shots serves as a nice summation both of some of the specific differences between theatre and film and of how the latter's remediation of the former speaks to the "doubled imaginariness of cinema" in general. That is, the cut that Lepage makes from Philippe in the locker room to André in the studio is one that could not be accomplished with the same seamlessness by a solo actor on stage. At the same time, the cinematic doubling of Lepage on screen is comprised of only virtual "images" that do not correspond to any physically present "bodies."[21]

Paradigmatically, then, what all of Robert Lepage's films show us is that the cinematic image is always already a doubled image. It is at once present and absent, mediated and remediating. It is Lepage's signal achievement as a director that he has consistently used both the content and form of his films, both their stories and the discourse or language of their telling, to elaborate a complex poetics of adaptation. Translating his own and others' stage work into screen images, he is uniquely positioned to demonstrate how we see in the theatre and how we see differently in film.

Portions of this chapter, in slightly altered form and in service of a much different argument, have appeared in my article "Space, Time, Auteur-ity, and the Queer Male Body: The Film Adaptations of Robert Lepage," *Screen* 46, no. 2 (2005): 133–53.

NOTES

1. Aleksandar Dundjerovic, *The Cinema of Robert Lepage: The Poetics of Memory* (London: Wallflower Press, 2003), 51.

2. See Bill Marshall, *Quebec National Cinema* (Montreal: McGill-Queen's UP, 2001); Henry A. Garrity, "Robert Lepage's Cinema of Time and Space," in Joseph I. Donohoe and Jane M. Koustas, eds. *Theater sans frontières* (East Lansing, MI: Michigan State UP, 2000), 95–107; Martin Lefebvre, "A Sense of Time and Place: The Chronotope in *I Confess* and *Le Confessionnal*," *Quebec Studies* 26 (Fall 1998–Winter 1999): 88–98; May Telmissany, "La citation filmique comme anachronisme," *Essays on Canadian Writing* 76 (2002): 247–62; and Dundjerovic, *The Cinema of Robert Lepage*.

3. See Garrity, "Robert Lepage's Cinema," 102; 105–06.

4. Gilles Deleuze, *Cinema 2: The Time-Image*, trans. Hugh Tomlinson and Robert Galeta (Minneapolis: U of Minnesota P, 1989), 54.

5. Richard Rushton, "Cinema's Double: Some Reflections on Metz," *Screen* 43:2 (2002): 109.

6. Christian Metz, *The Imaginary Signifier: Psychoanalysis and the Cinema*, trans. Celia Britton et al. (Bloomington: Indiana UP, 1982), 66–67. For further important discussions of the different dialectical relationships between the real and the imaginary, absence and presence, in theatre and film see: Walter Benjamin, "The Work of Art in the Age of Mechanical Reproduction," in *Illuminations*, ed. Hannah Arendt (New York: Schocken, 1968), 217–51; André Bazin, *What is Cinema?* vol. 1, trans. Hugh Gray (Berkeley: U of Calif. P, 1967), especially 76–124; Steven Shaviro, *The Cinematic Body* (Minneapolis: U of Minnesota P, 1993), especially chapter 1, "Film Theory and Visual Fascination," 1–65; Slavoj Žižek, ed., *Everything You Always Wanted to Know about Lacan (but Were Afraid to Ask Hitchcock)* (London: Verson, 1992); and, in the Canadian context, André Loiselle, *Stage-Bound: Feature Film Adaptations of Canadian and Québécois Drama* (Montreal: McGill-Queen's UP, 2003).

7. See Metz, *The Imaginary Signifier*, 66 and ff.; and Rushton, "Cinema's Double," 109.

8. The terms "remediation," "immediacy," and "hypermediacy" I borrow from Jay Bolter and Richard Grusin, who argue that new digital media, in particular, have achieved their cultural significance in part by

"remediating," or cannibalizing and refashioning, older visual media, at once seeking transparent immediacy by denying the residual presence of the older media and incorporating this presence within a new hypermediated environment; see their *Remediation: Understanding New Media* (Cambridge, MS: MIT Press, 1999). While Bolter and Grusin are unfortunately less than generous in acknowledging his influence, their work is undeniably indebted to the earlier thinking of Canadian media theorist Marshall McLuhan, one of whose "laws of media" was the principle of "retrieval," whereby the form of an older medium inevitably becomes the content of a newer one (as when, for example, movies are rebroadcast on television); see Marshall McLuhan, *Understanding Media: The Extensions of Man* (Toronto: McGraw-Hill, 1964), and Marshall and Eric McLuhan, *The Laws of Media: The New Science* (Toronto: U of Toronto P, 1988).

9. Robert Stam, "Beyond Fidelity: The Dialogics of Adaptation," in *Film Adaptation*, ed. James Naremore (New Brunswick, NJ: Rutgers UP, 2000), 64.

10. Dominique Lafon, "Pour servir à la petite histoire d'un mélodrame québécois: la leçon d'un tapuscrit," *L'Annuaire théâtral* 17 (1995): 49. See, as well, Michael Vaïs, "Robert Lepage: un homme de théâtre au cinéma," *Jeu* 88, no. 3 (1998): 125.

11. In conversation with Rémy Charest, Lepage has described the recurring character of Pierre as his "alter ego," someone who makes connections between the various threads of Lepage's theatrical and cinematic narratives, and between those narratives and the audience, "[h]is naive approach towards the events he encounters [reflecting] the spectator's position." See Lepage, *Connecting Flights*, with Rémy Charest, trans. Wanda Romer Taylor(London: Methuen, 1997), 33, 34.

12. Deleuze, *Cinema 2: The Time Image*, 81.

13. See Marie Brassard and Robert Lepage, *Polygraph*, trans. Gyllian Raby, in *The CTR Anthology: Fifteen Plays from Canadian Theatre Review*, ed. Alan Filewod (Toronto: U of Toronto P, 1993), 647–83.

14. Loiselle, *Stage-Bound*, 197.

15. Robert Lepage and André Morency, *Nô* (Laval and Montreal: Les 400 Coups/ Alliance Vivafilm, 1998), 87; my translation.

16. Ibid., 87; my translation.

17. Ibid., 87; my translation.

18. Christopher Gittings, *Canadian National Cinema: Ideology, Difference, and Representation*. (London: Routledge, 2002), 191.

19. Metz, *The Imaginary Signifier*, 49.

20. Patricia White, *Uninvited: Classical Hollywood Cinema and Lesbian Representability* (Bloomington: Indiana University Press, 1999), 197.

21. See, in this regard, Shaviro, *The Cinematic Body*, 46.

10

Straight Outta' Hogtown
Sex, Drugs, and Bruce McDonald

AARON TAYLOR

Pictures I like:

1. *naked women. snapshots of people when they were kids*
2. *my friends. people screaming*
3. *famous people looking bad and drugged out. any picture with Brigitte Bardot in it*
4. *famous people running from photographers. the moon*
5. *musicians in black and white. really big pictures*

—BRUCE MCDONALD[1]

IT MIGHT AS WELL BE A CHECKLIST. Any given work by Bruce McDonald will be an exercise in audaciousness and scale, in which raving lunatics, nostalgic romantics, fading rock stars, desperate and wasted celebrities, intimately familiar faces, and beauteous exhibitionists are all set adrift and floating through their own personal (and sometimes literal) lunar landscapes. To the popular press he's Canada's "Outlaw Filmmaker." Nearly every journalist makes note of the prominent false tooth, the perennial scruff, the ubiquitous cowboy hat (worn by various characters in nearly all of his films from 1996 on). None of them fail to mention "the big chunk of hash" he promised to buy with his $25,000 prize for Best Canadian Feature at the 1989 Toronto International Film Festival. The image serves a purpose, standing out in an otherwise nondescript landscape of bland English-Canadian filmmakers (the vaguely nerdy personae of the grand triumvirate—Cronenberg, Egoyan, and McKellar—being a collective case in point). McDonald, quite simply, is a character. Showman, rebel, *enfant terrible*, rock n' roll *auteur*, these various guises are instrumental in both selling and attracting much-needed (and deserved) popular attention to his vibrant hybrids of underground dynamism and pop virtuosity.

Perhaps the cultivation of this persona accounts for the severity of the criticism levelled at much of his work. After hearing that McDonald and producer Colin Brunton had secured funding for their second feature, *Highway 61* (1991), John Harkness of NOW magazine wrote: "Giving these guys a million dollars to make a film is like giving a loaded pistol to a six-year-old."[2] Critics attacked *Picture Claire* (2001) with a singular vehemence: *Eye Weekly*'s Jason Anderson was particularly harsh, calling the film "a dog's breakfast of convenient coincidences, noir clichés and easy art-world satire."[3] A ten-million-dollar debacle, the film is still invoked as the Canadian epitome of misguided ambition on a grand scale—its disastrous commercial failure was widely blamed for Alliance Atlantis's subsequent retreat from feature production. And yet, McDonald is his own worst critic. In *Claire's Hat* (2002), his hilarious and heartfelt film essay on *Picture Claire*, McDonald asserts with brusque magnanimity, "I fucked up my own movie." At the same time, his shouldering of the entire burden of responsibility is hardly equitable—especially considering screenwriter Semi Challas's poor plotting and producer Robert Lantos's insistence on casting third-tier American "stars" in the principal roles.

Undoubtedly, McDonald has helmed his share of unsatisfactory projects, but it would be a mistake to interpret the redirection of his creative energies toward television as a form of retreat. In fact, he has reinvented himself as a superlative director of high-quality and inventive television programming. Witness his live-to-air teleplay for CityTV *American Whisky Bar* (1998), the critically lauded comedy series *Twitch City* (1998–2000) for CBC, the experimental Robbie Robertson documentary *Road Songs* (2001), and his outstanding work directing episodes of *Degrassi: The Next Generation* and *Queer as Folk*. Despite these achievements, an implicit air of condescension pervades most critical discussions of his work—a smug assumption that he has been expelled from the limelight of feature film production to the hinterlands of television. Nearly every article in the popular press that mentions McDonald refers to him as "the director of *Hard Core Logo* (1996)," his last major commercial and critical success.

But to characterize him as an also-ran is not merely to overlook his most recent accomplishments. Indeed, his latest film, *The Love Crimes of Gillian Guess* (2004) is perhaps his most ambitious work to date. Such arch dismissals also reveal certain firmly entrenched biases in Canadian film criticism. While his work is certainly not invariably unproblematic, the single-mindedness of the critical attacks against McDonald seems to situate the director as "the victim of the success of the art-film movement in Canada."[4] And yet to label him a victim of English Canada's supposed preference for middlebrow, boutique cinema is doubly unprofitable. Such criticism corroborates the positioning of an *auteur*-driven "national" cinema as the ideal benchmark for measuring a work's "success" or value and also creates a false antinomy between the "popular" and the "refined." What should be emphasized instead is how McDonald's use and exploration of popular forms is central to his achievements as an artist. Indeed, what makes his films interesting is the intersection of pop and experimental proclivities, resulting in a consistent critical investigation of North American popular culture.

McDonald's best works are more than mere exercises in adolescent iconoclasm—tipping various international sacred cows such as British punk romanticism, the American road mythos, and the Canadian Griersonian tradition. His films are informed by and explore American pop culture, but are not mere mediations on Canadian-American relations. Borderlines and dualities haunt his work, usually serving as sites of confrontation. Thresholds are often places of instability, even violence, in his films, and such anxious liminality accounts for a number of things: the recurring appearance of characters who are on the verge of self-transformation but do not always successfully reinvent themselves; the director's own preoccupation with the interchanges between film and reality; a penchant for probing the boundaries of documentary; the inspired tensions between classical aesthetics and formal experimentation (the structure of most of his work seems informed by rock and roll). It is a cinema of perpetual motion, dissatisfied with and suspicious of precincts and stasis, in which the peripheries are the filmmaker's distinctive territory.

■ McDonald and the Toronto New Wave

McDONALD EMERGED as one of the most prominent directors from the generation of filmmakers that Wyndham Wise and Cameron Bailey (in a nationalistic spirit) have dubbed "the Toronto New Wave": a group of filmmakers who produced their first work in or around Toronto in the mid-1980s and achieved mainstream success by the early 1990s. Atom Egoyan, Don McKellar, and Patricia Rozema emerged on the scene at this time. High-profile documentarians Peter Lynch, Ron Mann, and Alan Zweig made their first films. Srinivas Krishna, Deepa Metha, and Clement Virgo offered alternatives to the WASP hegemony. Daring and aggressive queer polemics were introduced by John Greyson and Bruce LaBruce. Peter Mettler, Jeremy Podeswa, and David Wellington also produced notable debuts. Collectively, the Toronto New Wave turned its back on traditionalist representations of urban Canada, contributing to the formation of a recognizable national cinema that finally made its presence known in the international market.

This new wave was "urban, intimate, underdog, migrant. Educated and art-fuelled. Not political. Not commercial. And not literary."[5] It strove to produce works that were often intensely personal or, at least, resolutely unconventional, and it resisted the ethnographic impulses of National Film Board productions, as well as the grindhouse mentality of corporate filmmaking at the time. As a result, the filmmakers associated with the movement initially found themselves on the margins of the local industry. In 1982 the Toronto Festival of Festivals rejected McDonald's and Egoyan's student films, "Let Me See..." and "Open House." Hoping to attract an audience leaving a Fassbinder gala, they projected their films with a rented generator and a 16mm projector on the sidewalk by a store next to the Uptown Theatre's ticket window. CityTV arrived with a film crew and covered the tuxedoed hucksters' attempts to draw in the crowds. It would only be a handful of years before Egoyan and McDonald enjoyed their own respective places in the sun: *Family Viewing* would win Best Canadian Feature Film at the festival in 1987, and *Roadkill* scandalously beat out *Jesus of Montreal* for the same prize in 1989. *Roadkill* also marked the screenwriting and acting debut of McDonald's most frequent collaborator, Don McKellar, who catapulted to fame soon afterward.

McDonald is undoubtedly the new wave's most vocal cheerleader, passionately championing the work of his colleagues as frequently and noisily as possible. Originally from Kingston, Ontario, he began experimenting with Brownie 8mm cameras during his adolescence in the Toronto suburbs of Rexdale. An early love of horror inspired the no-budget zombie short that he filmed with his friends, and some of his amateur work was screened at the 1978 Toronto Super-8 Film Festival. While enrolled with Peter Mettler in Ryerson University's film program, he produced his first serious works, the short films "Merge" and "Let Me See." Although denied acceptance to the Toronto Festival, the latter would win the Norman Jewison Award for Best Student Film at the 1982 CNE, while McDonald simultaneously threw himself into the development and promotion of the emerging independent scene. Ron Mann gave him his first industry job as a production assistant on *Poetry in Motion* (1982), his sophomore feature documentary that presents spoken word performances by and interviews with such sub-cultural giants as Charles Bukowski, William Burroughs, John Cage, Allen Ginsberg, and Tom Waits.

During these crucial formative years, McDonald helped to found the Liaison of Independent Filmmakers of Toronto (LIFT), serving on its board of directors for three years. A non-profit film cooperative dedicated to assist aspiring filmmakers through access to equipment, workshops, and production grants, LIFT was established in 1981 and still functions as one of the best sources for peer networking in Canada today. McDonald virtually lived there while working on sound for Mettler's *Scissere* (1982)— a film he still cites as being one of the major influences on his early work.[6] Establishing himself as an editor of considerable ingenuity, he would co-edit many defining new wave films, including Egoyan's first three features, Ron Mann's *Comic Book Confidential* (1988), Mettler's second feature, *The Top of His Head* (1989), as well as Colin Brunton's hilarious, Genie-winning short, *The Mysterious Moon Men of Canada* (1989).[7]

Given his level of involvement in the work of his contemporaries, it is unsurprising that McDonald would be the new wave's most vociferous advocate. The period between 1983 and 1988 were pivotal years for the group: most of the filmmakers produced their first major features thanks to invaluable new sources of income from the Ontario Film Development Corporation, Telefilm's Feature Film Fund, generous provincial tax credits, and grants from the Ontario Arts Council. In the fall of 1988, *Cinema Canada*'s regular editor invited him to edit the issue that became the famed "Outlaw Edition." McDonald invited his peers to promote their work in the magazine, and he himself contributed a pair of editorials, one of them challenging the CBC to provide a late-night forum for shorts by independent filmmakers.[8] "We are paving the ground for the creation of the new Canadian Feature Film," McDonald wrote, and given the number of works of impressive creativity and quality, it was hard not to be swayed by his rhetoric.[9] Animated by a seemingly ungodly work ethic, McDonald worked at LIFT and drove a cab during the day, while also writing for *Nerve* and *Cinema Canada* and directing the sixty-minute *Knock! Knock!* (1985)—a mockumentary about a character obsessed with trying to find a way for Ronald and Nancy Reagan to give him a personal tour of their bedroom. A documentary director named Bruce films his efforts, but he abandons the project during early shooting and disappears. However, the shoot still manages to continue without the director's presence. Several of McDonald's preoccupations begin to coalesce in this early work: his satirical play with elements of American pop; his distrust of the documentarian as authority figure; his representation of the filmmaker as an intrusive buffoon ("Bruce" resurfaces again in *Roadkill* and *Hard Core Logo*, and more transparently in *Fort Goof* and *Claire's Hat*).

During this critical period, he met one of his idols, Norman Jewison. McDonald had secured a job as Jewison's driver on *Agnes of God* (1984), which was being filmed around Toronto and the Rockwood area. As McDonald careened along the icy highways toward the location for the morning's shoot, Jewison would regale him with tales of Hollywood decadence and petty bitchery. In his subsequent open letter to Jewison, McDonald voiced his admiration for the director, not so much for his formal influence or continued commitment to the tradition of the social-problem film but for his professionalism and expertise in coaxing the best possible work from a diverse range of people. At the same time, McDonald took the opportunity to promote the burgeoning new wave that was "just beginning to dance" and beseeched Jewison for his assistance in providing aspiring independent filmmakers with the means to realise their ambitions.[10] Jewison seemed to take the appeal to heart: he contributed the funds McDonald needed to finish *Knock! Knock!*, personally vouched for McDonald when he and his colleague Brunton applied to the Ontario Film Development Corporation (OFDC) for $120,000 to make *Roadkill*, and hired McDonald to direct *Dance Me Outside* (1994).[11] Most important, he founded the Canadian Film Centre in 1986, an institution that provides professional training and funding to aspiring filmmakers.

■ *Roadkill* (1989)

McDONALD'S FIRST COMMERCIAL FEATURE began as a documentary about Toronto post-punk favourites, A Neon Rome. After lead singer and avowed Buddhist Neil Arbic took a vow of silence before principal photography had started, McKellar was brought on board to help transform the film into a feature instead. What followed was the first instalment of McDonald's unofficial "road trilogy" and the film that made his reputation: *Roadkill* (originally titled, "All the Children Are In" to help secure funding from potential backers who might be turned off by a film named after furry roadside casualties). The film was budgeted at $198,924 and shot with a crew of ten in thirteen days. It was printed just in time for its debut at the Toronto Film Festival and distributed by Cinephile—an independent company run by Andre Bennett, who had marketed early features by Egoyan, Mettler, Rozema, and Krishna.

Valerie Buhagiar stars as Ramona, an intern for ruthless rock promoter Roy Seth, who orders her to track down the Children of Paradise—a band who have gone AWOL from their tour of Ontario.[12] Unable to drive, Ramona has never ventured north of Toronto. During her quasi-odyssey over the course of an Easter weekend, she is assisted by (and receives driving lessons from) several guides: Buddy (Larry Hudson), a cabbie who may have been the driver for a number of rock's biggest icons (Joey Ramone tries to get a lift from him at the film's end); Bruce Shack (Bruce McDonald), a gonzo filmmaker who is supposed to be filming the Children but finds Ramona a more interesting subject; Russell (Don McKellar), an aspiring serial killer who condemns rock 'n' roll as "an act of violence"; Luke (Mark Tarantino), a fifteen-year-old with whom she finds paradise by the dashboard light in an abandoned drive-in; and finally, the missing singer, Matthew (Shaun Bowring), who is silently seeking transcendence.

Ramona eventually rounds up the band—and learns to drive—but in the film's surreal climax, they are all blown away during their final gig by a gun-toting Seth (he also executes Bruce and Russell for good measure). The animus between corporate and artistic interests that McDonald articulates in his promotion of the new wave thus animates his feature-length debut (as well as his later projects, *Hard Core Logo* and *Platinum*). "Ramona! Tomorrow morning at the office," Seth orders after the massacre. "Nine o'clock. Don't be late." But the crowd isn't interested in suits; they're here for a show, dammit. And as they bang on table tops with their beer bottles, Ramona takes the reins: "Are you feelin' alright?" she intones into the bloodied microphone. "Lemme' hear you say, 'Yeah!'" The next morning, she clambers into the car Luke has given her and drives off into the "idiot wilderness," continuing her journey through a privately mythological northern landscape, steering clear of defenceless rabbits along the way.

Roadkill is a raucous attempt to reconfigure the conventions of the road film for a local audience—part "home" movie, part generic in-joke. It is, first and foremost, McDonald's love letter to Ontario indie rock: Nash the Slash both writes the score and drives Russell into a rage with his violin-burning performance, the Leslie Spit Tree-O also has a cameo (they show up again in *Dance Me Outside*), and the soundtrack is comprised almost entirely of local acts including the Cowboy Junkies, Handsome Ned, the Sidewinders, and Suffer Machine. The late, lamented godfather of American punk and the DIY aesthetic, Joey Ramone, also contributes a song. Joey Ramone is something of a totemic figure for McDonald, and his music features prominently in the filmmaker's next three films. He even shows up to plug a reunited Hard Core Logo.

McDonald's foregrounding of local talent should not be taken as idle patriotism; it is the local, the marginal, rather than the national, that is being celebrated here. If anything, the film lampoons "official" English-Canadian culture (or its lack thereof) "by delivering an emphatically understated commentary on the absence of anything emphatic."[13] Notably, the film opens with a spoof of the Canadian Wildlife Service's *Hinterland Who's Who*, which was broadcast on Canadian TV throughout 1960s and 1970s. Accompanying a close-up of a northern cottontail, a sonorous voice-over waxes soporific on the rabbits' mysteriously "declining population" but is interrupted by Bruce's hellish Winnebago, which comes screaming along the highway like a refugee from *The Road Warrior* toward the twitchy-nosed critter. Run for your lives! It's McDonald versus the cultural establishment! When his films are considered this way, it becomes clear that McDonald is not without his politics and that they represent more than just "an intense cultural nationalism, linked to a notion of do-it-yourself self-sufficiency."[14] Nearly all of his films represent and reflect upon the frictions that arise when socially aggrieved subjects attempt to find a place for themselves within, or apart from, a hegemony. To some degree, all of them touch upon issues of class, race, ethnicity, and gender, as well as the power differential that exists between those who serve and those who eat.

Rebellion, the circumvention of authority, and defiant self-definition are all staples of the road film. The genre typically sets up a tension between the ideological poles of individualism and populism and also "use[s] the road to imagine the nation's culture" as either homogenous and coherent or irreconcilably disconnected and reactionary.[15] Given that Canadian highways stretch across a cultural landscape that has always been heterogeneous and fragmentary, the anxieties driving American cult classics like *Easy Rider* (1969) and *Two Lane Blacktop* (1971) do not necessarily apply here, or at least, not in the same ways. On the one hand, the genre is well-suited for exploring the margins of North American society, and we might point to the number of outlaw and counter-cultural heroes that crop up in the Hollywood road movies of the late 1960s and early 1970s as evidence. If its "generic core is constituted...by a *tension* between rebellion and conformity," the manic energy of the road film is derived from the precariousness of its characters' social positions.[16] To put it more prosaically, the road movie dramatizes the circumstances of subjects who are both in search of, and fugitives from, the American Dream.

On the other hand, however, there is nothing distinctly or uniquely *American* about the journey, the image of the fugitive, nor the road movie itself. Cultural theorists might claim that "the road movie is...like the musical or the Western, a Hollywood genre that catches peculiarly American dreams, tensions, and anxieties, even when imported by the motion picture industries of other nations," but there is no reason for imperialistic claims of this kind.[17] Given the fundamentally diasporic aspect of Canada's cultural identity, the road movie is perhaps well suited to represent the exilic and migrant impulses within our (loosely knit) national fabric. In turn, however, it seems altogether too colonial for critics like Geoff Pevere to forward the counterclaim that the road movie is "a deeply Canuck form," if only for the number of canonical works that loosely adhere to the generic description.[18] Similarly, Katherine Monk's assessment of the Canadian road film is marred by fatuous comparative analysis with Hollywood product: "where the classic romantic road movie shows us men or women finding a sense of newfound freedom, the Canadian road movie shows us men or women learning all about the impossibility of escape."[19] Even the most cursory of surveys through the history of Hollywood road films should reveal that Canada hardly has a monopoly on failure and disenchantment. In the vast majority of road movies, Canadian or otherwise, the Grail object at the end of the teleological quest narrative is never achieved.[20]

Such failures, interruptions, or renunciations are typical in McDonald's work. In his films, the road is configured as both a *tabula rasa* and a mythological space that exists within ideology, and at the same time, outside of it. It is an (un)place where the individual is able to experience mobility in shaping her identity since she is not rooted to any geographic location, and the concept of "centre" is continually being displaced. Ramona is the first of McDonald's protagonists to attempt an escape from the prison house of a received subjectivity. In a montage sequence, she tries on various outfits Bruce's miscreant film crew have stolen for her, but she will eventually choose a look of her own. After applying her makeup in a Thunder Bay motel, she etches a minimalist, lipstick self-portrait on the bathroom mirror. Her signature: "RAMONA LIVES!"

■ *Highway 61* (1991)

GIVEN HIS FILMS' TENDENCY to promote the circumvention of binary logic in the formation of self-identity, it is ironic that scholars often characterize McDonald's next film, *Highway 61*, as a meditation on Canadian–American relations. Originally titled "Blonde on Black" (a nod to Bob Dylan's seminal *Blonde on Blonde*), it had a projected cost of $222,689, but as the project developed, McDonald and Brunton eventually produced the film for $1.48 million with funding from the OFDC, Telefilm, The Canada Council for the Arts, Britain's Channel 4 and Cineplex (which also marketed the film in Canada).[21] McDonald's initial idea to trace the genealogy of American popular music along the famed stretch of highway that runs from Thunder Bay to New Orleans evolved from an experimental history to a classically structured road flick.[22] Buhagiar and McKellar return as Jackie Bangs (a professed "fugitive from a heavy-metal road crew" and Wilmington, Manitoba, native) and Pokey Jones (a barber and would-be cornet player from Pickerel Falls, Ontario). Soon after Pokey finds a frozen corpse in his backyard, Jackie arrives in Pickerel Falls with a pouch full of stolen cocaine. Claiming the corpse, "Jeffrey," is her brother, Jackie stuffs it with the dope at the local mortuary, and guilt-trips the naïve Pokey into giving her a ride to New Orleans with the coffin lashed to the top of his 1966 Ford Galaxie-500 (inherited from his dead parents, but never taken out of the driveway). Pokey uses the opportunity to leave Pickerel Falls for the first time and trace out his beloved history of American pop music firsthand.[23] Along the way, they are pursued by Mr. Skin (Earl Pastko), a psychopath who believes he is the devil and is intent upon snatching "Jeffrey" in order to claim his soul.

Out of all of McDonald's films, *Highway 61* has attracted the most attention from film scholars. Academics typically interpret the film according to a post-colonial paradigm as a straightforward criticism of the American Empire's cultural bankruptcy. George Melnyk, for example, finds that "no other English-Canadian film of the 1990s spoke so critically of the escape-from-Canada mindset, so favourably of its down-home Canadian naïveté, and so confidently of the importance of being un-American."[24] Similarly, Rochelle Simmons believes that the film draws distinctions between a vulgar, consumerist monoculture and an innocent, introspective, and pluralist (albeit colonial) culture.[25] But the film is not just another fantasy of "our" resistance to those tawdrily seductive southern "others," *à la My American Cousin* (1985). Certainly, the scrap yards of Minnesota that cinematographer Miroslaw Baszak (another McDonald regular) captures in putrescent detail undermines Pokey's wonderstruck narration, but they are no more attractive than what passes for the downtown core in Pickerel Falls. Christopher Gittings is closer to the mark when he argues that McDonald demonstrates how the American cultural terrain is unavoidably imbricated within the Canadian imagination, that "the presence of its iconography in physical and psychic Canadian landscapes can become naturalized and is not always readily recognizable as something foreign."[26]

What this means is that *Highway 61* represents American pop music, "not simply a colonizing force but a force that blends and is transformed by its context of reception."[27] Like *Roadkill*, the film is a tribute to popular music but makes several clever inversions: Nash the Slash provides a southern blues-inflected score; Van-punk pioneer Art Bergmann plays a reclusive, chicken-shooting rock star; and ex-Dead Kennedys frontman, Jello Biafra, is featured in a cameo as an over-zealous border guard. McDonald's signatory foregrounding of intertexual elements is particularly inspired here. The substantial rhetorical significance freighted by each performer serves to undermine the cultural "authority" of American music. With a Toronto prog-rocker playing the blues, an elder statesman of Vancouver punk masquerading as an American pop icon, and a political dissident representing Yankee homeland security, it becomes clear that US rock 'n' roll is being celebrated *and* appropriated by Canadian subjects seeking to carve out their own personal identities. It is significant that Pokey's French-Canadian pal, Claude (Johnny Askwith), declares that his cover band performs both Guns n' Roses and BTO (or, "Bay Tay Oh," as Claude puts it), just as it is noteworthy that Pokey's own musical talents finally emerge when he plays a Dixieland dirge during "Jeffrey's" bayou funeral. For McDonald, borders are not boundaries that constrain, but thresholds to be traversed.

■ *Dance Me Outside* (1995)

WHAT, THEN, might we make of McDonald's follow-up film, the straightforwardly earnest *Dance Me Outside*? Set on the fictional Kidiabinessee Reserve outside of Parry Sound, the film is a condensation of a number of short stories by W.P. Kinsella from the book of the same name. It is yet another *bildungsfilm* of sorts, with a teenaged Silas Crow (Ryan Rajendra

Black) writing about a number of events in his community in order to gain entrance into a Toronto mechanics' school. Maintaining McDonald's reliance on voice-over narration as a structural device, Silas offers a first-person account of the circumstances that surround the rape and murder of another teen, Little Margaret (Tamara Podemski). When the perpetrator, a local white thug named Clarence Gaskill (Hugh Dillon), is convicted on a charge of manslaughter and released a mere two years later, Silas and his best friend, Frank Fencepost (Adam Beach), plan revenge.

One of the film's most ambitious aspects is its aspiration to address sensitive issues of race as well as gender within a commercial forum (Jewison's influence is evident here). Indeed, although the narrative is usually focalized through the male characters, the community is clearly held together by a very resourceful matriarchy. In a major subplot, for example, Silas's sister, Illianna (Lisa LaCroix), conspires to become pregnant without the help of her impotent white husband, Robert McVey (Kevin Hicks). Just as meaningfully, it is Silas's sometimes girlfriend, Sadie Maracle (Jennifer Podemski), who attempts to politicize the community, and even organizes several young women to pre-empt the men's efforts at vengeance: they slit Gaskill's throat themselves. The film's decision to represent the sizeable difficulties inherent in collective political mobilization is quite brave. After activist Hobart Thunder (Vince Manitowabi) gives a speech at the community centre, Silas and Frank trash his car by mistake. More pointedly, the "Feds" whom they thought were harassing Thunder turn out to be part of his act.

Strangely enough, however, critics frequently call McDonald to task on what they perceive to be his apolitical tendencies. McDonald himself has commented that he wanted "to try and make a teenage movie rather than try to position [Dance] as some kind of movie about Native life."[28] Accordingly, in his assessment of the film as an adaptation, Bart Beaty claims that McDonald "has sacrificed the social significance of the source book in order to reach the broadest possible audience," and even the Canadian Film Encyclopaedia entry on the film claims that it is "less concerned with politics than with people."[29] The debatable status of Kinsella's book's "social significance" aside, Beaty's argument is founded upon questionable assumptions that popular film is inherently apolitical. He finds that in moving toward domestic melodrama and away from the author's unornamented prose style, McDonald depoliticizes the material. But why should the latter be conceived as more suitable, or more political, than the former? Claims of this kind are in keeping with the old guard's insubstantial and elitist preference for the documentary, the avant-garde, the realist film, and the art cinema (echoing the manifestos of John Grierson in the 1940s, and those of Bruce Elder, Peter Harcourt, and Peter Morris in the 1980s).

The film's seemingly simple classical orientation is quite deceptive, then. Even its gentle lampooning of white liberalism is not as straightforward as it seems. In order to preoccupy McVey while Illianna attempts to conceive with her former lover, Gooch (Michael Greyeyes), Silas and Frank invite him to a hilarious "Indian Naming Ceremony" of their own invention. There, the white defence lawyer discovers his inner "animal spirit" ("I AM THE WOLVERINE!" he shrieks) and is dubbed "Bob Firechief," while Silas, Frank, Wendel, and Pete dance around him, singing, "Hey-ya-Yah-ya!" But while Gittings characterizes McVey's interaction with Illianna's family as an example of a "pathetic and impotent colonial gaze," the "Naming Ceremony" sequence is more complex than a mere critique of compromised liberal humanism.[30] Gittings fails to note the rather remarkable sequence that occurs immediately afterward. McVey rushes into the woods, followed by the boys—their pseudo-chanting giving way to cries of real exuberance. On the soundtrack, the Royal Scots Dragoon Guards haul out the bagpipes and strings, and "Amazing Grace" plays over tracking shots of running, silhouetted men and close-ups of flaming torches. Meanwhile, McDonald cross-cuts these shots with Illianna and Gooch's tryst ("Please don't love me," she implores). They reach mutual climax just as McVey hurls himself off of a cliff into the water, with Illianna's moans heard overtop of his descent. Silas and Frank delightedly follow. This Scottish military hymn forms a kind of musical bridge between two cultures, with mockery giving way to brief harmony and the shadow of assimilation momentarily dispelled (Ma Crow will become a grandmother after all).

But the sophistication of the sequence does not end there. Gooch drops Illianna off at home, and abruptly proclaims, "I don't love you." Her reply, "I know," is tenderly sardonic, while the magisterial bagpipes of the Royal Scots give way to the cedar flute of the Navajo-Ute musician, R.

Carlos Nakai. "Amazing Grace" becomes elegiac here, its emancipatory associations brought to the foreground. Just as Gooch is now free of his combined envy of and contempt for Illianna's marriage and social position, McVey has shed the cultural inhibitions that prevent him from truly engaging with Illianna's family. In a brief insert, a curious racoon noses his discarded glasses, as if to signify his emergence from the blinkered world of Bay Street. McVey even wins the respect of Frank and Silas: the three of them belt out Cher's (inexplicable) hit, "Half Breed," in Silas's truck on the way home, and they voice their admiration to Illianna after depositing her husband on the Crows' front porch. "You should've seen this guy," Frank grins, and Silas agrees, "He was pretty cool." McVey surveys the night sky with newfound wonder as he nestles in her lap, and she kisses him with no small measure of affection. We fade out on a starlit sky that shines down on lawyers and braves alike with equal magnanimity.

■ Hard Core Logo (1996)

McDONALD'S ADAPTATION of Michael Turner's experimental novel Hard Core Logo also explores characters who are marginalized by "respectable" society—this time, his focus is on the white, male underclass of punk rock. Just as Roadkill is a tribute to the Ontario indie scene, Hard Core Logo is a heartfelt, but unromantic, ode to Vancouver punk. Tremendous Canadian punk was being produced on the west coast in the late 1970s and early 1980s by the Modernettes, No Means No, the Pointed Sticks, the Young Canadians (of whom Art Bergmann was a member), and the most influential of them all: D.O.A. Turner's experimental novel is loosely inspired by D.O.A.'s exploits—Joey Shithead is clearly the model for the Hard Core's Joe Dick (Headstones' ex-frontman Hugh Dillon)—and the band makes an appearance in the film, playing a set at HCL's reunion gig. McDonald adapts the book as a pseudo-documentary, calling the film "Spinal Tap's mean little brother."[31] To help perpetuate the illusion of authenticity, the DVD release includes a mock fanzine and tribute album.

McDonald's recurrent conceit of the filmmaker as interloper is at its most sophisticated here. Playing himself, he and his film crew document Hard Core Logo's reunion tour: the loutish Pipefitter (Bernie Coulson) on drums, the schizophrenic John Oxenberger (John Pyper-Ferguson) on bass, rock star wannabe Billy Tallent (Callum Keith-Rennie) on lead guitar, indefatigable powerhouse and all-round asshole Joe Dick on rhythm guitar and vox. Their tour is ostensibly in support of their mentor, punk legend, Bucky Haight (a regally emaciated Julian Richings), who they claim had his leg shot off in a robbery attempt. Along the road, the band begins to self-destruct: a pair of groupies make off with their cash; John forgets his medication and suffers a mental breakdown; Bucky disowns Joe for exploiting him; and Billy secretly plans to abandon Joe to play in an up-and-coming LA band, Jenifur. The Hard Cores continually antagonize the film crew with their confrontational attitude, and a fed-up "Bruce" seeks payback. Betraying Billy's confidence, the director breaks the news of Billy's imminent departure to Joe before their final gig. After rounding off their set with, "Something's Gonna' Die Tonight," Joe goes berserk: he attacks Billy and subsequently shoots himself in the head outside the club.

The film offers an embarrassment of riches for Canadian film scholars predisposed to thematic analysis. Perennial favourites include the depiction of failed masculinity and the tragedy of arrested development, the representation of both urban and natural landscapes as hostile and alienating, the siren song of American glamour vs. the folkish warbling of Canadian integrity (or, as Joe puts it, "Billy wants the models and limousines; I'm happy with the taxi cabs and hookers"). But McDonald is not interested in simply re-treading Can-Lit clichés; two of his own authorial preoccupations crystallize in *Hard Core Logo*: the moral interrogation of the documentary impulse and the agonies of attempted self-transformation.

It is significant that the director is situated as a disembodied voice that only speaks off-camera. The filmmaker physically absents himself from the events he records, as a consequence, abandons his ethical responsibility to the situations he is complicit in creating. Just as Bruce Shack violates Ramona's privacy by filming her as she sleeps (a situation that recurs in *Picture Claire*), and harasses her to appear in his "movie about *real* life," so too does *Hard Core Logo*'s "Bruce" violate the trust that the various band members attempt to establish with him. It is as if McDonald is exposing the contradictions implicit in the so-called non-judgementalism of American direct cinema, or, closer to home, Alan King's self-congratulatory attempts at empathy in *Warrendale* (1967) and *A Married Couple* (1969).

This particular "Bruce" either vengefully violates King's (morally questionable) non-interventionist principles or takes them to absurdly irresponsible lengths: rather than helping John find his lost medication, he merely continues to shoot the distraught bass player tearing through his suitcase. The film is, in some sense, a cautionary tale to filmmakers working in the tradition of direct cinema—a metaphoric application of the uncertainty principle to documentary ethics: the observation of an event will change the nature of the event observed.

McDonald also documents the unhealthy insularity of a protracted adolescence, as all of the characters are victims of their inability to change. One lyrical vignette encapsulates each of the characters' personal pathologies in a succession of brief close-ups. As their rented van chunders along the highway, John's voiceover is heard, contemplating the compulsion that drives men to continue using juvenile punk monikers into their mid-thirties. A statuette of the Virgin Mary encapsulated in a broken plastic bubble is stuck to the dash—a bleeding heart exposed to the poisoned air. She is juxtaposed with a curling trophy, slightly out of focus in the foreground, as the median lines roll past through the windshield. The image evokes teenage dreams of success and affirmation forever out of reach.

Billy lounges in the back, laughing at Chester Brown's wry, but heartbreaking comic about the hopelessness of pubescent love, I Never Liked You.[32] Over a hand-held close-up of keys lodged dutifully in the ignition, John wonders at what age the "boys" will stop using their punk handles: "Forty? Fifty? Sixty?" Needless to say, Joe will crash the car, so to speak, long before the engine refuses to turn over, and he turns his head from driving to glance at Billy—that obscure object of his desire. Cut to the back of Pipefitter's head and then to an extreme close-up of his dangling hand as he sleeps, oblivious to the world as always. John is sure that Pipe "can't even remember his real name." As he writes in his diary, John (ever the thankless bassist) notes that he was never able to find a suitable handle for himself. "Maybe I never had a self to throw away like those guys," he muses as a lap dissolve to the rushing landscape obliterates him from view. We close with an abstract view of trees merging into an indistinguishable blur through the passenger window, and Billy takes up the voice-over, declaring, "After a certain age, it's hard to make friends, and I've known Joe since I was thirteen, and I love him more than anyone I've met since." This admission stands in sharp relief to the last exchange between he and Joe: Billy contemptuously spitting bloody phlegm into his friend's face, Joe half-raising a bottle and two glasses to Billy's retreating back in a final, pathetic, conciliatory gesture.

The film is usually regarded as McDonald's best work.[33] At the very least, it marks a turning point in his aesthetics. *Roadkill* was a scruffy, 8mm paean to DIY moviemaking in black and white, shot through with low-fi surrealist flourishes, but *Hard Core Logo* is a bonanza of visual tomfoolery. McDonald and his collaborators mix colour and black and white stocks; manufacture "found" Super-8 footage of early band performances; concoct a wild "acid" sequence; employ complex dissolves, superimpositions, and graphic inserts; and play around with various split-screen effects on the Avid.[34] His early skills as an editor are evident here. Of all his contemporaries, McDonald is probably the most daring in his use of montage, with a yen for odd juxtapositions, sudden interruptions within the linear flow of time, and violent insertions of text or graphic effects. Fittingly, then, his next film would be a *tour de force* of split-screen hyperactivity and rapid-fire montage.

■ *Picture Claire* (2001)

WHATEVER ELSE one might make of *Picture Claire*, the film makes for delirious eye candy. Miroslaw Baszak's cinematography transforms Kensington Market into a neon-drenched fever dream. More impressively, at several critical junctures in the plot, the image is shattered into dozens of overlapping, miniscule frames that cover the action from a variety of angles and distances before gradually being replaced by images from the succeeding scene. The dizzying aesthetics are well suited to the fish-out-of-water story, which represents Toronto from the perspective of Claire Beaucage (Juliette Lewis), a monolingual Québécoise on the run. Fleeing from a violent ex-boyfriend in East Montreal, Claire arrives in the Kensington district in search of Billy (Kelly Harms), a photographer who impulsively invited her to live with him in Toronto after a one-night stand. When she accidentally becomes involved in the aftermath of a jewel heist, the film descends into the narrative convolutions of *film noir*.

Billy's neighbour, Lily (Gina Gershon), is one of the heist's perpetrators, and in a reverse-double-cross, she murders her partner, Eddie (Mickey Rourke), in a donut shop and makes off with his share of the diamonds. To add to the turmoil, she is pursued by a pair of hitmen intent on recovering the loot. While merely trying to reunite with Billy, Claire finds herself a murder suspect, the accidental recipient of some hot rocks, and the unwitting target of one of the contract killers, Laramie (Callum Keith-Rennie). At the film's climax, the misogynist goon shoots Lily dead but is in turn blown away by Claire. Tired of Toronto's nightmarish hostility at this point, Claire leaves a befuddled Billy with a kiss (and the hat she appropriated from Lily) and heads off to sunnier climes.

What is of interest here is the way in which the narrative can be viewed through various overlapping lenses—cultural, commercial, and formal. To begin with, one might read Claire's exploits as separatist fantasy. As the narrative is predominantly focalized through Claire, Toronto is accordingly represented as a madhouse full of violent, ineffectual Anglos who are openly hostile toward her broken attempts at communication, if not outright intolerant of her presence. Her hopeless "dialogue" with an attendant at Union Station sets the tone for bicultural relations throughout the entire film: her request for a "lock-air" to store her baggage is met with total incomprehension. It is little wonder that she prefers her private dreamscapes to Hogtown. At several points she imagines herself a Debussian waif adrift on a sovereign lunar satellite.

And yet, such a reading must be circumscribed by the conditions of production. For Claire is notably *not* "authentically" French Canadian. In keeping with Hollywood business mentality, producer Robert Lantos prioritized commercial interests over narrative plausibility in casting a well-known Californian as Claire. Restricting Lewis's dialogue to a handful of lines is not so much a comment on the repression of Québécois culture in Canada as it is a technical necessity. Moreover, the grafting of a Hollywood caper plot onto a narrative whose subtext might otherwise have concerned itself with the specifically Canadian politics of intercultural romance reveals the short-sightedness of the producers. The assumption here is that Canadian audiences prefer familiar generic conventions to art that addresses local concerns. Lantos's desire to produce a popular thriller that can be sold to American markets trumps whatever use-value the caper plot may have to the film as a politically inflected work of art. This is not so much an example of the colonized imagination at work as it is a willing subservience to a commercial market dominated by the majors. The results are kaleidoscopic: American actors playing Canadian characters created by Canadian filmmakers working in an American mode in the hopes of appealing to a Canadian audience accustomed to American films. It is absolutely fitting that McDonald frequently applies a split-screen technique that breaks the singular frame in *Picture Claire* into a multitude of conflicting, schizoid images.

Admittedly, the $10-million production was a box-office fiasco, and McDonald takes much of the blame upon his shoulders in his Godardian follow-up documentary, *Claire's Hat*. Although he is not above slinging a little mud at "Darth" Lantos and playfully reads *Picture Claire* as an allegory of his relationship with the super-producer, the disaster is not entirely of his making. In many ways, a film like *Picture Claire* is doomed from its very conception. Geoff Pevere has pointed out that Canadian popular genre films are not appraised according to their own merits, nor situated within the larger context of a national cinema, but instead "are routinely hauled by Canadian critics onto the Hollywood chopping block and there condemned to death for failing to measure up."[35] This condition is in keeping with what Jim Leach calls "the aesthetics of failure"—a formal tendency of Canadian cinema to allude to Hollywood product and the European art cinema, which only draws viewers' attention to our cinema's inability to imitate these cultural juggernauts satisfactorily.[36] Certainly the blinkered vision of Canadian mini-major distributors cannot help matters either. Alliance Atlantis owns the rights to *Claire's Hat* and allows McDonald to screen the film privately, but ironically, the current executive chairman, Michael MacMillan, refuses to distribute it, a decision that effectively prevents the documentary from helping to recoup any of *Picture Claire*'s lost costs.[37]

■ *The Love Crimes of Gillian Guess* (2004)

McDONALD'S LATEST (and most sophisticated) feature film is *The Love Crimes of Gillian Guess*. The film is loosely based on the story of the real-life Gillian Guess, a female jurist in Vancouver who was found guilty of obstruction of justice in 1998 and sentenced to eighteen months in prison after having an affair with accused killer, Peter Gill. Commissioned by Vancouver's Force Four Entertainment (to whom Guess sold the rights to her story) and written by Angus Fraser (of *Kissed* fame), *Love Crimes* was originally intended as a TV movie for CHUM-City, but blossomed into a $3-million spectacle. Joely Collins (daughter of a certain ex-frontman for Genesis) tears into the role of Guess, appearing on a late-night Vancouver talk show that just might be one of the circles of hell. It is hosted by the Mephistophelean Bobby Tomahawk (a perfectly cast Hugh Dillon), who engages Guess in caustic repartee as she offers a fantasy version of her affair with Gill (Ben Bass, who steals each and every scene he appears in). However, as the show drags on, her self-assured bluster falters and oblique images of a past enshrined in pain and loss begin to emerge. The film debuted to favourable notices at the 2004 Toronto International Film Festival and has been picked up for distribution by Montreal indie Cinema Libre after being overlooked by both Alliance Atlantis and ThinkFilm (of which Robert Lantos is 50 per cent owner).

Love Crimes is not your average movie-of-the-week. It is certainly a far cry from McDonald's previous true-life tale of transgressive femininity, *Scandalous Me: The Jacqueline Susann Story* (1998). Rather than fall back on the representational norms that CTV executives insisted upon for *Scandalous Me*, McDonald subjects the classical discourse of televisual melodrama to violent, Brechtian dislocations. McDonald and *Hard Core Logo* DOP Danny Nowak mix formats wildly again, using overexposed 35mm for the fantasy sequences, degraded 16mm for those taking place in Gillian's recent past and adolescence, and 8mm shot through gelatine-smeared glass for her secreted memories of childhood that are brutally wrenched into the light. Graphic intertitles burst onto the screen like percussive bombs. Frequent mickey-mousing sound effects in the courtroom and on the Bobby Tomahawk show link the two arenas of judgment as modern-day coliseums. An extended animated sequence represents murder as hyper-violent enter-tainment for the masses. Gill's seduction of Guess in a fast-food restaurant is transfigured into music-video romance, with a little help from Josh Rouse's "Feel the Love Vibration" (the pair dance in their jammies and play guitar on the moon as babies pop out of craters). McDonald's penchant for using intertextual material to comment upon the action is even more exaggerated here: Gillian's son, Alan, watches Mario Bava's *Black Sunday* (1960) on the television; and the infamous shot of a mask of spikes being hammered into a woman's face suddenly fills the entire screen. Most impressive of all is the editing, which surges back and forth through time in angry fits and starts. The aggro-aesthetics of Oliver Stone and Quentin Tarantino come to mind here, but so, too, does that of Godard and his meditations on gender as a constructed social position and on cinema itself.

Love Crimes's most fascinating aspect is the way in which elements of Gillian's fantasies of self-transformation from working-class single mother to glamour queen are gradually revealed to be constructed from moments of past trauma. These buried instances, however, begin to intrude upon her fantasy world and threaten its very integrity. A friend from her adolescence, who commits suicide after an unwanted pregnancy, continually reappears, as does a man who is eventually revealed to be Gillian's estranged father. The line, "I'm dangerous; men like that," initially serves as her credo but recurs in more and more degrading situations, until its origins are revealed—a nine-year-old Gillian (Jessica Amlee) finds her mother drunk in the kitchen following her husband's departure, wearing the leopard-print halter top her daughter will favour when she grows up. Recalling the symmetries that Dorothy establishes between real and fantasy worlds in *The Wizard of Oz* (that most archetypal of road movies), *Love Crimes* demonstrates the inexorability of the Real even within the most elaborately imaginative attempts at escape.

Toward the end of the film, the young Gillian is left abandoned in the desolation of her father's wake, framed between the vertical thrust of skeletal trees. The camera pulls back to an extreme long shot, and she is barely visible in the grey oblivion at the edge of Stanley Park. With a shock cut, we are in the interior of the present-day Gillian's car, and this is the first time she is filmed without the lens of fantasy—all caked foundation, tacky lip-liner, and cheap dress suits. There is little connection between the little girl of the previous scene and the woman revealed here. Following Bobby Tomahawk's final assessment—that Gillian yearns for the brightness of spotlights and flashbulbs as a retreat from the "cold empty spaces" of loss and failure—the narrative discourse begins to wind backwards. Multiple images of Gillian are glimpsed, fragmented and contradictory. There is violence here akin to the steel of a knife slicing through an onion's layered flesh—revelation moving brutally toward evisceration. In the film's final scene, the young Gillian opens the door to the motel room in which her father is sequestered with his secretary. A voice-over of the young Gillian giving a definition of fantasy as "something you have when you're awake" is heard. Instead of a primal scene, she discovers the Bobby Tomahawk show—just in time to watch the adult, fantasized version of herself being thrown to the audience, who promptly tear her to pieces. As the coliseum disgorges its spectators, the young Gillian dances alone within the cocoon of a spotlight until a fade to black obliterates everything.

Love Crimes methodically pieces together and disassembles its protagonist's various personae. Bobby Tomahawk is interested in exposing the "real" woman behind the "She-Bitch of Babylon," but such a paternalistic will to mastery is frustrated by the disaggregated nature of the self. No essential femininity is there to reveal; only glimpses of various faces that have each assumed the mantle of "identity" for Gillian at some point in time.

GEOFF PEVERE WRITES of "McDonald's essential humanism"—that it "ensures [the] growth and survival" of his characters.[38] But as his career develops, his alleged belief in the capacity of individuals to outstrip external adversities in the interest of self-improvement gives way to a less smugly rationalistic worldview. Highways no longer lead to predetermined destinations. Pop songs lose their reliable three-chord progression and verse-chorus-verse predictability. We may believe that we are catching glimpses of familiar road signs or hearing the same time-honoured riffs. Nationalists may want to read thematic motifs as referents to stereotypically Canadian standbys: the seduction of American culture, the prevalence of the Griersonian ethos, the Canuck as polite, self-deprecating ironist. The tendency in most scholarship on McDonald's work is to apply these familiar ready-made interpretive paradigms, but the filmmaker's general irreverence toward entrenched and inflexible approaches to self-definition should dissuade such readings. His characters are always already in the process of shedding their skins, and if they fail to change, they are often destroyed. The promotional tagline for *Roadkill* reads: Move or Die.

While always preoccupied with the specifics and the eccentricities of place, McDonald's eyes remain fixed upon the horizon in an expansive view that far outstrips the blinkered vision of filmmakers working in a more nationalistic vein. If one wishes to draw him into the folds of a national canon, it would be no small act of imagination to picture him kicking and screaming all the way.

Yes, there is a kind of "Canada" being represented in McDonald's films, but it is more like a kind of *never-where* populated by shape-shifting transients, always and forever strangers in a strange land. The only true nations to speak of here are those fragile, private kingdoms, erected haphazardly by dreamers, lovers, and other fools. His films wind through these interstitial twilight zones that lie just outside of charted territories. There's a danger of getting lost out there, amidst the aspiring serial killers and would-be devils; the desperate, hungry artists and the suburban refugees, driven from their bungalows by nameless nomadic compulsions. But if it weren't dangerous, it wouldn't be a place worth visiting—a haven for outlaws and other visionaries. Bruce McDonald country.

AUTHOR'S NOTE

This chapter was written in a cabin on Rabbit Lake, Ontario, under the influence of Broken Social Scene, Sarah Harmer, the New Pornographers, the Rheostatics, Stars, The Tragically Hip, and a bottle or two of Sleeman's cream ale. Thanks to Bruce McDonald and Dany Chiasson, Lucy Johnson at Accent Entertainment, and Julie Lofthouse at the Film Reference Library for their invaluable assistance.

NOTES

1. Bruce McDonald, "Pictures," *The National Post*, 24 May 2004, D6.
2. Colin Brunton, "*Roadkill* and *Highway 61* or How I Got My Job at the Canadian Film Centre," Case Study for the Fall Lab, Canadian Film Centre 13 October 1992, 3.
3. Jason Anderson, "*Picture Claire*," *Eye Weekly* 10, no. 49 (13 September 2001): 18.
4. Steve Gravestock, "Outlaw Insider: The Films of Bruce McDonald," in William Beard and Jerry White ed., *North of Everything: English-Canadian Cinema Since 1980* (Edmonton: University of Alberta Press, 2002), 253.

5. Cameron Bailey, "Standing in the Kitchen All Night: A Secret History of the Toronto New Wave," *Take One* 9, no. 28 (2000): 10.

6. Mettler, in turn, would act as cinematographer on *Knock! Knock!* and McDonald's first episode for the CBC's *Life and Times* series, *Train of Thought: The Life and Times of Norman Jewison* (1997).

7. Brunton also credited him as co-producer, and the two would team up to produce McDonald's first two features, *Roadkill* and *Highway 61*. Allegedly, Brunton returned his Genie Award after *Highway 61* was snubbed for major awards by the Academy of Canadian Cinema and Television. McDonald, in turn, has served as producer on McKellar's first short *Blue* (1992), the short-lived CBC series *The Rez* (1996), Wolfgang Scholz's *Verlorene Flügel* (1999), James Dunnison's *Stuff* (1999), and Ron Mann's *Vinyl* (2000). Patricia Rozema also names him as a "Friend of the Film" in the credits of *When Night Is Falling* (1995).

8. Stan Fox had successfully programmed a similar show for CBC Vancouver in 1968, called *Enterprise*, which featured the early work of a vibrant west-coast avant-garde that included Gary Lee-Nova, Al Razutis, David Rimmer, Tom Shandel, Al Sens, and Anne Wheeler.

9. Bruce McDonald, "Listen, you screwheads," *Cinema Canada* 156 (October 1988): 4.

10. Bruce McDonald, "Dear Norman, What is to be done?" *Cinema Canada* 122 (September 1985): 11.

11. He also served alongside McDonald as executive producer of all nineteen episodes of *The Rez*, a television spin-off for the CBC of *Dance Me Outside*.

12. In keeping with McDonald's predilection for intertextual references and reflexivity, the band's name is a nod to one of Marcel Carné's best films, *Les Enfants du paradis* (1945).

13. André Loiselle, "The Radically Moderate Canadian: Don McKellar's Cinematic Persona," in Beard and White, *North of Everything*, 257.

14. Gravestock, "Outlaw Insider: The Films of Bruce McDonald," 253.

15. Steve Cohan and Ina Rae Hark, "Introduction," in Steve Cohan and Ina Rae Hark, ed., *The Road Movie Book* (London: Routledge, 1997), 3.

16. David Laderman, *Driving Visions: Exploring the Road Movie* (Austin: University of Texas Press, 2002), 19–20.

17. Cohan and Hark, *The Road Movie Book*, 2. Similarly, Laderman claims that "the very birth and adolescence of America seems crucially founded upon the notion of the journey, which thus becomes an essential feature of *American* cultural identity." Laderman, *Driving Visions*, 7; my italics.

18. Geoff Pevere, "Letter from Canada," *Film Comment* 28, no. 2 (1992): 64.

19. Katherine Monk, *Weird Sex & Snowshoes and Other Canadian Film Phenomena* (Vancouver: Raincoast Books, 2001), 99.

20. See, for instance Henry Fonda and Sylvia Sydney in *You Only Live Once* (Fritz Lang, 1937), Warren Beatty and Faye Dunaway in *Bonnie and Clyde* (Arthur Penn, 1967), Geena Davis and Susan Sarandon in *Thelma & Louise* (Ridley Scott, 1991).

21. *Highway 61* is, of course, a tribute to another Dylan classic, "Highway 61 Revisited." McDonald claimed that he wanted to adapt Dylan's "peculiar logic of time" to the film, but settled for having the two central characters make a brief off-road pilgrimage to the musician's childhood home instead.

22. His 1987 grant application to the Canada Council cites a wide array of decidedly non-Hollywood formal influences, including Joseph Campbell, Bruce Elder, William Faulkner, Michael Ondaatje, Anais Nin, Alain Renais, and John Kennedy Toole.

23. Aside from the birthplace of Dylan, several other historic locations can be found along Highway 61: New Orleans is the birthplace of jazz pioneer, Buddy Bolden, and the legendary Louis Armstrong; Louisiana was home to famed band leader and trombonist, Kid Ory; Memphis gave rise to both the Sun and Stax/Volt studios (Elvis made his best recordings with the former, while the latter produced albums by Otis Redding, Sam and Dave, and Booker T and the MGs).

24. George Melnyk, *One Hundred Years of Canadian Cinema* (Toronto: University of Toronto Press, 2004), 214.

25. Rochelle Simmons, "Border Crossings: Representations of North American Culture in Bruce McDonald's *Highway 61*," *Cineaction* 61 (2003): 58–61.

26. Christopher E. Gittings, *Canadian National Cinema* (London: Routledge, 2002), 154.

27. Chris Byford, "*Highway 61* Revisited," *Cineaction* 45 (1998): 16.

28. Angela Baldassarre, "Bruce McDonald," *Reel Canadians* (Toronto: Guernica, 2003), 77–78.

29. Bart Beaty, "Imagining the Written Word: Adaptation in the Work of Bruce McDonald and Nick Craine," *Canadian Journal of Film Studies* 13, no. 2 (2004): 31. See also "Dance Me Outside," *Canadian Film Encyclopedia*, www.filmreferencelibrary.ca/index.asp?navid=14, 2003, accessed 25 June 2005.

30. Gittings, *Canadian National Cinema*, 212.

31. Noel S. Baker, *Hard Core Roadshow* (Concord: Anansi, 1997), 139.

32. McDonald's dream project is an adaptation of Brown's disturbing surrealist masterpiece, *Yummy Fur*—the adventures of an accident-prone clown who awakes one morning to find the head of Ronald Reagan attached to his penis. After various attempts at attracting finances, it has yet to be filmed, despite a brilliant screenplay by McKellar. Note to Bruce if he's reading: mastermind a bank heist if you have to! Get it made!

33. The Bravo!FACT commissioned short, "Elimination Dance" (1998)—a collaboration with McKellar and Michael Ondaatje—is usually cited as a close second. An absurdist dramatization of Ondaatje's poem, it features McKellar and Tracey Wright as contestants in a marathon dance-off "based on revenge, jealousy and retaliation." A lime-suited announcer (played by *Hard Core* scribe, Michael Turner) reads proclamations from cards drawn at random, and contestants must leave the dance floor if his announcement applies to them. One contestant hangs his head sheepishly after the announcer reads: "Those who have been penetrated by a Mountie" and has his face slapped by Valerie Buhagiar.

34. Similarly, two of his television projects, *Platinum* and *Road Songs: A Portrait of Robbie Robertson*, are not so much telefilms as they are virtual split-screen collages, inspired by the use of sampling in hip-hop and electronica. In an interview about *Platinum* for *The Globe and Mail*, McDonald chortled, "I would hope the CBC gets lots of letters saying 'What the hell was that all about? I couldn't follow it! I didn't know what was going on!'" See Douglas Bell, "Bruce McDonald Goes Platinum," *The Globe and Mail*, 11 October 1997, C6.

35. Geoff Pevere, "The Rites (and Wrongs) of the Elder *or* The Cinema We Got: The Critics We Need," in Douglas Fetherling, ed. *Documents in Canadian Film* (Peterborough: Broadview Press, 1988), 333.

36. Jim Leach, *Claude Jutra: Filmmaker* (Montréal: McGill-Queen's University Press, 1999), 32.

37. Crow's Theatre has staged a dramatic adaptation of the documentary by Jim Millan and A. Sahy Hahn entitled, *Director's Cut: Planet Claire*. The play ran in Toronto from March to April 2005 at Buddies in Bad Times Theatre.

38. Pevere, "Letter from Canada," 64.

11

Living In/Between

The Cinema of Léa Pool

JENNIFER L. GAUTHIER

When I arrived in Quebec, in North America, the sound of an ambulance struck me; it was not related to a personal memory. For me it's an image of the search for something deeper, farther on, something between death and life. Whether it's heading for a hospital or a hotel, the ambulance is linked to urgency, to transition. It is an element of the unknown, injury, loss of autonomy, transformation. It is the passage from a state of suffering to what is in principle a state of healing.
—LÉA POOL[1]

■ A Sense of Place

LÉA POOL IS NOT A NATIVE CANADIAN; born in Switzerland in 1950, she immigrated to Montreal when she was twenty-five. After earning a bachelor's degree in communications at the Université du Quebec à Montreal, she began her filmmaking career. Since 1978 she has directed eight feature films, several short narrative films, and documentaries both for television and the big screen. In addition to directing, she has also written or co-written the screenplays for twelve of her films.

Her immigrant status allows her a unique position from which to view and reflect upon Canadian and Québécois culture. As an outsider, she is perhaps less hesitant to expose the ambiguities of life north of the forty-ninth parallel and the specific challenges that come with being a Quebecer. Her ruminations about hearing an ambulance for the first time seem to capture many of the themes that her films have dealt with for the past twenty-seven years. Pool explores liminality and states of transition, always foregrounding the corporeality of these experiences. She has developed a characteristic style, evident throughout her body of work, which challenges conventional storytelling by prioritizing her characters' psychological development and inner states of being over the simple rise and fall of the narrative. Garnering numerous festival prizes, critics' awards and audience acclaim, Pool's work speaks to Canadians, Quebecers, and audiences around the globe.

For Pool, place is paramount. "What is certain is that places have always been a dimension of the story in my work," she has said.[2] In her films, setting plays the role of a character, or more accurately, the setting for the story often defines the characters; the characters grow out of the setting. Places carry meaning and this meaning seems to seep into the very soul of her characters, affecting them like emotions and events might. These places are not always safe or comforting; in fact in several of Pool's films, the setting evokes feelings of anxiety and confusion. Places serve not only as the backdrop for identity crises; they often instigate or provoke the crises.

In many of her films, Montreal is a favoured setting. The films reveal a fascination with the city, an attempt to get to know it like a friend or a lover. Coming to Quebec, Pool settled in Montreal, and that city has had a formative effect on her life, just as it does the characters in her films. In her early films, *Strass Café* (1980) and *A Woman in Waiting* (1984), Pool creates nameless cities that cast an aura of placelessness; the setting is at once nowhere and everywhere, as if to suggest the universality of the character's search for self. The urban setting in *Strass Café* is indistinct, as are the characters, referred to only as *elle* and *lui*, whose shadowy existence takes on a kind of urgency through Pool's spoken narration. In *A Woman in Waiting*, Andrea, a director, wanders through the grey cityscape, taking pictures as she scouts locations for her films. One can imagine Pool doing just this for her own films. Like her character, Pool sees the city with an artist's vision, picking out its aesthetic qualities, its poetic spaces, and searching for its soul.

Pool began to sharpen her focus on Montreal with the film, *Anne Trister* (1986). However, in this and other films she refuses to romanticize the city, choosing instead to shed light on its haunting qualities. Fleeing the death of her father in Switzerland, Anne comes to Canada in search of peace. She moves through her environment like a phantom, the vacancy in her face like the empty windows she passes. For Anne, Montreal becomes the backdrop for her desperate attempt to reconstruct herself. The city serves a similar function in *Straight for the Heart* (1988), based on Yves Navarre's novel, *Kurwenal*. Pierre Kurwenal, a photographer, sees empty, bombed-out spaces when he looks at Montreal, one of the debilitating effects of the violence he has witnessed as a photojournalist on assignment in Nicaragua. Throughout the film, Pool intercuts scenes of Pierre's life in Montreal with his lovers, David and Sarah, and scenes of his experiences in Nicaragua. This strategy reveals the powerful effect of these two places on Pierre's psyche. Many of the spaces he inhabits in Montreal are dark, shadowy rooms and streets that make it difficult to connect with other people. Pool places Pierre in these dimly lit settings to underscore the chaos and confusion in his mind. He returns from his latest trip to find that his lovers have moved out of the apartment they shared with him and have cut him out of the relationship.

In *Set Me Free* (1999) Pool narrows her lens to a specific neighbourhood in Montreal. Mile End forms the backdrop for Hanna, the film's thirteen-year-old narrator, who lives with her mother, father, and brother in a sparsely furnished apartment but feels the influence of many other places. As the film opens, Hanna is visiting her grandmother and her uncle in the country, a place of refuge and retreat from a tension-filled home life. Hanna struggles to define her own identity under the influence of her father's Jewish heritage, her mother's Catholic upbringing in Quebec, and American and French popular culture. Montreal's urban landscape becomes a place for Hanna to lose herself and to hide from her own developing womanhood.

While Pool's other films are not set in Montreal, the power of place is still palpable. *The Savage Woman* (1991) is set on the edge of a Swiss mountain range, at a lake created by a large dam. Fleeing from a confrontation with a violent lover, Marianne, as the main character calls herself, crashes her car into a river and floats downstream to end up in the countryside. Living first in the cabin of a local dam worker, Elysée, she then moves into his hunting lodge, living in the attic when the police come to search the area. Although it is a stunningly beautiful landscape, it is visibly cold and empty; it is devoid of people, except for Elysée and his fellow dam workers. Marianne is both physically and emotionally isolated, suffering from post-traumatic stress and a feeling of hopelessness. The dam serves as a metaphor for all that she has bottled up inside of her; we never know her real name or exactly what has happened to her. Only snippets of a radio broadcast alert us to the fact that she may be a Canadian nurse who stabbed her lover. She is isolated from the world; her only connection is Elysée, a fleeting, tenuous one at best. The wide open space of the countryside contrasts vividly with the confined space of the lodge's attic, where Marianne takes refuge in the winter.

Lost and Delirious (2000) takes place at a private girls' school outside of Toronto. The main characters are defined by and imprisoned within this environment. While the film chronicles the relationship of three girls, Mary, Victoria, and Pauline, it is really Mary's story. Mary is sent to boarding school by her father, three years after her mother dies. She begins the film as a meek, awkward girl, lacking self-confidence and self-awareness. The school represents for Mary her estrangement from her father; he has a new wife and no longer has time for his daughter. Mary is assigned to room with Victoria and Pauline, known as Paulie, who are lovers. Victoria comes from a strict family, which has expectations about her role as a society woman, while Paulie was given up for adoption when she was a baby. Although they come from very different backgrounds, the girls have found solace in one another in an environment that is protected from the outside world.

Pool shifts her focus yet again in *The Blue Butterfly* (2002). The opening scenes take place in Montreal, where the main character, Pete Carleton lives with his mother. But the majority of the film's action is set in the rainforest of Costa Rica, where Pete travels with famous entomologist,

Alan Osborn, to find and catch the Blue Morpho butterfly. Pete and his mother could not be less suited to the rainforest, at least initially. He is in a wheelchair, suffering from a brain tumour, and has been given three to six months to live. His mother, as he explains in a voice-over, hates insects of all kinds. The group stays at a small village on the edge of the rain forest, and they make daily expeditions in search of the butterfly. On one of these treks they have to cross what Osborn refers to as "a small swamp." While he carries Pete across on his shoulders, their Costa Rican guide lugs the wheelchair and offers aid to Pete's mother, who, halfway across, begins to protest that she feels something on her leg. Retreating quickly back to the banks, she lifts her pant leg to discover that her skin is covered with leeches. After this disaster, Pete suggests that he and Osborn continue to search for the butterfly on their own. Over the course of the journey, Pete spends more and more time out of his wheelchair, carried by Osborn in a special backpack designed by one of their guides. When he and Osborn fall into a cave, he must climb out and find his way back to the village on his own. It is during this journey that he experiences a kind of spiritual awakening that ultimately reverses his cancer; the forest and its spirits heal him.

■ Embodied Knowledge: Opening Up New Spaces for Empowerment

POOL'S FILMS OPERATE within a tradition of feminist cinema, both in their subject matter and aesthetic approach. While critics have been divided about the brand of feminism she embraces, her work undoubtedly challenges traditional representations of women. Her cinematic style eschews the objectifying gaze that typifies mainstream film; as a woman director she is clearly cognizant of the power of the apparatus and foregrounds this issue with characters who themselves wield cameras (Andrea in *A Woman in Waiting*, Anne in *Anne Trister*, and Hanna in *Set Me Free*). Mary Jean Green has called attention to Pool's tendency to subvert stereotypes of women with her woman-centred narratives and her stylistic innovation, as well as her focus on women's relationships with other women.[3] As Bill Marshall argues, Pool's work is powerful in its embrace of liminality. He goes on to suggest that in her films, the "blurring and dissolution of boundaries" opens up new spaces for empowerment.[4] Building upon these ideas, George Melnyk highlights Pool's European feminism, specifically her representation of characters who are rooted in the French literary tradition, "with its avant-garde, aesthetic and introspective view of sexuality, a sense of existential angst pervading human life and an understanding of the crises that face professional women operating in the dislocating universe of contemporary urban life, where the struggle between creativity and the self is vital but problematic."[5]

Most evident in Pool's films is the feminist notion of embodied knowledge. She has explained it this way:

> At the end of my adolescence I had the impression that the body was like a social envelope, without any relation to what one is inside. It was impossible for me to reconcile the two. In my first films, there's a voice that says one thing and a body that says something else. To me the body is complex, but not tortured. I like forms and movements that are purified, stripped bare, essential, so as to extract the body from the everyday world, enabling it to regain a free space, without contingencies. Body language is what is the least directed.[6]

Both male and female characters alike embrace a kind of feminist epistemology that privileges the body and its sensual interaction with the world over more detached and scientific ways of knowing. The notion of embodied knowledge is a response to the traditional Cartesian separation of mind and body and its impact on the Enlightenment's celebration of scientific objectivity and rationality. In 1976 poet Adrienne Rich asked a question in response to this tradition: "I am really asking whether women cannot begin, at last, to think through the body, to connect what has been so cruelly disorganized—our great mental capacities, hardly used; our highly developed tactile sense; our genius for close observation; our complicated pain-enduring multi-pleasured physicality."[7]

Feminist epistemology celebrates this kind of embodiment, or the idea that "people experience the world by using their bodies, which have different constitutions and are differently located in space and time."[8] Donna Haraway has contributed the notion of "situated knowledges" to feminist epistemology, arguing that "objectivity turns out to be about particular and specific embodiment, and definitely not about the false vision promising transcendence of all limits and responsibility."[9] The notion of embodied knowledge suggests that the truth will be different depending on an individual's perspective; it foregrounds the specificity of knowledge and its situatedness in a particular place and time. Pool's films offer individual and specific versions of the world, expressed through characters living in a particular place and time. These characters experience the world around them through sensual engagement, offering their own particular truths to the viewer.

These unique perspectives are most obvious in films that make use of voice-over narration. Andrea, Hanna, Mary, and Pete all address the audience directly, structuring the film as their own personal reflection on their lives. Andrea opens *A Woman in Waiting* by telling us that she has returned to Montreal to scout locations for her film, but she realizes that she has become a stranger in the city that she lived in for eighteen years. Throughout the film she describes her feelings of alienation and her search for truth as an artist. Hanna's voice-over is heard only when she is underwater, in both fantasy sequences and swimming with her brother in a lake. She reveals to us her desire to be carried away by the waves, to escape the changes that her body has initiated and that have altered her relationships with her family. *Lost and Delirious* opens with Mary's voice-over, as she explains her reluctance to go boarding school and her feelings of abandonment. She speaks to us at the end of the film also, creating a kind of bookend that calls to mind her opening statements; however her closing remarks suggest a new-found maturity and sense of peace. Pete's voice-over punctuates *The Blue Butterfly*; his comments provide an often ironic counterpoint to the visual images. The film opens with his question, "Why me?" and later he informs us that he has secrets from his mother, who he feels is too protective. As the film proceeds, Pete's voice-over provides us with insight into his thought process, his growing appreciation for the natural world, and his acceptance of his own mortality. In each of these three films, the adolescent's voice-over guides the viewer on the character's inner journey, demonstrating the very particular process that each goes through to become an adult.

For Pool's female characters, the body is a site of both mystery and knowledge. Their search for power is ultimately realized in a kind of embodied knowledge. Anne, Hanna, Paulie, Mary, and Tory all come to understand themselves through an awareness of the body and its potential power. In this way, Pool celebrates a kind of epistemology that privileges the sensual, the tactile, and the corporeal. Anne seeks the physical closeness of others in order to combat her grief, but she is also alienated by her sense of loss. She pursues an affair with her friend Alix, and through this relationship she ultimately finds her strength. *Lost and Delirious*, too, foregrounds the importance of this kind of physical closeness. Paulie and Tory delight in each other's bodies as they come to terms with their own physical changes on their way to becoming women. The languid love scenes in these films emphasize the role of the body and sensual experience in self-knowledge.

For Hanna, the changes in her body bring with them emotional upheaval. At the start of the film she experiences menses, the onset of her period signalling her transition from girlhood to womanhood. While she seems open to the new possibilities that this change will bring, her father is reluctant to let her grow up. Arriving back from her summer vacation with long hair, Hanna's dawning sexuality is evident, so her father takes her to the barber shop and has her hair cut off. This scene is particularly moving, as the camera slowly pans around Hanna, in a tight close-up of her face, watching her reaction to this violation of her new-found independence. Her body becomes the site of the battle between childhood and womanhood, between her own identity and those of her mother and father, the battle for control of her life. She experiments with her body—kissing first her brother and then a girlfriend—and later uses it to become someone else. Hanna styles herself after the character of Nana in Jean-Luc Godard's *Vivre sa vie* (1962); she imitates Nana's dance in the pool hall and her manner of walking and speaking. While these are harmless acts, she later puts herself in danger when she runs away from home and takes the imitation of the prostitute character further, ending up in a hotel room with a potential john.

Pete is imprisoned within a weakened body in *The Blue Butterfly*. Although his illness is a focal point of the narrative, he ultimately overcomes it. When his mother agrees to let him go on the trip with Osborn, he travels long distances, his wheelchair heaved in and out of boats of various sizes. During the adventure, he is carried through the forest, first in his chair and then on Osborn's back. Despite this attention to his body's weakness, he ultimately proves his physical and mental strength when he climbs out of a cave and walks through the forest in an effort to get help for Osborn, who has been wounded in a fall. This miraculous plot twist attests to Pete's ability to unite those aspects of his physical being that Adrienne Rich lamented as being "cruelly disorganized."[10]

Pool's is an embodied cinema that, as Haraway would agree, is "not about fixed location in a reified body, female or otherwise, but about... inflections in orientations."[11] In her films, Pool strives to bring audiences closer to her characters, to let us into their bodies and souls, to allow us to see the world from their particular place and time. As she notes, "When you are a critic you have to see films from a distance. In my films, this is not possible because you must get involved in the experience to be able to feel the film."[12] She has stated that "Film is a tool for investigation and an expression of self"[13] and also that "[she is] not interested in just making films. For me, films are a way to express something inside."[14] Pool's films allow her to explore not only what is inside of her, but also what is inside of each of her characters.

■ **Living Between**

POOL'S FILMS feature characters who are living in between; they embody a kind of liminality, existing between home and away, childhood and adulthood, dreams and reality, life and death. She has explained her vision in the following way:

> In all of my films, the departure point is very important. The change in the life of the main character, which is a turning point in their life.... Also, my main characters are always on the edge. You never know if they will fall off or continue. My characters question themselves and make the audience think about their own lives. This may disturb some viewers.[15]

Her characters exist in borderlands, states of being that are fuzzy, ill-defined, and ambiguous. Often these borderlands are defined psychologically. Her main characters in *A Woman in Waiting*, *Anne Trister*, *Straight for the Heart*, *The Savage Woman*, and *Set Me Free* are caught between reality and fantasy; the mind plays tricks on them, driving them to the edge of sanity. In *The Blue Butterfly*, Pete experiences a moment in the forest that challenges the limits of reality, and it is unclear to the viewer whether the sequence represents a dream or actual events.

Also betwixt and between is Estelle, the eponymous mysterious woman whom Andrea meets in the hotel in *A Woman in Waiting*. In the wake of a failed relationship, the details of which are not entirely clear, she retreats to a hotel and wanders listlessly through the city each day. Andrea invites her onto the set of the film, seeing in her the inspiration for her main character and ultimately blurring reality and fiction in her film. After three weeks of an aimless existence, Estelle departs on the train, finally deciding to move on to the next phase of her life. Marianne, the title character of *The Savage Woman* also inhabits a liminal space. She creates for herself an alternate reality with Elysée, snatching a few more months of life, but it is not her life. She has no identity except that which she makes up. At the end of the film, Marianne's body is found by villagers, washed up on the banks of the river, into which she had disappeared three months earlier. The whole film plays like an extended dream sequence, as Marianne exists for a brief time in between life and death.

Mental institutions figure in a number of Pool's films, foregrounding the blurry line between fantasy and reality. The last shot in *Straight for the Heart* captures Pierre's liberation from the asylum to which he had committed himself. This literal freedom echoes his emotional release from the devastation of his failed relationship. A pivotal scene in Andrea's film in *A Woman in Waiting* takes place in a "rest home." The film's star, a singer, is taken to the institution when her life becomes too much for her. Estelle watches the shooting of the scene and its resonance for her is overwhelming; she flees the set in horror. Hanna's mother is emotionally absent for much of Hanna's youth and is ultimately committed to an institution after a suicide attempt.

While *Lost and Delirious* does not feature a mental institution, it does take place in another kind of institution, one which similarly attempts to normalize behaviour and identity. As the title suggests, all three girls struggle to maintain their emotional stability throughout the film. Mary is dealing with the death of her mother and a strained relationship with her father while adjusting to living away from home for the first time. For Tory, the struggle is against social and parental expectations, which are at odds with her desires. She is better able to handle these constraints than is Paulie, however, who cracks under the pressure. As the film progresses, Paulie seems to descend into madness. Ms. Vaughn, the headmistress, suggests that Paulie get some help from a counsellor to deal with her feelings, but Paulie refuses, attributing her behaviour to "mad, passionate love that crosses all boundaries," a sentiment inspired by Shakespeare's *Antony and Cleopatra*. Paulie begins to live in a fantasy life, believing that she is becoming a raptor she has rescued. In this liminal state between reality and fantasy, she stabs the young man that Tory is dating and throws herself off the roof of the school.

Pool tends to focus on the in-between moments of the life cycle, and notes that she has preferences. "All ages of life are represented in my films, but the child and the adolescent are the motors," she has said.[16] Adolescents feature most prominently in *Set Me Free*, *Lost and Delirious*, and *The Blue Butterfly*. These films are among Pool's most moving because they reconstruct the precarious moments between childhood and adulthood. All three films also represent the struggle between life and death. Throughout *Set Me Free*, Hanna is living in between childhood and adulthood. Not yet a woman, but no longer a girl, she struggles to come to terms with her changing body and sense of self. Her liminality is compounded by the fact that she is torn between the cultural influences of her mother and her father, between her real life and her fantasies. Her father is Jewish and lives in a kind of self-exile in Montreal, while her mother is a Catholic Québécoise.

Hanna uses her mother's surname, Riel, as her parents are not married. The name is reminiscent of an infamous figure in Canadian history, Louis Riel, the Métis who led a failed uprising in 1885. With this reference, Hanna is likened to the mixed heritage figure who occupies a significant place in Québécois history. On her first day of school, Hanna's teacher asks her a series of questions to determine her identity. In responding to her teacher's questions, Hanna states that her father is "patriote," for which the English subtitles read, "He has no country, he is not from anywhere." While this translation underscores her father's self-exile from his homeland, it also refers literally to another failed uprising that marks the history of Quebec, the rebellion of *les patriotes* in 1837–38. These cultural references underscore the difficult task of defining a distinct identity in the face of powerful influences.

Hanna's liminal status is also suggested by her strong, but misguided, identification with Nana in Godard's film. Her emotional connection with Nana blurs the line between fiction and reality and is further complicated by the fact that Nana, as played by Anna Karina, resembles Hanna's teacher. As was mentioned above, Pool intercuts scenes of Hanna imitating Nana's playful dance around a pool table at a bar to underscore Hanna's identity crisis. As the film progresses, Hanna takes on more of Nana's characteristics, going so far as to let a stranger bring her up to his hotel room. The oscillation between fantasy and reality results in Hanna's descent into self-doubt and confusion. She runs away from home and wanders the streets of Montreal, only to be rescued by her teacher. This experience signals the death of her childhood and the beginning of her life as a woman. It also marks the death of her fantasy life and the beginning of her acceptance of reality.

Mary, Paulie, and Tory, too, are all struggling with the passage from childhood to adulthood; *Lost and Delirious* chronicles their "growing pains." Pool links this stage of development to the fight for life itself; in effect, the girls exist between life and death. They must learn how to love and how to live without love in order to survive as adults. Pool suggests that the loss of childhood is a kind of death, one that requires strength to overcome. Paulie cannot face womanhood after losing Tory; her suicide represents her choice not to grow up. In contrast, Mary triumphs over death; her passage into womanhood represents not only her triumph over the death of her mother, but also her survival of the tragedy of Paulie's suicide.

Although he is just a child, Pete is thrust prematurely into an adult role because of his cancer. He is forced to face his mortality at a young age, which seems to give him a kind of wisdom and maturity that belies his youth. Having been given a short time to live, he exists between life and death. *The Blue Butterfly* chronicles his effort to live his life fully before he dies. However, through his journey his life is miraculously restored. In the dream-like sequence described above, Pete has passed out from the physical exertion of running through the forest. When he loses consciousness, he is visited by Natives painted in fluorescent colours, who tower over him as he lies on the ground, helpless. They touch his head with their spears and his scar disappears. After this figurative death he is resurrected, his cancer mysteriously gone.

■ Far From Home

POOL'S CHARACTERS are often stranded in an unfamiliar place or exiled from their homes. While some of her characters struggle to get home, others exude a sort of aimlessness, a lost quality. She has stated that this focus comes from her own situation. "It's an important part of my identity to have lived with a father who was stateless, completely out of step, who never found his anchorage. This is something I carry within me to a remarkable degree."[17] For some characters the exile is self-imposed, part of a search for self that necessitates an escape from the familiar. All of Pool's films chronicle the experience of rootlessness and transience, whether temporary or permanent, and the impact that this experience has on individuals and families.

"For me, going from one country to another is not the most important part of exile," she has said. "It's more a question of how you feel in society and in front of other people and how you try to find your own values and identity."[18] To emphasize these states in both their physical and psychological manifestations, liminal sites often figure in Pool's films: train stations, subways, hotels, and truck stops, for example. Andrea describes the locations she seeks for her film in *A Woman in Waiting* as "places you never stay in: theatres, railway stations, hotels."[19] Again, Andrea's artistic vision echoes Pool's own.

Many of Pool's characters deal with feelings of isolation and abandonment. They attempt to carry on normal lives, but their inner turmoil keeps them at a distance from those around them. Estranged from their friends and relatives, in some cases they are also ostracized by their communities. As Pool has noted, these feelings amount to a kind of psychological exile. Anne is adrift after the loss of her father, and repeated scenes of her walking through a desert emphasize her isolation and self-exile. She has exiled herself from Switzerland, much as Pool did, to come to Montreal. Marianne, too, chooses self-exile, while Pierre is exiled from all that is familiar to him by his lovers. Hanna's self-induced exile from her own life is precipitated by her father's overbearing expectations and her mother's emotional distance. An outcast in school because of her parents' non-traditional relationship, Hanna does not fit into society's prescribed roles. Hanna's solution to her identity crisis is to retreat into a kind of fantasy world, which she thinks will offer protection from the stresses of her everyday life: poverty, her mother's mental illness, and her developing womanhood.

All three girls in *Lost and Delirious* are lost in some way: searching for a sense of self and validation of their identities. They seek answers to the question, "Who am I?" Like Hanna, Mary struggles with the issue of naming. When she arrives at school, she introduces herself as "Mouse," her father's nickname for her. As the film opens, it fits her; she is timid and shy. When she tells Paulie and Tory the story of her mother's death, Paulie names her "Mary Brave," and throughout the film calls her "Mary B." for short. Later, when the school's gardener asks her name she replies, "It's in transition." Tory and Paulie struggle to come to terms with themselves as sexual beings. As an orphan, Paulie knows nothing about herself and must construct her own identity. Her ultimate suicide suggests that she wasn't successful in this attempt; she remained lost. In contrast, Mary finds herself and reconnects with her father.

In *The Blue Butterfly*, it is Alan Osborn, the entomologist, who is an exile. As he reveals to Pete's mother, he has a daughter who he has not seen since she was a baby. Osborn is an exile from the world of human beings, as his life revolves around insects, not people. His relationship with Pete forces him to reconsider his choices and brings him back into the world of humans. For Osborn, like Hanna and Mary, the state of exile is only temporary, but for other characters in Pool's films it is a more permanent situation.

■ Feminist auteur

WITH FIFTEEN FILMS under her belt, several of which she also wrote or co-wrote, Pool has developed a distinctive cinematic style. Because her films chronicle the psychological lives of her characters, this style, particularly in her early films is devoted to evoking moods. "I'm not much of a storyteller," she says modestly. "There are other directors who are better at telling stories than me. But that's not my special ability. For me, it is more important to express the feelings, emotions, and psychological sides of the characters."[20] Her early works are highly impressionistic, blurring the lines between fantasy and reality with dream sequences and circular narratives. "In terms of style, I just try and give a very strong point of view. Only then can you find this larger emotional scale. But for a strong point of view, it's so important to open oneself so you can get the universal. That's why I like very simple shots..." she reflects. "I have nothing left to prove, I'm a good filmmaker. I can relax a little. I don't need the fancy camera moves to find new ways of filming. I can relax a little now and enjoy the pleasure of living."[21]

In all of her films, the camera elevates the setting to the status of a character. Place is not just an aesthetically beautiful backdrop, but an important catalyst for the narrative. Pool's style cements her characters into specific places and times, emphasizing the particularity of their experiences and emotions.

A Woman in Waiting and *Straight for the Heart* are particularly striking in their evocative use of cinematography. In both films, the surrealistic style enables the viewer to feel the protagonists' inner pain as they straddle the line between sanity and madness. The slow, languid panning shots of Montreal in *A Woman in Waiting* underscore both Andrea's and Estelle's searches for meaning. Pool interrupts these sequences with stills to highlight the importance of certain places. Photos of the interior of the hotel and empty urban buildings emphasize the transience of the characters' lives.

While the camera's movement in *Straight for the Heart* is less frequent, when it occurs, it is faster and somewhat jarring, suggesting Pierre's frantic and confused mental state. The abundant stills in *Straight for the Heart* not only echo Pierre's profession, but also serve to document the decay of the world around him. As he takes photos at a dinner party given by his editor, he captures the "other" like an anthropologist documenting a foreign culture. This scene suggests that he is an outsider in his own city, just as he was in Nicaragua. Throughout the film, the narrative is punctuated by images of his trip and of happier days with David and Sarah. Pierre's photographs disrupt the flow of the narrative, disorienting the viewer, much as Pierre himself has become confused by the disruption of his life. These interruptions also underscore Pierre's liminal state between the past and the present, between his desires and reality. To highlight his psychological turmoil, Pool uses frequent close-ups on his face; it is often twisted in pain or frozen in disbelief. His feelings of entrapment intensify when he commits himself to a mental institution; in a stunning long take, Pool captures Pierre's anguish as he lies on the floor of his room in a foetal position.

In *The Savage Woman*, Pool also uses the camera to create a sense of isolation, but in the midst of a wide open space. Panoramic shots of the landscape predominate early in the film, figures dwarfed within them or absent entirely. The scale of the film is larger than that of Pool's previous works, creating a distance between the characters that lingers even when they are later confined in tight spaces. The vast landscape is an arctic one, the snow and the ice-blue water of the lake glisten in the natural light, creating a kind of pristine beauty that contrasts with Marianne's damaged psyche.

While many of her themes are consistent, Pool's overall style has changed over the course of her film career. The focus on atmosphere and mood rather than narrative goes hand in hand with her slow pace and languid camera work. Lengthy sections of the early films are without dialogue or completely silent; characters do not speak to one another, but instead exist next to each other in isolation. The plots are not a tightly woven series of causes and effects; gaps and unexplained occurrences leave the audience uncertain of character motivation. As she herself noted in an interview in 1989, her films borrow their form from European art cinema: "Films in America flow from one point to another in a straight line. My films progress in a cycle. There is not really a beginning and a definite end. For the audience, it's a little bit difficult perhaps because they are used to seeing films that have an introduction and a climax or conclusion. But I don't think life is like that at all."[22] This circular and open-ended narrative structure works to foreground the psychological twists and turns that her characters take. In general, *A Woman in Waiting*, *Anne Trister*, *Straight for the Heart*, and *The Savage Woman* evoke in the viewer feelings of detached disorientation that echo the protagonists' sense of alienation and confusion.

Set Me Free was a turning point in Pool's career. Made for just over CAD $3 million, it was her first international success, bringing her critical and popular acclaim all over the world. This film set the stage for her embrace of a more commercial aesthetic, which focusses on plot development and employs a logical progression of events. *Set Me Free* is widely accessible with its familiar story, likeable young heroine, and linear plot development. With few gaps in the narrative, characters and their actions are easy to understand and identify with. Additionally, Pool draws in a global audience with her inclusion of Canadian, French, and American popular culture. Despite its departure from her early impressionistic style, the film does retain traces of Pool's emphasis on psychology and the inner states of her characters. A recurring sequence in the film of a lone bicycle rider pedalling in circles disrupts the flow of the narrative with its dream-like quality.

Pool's films after *Set Me Free* utilize fewer impressionistic devices; they are less apt to blur the lines between fantasy and reality, and in general, they take a more straightforward approach to narrative development. *Lost and Delirious*, although not as resounding a success as *Set Me Free*, also embraces a more commercial, mainstream aesthetic. Based on a popular Canadian novel, Susan Swan's *The Wives of Bath*, it was Pool's first film in English, and its setting helps it fit neatly into an accepted genre. While it openly tackles the sexuality issues that Pool raised in some of her earlier films, it is not a ringing endorsement of lesbian experimentation. Paulie's punishment and death suggest a more traditional approach to this subject matter as heterosexuality triumphs in the film when Tory redefines herself for her parents and society. Also, the film stays squarely in the realm of reality, never delving into the characters' fantasies and desires with dream sequences or surrealistic cinematic techniques. The gaps in the narrative that do exist seem to be the fault of the screenplay, not an intentional strategy on Pool's part. Paulie's relationship with the wounded bird is never fully explained, but neither is it overlaid with the same kind of mystical spirituality that Pool injected into her early films.

This attention to mainstream accessibility seems to characterize Pool's latest film, *The Blue Butterfly*, as well. Her most expensive film to date (CAD $13 million), its sentimental tone and formulaic story seem out of character for Pool. However, the director has noted in the press that she welcomed the opportunity to make a family film as the mother of an adopted child.[23] Despite its generic storyline, the camera work in *The Blue Butterfly* is striking, alternating between wide shots of the landscape in the rainforest and extreme close-ups of insects, birds, and plants. The style of the film melds large-scale and small-scale images to evoke Pete's dawning sense of the world around him. The film's grand scale is suggested in its production locations, which spanned the continent, ranging from Montreal to Costa Rica. Pool evidently rented a helicopter or a small plane for some scenes. An overhead shot, for example, captures Pete, his mother, and Osborn travelling down the river as it winds its way through the frame.

The film's large-scale production values are contrasted with the intimate scale of its narrative. It is ultimately a very personal story of transformation, focussing on Pete and his relationships with his mother and with Osborn. As he learns to value everything in life, not only the blue butterfly, his growing awareness is echoed in the shots of tiny insects that go unnoticed by the naked eye. The close-ups serve as a kind of scientific documentation of the variety of species (both animal and plant) found in the rainforest. This technique goes hand-in-hand with the generally life-affirming message of the film and provides evidence for Pete's growing realization that everything around him is a miracle.

Unlike Pool's previous films, *The Blue Butterfly* takes advantage of special effects, or, rather, the effects in this film are created digitally rather than in camera or during the editing process. This use of new technologies suggests Pool's changing interests and her desire to appeal to a different type of viewer. Throughout the film, the Blue Morpho butterfly is superimposed on the action digitally; it glows with an otherworldly presence and stands out from the forest in its intense colour and luminosity. Pool's use of magic realism sets the film apart from standard Hollywood fare and from the rest of her oeuvre. While her films have often embraced the fantastic, they have done so in a more understated fashion, never resorting to what might be described as gimmicks. With its stunning natural beauty, *The Blue Butterfly* is reminiscent of *The Savage Woman*, however, while the earlier film was replete with emotional intensity and inner turmoil, Pool's most recent effort seems hollow, all surface and very little substance.

■ Canadian or Québécois?

I'm a Quebec filmmaker, this is clear to me; I've made nearly all my films in Quebec by choice. When I arrived in Montreal in 1975, this search for a national identity by the people of Quebec was stimulating. It gave a meaning to my own questions.[24]

POOL IS ONE OF CANADA'S most prolific filmmakers. She has garnered prizes and acclaim for Canadian cinema all over the world. However, it is clear that her films speak most intimately to Quebecers. In their in-betweenness, her characters echo Quebec's liminal status as a province within the nation-state of Canada and a collectivity with national char-acteristics. Some Quebecers believe that their province exists in a kind of colonial relationship with Canada, while others embrace the benefits of a federalist system. As the quote above suggests, Pool felt a kind of affinity for the province and its identity crisis when she came to Quebec from Switzerland in 1975. Because she is an outsider, she is able to observe her adopted culture from a distance and reflect openly on its conflicted nature. While many of her films have an autobiographical component, Pool has noted that in her later career she is less in need of "transferring directly to the screen what she herself lives."[25] Pool's work reflects the mix of European and North American cultural influences that shape Quebec. Her films are inflected with a European art cinema sensibility, but she also draws upon American popular culture to situate her characters in a distinct Québécois context.

Many of Pool's characters are struggling to construct or preserve a distinct identity. In this way they mirror Quebec's struggle. This is particularly true of Hanna in *Set Me Free* and Paulie and Mary in *Lost and Delirious*. All three women fight against powerful social forces to define their own identities. For other characters, like Pierre in *Straight for the Heart*, Marianne in *The Savage Woman*, and Pete in *The Blue Butterfly*, the struggle is to preserve a sense of self in a situation that threatens to destroy it. Her evocation of identity crises also speaks to the experience of all Canadians. Pool's char-acters work to construct unified selves in the face of competing allegiances. The schizophrenia that some scholars attribute to the nation of Canada is mirrored in several of Pool's protagonists, including Anne Trister, Pierre Kurwenal, Marianne, Hanna, and all three young women in *Lost and Delirious*. Each of these fictional characters is struggling with the question, "Who am I?" which has been a recurring theme in Canadian society since its founding. The hybridity that defines a multicultural nation like Canada is evident in Pool's films. As Hanna makes clear to her teacher in *Set Me Free*, she is the product of two different cultural traditions.

Pool's concern with self and identity links her work to much of Quebec cinema that has preceded it. In the 1960s, Québécois filmmakers sought to use film to explore issues of individual and community identity, and in the process they carved out a unique sense of self for Quebecers. In their quest to discover themselves and construct a new, more complete identity in the face of trauma and conflict, Pool's characters follow in the footsteps of their cinema-direct predecessors. Most obviously, Hanna's journey echoes that of Benoît in Claude Jutra's masterpiece, *Mon Oncle Antoine* (1963). Like Benoît, Hanna seeks to understand the world around her and find a place within it. Forced to face the unpleasant realities of life and withstand the pervasive influence of authority figures, both she and Benoît eventually come to terms with these constraints and develop a kind of provisional, mature self. The recurring theme of existential crisis also brings to mind Claude's path to self-understanding in *Le Chat dans le sac* (Gilles Groulx, 1964). Claude's remark in the film, "I am Québécois so I must find my own way," could have been spoken by several of Pool's characters some thirty years later. While Pool embraces some of the prevalent themes of Quebec cinema, her style departs from the documentary aesthetic of the 1960s. Over the course of her career she has been more interested in blurring boundaries between dreams and reality than in depicting the Real itself. Additionally, her meticulous control over the construction of the image departs from the more spontaneous aesthetics of the Quebec cinema pioneers.

Pool's role as a woman filmmaker in Quebec is a crucial one. In a staunchly patriarchal culture, she gives voice to Québéc women. She celebrates the Québécoise who seeks empowerment but is hampered by social and psychological barriers. Pool's films bring women's issues to the forefront; she highlights not only women's efforts to construct a coherent sense of self, but also women's desires and the importance of embodied knowledge. As a woman director, she also offers a different perspective on the province and its history. Her male characters evidence a kind of vulnerability that is absent in much of Québécois cinema; in fact her male characters have more in common with English-Canadian heroes, who are sometimes ridiculed by critics for their ineffectuality.

Just as Pool reflects Quebec's multicultural influences, her career also evidences a kind of cultural hybridity. Her films have been made with both Canadian and international financing. At the federal level, the National Film Board, Telefilm Canada, and Radio-Canada have supported her work, and at the provincial level, she has received funding from the Ontario Film Development Corporation and Quebec's various film funding agencies. Several of her films have been co-productions between Canada and Switzerland, including *Straight for the Heart*, *The Savage Woman*, and *Desire in Motion*. *Set Me Free* was made in partnership with Canada, Switzerland, and France.

Pool's work demonstrates the impact of globalization on the film industry and, more specifically, on small national cinemas. *Lost and Delirious*, Pool's first English-language film, was seen by many critics in Quebec as a kind of betrayal.[26] Both critics and policymakers have agreed on the value of Québécois films made in French, identifying their important contribution to the preservation of a distinct culture. However, her decision seemed to be part of a wider trend; both Denys Arcand (*Stardom*, 2000) and Robert Lepage (*Possible Worlds*, 2000) directed English-language features that were released around the same time.

The issue of English-language production is a complicated one. Ten years before making *Lost and Delirious*, Pool was asked about the possibility of directing in English, and she seemed ambivalent about the idea: "If my new film were produced in English, it would be easier to sell to the distribution...I cannot feel the same and direct the same way with English-speaking actors because the mood is essential to all my films. I don't think I could direct the same mood in another language."[27]

Set Me Free gained worldwide attention for Québécois film and gave Pool access to more funding and wider audiences for her next project. It makes sense that *Lost and Delirious* would be made in English, not only because of Pool's career trajectory, but also because of the film's source material. However, this logic has not convinced her Québécois critics, and Pool has had to defend her choice not to film in French. Her response

highlights the sensitivity surrounding this issue and its political reper-
cussions in the province:

> The idea that, if you speak English, and you make a film in English, you're a
> different person—that's completely stupid. I'm sure they will be looking a little
> closer at me, to see if I have not sold my soul to Hollywood. But the reason I made
> this film was that it was very close to me, to what I do. Of course, I knew that if we
> made the film in English it would be easier to get the money. I knew it was easier
> to find the name actresses. But when I was asked why I made this film in English,
> it was because I didn't want to translate it into French. That's the main, main
> reason. It's a screenplay by an American playwright, Judith Thompson, based on...
> Susan Swan's Wives of Bath. What else would I do?[28]

Roger Frappier, a Québécois producer who has worked with Pool offers a
different take on this difficult issue: "Does English prevent a Francophone
director from expressing his vision of the world? Isn't it preferable to
accept the making of films in English, rather than see our filmmakers
progressively exile themselves?"[29]

Making an English-language film also afforded Pool easier access to
distribution and exhibition; she notes that the film had already interested distributors before it was finished and that "in French, it would
have been impossible."[30]

Working in English has allowed her to tackle new challenges and to
develop her creativity as a filmmaker; at the same time, however, Pool's
career trajectory speaks to the ongoing marginalization of national cinemas
and, more specifically, of foreign-language films in the world market.
As Pool's situation has demonstrated, English-language films are easier
to fund, distribute, and market; they also allow for higher budgets and
widely known actors (Pool worked with American teen sensation Piper
Perabo in Lost and Delirious and veteran star William Hurt in The Blue
Butterfly). In general, Pool's cinema speaks to the ambiguity in Quebec's
relationship with the global market that Marie-Christine Abel identifies
when she suggests that "to be Québécois is, in every way, by definition,
to be very open to the world; it is to dream of leaving Quebec.... Our
cinema, naturally, is made by those who stay, or return, or even come here
from elsewhere to translate this love-hate relationship."[30]

All translations from the French are by the author.

NOTES

1. Eric Fourlanty, "Léa Pool: Director's Sheet," (Pro Helvetia/Arts Council of Switzerland, 2000), unpaginated.

2. Mario Cloutier, "Le film, c'est un outil de recherche et d'expression de soi," *Cinebulles* (Spring 1994): 32.

3. Mary Jean Green, "Léa Pool's *La Femme de L'hotel* and Women's Film in Quebec. *Quebec Studies* 9 (1989–90): 49, 52, 56.

4. Bill Marshall, *Quebec National Cinema* (Montreal: McGill-Queen's University Press, 2001), 233.

5. George Melnyk, *One Hundred Years of Canadian Cinema* (Toronto: University of Toronto Press, 2004), 177.

6. Fourlanty, "Léa Pool: Director's Sheet."

7. Adrienne Rich, *Of Woman Born: Motherhood as Experience and Institution* (New York: W.W. Norton, 1976), 284.

8. *Stanford Encyclopedia of Philosophy.* Available at http://plato.stanford.edu/emtires/feminist-epistemology/#si (accessed 15 June, 2005).

9. Donna Haraway, *Simians, Cyborgs, and Women: The Reinvention of Nature* (New York: Routledge, 1991), 190.

10. Rich, *Of Woman Born*, 284.

11. Haraway, *Simians*, 195.

12. Aaron Bor, "An Interview with Léa Pool," *Quebec Studies* 9 (1989–90): 68.

13. Cloutier, "Le film, c'est un outil de recherché et d'expression de soi," 32.

14. Bor, "An Interview with Léa Pool," 68.

15. Ibid.

16. Fourlanty, "Léa Pool: Director's Sheet."

17. Ibid.

18. Bor, "An Interview with Léa Pool," 64.

19. Ibid., 66.

20. Katherine Monk, *Weird Sex and Snowshoes and other Canadian Film Phenomena* (Vancouver: Raincoast Books, 2001), 205.

21. Ibid., 65.

22. *The Blue Butterfly* press kit, Galafilm, 2004, unpaginated.

23. Fourlanty, "Léa Pool: Director's Sheet."

24. Marie-Christine Abel, André Giguère, and Luc Perrault, *Le Cinéma Québécois à l'heure internationale* (Montreal: Stanké, 1990), 243.

25. See Odile Tremblay, "Tourner en anglais au Québec," *Le Devoir* 10, 11 June 2000, B1 and B3.

26. Bor, "An Interview with Léa Pool," 65.

27. Murray White, "Where Films Made in English Can Seem a Cultural Betrayal," *The New York Times*, 17 September 2000, sec. 2, pp. 11, 16.

28. Abel, *Le Cinéma Québécois a l'heure internationale*, 182.

29. Tremblay, "Tourner en anglais au Québec," B1.

30. Abel, *Le Cinéma Québécois a l'heure internationale*, 25.

12

Woman with a Movie Camera

Patricia Rozema's Revisionist Eye

BRENDA AUSTIN-SMITH

FOR SOMEONE CAREFULLY SHELTERED from cinematic images as a child, who did not even step into a film theatre until she was sixteen years old, Patricia Rozema has fashioned a remarkable career as a film screenwriter, director, and editor in a country in which home-grown filmic fame and fortune, particularly for a woman, is a challenging achievement. Rozema is one of Canada's most recognizable and successful film artists, famous for works in which the wilful imagination asserts itself despite bureaucracy, convention, and social expectation. As a writer and filmmaker, she is drawn to romantic figures whose artistry persists despite various obstacles, from institutionally derived notions of artistic standards to religiously supported ideas of appropriate sexualities. The motive for the determination of these characters is usually a lived conviction, a deeply felt secular faith in their own understanding, and a practice of creativity that imbues their local rebellions and resistances with a tinge of the protestant. Rozema is also known for her often sumptuous visual style, her juxtaposition of conventional protagonists and audacious storytelling techniques, and her sweet-tempered postmodernism, which often resolves challenges to received practices and opinions conclude in often magical happy endings.

Throughout her work, Rozema has retained a feminist eye for the stories of compelling female characters. However, her avoidance of protagonists who present themselves as revolutionary or startlingly exceptional marks her interest in artists of the everyday, rather than in iconoclastic figures who break completely, either creatively or socially, from everything and everyone around them. Indeed, many of Rozema's films attend to the loneliness and solitude involved in creativity. One need only think of Anne Vogel, the filmmaker in "Passion" (1985), whose creative work is tied to the break-up of her relationship, or Polly Vandersma, in *I've Heard the Mermaids Singing*, whom we see in her nightgown, alone in her apartment kitchen eating canned peas.

Being alone, outside of or apart from familial and intimate relationships, runs like a quiet threat through the lives of Rozema's women artists in particular. One of the ways in which a belief in art sustains many of these characters is that it offers them the possibility of community and belonging. A relationship with another person, though, or incorporation into any larger group, such as Fanny Price's absorption into the Bertram family in *Mansfield Park*, is subject to the demands of the artist figure's integrity, an ethical calling that trumps all other obligations; only in some filmic treatments of this situation does Rozema present her protagonists as fully able to reconcile intimate happiness with a life in art.

Patricia Rozema was born in 1958, in Kingston, Ontario, to an immigrant Dutch family, but grew up in the industrial town of Sarnia. Raised in a strict Calvinist religious environment, Rozema attended Lambton Christian High School, where she won prizes for her dramatic talents in school productions. In interviews, Rozema has described the effect her conservative upbringing had on her viewing experiences, recalling that her parents disabled the television set whenever they left their children home alone. Rozema grew up watching Disney, and saw the film *Snow White* on the small screen, but her first experience of a movie theatre screening was when a date took her to see *The Exorcist* in 1973. For someone who believed in the devil at the time, the experience was rattling.

In the mid-1970s Rozema moved from southern Ontario to Michigan, majoring in philosophy and journalism at Calvin College. It was here that her emerging sexual identity as a lesbian coincided with a decided break from all things religious. After graduation, she worked for a time in television in both Chicago and New York, and then secured a position with the CBC's *The Journal* in the early 1980s. It was only after having been laid off from the CBC that Rozema took a five-week course in film production at Ryerson, which yielded her first short work, "Passion: A Letter in 16mm," in 1985, which won second prize at the Chicago International Film Festival.[1]

In the years since that debut, Patricia Rozema has written and directed four more shorts, four feature films, made a segment of a television series, filmed Samuel Beckett's *Happy Days*, and become an executive producer of television and film projects. She has worked with outstanding artists in Canadian theatre and film, such as Linda Griffiths, Sheila McCarthy, Kate Nelligan, Paule Baillargeon, and Pascale Bussières, as well as artists from a diversity of creative fields, including the cellist Yo-Yo Ma, playwright and actor Harold Pinter, and the skaters Torvill and Dean. Her career as a writer-director was given almost unbelievable momentum by the release of her first feature, *I've Heard the Mermaids Singing* (1987), which received a six-minute long standing ovation at its Cannes screening, won the Prix de la Jeunesse, and turned Rozema into a made-in-Canada success story. That momentum stalled in 1990 with the release of *White Room*, and it was not until 1995 that *When Night is Falling* re-established Rozema's reputation among critics and viewers. It was in her spunky adaptation of *Mansfield Park* (1999), though, that Rozema's confident eye was able to turn its revisionist gaze not only to Jane Austen but also to the themes and formal strategies that have characterized her own film work since the mid-1980s, and to bring them to fully satisfying cinematic fruition. There is something about Rozema's relationship to Austen's ironic humour, as well as to the outsider protagonist of *Mansfield Park*, Fanny Price, that enabled Rozema to work through her own cinematic iterations of artistic struggle and finally, it seems, to achieve her most convincing and accomplished expression of those abiding preoccupations.

Many of the enduring concerns of Rozema's oeuvre, such as creative integrity and commitment, and the sometimes uncertain differences between the marginal and the independent artist, are present in her first short film, "Passion: A Letter in 16 mm." Starring Linda Griffiths as Anne Vogel, a documentary filmmaker addressing an unidentified lover, the film explores Anna's struggle to reconcile her desire for success with her wish for intimacy. In conforming to a certain image of what she thinks she is supposed to be, Anne has jeopardized her relationship, though her art has flourished. Anne's filmic love letter is both an attempt to communicate with the estranged lover and a demonstration of Anne's facility with the medium she has chosen as her emotional vehicle. The film also introduces the viewer to Rozema's "signature" narrative strategy of a character interrupting the story in order to deliver insights to the camera in direct address.[2] Agata del Smoluch del Sorbo writes that this film "stretches the boundaries of film-making as letter-writing," while introducing the viewer to the confessional mode that structures Rozema's subsequent art-house hit, *I've Heard the Mermaids Singing*.[3] The first-person address to the camera perfectly dramatizes Anne's intense relationship to art, for it is only through her chosen medium—film—that Anne can address her lost love, using the very mechanism of their estrangement to communicate. It is sadly ironic that viewers of "Passion" experience it as an "intimate" film, whereas Anne's fictional, off-screen lover might dismiss it as yet another proof of the distance that lies between them.

The success of her first short film propelled Patricia Rozema into her next project, the writing and directing of her first feature-length film, *I've Heard the Mermaids Singing*. Told almost completely in flashback, the film takes the form of a video-confession made by a frumpy, self-conscious woman to an unnamed audience. The film stars Sheila McCarthy as thirty-one-year-old Polly Vandersma, a temporary secretary, self-described as "organizationally impaired," who has a mangy haircut that could only be self-inflicted. Polly, who rides through the city of Toronto on her bicycle, snapping pictures of buildings, workers, mothers with prams, and kids playing street hockey, is an odd but strongly appealing protagonist. Rozema herself was tired, she said, of "successful women" pictures in which the heroines were endlessly capable and conceived Polly as an unconventional antidote to the type.[4] Polly is hired by the ultra-sophisticated Gabrielle St. Peres (Paule Baillargeon), curator of The Church Gallery, and is smitten by all that the worldly, beautiful, and cultured Gabrielle represents. It is, as critic Rita Kempley wrote in her review of the film, "an affair of the mind" in which Polly enacts the fascination of English Canada with French-Canadian culture.[5]

Though in her work life Polly is insecure, gauche, and inept, in private she enjoys a vivid fantasy life in which she walks up the sides of buildings, flies while wearing a toque emblazoned with a maple leaf, and walks confidently on water with Gabrielle, the two of them in period costume. The black and white fantasies, which arise whenever Polly gazes dreamily at her own photographs (the ones Gabrielle rejects as "the trite made flesh"), still depict Polly as waifish and somewhat awkward but also as powerful, for example, when she conducts an imaginary orchestra that depends upon her signal to play the last note. These compensatory daydreams can be read allegorically in relation to the Canadian film industry's desire for recognition in an environment dominated by Hollywood, while, as an adorable loser, Polly is also a female version of the ineffectual men who populate Canadian feature films.[6] The film's knowing use of first-person video narration acknowledges the history of documentary forms in Canadian cinema and indicates Rozema's self-consciousness about the role of media in the construction of identity, particularly in the construction of artistic identities that are markedly unconventional. Robert Cagle, for example, notes that in "Passion," *Mermaids*, and in her second feature, *White Room* (1990), Rozema's characters are "outsiders, alienated from the world around them; their only access to happiness is through media(ted) formulas for fantasy—formulas imposed upon them from elsewhere."[7] One of the ways in which *Mermaids* explores the tension between artistic insecurity and creative freedom is in its experimentation with the formulas of narrative cinema. Though the story is populated by characters unsure of their creative instincts, Rozema confidently disrupts the conventions of mainstream film, inserting rough video footage, fantasy sequences, and first-person narration into the film's formal unfolding, suggesting something about the artist Polly might become in the future, if she continues to trust her own vision.

It is in her resistance to formulas having to do with what constitutes artistic talent and success that Polly distinguishes herself from the other characters in *Mermaids*, as well as from Anne in "Passion." Polly's facility with her own camera, as well as with the video camera she sets up in the gallery and later smuggles home for her own use, demonstrates her comfort with the technology of visual fantasies, not to mention her imaginative re-appropriation of the cinematic apparatus to tell her own story from her own point of view. It is important, too, that though Polly destroys her camera and her pictures after her artwork is dismissed by Gabrielle, she maintains her integrity as an artist in the face of Gabrielle's pretentiousness and dishonesty, refusing, finally, to trade her direct apprehension of the world around her—documented in her photographs—for the fame and success that come, temporarily at least, to Gabrielle.

In the climactic confrontation with Gabrielle, Polly throws hot tea in the curator's face after learning that the mysteriously beautiful, glowing pictures Gabrielle has passed off as her own are actually the work of Mary Joseph (Ann-Marie MacDonald), Gabrielle's lover. It is a violent act out of proportion to the situation. Gabrielle and Mary Joseph's collusion is, after all, a small art crime whose only obvious victim is Polly's naïve and heart-felt belief in Gabrielle. The curator stands not only for a kind of talentless egoism that revels in its tiny power to pronounce on the creative efforts of others but also for the external validation or authority that artists seek to the detriment of their art. In the process of absorbing the truth about Gabrielle, Polly recovers faith in her own creative ability and is able once again to share her pictures with Gabrielle and Mary Joseph, who appear at her apartment in a scene of forgiveness as the film concludes. The reconciliation scene is a fabulous one, as Polly invites Gabrielle and Mary Joseph to step through a fantastic door that leads to an equally magical forest. Though this seems an improbable way to end the film, the tactic reinforces *Mermaids*' bi-fold message: fidelity to the imagination is the artist's first and only obligation and the artist's commitment to the existence of this realm can make it visible to others. Rozema's tendency to magic realism, particularly as her films conclude, surfaces in other, later works, leading del Sorbo, among others, to characterize them as "elegant fairy-tale like stories."[8]

A small Canadian film made on a shoestring budget of CAD $350,000, *Mermaids* went on from its triumph at Cannes to open the 1987 Toronto Festival of Festivals, play in over fifty US cities, make millions of dollars in profit, and end up at #17 on the *Variety* billboard.[9] As Lee Parpart writes, though, the success of *Mermaids* had an ambiguous effect on the funding scene for other domestic films:

> Canadian film funding bodies responded by funneling more resources into artist-driven films, hoping for another hit, while Mermaids' unusually high profits gave arts bureaucrats an excuse to drive budgets down on other projects. If Rozema and Raffe could produce an international hit for less than half a million dollars, they argued, other Canadian auteurs-in-waiting should be able to do the same.[10]

With her place in the company of other Toronto New Wave directors, such as Atom Egoyan and Bruce McDonald, established, Rozema released *White Room* in 1990. As Parpart notes, Rozema's second feature was "nothing less than a critical disaster," due, in part, to viewer dismay at encountering this "serious, at times painful, meditation on voyeurism, deception, and the high costs of fame," many of the same ingredients that *Mermaids* had treated with "gentle whimsy."[11]

In *White Room*, Rozema replaces direct address by a character with a soft-speaking narrator who uses the familiar incantation of fairy tales to introduce Norman Gentle (Maurice Godin), the male protagonist: "Once upon a time there lived a young man who lived an exciting life. The only problem was, it was all in his head, and when he tried to put words on it, it always slipped away." Norman shares a lack of identity and artistic direction with Polly Vandersma, though the mermaids of inspiration clearly speak to him, indicated onscreen by the sudden intrusion of mind-screen images that represent the intense visions—like those of a rearing horse—he wishes to represent through his chosen medium, writing. In Norman's case, the harmless voyeurism associated with Polly, who in *Mermaids* awkwardly spies on a couple making out in a park, becomes more clinical in its perversion. The result is his inadvertent witnessing of the rape and murder of Madeleine X, a famous pop star. Norman's transfixion before the spectacle of the murder he sees from the yard behind Madeleine's glass-sided house becomes a pathological extension of his writer's block. Indeed, as a protagonist, he is negatively characterized by his general aimlessness and passivity, both as an artist and as a character, drifting from the orbit of one strong woman, his friend Zelda

(Sheila McCarthy, as a darkly inflected version of Polly), to that of Jane (Kate Nelligan), a beautiful and traumatized recluse who has lent her voice to the career of the murdered singer. Norman shares with Polly Vandersma a fascination with a remote, sophisticated older woman. He begins by stalking Jane, then he helps her reclaim her garden from the organic riot to which it has fallen victim and finally becomes her lover.

The ambition of White Room is obvious in its mixture of cinematic and literary narrative strategies, which Robert Cagle argues are brought together in a "treatise on desire and repression." He also quotes Rozema, who claims that the film presents a self-conscious "journey through genres," from murder mystery to comedy to pastoral romance.[12] It is this rapid shift in generic direction, however, that gives the film its lurching sense of tone. In one scene, Norman is gamely working for the whacky Zelda in a strangely isolated newsstand, and in the next scene he is shadowing the mysterious Jane as she wafts across courtyards in her black headscarf and dark glasses. It is this air of deliberate portentous-ness—an ungainly combination of over-determined symbolism (the restored garden, Norman's visions, the white room itself in which Norman and Jane make violent love) and under-motivated characters—that made the film a puzzle for viewers who criticized it for its lack of subtlety.

On the other hand, critics such as Lee Parpart and Deborah Knight have defended the self-reflexivity of White Room. Knight sees the film as an exploration of "story-telling as *fabulation*" in which the principles of realism may be suspended.[13] For Knight, White Room's turn to magic realism allows the film to dramatize those facets of human experience that "threaten either to transcend or to escape capture in representational systems," a reading that permits Norman's creative block to be seen as something more complex and significant than mere impotence.[14] Building on Knight, Parpart sees the film as launching a critique of "androcentric story structures," pointing out that Norman's role as a well-meaning young man with a traditional approach to narrative becomes, because of his innocence and naïvety, fatal to two of the women in the film.[15]

White Room and Mermaids express uneasiness about artistic success, dramatizing it through the splitting or multiplication of artist figures, one of whom is struggling, blocked, or otherwise marginalized.[16] In these two films, the true artists, Polly, Mary-Joseph, and Jane, are those who create in a spirit of disinterest, unconcerned that someone else takes credit for their work. Far from seeking attention, they avoid and even flee from it. Attached to each of these artist characters is another would-be creator, such as Gabrielle, Madeleine X, and to some extent, Norman, who is focussed on the trappings rather than the essence of art. The romantic and sexual resonances of these artistic triangles are central to both plot and theme, as the characters strive to form generative connections between erotic and creative energies. While *Mermaids'* light touch lets these figures achieve reconciliation, *White Room* does not. It is only after consummating his obsession with Jane that Norman defeats his writers' block, but the prose that spills out of him onto the page is still drenched in clichés. And the nightmare-fairytale conclusion that allows Norman to wish Jane back to life is a forced march of a happy ending, one with strings left attached and visible.

Despite its lukewarm reception, Rozema herself remains happy with *White Room*, predicting that it will one day receive more positive notice and pointing out that the film received several prizes in France, Germany, and Japan, and earned three Genie nominations in Canada.

Two years after the release of *White Room*, Rozema returned to the short film format, with a quirky treatment of English-Canadian anxiety in relation to the legendary sophistication of French-Canadian culture. "Desperanto" (1992) was one of a six-part compilation feature made by some of Canada's most well-respected directors, including Léa Pool, Denys Arcand, and Atom Egoyan. Rozema's early muse, Sheila McCarthy, appears once again onscreen as Anne, an Ontario teacher who visits Montreal in search of the romance and mystery she associates with all things French-Canadian. While in Montreal, Anne crashes a party even though she cannot understand French. Misunderstandings and embarrassment follow, culminating in Anne faking a fainting spell, during which she imagines the party as a film, with sub-titles appearing helpfully below the frames. Though Rozema protests that she doesn't like Hollywood endings, "Desperanto" resolves its protagonist's difficulties through magic, a tactic that in many of her films guarantees her characters as much happiness as Hollywood would allow, if without the realism.

Rozema's next feature, which combined frankness and romance in its presentation of sexuality, brought her once again to the attention of the mainstream. *When Night is Falling*, released in 1995, was regarded by viewers and critics alike as Rozema's "comeback" movie. Rozema's continuing interest in emotional triangles finds expression in the story of Camille (Pascale Bussières), her fiancée, Martin (Henry Cznerny), and Petra Soft (Rachel Crawford). Camille and Martin are professors at a religious college who must marry in order to take up a coveted chaplaincy as a couple. Petra is a free-spirited performer in the visiting Sirkus of Sorts who meets Camille by chance in a laundromat, and develops an immediate attraction to her. Petra contrives another meeting by deliberately switching their laundry, which forces Camille to visit the circus to retrieve her clothes and results in a shared drink in Petra's funky trailer. At first, Camille rebuffs Petra's bold advances but, over the course of their meetings, she is gradually pulled by the force of her own emerging desire to become Petra's lover.

The opening minutes of the film signal its future direction in a slow camera pan that moves from a shot of Martin's class, in which he is lecturing his students about the need for absolutes in human life, to a shot of Camille, teaching her mythology students that people crave transformation. The shot forecasts Camille's eventual abandonment of Martin and the life of conservative Christianity he represents, suggesting that Camille's discontent has profound spiritual, as well as sexual, roots.

Camille's journey from straight mythology professor to erotically awakened lesbian begins with the sudden death of her dog, Bob, but is tied up, as all of Rozema's films are, with matters of art and ethics. Camille is weeping disconsolately while doing her laundry when Petra first sees her, touching her arm in a gesture of comfort. It is a first reaching out from one world to another, one that soon draws Camille to a scruffier part of town in order to return Petra's clothes to her. Stumbling through the entrance to the circus, Camille wanders backstage before being mistakenly ushered through a curtain, where she finds herself standing in a spotlight, fielding questions from someone who thinks she is auditioning for a spot. And of course, she is, though she is not fully aware of it. Stephen Holden, in his *New York Times* review of the film, remarks on the "images of gymnastics, daredevil sports and circus stunts to evoke

Camille's terrified erotic leap of faith," while Linda Lopez McAllister suggests that in the circus scenes Rozema is citing the "Acrobats" segment from Laura Mulvey and Peter Wollen's *Riddles of the Sphinx* (1977).[17] What is clear is that the circus is an idealized version of other spaces and institutions, like the Church Gallery in *Mermaids* or the music industry in *White Room*, which is associated with creative display or performance. In Rozema's work, these places are often corrupted by commercialism and rigidity. The artist figures who challenge these conditions find themselves marginalized and must strive to transform their outsider status into a productive independence. Polly seems well on her way to this sort of life, while both Madeleine X and Jane do not achieve it and are destroyed.

Whether she realizes it or not, then, Camille is destined to join the circus, for the Sirkus of Sorts is an inclusive and utopian performance site that harbours misfits just like her. It stands in opposition to the college as a place of permission and exploration, where the transformations described in the mythology Camille teaches to her students are experienced first hand. Camille musters up the ethical courage to break away from the college, and, with it, from Martin, realizing that the moral rigidity of the institution to which she is about to commit her life is destructive to her. Petra, having established herself as an independent performer affiliated with the circus, is Camille's ideal lover-instructor, someone for whom sexuality and creativity are intimately related. Although the schematic contrasts between Camille and Petra can reinforce unfortunate associations between black lesbian sexuality and an exotic world of sideshows and freaks, Rozema's sustained focus throughout is on the "existential questions" of individual identity and the individual choices the two women make.[18]

When Night is Falling was filmed by Douglas Koch, Rozema's cinematographer on *Mermaids*, and even reviewers who found the plot contrived and the dialogue stiff commented on the superb compositions. Edward Guthmann, writing a positive notice in the *San Francisco Chronicle*, called Rozema "a fabulist with a strong visual sense," and her eye for the gorgeous shots of a stand of birch trees in winter or the structures that high-voltage towers create against the sky is undeniable.[19] Apart from gorgeous visuals, though, there is a streak of unbridled romanticism in the film that leads to unlikely and sentimental plot devices, such as having Petra reach Camille's frozen body before the ambulance does or showing Bob, Camille's dead dog, improbably shake himself free of the snow in which she has buried him and run off into the woods as the final credits roll. The film was just what Rozema's career needed, however. It won a Silver Bear at the Berlin Film Festival, Best Film at the Melbourne Film Festival, and several Most Popular Film awards around the world. Important too, for a director reluctant to identify herself primarily as a lesbian film-maker, the film's portrayal of "the whole wonderful world of lesbianism" won awards at several gay and lesbian film festivals, including Outfest in Los Angeles and the London G&L Festival. [20]

By this time in her career, Rozema had established a pattern of moving from feature filmmaking to short film work and back again, as if using the discipline and concentration of one form to replenish her energy and vision for the other. And so, in 1997 Rozema released the short film, "Six Gestures," as part of a television documentary, "Yo-Yo Ma: Inspired by Bach." The piece won both a Primetime Emmy and a Golden Rose award in Montreux, Switzerland. The film deftly and lyrically showcases Rozema's persistent attraction to inter-arts performances. Rozema films Ma per-forming Bach's *Suite No. 6* on a traffic island, on a roof-top, and in other Manhattan locations. Interlaced with these are segments featuring the skaters Jayne Torvill and Christopher Dean, along with Tom McCamus, as the narrator, Bach. The same year that saw "Six Gestures" produced, Rozema received a Crystal Award for Outstanding Achievement from the Canadian organization Woman in Film and Television.

Two years later the release of Rozema's fourth feature, an adaptation of Jane Austen's *Mansfield Park*, brought her the most international atten-tion since her break-out hit twelve years earlier. In the novel, the young, introspective, and prim Fanny Price, poor cousin of the Bertram family, comes to live with her wealthy relatives in their country estate Mansfield Park. She becomes a central member of the household, which includes Lord and Lady Bertram, their drunken firstborn, Tom, their gentle second son, Edmund, who wishes to become a clergyman, and two daughters, Maria and Julia. Fanny eventually falls deeply in love with her cousin, Edmund, while he becomes interested in another one of his relatives, the fascinating Mary Crawford, who, with her dashing brother, Henry, has also come to live on the Bertram estate. In contrast to Mary, Fanny is shy, introspective, and extremely passive. She is an unusual Austen heroine, which has made *Mansfield Park* the least-liked of Austen's novels and the most challenging to adapt for audiences desiring less pious, more arresting heroines. Nor is Edmund as immediately interesting as Henry Crawford, who is, in the novel, finally exposed as a rake, running off with Edmund's married sister, Maria. In the end, all of the initially attractive but morally vacant characters are dispatched from Mansfield Park, leaving Edmund to realize finally that Fanny is his heart's desire.

Uninterested in producing a deferential adaptation, one in league with the heritage genre familiar from Merchant-Ivory productions, Rozema made a number of contentious moves in bringing the novel to the screen, all of them undertaken after she had rejected the screenplay offered to her by Harvey Weinstein, of Miramax, in the original commission to direct the film. The most central was re-conceiving Fanny Price as a spirited rather than retiring young woman. The script Rozema produced re-fashioned Fanny in the image of Jane Austen herself, using excerpts from Austen's letters and journals as dialogue for the character of Fanny (Frances O'Connor), who is from the beginning the perfect match for her cousin, Edmund (Johnny Lee Miller). Imagining Fanny as a writer, Rozema also awarded her the authorship, in the film, of numerous stories taken from Austen's own collection of juvenilia. The result is a character who speaks her own mind, who defiantly rides her horse in the rain, and who challenges Lord Bertram's (Harold Pinter) authority to hand her over in marriage to Henry Crawford (Alessandro Nivola), a man she neither trusts nor loves. Most important, Rozema's Fanny questions the family's reliance upon its slave holdings in Antigua to generate its wealth. The film's emphasis on the role of the slave trade in financing the lives of the gentry in late eighteenth-century England was another bold feature of Rozema's production, though it was based on allusions made in Austen's own novel. Finally, Rozema loosened the corset of the costume drama by hinting at lesbianism in a scene between Fanny and Mary Crawford (Embeth Davidtz) and including an adulterous sex scene.

All of these deviations from and re-orientations of the novel set many Austen fans back on their heels, though just as many lauded the film for its vital interpretation of Austen's most challenging work. Claudia L. Johnson, in a review article in the *Times Literary Supplement*, for example, called it "an audaciously perceptive cinematic evocation of Austen's unblinking yet forgiving vision."[21] *Mansfield Park* was in part a *succes de scandale*, as voices rose in criticism and in passionate defence of her revisionist version of Austen. It is also, though, a beautifully made film that reprises the emotional and ethical dynamics of Rozema's previous work. In addition, Rozema's *Mansfield Park* makes use of its period setting, the convenient framing device of a time gone by, to balance tonal shifts between lightly ironic humour and strong social criticism more gracefully and effectively than has been the case in Rozema's other films.

Controversial and perverse as *Mansfield Park* may be to some Austenites, it is perfectly in keeping with Rozema's passionate cinematic exploration of the relations between convention, creativity, integrity, and happiness. The relational triangles that dominate Rozema's films are doubled here, with Edmund, Fanny, and Henry as the points of one, and Fanny, Edmund, and Mary as the points of the other. And while Rozema's Fanny demonstrates local resistance to her uncle and to Henry Crawford, she ends up quite conventionally, as in the novel, marrying her cousin and remaining at Mansfield Park. It is this combination of rebelliousness and conformity that seems to fascinate Rozema, drawing her to characters trying to carve out space between formless freedom and suffocating orthodoxy. As the most counter-intuitive heroine in the Austen canon, Fanny also speaks to Rozema's well-established fondness for unlikely protagonists. In Fanny, Rozema's attraction to ethical rebels, characters driven to act out, speak up, and break away because of their moral convictions, finds a complete incarnation. Fanny's characterization is a notable development for Rozema, for Fanny is someone in whom an ethically informed spiritedness and a fully matured creativity are combined, whereas in other films these qualities have been distributed, sometimes unhappily, between two characters, like Madeleine X and Jane in *White Room*. Nor does Rozema efface all signs of the novel's Fanny in order to realize her for the screen. Traces of the propriety and moral perspicuity that cause Austen's Fanny to recoil at the thought of acting in a play and to see through the social artifice of both Henry and Mary Crawford, are present, as well, in the film's equivalent scenes. However, these same character traits also fuel Fanny's objections to the Bertrams' ownership of slaves. In this way Rozema preserves the moral vision Fanny possesses in the novel while making it resonate with contemporary audiences. Some may take this to be pandering, but it is more fairly described as what all good adapters of texts do in finding the contemporary vernacular by which the essences of a great book become effectively cinematic.

Mansfield Park is a happy instance of Rozema's thematic and formal strategies coming together in remarkable narrative harmony. Awarding Fanny the status of both protagonist and narrator of the story is in keeping with Rozema's playful treatment of filmic and narrative frames, while serving as the most recent example of her signature style of direct address. The strong and witty narrative presence supplied by the novel is also an avenue by which Rozema can channel the famed Austen irony through Fanny, without appearing to manipulate or imprison her characters.

More than anything else, *Mansfield Park* is a cinematic culmination of Patricia Rozema's years of attentiveness to the conditions necessary to the production of an ethically grounded, personally significant art. In her films, artists, particularly, but not exclusively, women artists, must discover the idiosyncratic alchemy by which desire and vision become act or artifact, releasing them from marginalization and isolation into independence. When doubt, repression, and insecurity persuade these figures to compromise, they lapse into an inexpressiveness grimly conveyed by Jane's slit throat in *White Room*. In films in which this goal is advanced or reached, the artist-figure is enabled, like Polly, like Camille, and like Fanny, to counter the effects of aesthetic, sexual, and social restrictions on self-expression. This is not to suggest that Patricia Rozema has nothing left to say about these and other matters in whatever films she makes in the future. At present she is under contract to Miramax for two more projects. The confidence of her feminist and post-colonial approach to Austen, though, bodes well for her ability to resist the pull of convention and to continue making the kind of pictures that her most-beloved heroine, Polly Vandersma, would appreciate: the kind that give you a kick.

1. See Bruce McDonald, "Scaling the Heights," *Cinema Canada* 141 (May 1987): 12–15; and Michael Posner, *Canadian Dreams: The Making and Marketing of Independent Films* (Vancouver, BC: Douglas and McIntyre, 1993) for more details of Rozema's early film experience and *I've Heard the Mermaids Singing* production history.

2. Barbara Goslawski, "Patricia Rozema's *Mansfield Park*," *Take One* (22 December, 2006), http://findarticles.com/p/articles/mi_moJSF/is_26/ai_30086925, accessed 6 February 2007.

3. del Sorbo, Agata Smoluch. "The Polyphonic Nature of Patricia Rozema." *Take One* (December 2004–March 2005): 14.

4. Posner, *Canadian Dreams*, 3.

5. Rita Kempley, review of *I've Heard the Mermaids Singing*, *Washington Post*, 16 October 1987, http://www.washingtonpost.com/wp-srv/style/longterm/movies/videos/iveheardthemermaidssingingnrkempley_aoca47.htm, accessed 13 December, 2006.

6. See Karen Jaehne, "Independents: *I've Heard the Mermaids Singing*," *Cineaste* 16, no. 3 (1988): 23, on Polly's "Canadian-ness"; Geoff Pevere on her as a variant of the great Canadian male loser, "In Others' Eyes: Four Canadian Films Come Home from Cannes," *Cineaction* (Winter 1987–88): 22; and Mike Gasher on Polly as a positive image of the Canadian film artist, "Decolonizing the Imagination: Cultural Expression as Vehicle of Self-Discovery," *Canadian Journal of Film Studies* 2, no. 2–3 (1993): 99. Agata Smoluch del Sorbo also mentions Rozema's reinvention of "the iconic paralyzed artist figure" in her portraits of "strong, complex successful female artist characters" (del Sorbo, "The Polyphonic Nature of Patricia Rozema," 21).

7. Robert Cagle, "A Minority on Someone Else's Continent: Identity, Difference, and the Media in the Films of Patricia Rozema," in *Gendering the Nation: Canadian Women's Cinema*, ed. Kay Armatage, Kass Banning, Brenda Longfellow, and Janine Marchessault, 184 (Toronto: University of Toronto Press, 1999).

8. del Sorbo, "The Polyphonic Nature of Patricia Rozema," 14.

9. These details are taken from Lee Parpart's article "Political Alignments and the Lure of 'More Existential Questions' in the Films of Patricia Rozema," in *North of Everything: English-Canadian Cinema Since 1980* ed. William Beard and Jerry White (Edmonton: University of Alberta Press, 2002), 295.

10. Parpart, "Political Alignments and the Lure of 'More Existential Questions' in the Films of Patricia Rozema," 295.

11. Ibid.

12. Cagle, "A Minority on Someone Else's Continent: Identity, Difference, and the Media in the Films of Patricia Rozema," 189.

13. Deborah Knight, "Metafiction, Pararealism, and the `Canon' of Canadian Cinema," *Cinémas* 3, no. 1 (Fall 1992): 138.

14. Ibid.

15. Parpart, "Political Alignments and the Lure of 'More Existential Questions' in the Films of Patricia Rozema," 295.

16. In articles published the same year, Lee Parpart and I make similar observations on Rozema's attraction to divided artist figures. See Parpart, "Political Alignments and the Lure of 'More Existential Questions' in the Films of Patricia Rozema," 307, n. 6; and Austin-Smith, "Gender Is Irrelevant: *I've Heard the Mermaids Singing* as Women's Cinema," 219, n.41.

17. Stephen Holden, "Of a Circus, Church, and Lesbian Love," *New York Times*, 17 November 1995 http://query.nytimes.com/gst/fullpage.html?res=9905E1DC1239F934A25752C1A963958260, accessed 14 December, 2006. See also Linda Lopez McAlister, "The Women's Show," WMNF-FM 88.5 Tampa, FL., 9 December 1995, http://www.mith2.umd.edu/WomensStudies/FilmReviews/W/When-night-is-falling-mcalister, accessed 14 December, 2006.

18. Parpart discusses Rozema's political evasiveness in the context of what Rozema says is her interest in "more existential questions" at length in her article. I discuss some of the same issues in "'Gender is Irrelevant': *I've Heard the Mermaids Singing* as Women's Cinema," *Canada's Best Features*, edited by Gene Walz (Amsterdam: Rodopi Press, 2002), 209–33.

19. Edward Guthmann, "A Fabulist Tale of Desire: Sexual Awakenings in 'Night is Falling,'" *San Francisco Chronicle*, 24 November 1995, C5.

20. Rozema makes this remark in conversation with Edward Guthmann in "Director Finds Gender Does Matter," *San Francisco Chronicle*, 25 November 1995, C1, discussing the NC-17 rating given to *When Night is Falling*. The rating was later appealed, but denied. The film was finally released unrated.

21. Claudia L. Johnson, "The Authentic Audacity of Patricia Rozema's Mansfield Park (1999)," *Times Literary Supplement*, 31 December 1999, 16–17.

13

Mina Shum
The "Chinese" Films and Identities
JACQUELINE LEVITIN

[In Chan is Missing] *many courses of action are identified as being Chinese and others as being American, but a Chinese American course of action is difficult to identify.... Being Chinese American is not a matter of resolving a duality, for proposing to draw from two cultures inevitably results in not belonging to either culture.*
—PETER FENG[1]

What you are fighting against with your second film is the imagined film of your fans.
—MINA SHUM[2]

IN 2002 AUDIENCES EAGERLY AWAITED the release of Mina Shum's *Long Life, Happiness and Prosperity*. Like her acclaimed autobiographically driven first feature, *Double Happiness* (1994) and unlike her unsuccessful second feature, *Drive She Said* (1997), Shum's third feature promised Chinese subject matter. Pre-release publicity made clear that Mina Shum had even brought

271

back Sandra Oh, the praised lead of *Double Happiness*. Shum had already wanted the Korean-Canadian actor, who passes as the Hong Kong–born Chinese Jade Li in *Double Happiness*, for the lead in her second feature, though its story reprised only the feminist theme of *Double Happiness* not its ethnic plot. But conflicting commitments prevented Oh from taking the role and from bringing ethnic nuances to *Drive She Said*'s story of a bank teller whose life choices are put into question when she is kidnapped in a bank robbery. A non-descript plot without Oh, Shum's second film bombed at the box office. Perhaps everyone in the audience was surprised that Mina Shum had produced a "non-Chinese" film.

While she was studying theatre at the University of British Columbia, Shum was once assigned to play a role "that you would never be asked to play."[3] Like her surrogate, Jade, in *Double Happiness*—an aspiring actor who practises the part of Southern belle Blanche Dubois of *A Streetcar Named Desire* and Saint Joan of Arc—Shum must have thought that any role was a possibility for her despite being Chinese Canadian. The lesson, thus, in circumscribing her ambitions was shocking for her—the "first Chinese Canadian woman to have made a feature film in Canada" who never thought of herself as such.[4] Looking over her career, including the success of "Me, Mom and Mona" (1993),[5] an early short documentary about herself, her mother, and her younger sibling, Mina Shum likely interpreted the failure of her second feature as a lesson in not straying too far from ethnic subject matter. However, *Long Life, Happiness and Prosperity*, though entirely Chinese, was to have a critical and box-office fate not unlike *Drive She Said*. Interpreting Shum's record of successes and failures can reveal something about the enterprise of non-White and ethnic filmmakers making feature films in Canada today.[6] It would seem that critics and general audiences expect ethnic filmmakers to offer personal stories that reveal something about living in a multi-racial and multi-cultural society—which is particularly true of Canada today—and to do it in a lively and familiar format.

▪ Minorities and History

GAY FILMMAKERS often decry being trapped in gay-only subject matter, and other minorities similarly cite pressures that limit their choices.

Taiwan-born, but New York-trained, filmmaker Ang Lee[7] demonstrated that one need not be a member of the dominant culture to master the dominant culture's subject matter, but his experience has been quite unique. Others, such as Wayne Wang,[8] have not been as successful. Mina Shum, nevertheless, may not have been feeling particularly minority-like or ethnically challenged when she embarked on *Double Happiness* and *Drive She Said*.

While Canada is a country of immigrants, greater Vancouver has become home to Chinese immigrants in particular. In 1996 Chinese accounted for slightly over a quarter of the population of Vancouver, which included almost 45 per cent visible minorities. By the time Shum made *Long Life, Happiness and Prosperity*, the Chinese population of Vancouver was almost 30 per cent, and across the river in Richmond the percentage was even higher.[9] These numbers must have at least partially inspired the confidence Shum felt in embarking on her first Chinese-subject matter film, although her natural tendency for optimism has also played a part.[10]

The racial and cultural mixing of populations in Vancouver, however, has not been without tensions. The quick transformation of the composition of the city strained ethnic relations in the 1990s. It is useful to review both the recent and distant history of Chinese immigration in Canada to place the production of Shum's films in context for a better understanding of what making a Chinese subject matter film means in the framework of Vancouver and Canada.

■ Chinese Canadian History

CANADIAN IMMIGRATION POLICY for Chinese largely mirrors the American (racially biased) example: accepting of an influx of (male) Chinese workers to build a cross-country railway then severely limiting numbers via a head tax imposed in 1885;[11] passing the Chinese Immigration Act of 1923, which eliminated Chinese immigration altogether; eliminating the (anti)Chinese Immigration Act in 1947 in red-faced acknowledgement that the Chinese were allies in the war effort against Japan; overhauling immigration law in 1967 and adopting a point system that allowed assessment of the Chinese immigrant in the same manner as all other immigrants (leading to a new influx of Chinese immigrants; Mina

Shum's own family arrived in 1966 when she was less than a year old); and, finally, in 1994, creating an "investor" immigrant class through which a number of wealthy Hong Kong immigrants were permitted to come to Canada before the British colony reverted to Chinese ownership in 1997. In a further development, beginning in the late 1990s, wealthy Chinese immigrants began to be outnumbered again by poorer arrivals from mainland China.[12]

The various waves of Chinese immigrants, however, fall into only two groups when considering class aspects and attitude to their country of reception. Accordingly, the immigrants who arrived soon after 1967 differed little from early immigrants and those who came after 1947. Generally relatively poor, at the time of their arrival, these immigrants lived modestly, careful not to stand out "too prominently" or annoy the White population. This contrasts with the majority of Chinese immigrants arriving in the 1980s and early 1990s who were often wealthy and disinterested in keeping a low profile. This wave built a series of extensive Chinese malls where English signage was absent. Newspapers in the late 1980s ran story after story of a "Chinese takeover" of the real estate market in Vancouver[13] and the established (White) population expressed horror at the building of "monster homes" in their neighbourhoods and at the cutting down of trees that the new arrivals considered to "block the path of good fortune."[14] This climate of xenophobia is the context in which Mina Shum made *Double Happiness* (1994), a film that reaches out to say "we Chinese are harmless and essentially just like you." It should be noted, however, that at present anti-Chinese xenophobia has quieted down. New demographics, fewer financially competitive Chinese immigrants, and a well-integrated school system have lead to a new harmony between the Chinese and established White population.

■ **"Chineseness"**

WHILE MULTICULTURALISM is a relatively new concept in the United States, it has been official policy in Canada since 1971 and the government of Prime Minister Pierre Elliot Trudeau, and it means something quite different here as opposed to the US. Not wanting a "melting pot,"

Canada encouraged the sharing of aspects of a common culture while proposing to preserve cultural identities—though this often amounted to no more than conserving the folkloric and stereotypic aspects of a cultural diversity. Relevant to the films of Mina Shum is how "Chineseness" came to be regarded as a result. Multiculturalism fossilized the imported culture at the moment of importation. The continual influx of Chinese immigrants in recent years has nuanced "fossilization," but still most adult non-Chinese Canadians' knowledge of Chinese culture remains circumscribed to (a rather Westernized) Chinese cuisine; perhaps the ability to recognize a lion dance; and "dim sum." For the Chinese themselves, their fossilized imported culture has meant the preservation of the patriarchal family.

The title of Mina Shum's first film, *Double Happiness*, refers to the twice-written Chinese character that symbolizes unity and marriage. In her film, it also references the need to please the patriarchal family—making their "Happiness" by getting married to "a suitable boy"—while attempting to please oneself [15] relegated to a second "Happiness." Individual happiness, deriving from Western values of independence, places individual desires over the good of the family collective and thus contradicts typical Chinese social organization. The traditional Chinese social order is not only based on a rigid hierarchy inherited from Confucianism but also on the concept of "inside" and "outside." [16] The family group is the primary inside grouping. The power it derives from its membership is compromised when individual members do not organize themselves according to its collective needs, as defined by the patriarch. The individual might find the family's rules and hierarchies interfere with their personal desires and thus choose to break away, but this separation is not without consequence. Once outside, the individual no longer "belongs," no longer benefits from what the unit can provide. [17]

When I first met Mina Shum in 1991, the title for *Double Happiness* was "Banana Split." In Vancouver in the 1990s, "Banana" was the term the new, richer, and self-confident class of Chinese immigrants used to describe the older Chinese community. They chastised the first wave for not having preserved their culture, for not being "Chinese enough"—for being yellow on the outside and white within. The inability to read and write Chinese characterized this loss of culture. Chinese who lost their culture were no better than "ghosts"—the term the Chinese language uses for foreigners, a term that also communicates a troubled psyche.

More than merely a "banana," however, Double Happiness's Jade is a "split banana." Although seemingly optimistic about Jade's decision to leave her restrictive home, Double Happiness also seems to register Shum's self-doubts about the prospect of cutting family and thus Chinese ties. Nuances appear in the second audition scene, where Jade is presented to a Hong Kong producer. At stake is the possibility of a "real" role. Jade, however, fails to impress—not because of a lack of talent, but because, though able to speak fluent Cantonese, she cannot read the audition sides written in Chinese. Unsuitable for roles in "White" films because she is Chinese, she also does not qualify for Chinese roles because she is not "Chinese enough." Reflecting perhaps the internalization of the second wave's criticism, in this audition scene, Shum herself plays the producer who angrily denounces Jade, her fictional double. Significantly, too, Jade's exodus from the family home, though forced by her father's confiscation of her key, does not land her in the arms of her non-Chinese suitor. It is Jade alone in her apartment that we see. There is still time for a contemplation of cultural choices.

Normally, however, Mina Shum comfortably (nostalgically, perhaps, in Long Life, Happiness and Prosperity) identifies with the first wave of immigrants to Vancouver. She carefully defines the economic status of Jade's household—not from any Marxist impulse, but because she wants to claim her membership in the earlier group, those who, in Canada, were lower middle class and had to work their way up in the world. In Double Happiness, the father and provider of the household is a security guard; a well-placed camera angle allows us to read the insignia on his shoulder. In Long Life, Happiness and Prosperity, Shuck, the hero of the "Long Life" storyline, is similarly a security guard, losing his job just five years before reaching retirement age, just like Shum's own father.[18] The class to which Mark (the Caucasian who will become Jade's lover and initiate her separation from the family) belongs, is not made clear in the film. He looks like a badly dressed nerd but, she notes, he is a graduate student in English. Economic security may not define Shum's group, but it is still valued. Although an English major does not rate particularly well in her family's hierarchy of professions, to the theatrically inclined Jade, Mark is a suitably artistic choice. And he drives a sports car. The car might hint at a higher economic status or that he has hidden, non-nerd qualities. Either way, he is as suitable for Jade as a non-Chinese boyfriend can be. He is an outsider like herself. Like her, he has a domineering father; he even accuses Jade of having been set up by his father to abandon him to confirm his father's image of him as a failure and an incompetent.[19]

■ Audience Identifications

PETER FENG, in an article on Wayne Wang's early film, *Chan is Missing* (1981), tried to pin down how that film contributes to defining "Asian American." Feng rejects the hyphen in "Asian-American" and, following Trinh T. Minh-ha, promotes the space left empty where the hyphen usually is placed as the place of "becoming"—of definitions that cannot be fixed because they are in process. In the absence of a hyphen, he proposes, the two terms on either side are left to negotiate with each other.[20] While Feng proposes Asian American as the political label, a term based on race and useful in designating allies in the struggle against hegemonic power, "Chinese American" (or, we could add, "Chinese Canadian") he declares to be a "cultural label." Feng celebrates *Chan is Missing* for foregrounding the heterogeneity of Chinese American subjectivities and for what this then contributes to the political notion, "Asian American."

The characterization in Mina Shum's films could be said not to participate in the enterprise of heterogeneity; her films are non-political according to Feng's definitions. A notion of harmony, for example, permeates *Long Life, Happiness and Prosperity*. Individual differences are minimalized; the small community is understood to be unified, although individual members speak different dialects of Chinese.[21] In *Double Happiness*, while Jade rebels against a family she is careful to distinguish as "a Chinese family," all families are found to be patriarchal—her Chinese friend Lisa's as well as Mark's; the problem is posed as generational rather than cultural. Jade's difficulties with the producer from Hong Kong indicate that differences among Chinese do exist, but the producer is presented as an outsider to a Vancouver where racial and ethnic groups co-exist happily.[22] Though hegemonic power exists in *Double Happiness*, it is not directed only against Chinese; the bouncers outside the "No No" club discriminate equally against Mark, the White nerd. There are no racial barriers to understanding in *Double Happiness*; Jade's potential allies are not simply other young Chinese or Asians but also any sympathetic White. Allies can be anyone in the film's audience who empathize with rebellion against constraint or with being the "other"; the role of Mark opens possibilities for identification with the latter.[23] In contrast, points of identification for non-Chinese seem not to have been calculated for *Long Life, Happiness and Prosperity*. In that film, the "inside" leaves no open doors for would-be non-Chinese members. This may partially explain the tepid response the film received from (primarily White) critics and lack-lustre box-office success.

■ *Double Happiness*

IN A FOOTNOTE, Feng dismisses *Double Happiness* as belonging to that too-frequent trope, and possible essentialist cliché: the generation-conflict film.[24] However, one could argue that it is Shum's variation on the generation-conflict story in *Double Happiness* that makes it interesting in terms of audience identification strategies. Jade is a twenty-two-year-old living at home. Although she has ambitions to be an actor, her parents' ambition is that she marry a nice Chinese boy. They do not deny her a career, but their imaginings of an acceptable acting role is embodied by Connie Chung, an anchorwoman. In the Chinese-Canadian cultural pull, Jade—and we along with her—lean to the Canadian side because her experience of what Chineseness represents is repression and rigidity in the person of the father. He has already banished an elder brother, Winston, presumably for non-obedience in career plans or relationships.

The film's first scenes set the tone for audience identification. Sandra Oh, holding her own clapper board labelled with the name of her character, directly addresses the audience as Jade. The effect of the direct address is more like a confiding wink to the audience than a Brechtian alienation device. We, the audience, are not so much pulled out of the film as pulled into it, asked to identify with Jade's point of view. This direct address also serves to reference Mina Shum, an aspect reinforced throughout the film by stylistic devices such as rapid zooms, obviously tinted images, and slow-motion scenes that call attention to the signs of enunciation. Jade/Sandra Oh/Mina Shum tells us about her family.[25] "Just imagine them as any average family that you would see on television—but of course you wouldn't see them on television," she jokingly adds, sensitizing us to the Chinese reality, reminding us of the absence of Asians on Canadian and American television, a theme reiterated in the film in Jade's near-futile efforts to get roles as an actor. "We" non-minorities do learn some cultural sensitivity from the film, although the lessons are humorous and easy to take rather than angry. Jade/Oh/Shum then describes her family: "They're very Chinese, if you know what I mean." Jade's use of "they" others her family, her parents in particular, while conspiratorially aligning the Jade/Oh/Shum trio with the audience. This is reinforced in the scene that follows, where, perched on a Lazy Susan between the rice and the hoisin sauce, like a bump on a log that is a tabletop, we are introduced to "them" during a family dinner. "They"—really only the parents' generation—are "very Chinese" first because of language, their poor grasp of English. Swinging left and right on the Lazy Susan, we witness the father confusing Jade's sister's use of the word "fact" for another, improper, dinner-table word, and the unwarranted censorship that results. The patriarch's authority is thus from the start demonstrated to be inappropriate linguistically and culturally; limited English and cultural inflexibility render him blind and deaf to what is happening even at his own dinner table.

Shum not only others the parents in *Double Happiness*; she at times renders them quite ridiculous. Even the mother comes up for a thrashing. Although in her direct-address monologue—each family member has a monologue that allows us to penetrate their inner realities—we sympathize with her anguish over her banished son, Winston, we snicker when in her "real time" prayer to the Chinese gods for her lost son she petitions with equal fervour for the success of her tomato patch. Her prayer, surprisingly, is recited in English. It is impossible to tell whether the mother and father's wooden acting style that contributes to their ridiculousness comes from purposeful bad timing or from the actors' real inability to master the dialogue in English. Either way, it is well-calculated. The father, supremely confident in his superior knowledge, commands Jade to follow his direction in life. "I know this world better that you," he tells her. His claim is risible because Shum places the scene immediately after Jade discovers Ah Hong, the father's visiting boyhood friend, quietly communicating to his family back home by phone from the bathroom. He tells Jade that he dare not admit to father that the woman who is his wife was formerly his maid; "your father would say this is not a family." Even the friend considers the father to be incapable of understanding cultural compromises; the father's notions of Chinese culture have been idealized and fossilized through immigration.

Shum, however, would presumably like the audience to consider that things are not black and white but rather that they come in shades of grey. In her father's direct-address monologue, we learn that back in China, he, too, had ambitions that were suppressed. That knowledge is supposed to nuance our interpretation of his rigidity. As well, our siding with Jade in her strategies for dealing with him—she calculatedly presents him with red-bean cakes, his favourite, when he is angry with her—also help to soften our resistance to him: if we, too, have strategies for dealing with such fathers, our resistance need not be quite so dogmatic. This pattern for dealing with the father was already revealed in "Me, Mom and Mona" (1993). The film is basically an intimate conversation between Mina and her mother and sister interspersed with cut-away footage. Absent from the film is the father. In fact, much of the film tells secrets about the father and reveals strategies for how to deal with him. The daughters learn from the mother, and the mother—stronger and much livelier than the mother in *Double Happiness*—leads the charge. Shum's father has never seen "Me, Mom and Mona" and does not know what secrets it tells about him there.[26] Perhaps the reason is linguistic; he would not understand the little film. But one cannot help suspecting that he is a willing accomplice in the effort to "save face" for him; what he does not acknowledge knowing cannot hurt him.

■ **Plots and Fathers**

STYLISTIC INNOVATIONS such as the surprising Lazy Susan point of view remind us that Mina is not only one of "us Westerners." She is hip—a new-generation Chinese filmmaker, younger, more stylish than the Wayne Wangs and Ang Lees. Presenting herself thus was likely a marketing strategy (that worked). But, despite stylistic innovations, *Double Happiness* is classic and linear in its plot development and Hollywood-like in its conceptions of success and freedom as the reward for action.

It is useful to compare the narrative strategy of *Double Happiness* to the narrative strategies of recent American and Canadian Chinese women writers. Two plots seem typical of these writers, both revolving around the father. The first of these plots, which could be called the "ethnic plot," concerns the impotency of the father in his new North American setting. As out-lined by Shirley Geok-Lin Lim, in this plot, the traditional father, whose pride depends on being able to provide for and organize his family, is disempowered by a racist, classist, White North American society.[27] The novels document the father's humiliations, losses, and pathetic struggles.[28] The heroine in this plot may, herself, suffer racism and endure censorship when the father's impotency is turned against her, but finally she does not rebel because she realizes that society's threat against him is greater than the threat against her.[29]

In the second plot—what I will call the "gender plot"—the conflict between the father and the daughter is conceived as a conflict of gender roles. Here the ethnic patriarch is seen as villain and the ethnic woman as victim. These works are more clearly about rebellion and use feminist rather than ethnically identified codes, such as poetry written on the body. (Shum's "punk" stylistics could be viewed in this light.) These works are seen as more assimilationist; for women, the new culture offers more possibilities for liberation.[30] In *Double Happiness*, Mina Shum steers a safe course between these two seemingly incompatible plots.

As in both the ethnic and the gender plot, the father in *Double Happiness* is presented as the centre of the problem. In *Long Life, Happiness and Prosperity*, the first two of the three plotlines wait on the actions of the patriarch of the family—the butcher and the night watchman; women characters, in contrast, are incapable of changing the direction of the plot. In the third plot, the "Happiness" plot, Mindy attempts to bring happiness to her mother through Taoist magic. She succeeds but only when the she takes desperate measures and invokes the power of the fourth element, fire, a yang (male) symbol.

Shum identified herself at the time of the making of *Double Happiness* as belonging to the punk generation. As self-identified, punks were on the fringes of society, permissive toward women, anti-social, and law-less. Thus it is not surprising that Jade and Mark, her Caucasian lover, nerd, and fellow outsider, find each other in the literal fringes of the city, not in the postcard-like "Beautiful British Columbia" (as BC license plates proclaim) but in industrial landscapes, atypical locations for romance. These industrial landscapes are where both obviously feel at home. And it is in such a landscape that the young Mindy, heroine of *Long Life, Happiness and Prosperity*, goes about her daily life—just steps away from the idealized "Chinese village" where she lives.

Jade's story is one of rebellion and thus seems to belong to the gender plot. Yet, as has been noted, the film is not unkind to the father. Jade/Shum both rebels and does not rebel. Although in life, director Mina Shum left the family home, in the film plot she makes the leaving easier by creating a second father for Jade—Ah Hong, the father's cherished boyhood friend. Ah Hong plays the role of a surrogate father—a kinder, liberal (more Western-like) father who tells Jade to "find her own path." "Do you need me, dad?" Jade tearfully asks her undemonstrative real father at Ah Hong's going away dinner. "You are supposed to tell her that you need her," prompts Ah Hong. Her father's refusal even to concede to Ah Hong's prompting leads Jade then and there to announce that she has decided to leave home, aborting the feast that has set Chinese and non-Chinese spectators' mouths watering in mere contemplation. Ah Hong soon finds words of encouragement to comfort Jade. "It's a different path," he comments on Jade's decision; "it's a good one."

Rather than having been inspired here by autobiography, Shum claims to have invented this second father who gives the rebel daughter permission to liberate herself. A character from Hong Kong, he is not caught in the immigrant's rigid image of family and the patriarchal role. Images or "stereotypes" are interrupted by characters in *Double Happiness* and also in *Long Life, Happiness and Prosperity*. Ah Hong bounces on the bed when he arrives and gets the stodgy father to do so, too—not a common image of the adult Chinese male. Later, he gets the whole family to dance around crazily and sing Karaoke. In *Long Life, Happiness and Prosperity*, Kin, Mindy's mother, played by Sandra Oh, responds sarcastically to her daughter's urging to buy a lottery ticket, that "yeah, I've got horseshoes up my butt." Her graphic language surprises us and the film's middle-age women discuss new possibilities for sex now that the children have left home. A scene depicts Shuck's wife intimately sitting on the ledge of the bathtub as he bathes. There is also a seduction by Shuck's wife, and a seduction he, himself, will initiate when he gains a new lease on life. Having undignified fun and being sexual are not the images typically associated with "proper" Chinese. In both films Shum lets us penetrate homes, be confided to in direct-address monologues, and overhear frank conversations to get a different idea of what it means to be Chinese. She neatly cuts from Jade's family living room, where the wild Karaoke is taking place, to just outside the window. The animated scene now only fuzzily visible behind curtains reminds us that we are outsiders with only temporary insider privileges.

■ Long Life, Happiness and Prosperity

DOUBLE HAPPINESS allows Jade to successfully rebel, but it leaves the hard questions unresolved, such as: "In assimilating, is she Chinese enough?" Leaving home, her father demands that she surrender her key, effectively cutting her off from the home, the source of her Chinese identity. It is a moving moment in the film. Jade's brother has already been banished, and in Shum's own family a banished brother has never been rehabilitated. *Double Happiness* could be read as an attempt to argue his case. Thus, it is not surprising that, when returning in *Long Life, Happiness and Prosperity* again to make a "Chinese" film, Shum mythifies Chineseness.

Coming seven years after *Double Happiness*, Mina Shum describes *Long Life, Happiness and Prosperity* as a homage to her parents and to the working-class community in which her parents raised her. Although unacknowledged, as such, the film seems set in the past, before more recent immigrations, at a time when the Chinese community was harmonious and of a similar economic stratum—before the arrival of the special-category investor immigrant of the 1990s—and when Chinese life in Vancouver was more physically circumscribed. There is an almost timeless feel to the location where the film's action takes place—a place of village-size proportions, although set within an urban landscape, a place whose exact contours we do not see but which includes all the necessary Chinese ingredients: a butcher shop that prepares BBQ duck; a dim sum restaurant where Kin, the mother of Mindy, the twelve-year-old heroine of the film, works;[31] a corner store with a *feng shui* mistress in the back room; small houses only large enough for a single family; traditional Chinese culture in the form of Taoism.[32] It is a vision of Chinese-Canadian existence in which the tension between the two poles—Chinese and Canadian—is eliminated because the implications of the second term are missing. Although a passing train carries the words "Canada," a Canada of non-Chinese barely exists in *Long Life, Happiness and Prosperity*. Two White high-school-age boys, for example, pass in the background of one scene, bouncing a basketball. Shum exaggerates the noise of the bouncing ball, but the (now ex-) security guard, Shuck, sitting on a bench in the foreground, does not appear to hear the sounds nor notice their makers. Foreign ghosts, the boys seemingly do not exist.

Perhaps because of the large "community" of Chinese actors and the difficulty of bringing nuance to every portrait, *Long Life, Happiness and Prosperity* feels superficial, devoid of the subjective complexities of *Double Happiness* despite its claims.[33] Even Taoism is reduced to its magic aspects; absent are its moral and philosophical dimensions, the complex notions of harmony. Though Shum travelled three times to Hong Kong in preparation for this film, she seems to have absorbed little of a deeper Chinese culture. It is a postmodern notion of Chineseness that she substitutes for a culturally more substantial one in *Long Life, Happiness and Prosperity*.

The industrial landscapes are still present in this film, representing potential refuges should the future hold any difficulty for Mindy. Significantly, other characters are not associated with or seen in these industrial spaces except for Shuck and then only when he is looking for a place to commit suicide. Mindy could be Jade before she grew up and started wandering into the other term of her dual identity. For now, she appears to be "born culturally Chinese"—embracing Taoist magic as if by genetic disposition, certainly not through the influence of her Chinese-speaking, but seemingly very Canadian, mother. The film centres on Mindy's attempts to save her mother from her unhappiness. Deserted long ago by Mindy's father, Kin is poor, overworked, and lonely.

Mindy's magic does not cause her mother to gain riches at the lottery and achieve "Happiness via Prosperity"[34] as she had hoped, though elaborate Taoist magic indeed works because it makes the butcher win the lottery. Without the jackpot, her mother's happiness must be secured in another way. It is worth noting, however, that the coveted jackpot only brings $250,000—perhaps in line with jackpots in a nostalgic past but not enough to catapult a working-class woman into a higher class sphere (that would be an assault on Shum's nostalgic vision of community, which one does not leave). Accordingly, Jade's renegade double, the butcher's son, Peter, is to share in his father's new wealth.[35] With the lottery money, the father buys the butcher shop where he works and proudly makes his son his partner, but the son flees this imposed identity. His escape, however, is not, like Jade's, to the Canadian side of his duality. He desires to become a Buddhist monk. Hardly a falling away from Chineseness, the Buddhist Temple is just down the street.[36] In *Long Life, Happiness and Prosperity*, the failure of the patriarchal family as one's primary "inside" group is cushioned by the film's vision of a new primary group, the Chinese community.

Mina Shum uses many of the daring stylistics here that she used in *Double Happiness*. The mobile and startling camera of the first feature and a studied use of colour return, although these aspects are not as extensive here as in the earlier film.[37] Shum's style in *Long Life, Happiness and Prosperity* matches the subject matter; there are no Taoist-style "observations of nature" outside of the narrative-motivated storm of the film's denouement. The camera still takes pleasure in changing position in the first scenes as it follows Mindy practising her magic, shooting first from above then from below; but it does not draw attention to itself as the marker of enunciation in the same manner that it did in *Double Happiness*. Shum attempts to match the audacious Lazy Susan shot of *Double Happiness* in *Long Life, Happiness and Prosperity* by mounting the camera on the cart of a dim sum waiter. Our introduction to Mindy's mother occurs when the cart intrudes in the dim sum restaurant kitchen and Kin leans forward to shout at "us" in Chinese. Later, again in the kitchen, the cart flies out of control, throwing Kin into Alvin's arms and breaking Mindy's badly administered spell that made Alvin fall for Nelson, the butcher's boss, instead of for Kin. Although the subjective camera features are even more elaborate here than in *Double Happiness*, their effect is less remarkable than in the earlier film because used less consistently. We return again to a subjective-like shot only in the final images of the film: craning out, we move with the camera away and above Mindy and her mother's house now that "Happiness" has been achieved. Through this subjective shot, we, the audience, leave, as presumably we had arrived—from away. Mere spectators, we have never truly become participants in Shum's idealized Chinese community.

Is *Long Life, Happiness and Prosperity* an antidote to the less embraceable Chineseness of *Double Happiness* and a bridge to understanding the "other" via familiar cultural icons? It is true that traditional Chinese culture seems oppressive in *Long Life, Happiness and Prosperity*. Not all it's male characters are tyrants like Jade's father and Bing, the butcher; not all the women dependent, as the spirited Kin demonstrates. But the diversity it offers is village-sized; nothing here resembles the cultural variety that Feng valued in *Chan is Missing*. If a mate is needed for Ken, he can (must) be found within the community; there is no one else, no *Double Happiness* outsider-style Mark offered as an alternative. But Shum gives us no need for concern. Alvin is as endearing as Mark;[38] he brings cappuccinos. And if Kin is not immediately attracted to him, no matter; Taoist magic can fix that—Kin need not wander away.

But what made the rejecter of Chineseness in *Double Happiness* embrace it as she does in *Long Life, Happiness and Prosperity*? Making Chinese-subject-matter films is more fashionable now. In the new millennium, everyone has heard of Taoism, *Feng shui*, and *qi*—even if they do not know the details. After Ang Lee's successful *Wedding Banquet* (1993), many will be acquainted with the Chinese notion of "saving face." In the culture game "I caught that ethnic reference," some may even grasp the meaning of the pair of goldfish offered as a present by the suitor, Nelson, to Mindy's mom.[39] The fashionableness of a postmodern notion of Chineseness is likely the motivation for *Long Life, Happiness and Prosperity*'s nostalgic "Chinatown" with its "Chinese ingredients" and stock places familiar to a non-Chinese audience. A non-Chinese audience would enjoy the privilege of safely penetrating the all-Chinese restaurant scenes. ("Everyone knows, if a restaurant has only Chinese customers, it is bound to be authentic.") The, by now, familiar trope of the argument among Chinese over who will pay the restaurant bill here is even played twice: once for comic effect in the background of the dim sum restaurant where Kin and Alvin work, and once again with pathos between the jobless Shuck and his wealthier younger brother, who has just spoiled Shuck's hopes to be his partner by announcing that he is well-off enough to retire. In the corollary familiar trope, we observe Shuck's wife, Hun Ping, watching but obediently saying nothing about Shuck's inability to pay. Finally, returning to the aspect of *Feng shui* in the film, magic manipulations generally are in fashion now, especially in the hands of children, given Harry Potter's popularity. This fashionableness had only just begun when Shum made *Double Happiness*.

■ By Way of Conclusion

MOMENTS OF ROLE-PLAYING structure the narrative of *Double Happiness*. Throughout, identity is presented as performed. In *Long Life, Happiness and Prosperity*, characters reprise *Double Happiness*'s roles, offering pastiche performances of the earlier film. But rather than *Long Life, Happiness and Prosperity*, the real sequel to *Double Happiness*'s story is the performance that is Mina Shum's real life. In the narrative "Successful Filmmaker is Reconciled with her Family," Shum is accepted back into her real-life family because she has become successful in the business of film. As in Jade Snow Wong's *Fifth Chinese Daughter* (1945), the daughter manages to change her father's view of her, winning his approval by succeeding like a son. Rebellion in the real-life follow-up narrative is recast as male-style success.

Mina Shum's films have at least demonstrated that ethnicity need not always be cast as suffering.[40] Her theme of colour-blind casting in *Double Happiness* has also succeeded in making a Chinese out of Sandra Oh (everyone now seems certain that she is Chinese and not Korean). Thus Peter Feng's aspired-to label, "Asian Canadian," has been realized, though it seems here to have lost Feng's political dimension, not a victory against hegemonic power. Shum is about to embark on a new film.[41] As she describes it, it will have Chinese content.[42] But it promises to be no more "authentically Chinese" than *Long Life, Happiness and Prosperity*. Her story concerns a family of "immortals" living in the West. But as she describes it, the daughter's desire to give up immortality to "belong" appears to contain nothing of the social terror of exclusion (the inside/outside of Chinese society) that the notion of ghosts hinted at in *Double Happiness*.[43] It is the marketplace, the impact of globalization, that promises to dominate in this new film, and pastiche likely will rule again. Mina Shum wants to succeed in feature filmmaking, which these days, especially, means succeeding in the global market. In Canada today, making feature films—financing feature films—takes immense effort.[44] That she not only wants to succeed but must succeed for her father's sake, is just the kind of drive that might keep Mina Shum going in this trying profession.

NOTES

1. Peter Feng "Being Chinese American, Becoming Asian American: *Chan is Missing.*" *Cinema Journal*. 35, no. 4 (Summer 1996): 94.
2. "Guy Maddin said that what you're fighting against with your second film is the imagined film of your fans. I never thought of that until I got to Toronto and I realized: 'Oh, my god, they've been waiting for something else.' That hit hard." From Pamela Cuthbert, "Mina Shum Drives On," *Take One* (Spring 1998): http://www.findarticles.com/p/articles/mi_moJSF/is_19_6/ai_30066448 (accessed 19 September 2005).
3. Mina Shum obtained a Bachelor of Arts in theatre at the University of British Columbia in 1988 and a Diploma in Film and Television Studies in 1990. She then trained in directing at the Toronto-based Canadian Film Centre founded by Norman Jewison.
4. The description is typical of Canadian press concerning Shum's films.
5. The film won a Special Jury Citation Award when it premiered at the Toronto International Film Festival.
6. As Mina Shum reveals in an interview (Forthcoming in George Melnyk, ed., *The Young, the Restless and the Dead: Interviews with Canadian Filmmakers*), the serial aspect of the television programs she has directed has allowed her to step outside the constraints of ethnic identity.
7. Ang Lee's films include *Sense and Sensibility* (1995), based on the Jane Austen novel, *The Ice Storm* (1997), and *Brokeback Mountain* (2005), in addition to his films made in Chinese for which he is also celebrated: *The Wedding Banquet* (1993), *Eat Drink Man Woman* (1994), and *Crouching Tiger, Hidden Dragon* (2000).
8. Wayne Wang, who was born in Hong Kong, is most celebrated for his American-made Chinese-subject matter films such as *Dim Sum: A Little Bit of Heart* (1985) and *The Joy Luck Club* (1993). Among his non-Chinese subject matter films, critics and audiences prefer his off-beat productions such as

Smoke (1995) to his attempts at American-style genre filmmaking such as the thriller *Slam Dance* (1987).

9. These statistics come from the Canada 2001 census, http://www12.statcan.ca/english/profil01/PlaceSearchForm1.cfm and http://www12.statcan.ca/english/profil/PlaceSearchForm1.cfm (accessed September 2005).

10. "In terms of carving a cultural space, I never once assumed I couldn't sit at the big table," she told interviewer Lorraine Chan in 1994. "I felt I deserved to be there too, and that has always fuelled me. I never once assumed that they weren't going to accept me, I never put my energies into that kind of thinking." Positive thinking, she offers, can go a long way in resolving complex issues of identity. From "Lorraine Chan in Conversation with Mina Shum." *Reverse Shot* 1, no. 2 (Summer 1994): 34.

11. The amount the government collected from Chinese immigrants amounted to $21 million, just $2 million short of the cost of building the CPR itself.

12. See Peter S. Li, *The Chinese in Canada* (Toronto: Oxford University Press, 1998).

13. For example, the following appeared in the real estate section of the *Vancouver Sun*, 21 September 1996: "Research shows local Asians or immigrants purchase 60 per cent of residential properties sold in Vancouver east and Richmond, 50 per cent of homes sold in Burnaby and 40 percent of homes in Coquitlam. About 70 per cent of Greater Vancouver homes selling for $1 million or more are bought by Asians." From Wyng Chow, "Independent firm takes aim at booming Asian market," *Vancouver Sun*, 21 September 1996, E1.

14. *Feng shui* advises on the placement of trees in relation to entries and other physical alignments to improve well-being, relationships, health, and prosperity.

15. See http://www.canadianheritage.gc.ca/progs/multi/inclusive_e.cfm, accessed August 2005.

16. Confucianism as set down in China in fifth-century B.C. gave rules for the social order and also stipulated responsibilities that came with position. Accordingly, the emperor ruled over the population, father over family, older brother over next younger brother, the mother over daughter-in-law, etc., with the responsibilities that came with that privilege.

17. This system is very much alive in China today. Parents very frequently borrow money to pay their (usually one) child's education. It is an investment in their own economic future, since the child is expected to take care of his parents when they are old.

18. Shum's father was fired at the time Shum was finishing school.

19. Mark can also be said to be "feminized" and thus, perhaps, unthreatening. Feminization was commonly used by White filmmakers such as D.W. Griffith in *Broken Blossoms* (1919) to characterize the Chinese male.

20. Peter Feng, "Being Chinese American, Becoming Asian American: *Chan is Missing.*" *Cinema Journal* 35, no. 4 (Summer 1996): 88–118. See especially n2.111. Thus Peter Feng's aspired-to label, "Asian Canadian," has been realized, though it seems here to have lost Feng's political dimension, not a victory against hegemonic power. See also Trinh T. Minh-ha. *The Moon Waxes Red: Representation, Gender and Cultural Politics* (New York: Routledge, 1991).

21. By chance, Mina Shum notes, actors Chang Tseng and Tsai Chin, who play husband and wife Shuck and Hun Ping Wong, speak the same Shanghaian dialect; differences in dialect between characters are not evident in the subtitled version of the film.

22. Notably, Jade's sympathetic agent is darker skinned, kinky-haired, and obviously non-White.

23. It is interesting to note the commercialization of the character of the "other" in the role played by Kevin Spacey in the immensely popular *American Beauty* (1999).

24. Peter X. Feng, "Decentering the Middle Kingdom: *China—Land of My Father* (Felicia Lowe, 1979), *The Way to my Father's Village* (Richard Fung, 1988), *Made in China* (Lisa Hsia, 1986)," *Jump Cut* 42 (December 1998): 122–34.

25. That *Double Happiness* is autobiographical was the main message of all pre-release publicity and every review. Jade's is also Mina's and Sandra's story. Both left home at an early age, both questioned their parents' plans for them, and, in both cases, the father was the source of the tension. Mina Shum claims she made the film for the eighteen-year-olds—Chinese North Americans like herself—alone in their decision to leave their family, in order to show them that they are not alone.

26. Quoted in my interview with Shum in the forthcoming Melnyk, ed., *The Young, The Restless and the Dead*.

27. Shirley Geok-lin Lim, "Feminist and Ethnic Literary Theories in Asian American Literature," *Feminist Studies* 19, no. 3 (1993): 571–92.

28. Lim, Feminist and Ethnic Literary Theories," 580.

29. Examples include Jeanne Wakatsuki Houston and James Houston's *Farewell to Manzanar* (1974), Kim Ronyoung's *Clay Walls* (1984), and, in Canada, Denise Chong's *The Concubine's Children* (1994) and Sky Lee's *Disappearing Moon Café* (1990).

30. See, for example, Maxine Hong Kingston's *The Woman Warrior* (1975).

31. Kin reveals that she is twelve, but she appears and is dressed as much younger. She is "young for her age" as Shum often describes her own appearance. See, for example, Monique Harvey, "Achieving Double Happiness: An Interview with Mina Shum," The Peak 90, no. 12 (24 July 1995). http://peaksfu.ca/the-peak/95-2/issue12, accessed 28 February 2007. Here, Shum notes, "I'm only 29 and I look 13."

32. The vision contains all the necessary ingredients of Chinatown as a destination except that there are no White shoppers. There are also few young people; the only other child is a boy with a lost turtle. Shum's "Chinesetown" is disproportionately composed of the middle and old aged.

33. The number of actors is quite astonishing. Shum creates an ensemble piece, a celebration of Chinese acting skills.

34. "Long Life," "Happiness," and "Prosperity" are three gods to which Taoist-influenced Chinese pray for good fortune.

35. It is interesting to note that almost all the characters from *Double Happiness* find new characters to inhabit in *Long Life, Happiness and Prosperity*, typically with less depth due to the second film's numerous characters.

36. This character is reminiscent of followers of the Hare Krishna sect that tempted youth away in the 1970s to dance on the street. Another anachronism born of nostalgia?

37. According to *Reel West*, an industry publication, with three stories to tell and a plethora of locations, there was too little time for more audacious camera work. *Reel West*, http://www.reelwest.com/magazing/archives/vol17_2/shum.htm (accessed May 2002).

38. Alvin, the designated correct mate, again is feminized. This gendering is underlined by his Mindy-Taoist-magic-induced wooing of Nelson.

39. The doubles indicate happiness in marriage.

40. See J. Hagedorn, "Asian Women in Film: No Joy, No Luck," *Ms.* (January–February 1994): 74–79.

41. See my interview in the forthcoming Melnyk, ed., *The Young, the Restless and the Dead*.

42. Personal interview with Mina Shum, 10 August, 2005.

43. The Immortals are part of traditional Chinese culture and mythology; they are ubiquitous in sculpture.

44. We should remember that Mina Shum still belongs to the category "independent filmmaker." *Double Happiness* was made for CAD $1 million, *Long Life, Happiness and Prosperity* for under $3 million.

Future Greats

14

A Problem with Rules
Gary Burns
PATRICIA GRUBEN

AFTER A DECADE of studying fine arts, working in construction, and painting houses in Calgary, Gary Burns entered the film program at Concordia University in Montreal at the age of thirty. In the ten years after graduating in 1992, he made four feature films—*The Suburbanators* (1995), *Kitchen Party* (1997), *waydowntown* (2000), and *A Problem with Fear* (2003)—all with modest budgets but increasing critical and popular attention.

Before launching his feature-film career, Burns made two notable shorts. His twenty-minute graduating film "Happy Valley" (1992) won the Bellevue Pathé Award for Outstanding Achievement at Concordia. Returning to Calgary after film school, Burns received a KickStart Award sponsored by Telefilm Canada and the Directors Guild to make another short, "Beerland" (1995), which he described as "a deadpan comedy of cultural alienation."[1] Accolades for this short led to a grant from the Canada Council for *The Suburbanators*, whose success at the Toronto International Film Festival brought Burns to national attention in 1995. It was included in the Toronto film critics' Top Ten Canadian Films of 1996 and cited by

Canadian film writer Geoff Pevere in his book *Mondo Canuck* as one of "English Canada's Coolest Movies."[2]

Burns's early work fits into a broad genre of North American independent cinema that derives its aesthetic both from limited economic means and from a desire to portray everyday experience as truthfully as possible through casual, documentary-style staging, often combined with a dry, self-conscious wit. Naturalism in contemporary cinema owes a debt to Italian Neorealists such as Vittorio de Sica and Roberto Rossellini, who depicted life in post-war Europe from a position of cultural and political disillusionment. New German filmmakers of the 1970s, particularly Wim Wenders, further explored this sense of alienation in a country whose citizens had good reason to be cynical about the authority of parents and government. Many American filmmakers saw this European work in film school and saw it as more relevant to their own interrogation of traditional values and glib materialism than the polished, artificial style of Hollywood. A realist style was not only more attainable within the constricted budgets of student and independent filmmakers but it also seemed more honest in its exploration of mundane subject matter, the unaffected performances of its actors, and its political and philosophical themes. These films tended to handle narrative in a less dramatically "managed" way; their conflicts tended to be internal rather than overt, their endings often unresolved, as described by David Bordwell. In *Narration in the Fiction Film*, Bordwell notes that

> contemporary cinema...follows Neorealism in seeking to depict the vagaries of real life, to "dedramatize" the narrative by showing both climaxes and trivial moments, and to use new techniques (abrupt cutting, long takes) not as fixed conventions but as flexible means of expression.... In the name of verisimilitude, the tight causality of classical Hollywood construction is replaced by a more tenuous linking of events....
>
> Certainly the art film relies upon psychological causation no less than does the classical narrative. But the prototypical characters of the art cinema tend to lack clear-cut traits, motives and goals.[3]

In North America, the realist style developed not only from the work of these post-war Europeans neorealists, but was also from the films of

John Cassavetes, who used his training as a Method actor to develop a distinctively gritty, open-ended approach through improvisation with an ensemble of like-minded performers. Cassavetes's first feature, *Shadows* (1959), was shot with a hand-held 16mm camera and the script was developed in collaboration with the actors while shooting. After influencing Scorsese and others of his generation, Cassavetes's spontaneous style filtered down to another cohort of filmmakers like Richard Linklater (*Slackers* [1991], *Dazed and Confused* [1993]), Kevin Smith (*Clerks* [1994]), and to a lesser extent Jim Jarmusch (*Stranger than Paradise* [1984])—though with these filmmakers, the acting was influenced more by lack of experience than by Method training. In Canada, the realist style derives equally from the documentary background of the two most notable English-Canadian filmmakers of the 1960s, Don Shebib (*Goin' Down the Road* [1970]) and Don Owen (*Nobody Waved Goodbye* [1964]).

As this more relaxed and natural independent cinema evolved in Europe and North America, *auteurs* like Jean-Luc Godard developed an ironic, playful formalism that seemed paradoxically unaffected and yet self-conscious. Although Godard's visual puns and direct address to camera might seem to depart from realism, this spontaneity acknowledged the influence of both chance and the director's imagination in the process. In their own work two decades later, Linklater, Smith, and particularly Jarmusch used minimalism and irony to develop a less self-consciously formal style that reflected the humour of their generation. In Canada, Bruce McDonald and Bruce Sweeney each developed a distinctive comic aesthetic. McDonald and screenwriter Don McKellar derived their stoner humour in *Roadkill* (1989) and *Highway 61* (1991) from the naïveté of the characters and the absurdity of their adventures; Sweeney, in *Live Bait* (1995), *Dirty* (1998), and *Last Wedding* (2001), explored themes of male role confusion and perverse sexuality through psychodrama, often drawn from his own or his actors' lived experiences.

Gary Burns describes his work as not directly influenced by other filmmakers, but sanctioned by their successes. He credits Jarmusch and Linklater for the notion that films could be made with minimalist plots and rudimentary technology. As well, he was inspired by multiple subplots woven around a common place or theme in Robert Altman's *Nashville* (1975).[4] However, Burns denies that he is intentionally following any school of film style; rather, his work seems to reflect a generational North American zeitgeist.[5] "I've been really lucky, being based in Calgary, that I have never really had some mentor," he told the Calgary weekly FFWD. "I never wanted to be Atom Egoyan or David Cronenberg. There is no one here that I am trying to copy or follow."[6]

Burns's work is distinctive in the consistency of his subject matter as well as his style. All four of his feature films (*The Suburbanators*, *Kitchen Party*, *waydowntown* and *A Problem with Fear*) involve groups of estranged young people searching incoherently for meaning and commitment. All four feature young men confined in highly controlled atmospheres, resisting the numbing effects of conformity. Most notably in *Kitchen Party* and *The Suburbanators*, plots are assembled from the petty but significant frustrations of everyday life. Burns finds ironic conflict in condemnation of authority figures, not as an articulate political critique but as a late-adolescent resistance to rules made and enforced by others. The freedoms the characters seek include: the ability to buy dope without getting busted (*The Suburbanators*), to drink beer in the living room (*Kitchen Party*), and to escape the trivial responsibilities of office work (*waydowntown*). In *Kitchen Party*, getting stoned or drunk is an act of emancipation, even for the repressed and hypocritical parents—though for the parents, drunkenness unleashes only prejudice and fear, and is thus destructive rather than therapeutic. In *waydowntown*, Tom's cathartic act is to quit his job, but there are few clues as to what he will do with his newfound freedom.

Burns admits that, in his first three films, it was easier to write for an ensemble with multiple simple subplots than to probe deeply into the psyche of one character. "It is still easier for me to have lots of different stories going on at the same time," he told an interviewer in 2003. "None of them are very complex, but they all add to something more total."[7] However, over the course of his four films, Burns has gradually moved toward a closer examination of a single character's psyche. More complex, both narratively and psychologically, than either *The Suburbanators* or *Kitchen Party*, *waydowntown* features a narrator who struggles with his moral concerns, his sense of who he is, and his fantasies of escape. Finally, in *A Problem with Fear* (2003), we see the extreme consequence of institutional oppression on a deeper level in a character who is terrified by contemporary life; yet for the first time in a Burns film, the character is finally able to commit to a meaningful relationship with his equally neurotic girlfriend.

Another common feature of Burns's work is that virtually all his films are set in Calgary, yet for the most part they are geographically anonymous. Their architectural and cultural blandness creates the impression that we could be anywhere in middle-class North America and that the dilemmas of these young, befuddled characters are universal. Rather than play alienation off against the geographic and cultural specificity of the setting, as happens in films such as *Goin' Down the Road*, *Lost in Translation* (2003), or *Desert Bloom* (1986), Burns's four films exaggerate the utter featurelessness of their seemingly ahistorical landscapes: suburban golf courses and strip malls, or downtown offices and shopping centres. The only exception to this anonymity is the parody of pioneer life at "Western Days" at Westgate Mall, a major location in *The Suburbanators*. There, a grinning ersatz cowboy twirls his lariat in the parking lot while geriatric square dancers and a barbershop quartet try to drum up business inside the mall.

Looking at the four feature films consecutively, we see an evolution of both formal and psychological sophistication, and an increasing mastery of cinematic technique. As Burns's ironic style developed, the work revealed his increasingly sophisticated approach to representation, framing, and narrative structure. From the start, his deceptively unpretentious framing has featured beautifully composed and often witty images, like the artful overhead shots of vacuum cleaner tracks on the pristine, off-limits beige carpet in *Kitchen Party*; an elastic telephone cord stretched across an empty wall to an unseen speaker in *The Suburbanators*; or the solitary smokers confined in the glass cubicles of *waydowntown*'s urban mall. These visual markers are seamlessly integrated into the naturalistic acting and narrative style of Burns's early shorts and features, and lead to a more and more expressive and kinetic *mise-en-scéne* in the latter two.

■ *The Suburbanators* (1995)

As BURNS DESCRIBES IT, it was a bit of a shock when he realized that to make a film he'd have to write a screenplay:

I could say I was almost illiterate. Well, I could write a paragraph but I had never written anything, really. So the first film I made [Happy Valley, 1992] I tried to make a real anti-narrative.... I made a film about two guys walking across town, made them Arabic, and I didn't subtitle their dialogue, so their performances wouldn't have to be very good and the dialogue wouldn't have to be very good. I've always tried to do what I had to do to make it work.[8]

Characters speaking Arabic reappear in *The Suburbanators*, a deadpan comedy that follows three groups of young men over the course of a day. Two of the groups—Al and Bob, and Eric and Carl—want to score some pot from the same dealer but are distracted by trips to the barber and the video arcade, a trivial accident with a lit cigarette, and—just when the score is in sight—a police raid at the dealer's house. The third group—Karim, Salah, and Roger—must get into a locked apartment to retrieve the musical instruments they need to play at a club that night. A suspicious building manager won't let them in, and they spend the film plotting (in Arabic) to get past him.

Like real life, *The Suburbanators* is full of non-sequiturs and half-finished conversations—the barber's complaint about a deadbeat leaving his driver's license at the shop as security for payment and never returning; Bob's musing on the question of whether "your car is your penis"; Carl's furious envy of another fellow who is "falsely modest" after winning a literary prize; and Al's constant dithering over his lack of commitment to his unseen girlfriend, Diane. Burns suggests deeper issues—as when Bob and Al avoid the barber's questions about their employment status—but never clarifies them; the endless debates about women are never resolved.

In its haphazard encounters with groups of confused suburban adolescents, its deflation of dramatic conflict, and its "real time" sensibility, *The Suburbanators* superficially resembles Richard Linklater's second feature, *Dazed and Confused*. Yet the latter film's plot, which follows several teenagers over the course of an evening at the end of the school year, is tighter and its outcome is not only more resolved but also more optimistic—perhaps largely because Paramount, the film's sponsor, pushed Linklater relentlessly toward a teen sex comedy, very different in tone from his ground-breaking non-linear first feature, *Slackers*.[9]

Burns, working with a total budget of about $100,000, was his own master in the making of *The Suburbanators*, with the freedom to create a minimalist dramatic arc and an unresolved, ironic ending. Although each character has a goal of sorts, all four main characters are easily distracted and thwarted by obstacles. When Carl offers Eric a joint he's managed to filch in their escape from the police, Eric declines to smoke it, saying, "I like the idea of having dope. I'm not so much interested in using it." Eric's remark is ironic, given that this has been his primary pursuit to this point in the film. In counterpoint to their quest for pot, Eric and Carl also laconically trail Susan, whose shoe Carl has accidentally burned when he dropped a cigarette. In the end, she gives them both the brush off and that's the end of it—another goal haphazardly pursued and unachieved.

Burns's characteristic mix of naturalism and formalist camerawork is established early in the film with a POV shot through the windshield of a car, introducing us to a totally anonymous neighbourhood. We don't see more than fragments of Bob and Al in the car until we've heard them talking for more than three minutes, and we don't learn their names for over half an hour. Significant events often take place outside the frame. One odd example is the scene in which Carl drops his cigarette on Susan's shoe. Rather than show us the event itself, Burns keeps the camera on a close shot of Al and Bob witnessing this event as they drive past. Later, when they see Susan walking alone, Al stops the car and offers her a ride. Burns shows us this scene only in a fragment through the rear-view mirror, with the two characters' heads cut off and only parts of their bodies visible. In several other scenes the audience overhears or witnesses only fragments of dialogue or images—an argument between Tim, the drug dealer, and his girlfriend; loud giggling from what sounds like lesbian sex play in a nearby apartment; a peek at a nearly naked young woman heading to her room after a shower. We glimpse moments of dramatic conflict or eroticism only through a window or down the hall.

The Suburbanators has no real climax; as Eric is carried off to the hospital in a slow ambulance after being hit by a car, Bob and Al continue to drive around looking for marijuana. In the end, the film renounces any claim to a "coming of age" plot, its characters left in limbo or defeated by forces of authority. The conclusion that has been denied us on screen is provided as an afterthought in the end titles. Over empty shots of the locations where the following events have presumably taken place, we read:

> *Eric is released from hospital with a bruised hip. Eric and Carl go to Eric's parents' place where they have pizza and play cards with Eric's mom and dad.*
>
> *Police question Kareem, Salah, and Roger at the restaurant where they're the house band. The next day's tabloid reads, "Immigrants rough up local landlord."*
>
> *Al goes over to Diane's where he manages to avoid any mention of their relationship. They watch a made-for-TV movie starring Lindsey Wagner.*
>
> *Bob gets drunk in a park by himself. He is arrested after getting into a fight with a group of teenage girls.*[10]

The Suburbanators compares favourably in subtlety and craft to other first features by Canadian auteurs—for example, Cronenberg's *Shivers* (1975) or McDonald and McKellar's *Roadkill*. It premiered at the 1995 Toronto International Film Festival and was invited to the prestigious Sundance Film Festival, as well. Along with its inclusion as one of the Top Ten Canadian Films of 1996, Geoff Pevere called it "the most promising first feature by a Canadian director to come along in years."[11]

■ *Kitchen Party* (1997)

BUILDING ON THE SUCCESS of *The Suburbanators*, Burns attracted a higher budget for his second feature, *Kitchen Party*, which was shot in 35mm. Still, the financing was difficult; the Alberta government shut down its provincial funding agency just as *Kitchen Party* was gearing up to shoot. When British Columbia Film offered support in its wake, Burns moved the production to Vancouver but was forced to shorten his shooting schedule and change some key crewmembers.[12] Like *The Suburbanators*, *Kitchen Party* is set in an anonymous North American suburb and follows the mundane antics of a group of adolescents. Burns's subtle formalism is introduced in the title sequence—in the image of the off-limits beige-carpeted living room and its perfect patterns of vacuum trails—contrasted, as in the earlier film, with naturalistic performances and a meandering plot. Whereas *The Suburbanators* was constructed around three loosely related stories, *Kitchen Party* contains a somewhat more tightly interconnected parallel narrative. Scott (Scott Speedman) holds an anxious drinking party in the kitchen of his suburban home while his parents Brent (Kevin McNulty) and Barb (Gillian Barber) negotiate their own social minefields at dinner with the neighbours in an upscale golf-course development.

Kitchen Party's dramatic trajectory is clearer than *The Suburbanators's*, revolving around Scott's need to keep the house pristine. If he shows any signs of carousing—"so much as a bottle cap"—Brent will refuse to pay his way to Queen's University; he'll have to attend the local college and live with his bickering family for another four years. Besides his exaggeratedly uptight and abusive parents, Scott must also contend with his older brother Steve (Jason Wiles), a reclusive stoner who spends most of his life in the basement. While Scott's friends speculate about Steve's capacity for rape and murder, across town Brent gets into an altercation with his host, Lester (Jerry Wasserman), over Brent's conjecture that any of their sons might be gay. Meanwhile, Lester Jr., buying beer for Scott's party, backs his father's precious '78 Beaumont into four other cars. When his friend Tim asks, "Geez Les, what was that?" the glazed Les Jr. answers, "I have no idea." The police arrive and Tim is forced to conceal in his pants the loaded pistol that Lester found somewhere, while contorting himself in the driver's seat to prove his claim that the gas pedal was stuck.

During this mayhem, Steve erupts from the house with Scott's romantic interest, the clever, pretty and compassionate Tammy (Laura Harris). He attacks a couple making out in a parked car then rips up the golf course on his motorcycle. Even the sympathetic Tammy is disgusted by his destructive behaviour, but she is even more appalled by the refusal of either Scott or Brent to come to Steve's aid when he is arrested. Brent has already exposed himself as an authoritarian *poseur* whose only power comes from his control over the family finances. Scott declares his own nihilist rebellion by pouring beer on the perfect carpet just as his parents return home.

As in *The Suburbanators*, the authority figures are exposed as ineffectual goats; similarly, their children achieve no real liberation through their eruptions of impotent rage. Like his mother, Scott is obsessed with keeping the house clean; like his father, he is unable either to restrain or to extend compassion to his brother. Lester Jr.'s girlfriend, Crystal, is overprotective but powerless, like his own mother. It is clear that these kids will grow up to be much like their parents. Even Scott, the erstwhile protagonist, seems destined to follow his brother into meaningless acts of rage.

Burns described the origin of the script as a desire to portray the hierarchy of teenage society, "the strangely woven structure of teenage friends held together by a need to belong. It occurs during a period in our lives when we try to solidify our maturity and practice our 'adult' interaction, an often ill-conceived and clumsy pursuit, but still act out instinctive behaviour which adults often bury for the sake of decorum." Burns began writing with a list of "typical" teen types: "I was interested in showing awkwardness, naïveté, mean-spiritedness, callowness, follower mentality, but also the possibility of empathy and insight. It's an open-ended narrative of observations that doesn't provide answers."[13]

Kitchen Party premiered at the Toronto Film Festival and was invited to the prestigious New Directors/New Films festival in New York; *The New York Times* called it "the funniest, nastiest comedy of manners to come down the pike in months."[14]

■ *waydowntown* (2000)

BURNS ACKNOWLEDGES that his first two films were autobiographical, but "*waydowntown* was a bit of a departure. I've never worked in an office, for instance."[15] This time he had a writing partner, journalist James Martin, who *was* familiar with the business world. Burns's original idea was to shoot in a downtown tower on video, in one 90-minute take. "I thought it was going to be about architecture and revolve around a visual plot device." Then he heard about the Mike Figgis film *Timecode* (2000). Feeling his idea was no longer original, he changed it into a more character-driven narrative.[16]

The architectural feature of downtown Calgary that most intrigued Burns was the city's "Plus 15" walkway system, which connects a number of the downtown buildings, allowing people to stay inside and leaving the city streets devoid of life. He called this "a metaphor of sorts for modernism gone wrong."[17] Although he abandoned the idea of doing the whole film in one take, he did end up shooting much of it in video, finding it more flexible and less conspicuous for filming while the Eaton's Centre mall was open. He also liked the look of digital video, which he felt "gave the film an edgier look and heightened the sense of realism," as well as making it easier to add special effects and animation. The video, along with some sequences originally shot in film, was transferred to 35mm for theatrical release.

waydowntown begins with a classic skyline shot, as seen in hundreds of other films set in New York, Philadelphia, or Los Angeles. Here, the anonymity of Calgary's skyline parodies the cliché. This is followed by a split-screen montage of tense, nonverbal situations in elevators, mall shops, and a parking garage with people crammed together, trying to ignore one another and their unnatural surroundings. Gradually we come to recognize four of the characters in the montage as co-workers Randy (Tobias Godson), Sandra (Marya Delver), Curt (Gordon Curry), and Tom (Fabrizio Filippo), who are into Day 24 of a competition to see who can go the longest without leaving the building. Since they all live, work, and shop in the same interconnected downtown high-rise complex, they can function within its confines indefinitely. But their internment is becoming seriously disturbing and they've each bet a month's salary on the contest, so the stakes are high. It's typical of Burns to downplay the conflict in this dramatic device; the competition is mentioned cryptically but not clarified until nearly twenty minutes into the film.

The controlling force in the characters' lives is, as in Burns's earlier films, exposed as illegitimate and ultimately impotent. Here it is personified by Mr. Madder, the founder of the company they all work for—a senile kleptomaniac, protected by the office staff.

For the protagonist, Tom, as for Burns's earlier characters, smoking a joint is the only escape from a life of routine imprisonment. However, even getting high brings no respite; after toking up in the parking garage, Tom opens his car door to find a dead mouse, the first of several Burnsian jokes about the impossibility of natural life in an artificial universe. The film is full of such visual gags—the smokers isolated in glass cubicles; Tom's ant farm; Sandra's obsession with sniffing the perfume inserts in fashion magazines, a simulacrum of fresh air. Sandra's sweater is powder blue until she finally bursts outside; the next time we see her it's turned red, like suddenly re-oxygenated blood vessels.

Marijuana is perhaps the origin of the other image of liberation in the film, Tom's superhero fantasy. Early in the film, we see a pixilated sequence, with Tom's voice-over, showing a super-villain lifting the entire downtown core into the sky. In another scene, Tom glimpses a super-hero in costume patrolling the mall and fantasizes about himself flying along its corridors, until he's literally brought down to earth by bumping into Sandra. Finally, the city *is* apparently picked up by some villain or other, and the superhero must set it back to rights.[18] Tom's voice-over suggests that the evil actually comes not from outside, but from himself and others who behave in petty, selfish ways.

As Tom realizes the consequences of his thoughtless acts he tries, with mixed success, to right the wrongs. After suggesting to his competitor Curt that their co-worker Vicki (Jennifer Clement) is available for seduction, he has second thoughts and tries to stop Vicki from getting hurt. When he unwittingly jokes about an attractive woman to her boyfriend, throwing the poor fellow into a catatonic crisis, he tries to talk him out of it. He discovers that the only way to get the kleptomaniac Mr. Madder to give up his stolen goods is simply to ask nicely. Finally, after finding his colleague Bradley (Don McKellar) on the verge of suicide, he does his best to apologize for his many mocking insults.

The quietly desperate Bradley has spent the entire film trying to get up the nerve to smash his window with a jar of marbles and jump—the ultimate liberation and the source of the film's title.[19] At the end, just as Tom gives up on the bet, steps out onto the street and declares he's quitting his job, a jar of marbles hits him. He looks up and sees another jumper, who is rescued by the flying superhero just before he hits the pavement. Thus the film seems to end on a hopeful note, despite Tom's own ambiguous future.

waydowntown is technically and aesthetically more sophisticated than Burns's earlier films, surely a function of both experience and budget. It's far more kinetic as well, partly due to his partnership with cinematographer Stefan Ivanov. It has been Burns's commercially and critically most successful film to date, chosen Best Canadian Feature at the Toronto International Film Festival and released theatrically in the United States.

■ *A Problem with Fear* (2003)

FOR HIS FOURTH FEATURE Burns teamed up with his wife, Donna Brunsdale, a visual artist and filmmaker who had been art director on *waydowntown*, to write the script. As the earlier film had mirrored co-writer Martin's experience working in offices, *A Problem with Fear* seems to reflect the influence of working with this new writing partner, as it closely explores a male-female relationship. Like *waydowntown*, the film focusses on a young man who's been prevented from growing up by corporate exploitation—in this case, a company (Global Safety Inc.) that markets fear in order to sell its "Early Warning 2 Safe System™" bracelet, which sends off an alarm if danger is near. Laurie (Paulo Costanzo), who runs a magazine shop in a downtown mall, is paralyzed by fear of many things—elevators, escalators, crossing the street, spaghetti ("or any red sauce meat")—and, most of all, of commitment to his needy girlfriend Dot (Emily Hampshire).

Laurie's sister, Michelle (Camille Sullivan), an executive at Global Safety Inc., has given him a prototype bracelet, but it hasn't helped. In fact, when accidents start to happen all around him, Laurie becomes convinced that he is the cause. An elevator plummets to the ground, an escalator chews up a woman, a man is hit while crossing the street—all before his eyes. In each case, not only does the victim have a premonition of the accident, but Laurie does, as well. Michelle ridicules his fears, but knows there's some lethal problem with the bracelet. Meanwhile, the tabloids and TV news grind away to escalate the separate incidents into a systemic panic, and generate a "fear storm" in the city.

Laurie is pursued, then attacked, by Erin (Willie Garson), an employee of Global Safety Inc., who was injured in the elevator accident and is now convinced that the only way to stop the panic is for Laurie to kill himself. Laurie himself now believes he must overcome his fears in order to save everyone around him. He makes a list of his phobias—riding the escalator, the elevator, and the subway; and crossing the street by himself. As he faces and conquers each fear one at a time, he discovers that Dot has scribbled COMMITMENT on the bottom of the list. When Laurie has overcome all of his other terrors, he can finally accept a relationship with Dot; he grabs her and kisses her in exhilaration. But even here, Burns can't bring himself to give us an irony-free ending. As Sandy the TV reporter announces the discovery of confidential memos from Global Safety Inc., Dot starts jumping gleefully on a subway grating, a car screeches and Laurie fights off another panic attack—he's better, but the big bad world is still out there.

A Problem with Fear appeared after a summer of power failures, West Nile Virus scares, and SARS, as well as the ongoing bogeyman of global terrorism. It's built around the premise that Michael Moore proclaimed in *Bowling for Columbine* and *Fahrenheit 9/11*: big business and the media thrive on keeping us frightened and dependent. It launched the Canadian Perspective program at the Toronto International Film Festival but was less successful commercially and critically than *waydowntown*, with several critics remarking that Burns was revisiting the quirky critique of corporate consumerism that he had fully explored in the previous film. Its semi-comic premise is simpler and more predictable, yet it is still a witty, entertaining, and inventively shot accomplishment.

■ *Radiant City* (2006)

IN 2003 Burns wrote and directed *My Life as a Movie*, a mockumentary for Alliance Atlantis. The following year he directed the reality-based heist MOW *Cool Money* with James Marsters and Margot Kidder for USA Network. More recently, he co-wrote and directed a mini-series, *Northern Town*, about a meteorite that lands on a frozen lake, broadcast on CBC in fall 2005. His latest project is, *Radiant City*, a hybrid documentary on suburban sprawl for the National Film Board and CBC.

Radiant City starts off looking like a classic talking-heads exploration of a familiar topic: the horrors of suburbia as described by city planners, including the world-famous urban authority Jane Jacobs. But quickly Burns turns a corner into a witty critique of the conventions of this cinematic style. A few minutes into the film, a ten-year-old girl who has been describing her life to the camera says, "This is the part of the documentary where an expert in the field introduces us to the main argument or thesis." Sure enough, we cut to an interview with a writer on urban sprawl. The film soon becomes something of a battleground between the experts, who are universally contemptuous of suburbia, and the residents, who become defensive and even angry about their choices. As architect Christopher Alexander pontificates, a distraught mother, Karen, rushes to the hospital to comfort her daughter who has witnessed a friend's suicide. Karen lashes out at the filmmakers, "I suppose you'll want to use this as evidence that the suburbs are somehow destructive."

At the end of the film, the child, Jennifer, introduces us to her fellow subjects, revealing that some of them have been played by actors—but the actors admit that they, too, live in the suburbs and launch into a discussion of the primarily economic reasons for their doing so. Finally some of the actors/characters discuss the artifice of the film with Jane Jacobs, trying to convince her that she could in fact get a decent cup of coffee at the 7-11, but she is horrified by the suggestion.[20]

Radiant City was named as one of Canada's Top Ten films of 2006 by the Toronto International Film Festival Group.

BURNS REMAINS A DOWN-TO-EARTH CALGARIAN, where he feels comfortable working with low budgets and familiar crews. "In Calgary, I have an infrastructure I can depend on…I think it's easier and cheaper to make low-budget movies in a place like Calgary than it is in places like Montreal or Toronto."[21] Nevertheless, he claims to be a film-scene outsider even in Calgary. "I don't really know what's going on in Alberta from a film standpoint. I'm not a part of it. I'm not really part of anything. I don't crew. I don't work in the industry. My friends have nothing to do with the film business. I don't even go to see movies. I guess I'm just another alienated Canadian filmmaker."[22]

Given the global anonymity of North American culture, can Burns's critique of it—or anything else about his cinematic style—be seen as distinctively Canadian? The days when film scholars sought a quintessential "Canadian" identity in the expressions of Anglophone cinema are largely over, with academics acknowledging that films that express the motifs of geographic isolation espoused by Northrop Frye and Margaret Atwood have been privileged over others in developing a canon of Canadian cinema for scholarly work and university film studies courses.[23] Still, journalists such as Katherine Monk still look for "weird sex and snowshoes" (part of Monk's wry checklist including "hockey, beer, snow, outsider stance, potent women, passive men, pluralist perspective, orphans, emancipatory power of the imagination," etc.) to characterize the national cinema.[24]

As noted, Gary Burns's work shares a broad aesthetic and a set of values with other filmmakers of his generation who grew up white, middle class, and suburban—whether in Austin, like Richard Linklater; in New Jersey, like Kevin Smith; in Toronto, like Bruce McDonald; or in Calgary, like Burns himself. Whether his unpretentious diffidence can be attributed to prairie values is debatable. In any case, as Angela Stukator points out, much current writing on national cinemas emphasizes national culture as "a set of mutable and evolving characteristics which involve the film, the local audience, and the transnational audience," rather than the doomed project of seeking some universal cultural essence.[25] Are *The Suburbanators* and *Kitchen Party* more "Canadian" in their realism than the more stylish *waydowntown* or *A Problem with Fear?* Certainly it is clear that the support of Canadian funding agencies has been crucial in Burns's career and may have made a critical difference in enabling him to maintain his independence.

NOTES

1. *Kitchen Party* press kit, 14.
2. Geoff Pevere, *Mondo Canuck* (Toronto: Prentice Hall, 1996), 67.
3. David Bordwell, *Narration in the Fiction Film* (Milwaukee: University of Wisconsin, 1985), 206.
4. Interview with the author, 2 August 2005.
5. "Toronto Winner is a Maverick," *Toronto Star* (27 September 2000): 32.
6. Jason Lewis, "Fearless Filmmaker," *FFWD Weekly* (Calgary), 25 September, 2003, www.ffwdweekly.com (accessed 13 February 2007).
7. Ibid.
8. P. Pam Sawhney, "A Success Story for Slackers: An Interview with *waydowntown* Writer/Director Gary Burns." *Moviemaker* 2, No. 4, Issue 12. www.moviemaker.com/hop/12/screenwriting.html (accessed 13 February 2007).
9. John Pierson, *Spike, Mike, Slackers & Dykes: A Guided Tour Across a Decade of American Independent Cinema* (New York: Miramax Books, 1995), 181.
10. *The Suburbanators*, VHS release, 1995.
11. Pevere, *Mondo Canuck*, 67.

12. Laura Lind, "Real Life: Cautionary Tale of Two Provinces," *Eye Weekly* (Toronto) 21 August 1997, 21.

13. *Kitchen Party* press kit, 12.

14. Stephen Holden, "Anomie's Insidious Grip on Suburban Affluence," *New York Times*, 10 April 1998, 21.

15. Sawhney, "A Success Story for Slackers," 4.

16. "Toronto Winner Is a Maverick," 32

17. *waydowntown* press kit, 4.

18. The 1978 version of *Superman* with Christopher Reeve was shot in Calgary when Burns was a teenager, but he insists it was not a significant influence in his life.

19. A barista from the mall tells Tom a joke he's made up: "A 15 bus takes you downtown, a bottle of marbles takes you *way* downtown."

20. Gary Burns, *Perfect Radiant City*, final draft (as of 2 August 2005), unpublished, courtesy of the author.

21. Pevere, *Mondo Canuck*, 97.

22. "Toronto Winner is a Maverick," 32.

23. Peter Morris, "In Our Own Eyes: The Canonozing of Canadian Film," in Blaine Allan, Michael Dorland, and Zuzana Pick, eds., *Responses in Honour of Peter Harcourt* (Toronto: The Responsibility Press, 1992), 157–62.

24. Katharine Monk, *Weird Sex & Snowshoes and Other Canadian Film Phenomena*. (Vancouver: Raincoast Books, 2001), 67.

25. Angela Stukator, 104, "*Guide to the Cinemas of Canada*, *Take One's Essential Guide to Canadian Film*, and *Weird Sex and Snowshoes & Other Canadian Film Phenomena* (book reviews),"*Canadian Journal of Film Studies* 112 (Fall 2002): 101–05.

15

Coward, Bully, and Clown

The Dream-life of Michael Dowse

BART BEATY

WHILE ITS ONGOING SCHOLARLY RELEVANCE may be debated, Robert Fothergill's 1977 essay "Coward, Bully, or Clown: the Dream-Life of a Younger Brother" still casts a powerful shadow over the popular understanding of Canadian cinema, particularly as it is shaped by the Canadian arts press. While, over the past three decades, academic writers on film have increasingly turned their attention toward the high-minded or serious Canadian cinema found in the art houses and film festivals of major urban centres, reporters for Canadian daily newspapers have tended to emphasize an entirely different cinema, one that valorizes the loser as a distinctly Canadian hero. The "popular" Canadian cinema—from *Meatballs* (Reitman, 1979) to *Going the Distance* (Griffiths, 2004)—is championed by the Canadian press for its ability to speak to "ordinary Canadians." As such, the press strives to demonstrate the mass appeal of popular Canadian cinema, championing box-office receipts and promoting international success stories as evidence that Canada remains relevant in a global cultural marketplace. Within this framework of populist boosterism a very limited

notion of Canadian identity is advanced. Moreover, it is one that, arguably, film scholars have long abandoned. In short, Canadian arts journalists
find in Canada's popular cinema a continuing reliance on Fothergill's
observation that Canadian feature films depict "the radical inadequacy
of the male protagonist."[1] Perhaps the filmmaker who best exemplifies
the ongoing reliance of arts journalists upon Fothergill's conception of
Canadian identity is Michael Dowse. In his short career, beginning with
his first feature film in 2002, Dowse's work highlights the Canadian
stereotype outlined by Fothergill, while also distancing from it in strategic ways to position him as a decidedly international, not national,
filmmaker.

Born in Calgary in 1973, Dowse rose to prominence as a director based
on the success of his first feature-length film, *FUBAR* (2002), a film that
he also produced and wrote with the actor-writers Paul Spence and David
Lawrence. The success of this film led to a British-Canadian co-production set on the Spanish island of Ibiza, *It's All Gone Pete Tong* (2005). Taken
together, these two films have been heralded in the Canadian press as
simultaneously reinforcing and destabilizing the two main stereotypes
of Canadian cinema: a realist cinema rooted in documentary traditions
and a cinema of losers.

Of Dowse's two films, *FUBAR* is the one that most obviously works
within the thematic traditions of Canadian loser cinema. The film follows
the misadventures of a young filmmaker, Farrel Mitchner (Gordon Skilling),
who is shooting a documentary about two Calgary-based headbangers.
His subjects, the mullet-haired Dean Murdoch (Paul Spence) and Terry
Cahill (David Lawrence), work in low-skill jobs while spending their free
time binge-drinking beer. Dean is estranged from his girlfriend and the
mother of his child, forcing him to live with Terry as the two desperately
attempt to hold on to an adolescent lifestyle that is best expressed in
their personal philosophy of life, "give'r." When Dean is unexpectedly
diagnosed with testicular cancer, he and Terry decide to take to the road
with the film crew for a final pre-operative blow-out. While on this trip
to High River, Alberta, Farrel is killed in a swimming accident. The crew
finishes the film, following Dean through his operation, Farrel's funeral,
and Dean's chemotherapy. Successfully recovered from the cancer, Dean

and Terry return to a life of "give'r" at the film's end, saluting Farrel with a beer at the cemetery before resuming their everyday lives.

Following Fothergill's lead, it has been easy for commentators to read *FUBAR* as the story of eternally younger brothers. Dean and Terry steadfastly refuse to grow up. Their lives are contrasted in the film to that of their friend Tron (Andrew Sparacino), their former mentor who is now married and working as a welder. While Tron's encounter with his former friends leaves him longing for the carefree lifestyle that they still lead, it is clear that this longing is regressive. Dean is both a coward and a bully. He is terrified of dealing with the consequences of his cancer until he is forced to do so by his ex-girlfriend Trixie (Tracey Lawrence). He vents his frustrations on Terry, physically dominating him in a series of playful fights, before focussing his attention on Farrel, whom he goads into the diving stunt that eventually claims his life. Throughout the film, however, his position as a bully is strained by his illness and self-destructiveness, which emphasizes the frailty of his masculine position, making Dean at once bully, coward, and clown. Textually, *FUBAR* does little to mitigate the loser stigma attached to Canadian cinema. If anything, the film revels in the puerile humour of the characters that it supposedly satirizes. This is perhaps best revealed in the scene in which a parking-lot brawl breaks out among local High River residents who believe that they are actually participating in a documentary shoot and are hoping to provide a good show for the cameras.

The success of *FUBAR* brought Dowse to the attention of a group of British producers who hired him to write and direct a film based on their working title: *It's All Gone Pete Tong*. Since the film was neither initiated by Dowse nor concerned with quintessentially Canadian concerns, it offered Canadian critics and journalists an interesting counterpoint in terms of reframing the loser cinema in an increasingly global context. Frankie Wilde (Paul Kaye), the superstar protagonist of *Tong*, might be said to fill the role of the classic clown. Frankie is a British club DJ in residence on the island of Ibiza, home of several of the world's largest dance clubs and a vacation destination for European clubbers. Living a lavish lifestyle with a cheating wife and a massive cocaine addiction, Frankie falls on hard times when it becomes increasingly evident to those around him that he is going deaf as a result of long-term exposure to loud, thumping music. His doctors warn Frankie against excessive noise, but he loses his hearing completely after a freak accident in his recording studio. Unable to work, Frankie is abandoned by his wife and left to his own addictions. After unsuccessfully attempting suicide by firecracker (in a nod to Godard's *Pierrot le fou* [1965]), Frankie reclaims his life, first learning to read lips then learning to mix music through the close monitoring of sound vibrations. He stages a triumphant comeback with an album release and a star set at Manumission, the biggest club on the island. Then, without warning, he disappears from the scene, shucking off his celebrity status to teach music to deaf children.

The humour in *Tong* largely shifts over the course of the film. In the first act, it is mostly about Frankie's extreme lifestyle and the difficulty that his failing hearing causes. In these scenes he is portrayed as a buffoon, completely ignorant of his surroundings and out of touch with the world. In the second, more depressing, act, the film adopts a much darker tone as Frankie sinks into the depths of addiction and despair. The lightness returns in the third act, however, propelled by Frankie's crazed manager, Max Haggar (Mike Wilmot), who sees in the DJ's comeback an opportunity to return to the lavish excesses of the film's opening through the marketing of bobble-head dolls, energy drinks, and high-concept music videos. Thus, *It's All Gone Pete Tong* opens, like *FUBAR*, with a critique of the main character(s). However, unlike the earlier film, it allows the characters to evolve into something resembling maturity and even adopts a sentimental tone. While *FUBAR* is a film in which the main characters overcome adversity without changing their nature, *Tong* is the story of a clown who, through a sudden tragedy, has his life turned upside down and re-emerges from the darkness of depression a better person in every aspect of his life. In this way, it is an uplifting story of self-actualization.

Fothergill argued that "it is very rare indeed to find an English Canadian film in which a male character of some worth and substance is depicted as growing towards self-realization, achieving or even working towards a worthwhile goal, playing a significant part in any kind of community, or establishing a mature loving relationship with a woman."[2] In *It's All Gone Pete Tong*, Frankie Wilde accomplishes all four, yet Canadian critics were steadfast in their refusal to cede the film's quintessential Canadianness.

While it is clear that *FUBAR* more easily fits the established stereotypes of Canadian cinema than does *Tong*, which is, after all, the story of a British man living in Spain, a hit-oriented Canadian press sifted through *Tong* searching for nationalist signifiers. Indeed, while there are no Canadian characters in *Tong*, nor Canadian settings, and while the film's conclusion is at odds with the central mythology identified by Fothergill and frequently championed in the press, the film is nonetheless claimed as distinctly Canadian insofar as it draws upon satiric and cinematic sensibilities that can be recuperated for a nationalist sensibility.

Both of Dowse's films rely on differing conceptions of the Canadian documentary tradition, which are then mocked. *FUBAR* is a reasonably straight take on the mockumentary tradition, an aesthetic that is carefully foregrounded throughout. Farrel Mitchner is not presented as a particularly skilled filmmaker and neither is his film supposed to be well-accomplished. While his subjects are ragged and often out of control, the film itself shares an unpolished feeling with the characters with long sequences shot in low light and with an extremely unstable hand-held camera. The film's overall aesthetic is best described as chaotic, which seems to be very much in accord with the way that Terry and Dean live their lives. The unprofessional look of the film works to heighten the sense of realism, reinforcing the idea that these are unstaged and improvisational moments caught on tape. Of course, in reality this was also very much the case. *FUBAR* was created without a script by actors who improvised the general narration and dialogue. Further, in the sequence shot in High River, the actors were improvising with non-actors who were told that the filmmakers were making a "real" documentary, rather than a fictional mockumentary. In this way, *FUBAR* works to blur the documentary/mockumentary distinction, beginning as a parody of the depiction of Albertan headbangers and subtly shifting into the real thing on occasion.

It's All Gone Pete Tong, on the other hand, mimics the television biography style popularized by such shows as *Behind the Music*. Featuring interviews with a number of real DJs as themselves (Carl Cox, Tiësto, and, of course, Pete Tong), as well as actors playing the roles of journalists, record company executives, and other interested media personnel, *Tong* unfolds much of its background material using direct address by experts to the camera.

At the same time, none of the major characters in the film are interviewed, and the film steers clear of a documentary-style approach in the main dramatic sequences. Shaking the documentary aesthetic moves *Tong* a step away from the realism of *FUBAR* and into more subjective territory. This is accomplished through the creative use of sound editing to represent Frankie's increasing deafness and the actualization of his cocaine habit in the form of the coke badger. The latter shifts the film on occasion into the realm of fantasy. This shift not only offers more creativity in cinematic story-telling terms but it also allows for a deeper exploration into the psyche of the character, revealing something more than the simple loser archetype that Dean personifies.

While stylistically *FUBAR* works within a realist tradition that is often assumed to be particularly Canadian, the film offers a commentary on a conception of filmmaking perhaps even more than it does on its characters. While the "director" in many faux-documentaries is concealed from the camera in an effort to create a *cinéma vérité* feeling, Farrel Mitchner is a major character in *FUBAR*. Significantly, the film opens with footage of Farrel screening an experimental short film for Dean and Terry, who ridicule his arty pretensions, calling on him to "turn down the suck." If Farrel's early efforts turn out to be not the cinema Dean and Terry need, his shift to the documentary mode recasts him in the role of participant-observer, endlessly challenging Dean and, in turn, being challenged by him. Through the figure of Farrel, first-time Calgary filmmaker Dowse paints a picture of a first-time Calgary filmmaker struggling between his own high-art aspirations and a deep desire to tell an authentically Canadian slice-of-life story. What separates the portrait from straight autobiography is the fact that *FUBAR* was a truly collaborative project between Dowse, Spence, and Lawrence, while Farrel's film relies to a much higher degree on manipulation. Farrel is not content to merely observe his subjects but frequently goes behind their backs to learn more about them (through interviews with Tron, Trixie, Dr. Lim, and Terry's employer) or to create drama, as when he confronts Trixie with the news of Dean's cancer. The end result is a portrait of a filmmaker who is himself something of a coward and a bully. Farrel is not a mature masculine character to be looked up to, but a petulant wannabe and possibly fraudulent artist who finds himself in (literally) deeper water than he anticipated. The portrait of the Canadian artist painted by the film is remarkably unsympathetic and bleak; ending, as it does, with his death by drowning.

A very different image of the artist is offered by *It's All Gone Pete Tong*. Where Farrel is doomed to failure, Frankie is already a tremendous success. Central to the film's concern are the importance of the artist's ability to maintain himself as an active creator and the notion of the "authentic" cultural player. Frankie's deafness challenges his ability to continue working, and for a while the film promises an ending as bleak as the one for Farrel. However, his re-dedication to his art, and his ingenuity, save Frankie from death. As a result of his deafness, Frankie is ironically elevated beyond his former talent, producing a superior record through his unique ability to see rhythm in everyday movements, which grants him a greater connection to the world and to his music. In a sense, losing his ability to hear transforms Frankie from hedonist to humanist. While Faithless' 1999 club hit intoned "God is a DJ," in *Tong* it is clear that the DJ has become a god. Nonetheless, despite his divine gifts, Frankie's career is threatened by Max, the leech-like manager who attaches Frankie to a series of crassly exploitative commercial developments that undermine his new-found sense of self. Pressed by Max to churn out bobble-head dolls in his image, Frankie rejects these false idols, choosing to play one comeback gig and then disappear. This disappearance turns Frankie into a mystical figure within the dance music scene, with journalists wildly speculating on the various possibilities of where he might be now. From *FUBAR* to *Tong* we find an inversion of the portrait of the artist. In *FUBAR*, Farrel is something of a leech, attaching himself to his more interesting subjects in an effort to make his own name as a filmmaker. In *Tong*, on the other hand, Frankie is forced to recognize and then distance himself from those aspects of the cultural industry (his management, his record label) that threaten his creative and personal autonomy. Thus, the artist-protagonist's journey in each of the two films takes him in significantly different directions.

The ending of *It's All Gone Pete Tong* suggests the uplifting possibility that one man can overcome his personal demons and learn to put others before himself, living in greater harmony with the world. Yet the tone of this ending is somewhat at odds with the rest of the film, which seems to be more of an ironic take on the cult of celebrity and the excesses of the celebrity lifestyle. This is perhaps a response to the sudden fame Dowse himself achieved following the release of *FUBAR*. The irony of *FUBAR*'s success is that while the film itself ultimately seems to revel in working-class excess, it found its audience within the festival and art-house circuit, well-removed from the culture that it celebrates, however tongue-in-cheek, on the screen. Debuting at an elite film festival and enjoying a theatrical run exclusively in art house cinemas, *FUBAR* is not so much a film for 'bangers but for those with the cultural capital required to both understand and mock that particular subculture. However, the joke, in the end, may be on them. The film's take on the bully-coward-clown archetype in Canadian cinema is inflected by generations of intervening Canadian (and foreign) cinema, which has raised its know-ingness to arch heights. As a parody of both the documentary, that central Canadian film genre, and the process of creating independent cinema, *FUBAR* positions itself as an ironic commentary on Canadian culture through the celebration of two of the least praise-worthy lead characters since Pete and Joey travelled from Cape Breton to Yonge Street in *Goin' Down the Road* (1970). Early on in *Tong*, on the other hand, the film signals an ironic disposition that is subsequently overturned with the introduc-tion of Penelope (Beatriz Batarda), Frankie's lip-reading instructor and love interest. The uplifting ending that is associated with Frankie's return to greatness and the love of a good woman strips most of the irony from the film, abruptly changing its direction. Dowse himself has rejected the "post-ironic" label for his work, but it is nonetheless clear that from *FUBAR* through to *It's All Gone Pete Tong* there is a general migration of sensibility moving from irony toward something more heartfelt. What's more, that sympathy ultimately goes to the artist working against the system.

It is clear that Dowse's personal trajectory in the two films is equally central to our understanding of the films. *FUBAR* is an avowedly local film. Written, shot, produced, and financed in Calgary by Calgarians, the film evinces a local sensibility to the degree that, when it was picked up for distribution by Odeon Films, it generated something of a minor national phenomenon. *Tong*, on the other hand, is arguably better clas-sified as a British film than Canadian, despite the fact that it maintained enough Canadian participants to bring in some level of funding from

Canadian agencies. The film was created primarily for the UK box office by British producers looking to cash in on that country's large dance music and club scene. In the UK, the film opened on more than two hundred screens, as compared to ten in Canada, and it opened in Canada only after its run in the UK and the United States had ended. So, to what degree can *Tong* be properly termed a Canadian film? Is the fact that writer/director Dowse is a Calgary native sufficient? Or the fact that it is a British-Canadian co-production? Both of these suggestions feel extremely hollow. Yet there is a strong tendency in the commentary on the film to read it as a distinctly Canadian popular success story. If so, does it come from the film itself or from an earnest, if naïve, desire on the part of the Canadian cultural reporters to imprint nationalism on any text that it can find?

The critical reaction to Dowse's two films is indicative of the consolidation of an affirming nationalist culture impulse in Canada. Reviews of *FUBAR* were generally mixed, leaning to the positive end of the spectrum. Critics who championed the film relied on the testicular cancer storyline as the film's strongest virtue, a plot device that some felt elevated the film from the merely moronic to a state of enlightened pathos. Writing in the *Toronto Star*, Daphne Gordon argued that *FUBAR* "is a hilarious ode to the random stupidity of headbanger culture and a touching story about two friends who face death together," while *Exclaim!*'s Noel Dix notes: "It's this saving grace that really separates *Fubar* from being some idiotic amateur film, turning it into a touching, yet extremely amusing cult classic."[3] At the same time, however, a number of Canadian critics found that the film did indeed err toward the idiotic and amateur. Cam Fuller, writing in the *Saskatoon Star-Phoenix*, suggested that the film "remains more of a curiosity than a bona fide comedy," and the *Calgary Herald*'s Heath McCoy argued that because the film is "grounded in ugly, white trash reality," that "a lot of these gags are hard to swallow."[4] This critical back-and-forth about the merits of the film would be no different from the reviews of any other comedy, were it not for the insertion of a nationalist imperative into the discussion. It serves to completely reorient the concerns away from the aesthetic and ground them anew in civic-minded rhetoric. Todd Babiuk, writing in the *Edmonton Journal*, exemplified the nationalist discussion of *FUBAR* when he wrote: "*Fubar* isn't perfect.

It's clear that most of the dialogue is improvised, and some scenes are more successful than others. Even so, with limited resources, no beavers and no recognizable stars, Calgary's Broken Tranny Productions has released the best Canadian movie of the year."[5] That Babiuk suggests in the same breath that FUBAR is both flawed and the best thing that Canadian film-makers will accomplish during the year is indicative of the greatly diminished expectations for Canadian film that exist among the nation's film critics and, perhaps, the Canadian film-going audience.

For many critics, FUBAR could be read as a distinctly Canadian take on the male anti-hero. These readings were amplified through the film's perceived participation in a distinctly Canadian comedic lineage. Thus, both Michael Reid and Jay Stone compared Dean and Terry to the McKenzie brothers, the beer-drinking hosers played by Dave Thomas and Rick Moranis on SCTV in the early-1980s, while the Toronto Star's Peter Howell compared them to the Saturday Night Live headbangers Wayne and Garth, characters created by Canadian comedian Mike Meyers.[6] While the assumption that the beer-drinker and the headbanger are uniquely Canadian seems dubious, particularly given that Wayne and Garth came from Aurora, Illinois, it is one that critics not only took for granted but actively cele-brated. In an Edmonton Journal feature, Todd Babiuk claimed the headbanger as not simply Canadian but, more specifically, an Albertan archetype:

> A proud beast walks in our province. He lives in the cities and in the towns, working on the rigs or in factories, building houses and grain elevators and clearing asbestos from office towers.
>
> On the weekends he scores weed and drinks Pilsner.
>
> He cruises in trucks with rebuilt engines and custom mufflers, and changes lanes without employing the signal light....
>
> He is the modern headbanger.[7]

While attempts to claim the headbanger as distinctly Canadian, or even distinctly Albertan, fly in the face of logic and evidence, numerous critics clung to the notion that FUBAR represented a tried-and-true Canadian sensibility. Michael Reid, for example, argued that "FUBAR is, for starters, so irreverently Canadian it deserves a special Heritage Canada award."[8] For Reid, and others, this particularly nationalistic reading of the film is derived from the legacy of Robert Fothergill and the assumption that Canadian culture is a loser culture. Dowse cannily played up this notion in interviews, telling the *Ottawa Citizen*'s Jay Stone: "The Americans celebrate the overachiever, while Canadians look to the person they can relate to," a comment that assumes that Canadians relate to marginalized losers from a working-class, white, masculine suburban subculture.[9] Yet for those who do identify, the equation of *FUBAR* with particularly Canadian cultural values is a seductive force. The *Charlottetown Guardian*'s Donnie Killorn, for example, exalted the film for its ability to distill a purely Canadian essence:

> Canadian cinema has always been a bit of an oxymoron. We're really good at making American movies for them, but haven't quite got the hang of making our own.
>
> My vocabulary fails me when trying to describe how good this movie is.
>
> While its run at City Cinema has ended, I believe the theatre will bring it back for another viewing. If not, rent FUBAR the first weekend it becomes available. And when it's over, put on the national anthem, send our flag up a pole and shotgun a beer in honour of FUBAR.
>
> Be proud of Canadian cinema.[10]

Here, Killorn reads the failures of Canadian cinema writ large onto the figures of Dean and Terry, allowing these headbangers to act as ideological stand-ins for an underachieving film industry. From this point of view, Canadian cinema is not merely a cinema of losers, as Fothergill might have it, but a loser's cinema.

Killorn's reading of *FUBAR* as a Canadian film to take pride in relies on its use of what are taken to be important Canadian archetypes. With *It's All Gone Pete Tong*, however, the Canadian archetype is notably absent. While one might assume that this would lead to a reduction of nationalist claims, this was not the case. With *Tong*, the international aspect of the film was largely seen by critics as evidence of an increasingly important role for Canada in the world or of a maturity in the film industry that was deemed absent only three years prior. One central difference between *FUBAR* and *Tong* is the fact that the former relies on an internationalized subculture erroneously claimed as nationally based by Canadian critics, while the latter relies on a subculture almost completely absent from Canada outside of Montreal, Toronto, and Vancouver. The international-ization of *Tong* allows a certain degree of nationalist confusion to enter the frame. Indeed, *The Chicago Reader* identified the British-Canadian co-production as an "Australian mockumentary," possibly a Commonwealth confusion or a slippage from the fact that Spence and Cahill revive Dean and Terry in *Tong* as Austrian, rather than Australian, heavy metal stars.[11]

For Canadian journalists, there was little doubt that *Tong* was a distinctly Canadian film, despite its distinctly non-Canadian setting and subject matter. Sandra Sperounes, writing in the *Edmonton Journal*, stated bluntly: "*Pete Tong* film is not only hip, it's funny, smart—and Canadian."[12] For Sperounes, the presence of Canadian actors (Spence, Cahill, Mike Wilmot) and a director born in Calgary, conspire to construct the film as not just a local production but also a specifically local narrative. For Katherine Monk, writing in *The Vancouver Sun*, however, *Tong* is situated within a Canadian comedic tradition, despite its lack of obvious Canadian trappings.[13] Needless to say, the distinctly Canadian comedic tradition identified by Monk as a cross between British intellectualism and American vulgarity is rooted, as Fothergill maintains, in "the film's themes of failure, self-effacement and finally, tolerance and growth in the face of massive obstacles." The desire to find distinctly Canadian traits in a film that was so clearly British was common to journalists across the country. For example, Jay Stone lamented the fact that Dowse had left Canada for greener pastures: "Come home, Michael Dowse: there's plenty of mate-rial here."[14] Vancouver's *WestEnder* went further and desperately adopted the film as its own, despite the near-complete lack of logical connections:

> Truthfully, the critically acclaimed tale of a DJ who loses his hearing has few ties to our city beyond the involvement of Vancouver's True West Films; it takes place in the legendary clubland of Ibiza, stars a British comedian, and was written by a Calgarian. But for a city whose cinematic reputation is often linked with clunkers like Eks Vs. Sever and Alone in the Dark, it's probably best that we grasp this tenuous link and call it our own.[15]

The *WestEnder*'s desire to claim *It's All Gone Pete Tong* as a local production was considerably amplified by the *Calgary Herald*, which saw in the film an opportunity to claim the first great Calgarian international cinema success story. The paper ran half a dozen stories about the film, each toasting it as a spectacular success story. When *Tong* won the City Award for Best Canadian feature at the Toronto International Film Festival, the *Herald* reported that "Writer/director Michael Dowse was back in his hometown of Calgary Sunday night to celebrate a big win."[16] In subsequent months the paper reported speculation that Paul Kaye would receive an Oscar nomination for his role as Frankie Wilde and that the film opened to "rave reviews" in the United Kingdom. Throughout their coverage, the *Herald* insisted upon the Calgary influence on the film, despite the fact that the filmmaker no longer lived in the city. The paper reported that "Director Mike Dowse is likely the only link between Calgary and the exotic island of Ibiza," which is "an island off the coast of Spain where international DJs, Eurotrash and jet-setting hedonists indulge in sex, drugs and club music. Although the former might be similarly described during the pique of Stampede, Calgary shares few commonalities with the hot and sunny isle of Ibiza."[17] Nonetheless, Dowse told the *Herald* that his years in Calgary had "given me a great sense of humour—that I carry with me no matter where I go," and Judd Palmer, speaking at *Tong*'s Calgary premiere, noted about *FUBAR* that "he took a miniscule budget and a crazy idea and turned it into something that made an impact. That's just good old-fashioned Alberta pioneer know-how."[18] When the Uptown Theatre, at which Dowse once worked, hosted a two-day retrospective of the filmmaker's (two-film) career, the *Herald* noted: "Seeing his funny headbanging mockumentary *Fubar* is almost a right of passage for Calgarians, and his latest feature, *It's All Gone Pete Tong*, is being called one of the best Canadian movies in years."[19] This civic boosterism and desire to claim Calgary as a city where somebody once made a movie mimics *FUBAR*'s own reticence to fully challenge the loser aesthetic. Rather, it elevates it to the level of cultural zeitgeist defined in narrowly parochial terms. The extent to which Canada's arts journalists cling to this notion is further evident by their insistence on squeezing *Tong* into *FUBAR*'s ill-fitting shoes.

In the 1970s, Fothergill suggested that Canadian features deal with the dream life of younger brothers, establishing male protagonists who are marked by underachievement and failure. Thirty years later *FUBAR* could be easily slotted into such a framework, since none of the three lead characters is marked by any kind of reasonable success, and two, Dean and Terry, seem to lack aspirations of any kind at all. By the same token, the first half of It's All Gone Pete Tong seems to offer a non-Canadian lead in what has been conceptualized as a quintessentially Canadian role, but by the film's end Frankie has transformed himself into a better person, something Fothergill works to place outside the Canadian cinematic context. Does this mean that Tong is not a Canadian film? Cleaving tightly to Fothergill's outdated typology, one could certainly make this argument. Yet I would suggest that the example of Michael Dowse's short film career better highlights the growing realization that nationalist conceptions of cinema, resting as they do on a populist critical shorthand, are outmoded and insufficient. As the reviews for both of his films demonstrate, the desire to make claims about the "Canadian character" of a film rests less on artistic or aesthetic concerns and increasingly upon sentimentalized civic discourses.

NOTES

1.   Robert Fothergill, "Coward, Bully, or Clown: The Dream-Life of a Younger Brother," in *Canadian Film Reader*, ed. Seth Feldman and Joyce Nelson (Toronto: Peter Martin Associates, 1977), 235.

2.   Ibid., 240–41

3.   Daphne Gordon, "Hey, dude, where's my beer? ; FUBAR mockumentary comes with buzz," *Toronto Star*, 23 May 2002, A26; Noel Dix, "Fubar," *Exclaim!*, 10 December 2002, http://www.exclaim.ca/index.asp?layid=22&csid=5&csid 1=1185, accessed 12 November 2006.

4.   Cam Fuller, "Much-hyped *Fubar* doesn't quite deliver," *Saskatoon Star-Phoenix*, 13 September 2002, D7; Heath McCoy, "FUBAR: Pair wrestles with life's realities," *Calgary Herald*, 24 May 2002, E3.

5.   Todd Babiuk, "*Wayne's World*, Alberta-style," *Edmonton Journal*, 6 February 2002, C1.

6.   Michael D. Reid, "Crude, rude and, admit it, a piece of our past," *Victoria Times-Colonist*, 13 June 2002, D6; Jay Stone, "The headbangers next door," *Ottawa Citizen*, 11 June 2002, B7; Peter Howell, "Mullet head flick with a heart of gold," *Toronto Star*, 24 May 2002, D06.

7.   Todd Babiuk, "Headbangers show heart," *Edmonton Journal*, 31 May 2002, E2.

8. Michael D. Reid, "Crude, rude and, admit it, a piece of our past," D6.

9. Jay Stone, "Quirky mockumentary fuelled by ale and f-word," *Ottawa Citizen*, 14 June 2002, D3.

10. Donnie Killorn, "*FUBAR* fine Canadian cinema," *Charlottetown Guardian*, 9 August 2002, C5.

11. J.R. Jones, "*It's All Gone Pete Tong*," *The Chicago Reader*, http://onfilm. chicagoreader.com/movies/capsules/28054_ITS_ALL_GONE_PETE_TONG, accessed 14 November, 2006.

12. Sandra Sperounes, "Putting the proper spin on a DJ's disintegration," *Edmonton* Journal, 24 June 2005, G1.

13. Katherine Monk, "When the scene destroys its king," *The Vancouver Sun*, 10 June 2005, D1.

14. Jay Stone, "Dowse spins funny DJ tale," *The Kingston Whig-Standard*, 29 July 2005, 21.

15. "'Mock biopic' of deaf DJ fools, inspires, and garners Leos," *WestEnder*, 9 June 2005, 17.

16. John McKay and Alexandra Burroughs, "Calgarian's film big winner," *Calgary Herald*, 20 September 2004, E1.

17. "Good Good Good Vibrations: It's all gone right for locally grown director," *Calgary Herald*, 10 June 2005, SW09.

18. Alexandra Burroughs, "Dowse's lean days All Gone," *Calgary Herald*, 10 June 2005, C1.

19. "Flick Picks: A weekly roundup of the week's best bets," *Calgary Herald*, 5 August 2005, D2.

16

Hanging in Plain Sight
The Problem Body in Thom Fitzgerald's Films

SALLY CHIVERS & NICOLE MARKOTIĆ

Journalists keep asking the same questions...like they don't believe you. Finally I was like, "Yes, fine. It's all true. I was fat, I hanged myself, I'm dead now. Happy?"

—THOM FITZGERALD[1]

THOUGH KNOWN AS A CANADIAN FILMMAKER, Thom Fitzgerald (born 8 July 1968 in New Jersey) grew up in New Jersey and New York. Rejected for an exchange program to Italy, Fitzgerald instead moved in 1986 to attend the Nova Scotia College of Art and Design after completing a BFA in performance and film in Manhattan at the Cooper Union for the Advancement of Science and Art. Though some critics turn to Thom Fitzgerald's films for hints about his own life experience, he quickly dispels the relation, claiming that his silver-screen creations match only his imagination. All his films push viewers to question the line between fantasy and real life, to cross the "normal/abnormal" border. Such a pointed challenge to film realism makes questions about his own "real life" difficult to pose, as interviewers have discovered. For example, Fitzgerald tells Matthew Hays, speaking of the connection between the dysfunctional family in *Hanging Garden* and his own relatives: "When I decided I wanted to be closer to my family and make some reconnection...I thought, What better way to do it than in my imagination? It'll all go swimmingly if I do it on paper rather than in real life."[2] Or, as he expresses it elsewhere, "I fantasized about a family reunion... Then I thought, fuck it, I'll just write a movie about one. That's easier."[3] While it is tempting and perhaps apt to read his most influential film biographically, his career following that break-out success consists of efforts to disallow audiences the biographical connection.

Best known for his impressive feature-film debut, *The Hanging Garden* (1997), Fitzgerald learned the subtleties of Maritime irony and deadpan caustic humour during the decade prior to its release, which he spent studying painting, performing in theatre, and making films in Halifax. The tenuous distinction between fact and fantasy, between one possible narrative and one impossible one, is pivotal to the massive success of *The Hanging Garden*. Such distinctions show up even in his award-winning (Goldstar Award, Atlantic Film Festival) student film, "The Movie of the Week" (1990), which features a character who confuses television events with real ones. Two short films, "Cherries" and "Canada Uncut," released in 1995, show his development as both a Canadian filmmaker and a director with a sense for revitalizing the mundane while courting controversy. Produced with the help of Shortworks, a film and video production workshop funded by CBC, Nova Scotia Film Development Corporation (NSFDC), and Telefilm Canada, and awarded to aspiring filmmakers, "Cherries" grows from Fitzgerald's work with the Charlatan Theatre Collective and is an adaptation of a stage production featuring a woman who celebrates each menstrual cycle by baking a vulva-shaped cake. "Canada Uncut," an intense satire of Canada customs agents, became the title short film for curators Shawna Dempsey and Lorri Millan's film festival, subtitled "the Roaring '90s." Dempsey and Millan explain:

> The 1990s was an exciting time to be making media work. It clearly mattered to the audience. Together, we were forging a vocabulary of what it looked like to be openly, unapologetically gay. This program reflects the energy and diversity of that

time. But this work is more than historically significant. It remains great film and video, and is not only an essential part of our gay history but the history of Canadian art as well. [The filmmakers included in our show] are not simply of an era. However their significance in the 1990s was unmistakable, as they pushed the boundaries of the film and video media while providing the visual imagery for a public, gay identity.[4]

While many critics have quickly designated Fitzgerald a gay filmmaker based on the subject matter he puts on screen, and he is happy enough with that designation, he also continues to mock the relationship that designation has to his "real life": "My own Kinsey identity is pretty fucked up," he cheerfully offers. "I've never identified myself as gay. But I'm such a big fruit, everyone assumes I'm a Kinsey 6 [exclusively homosexual]."[5] Fitzgerald places himself more in the middle of that scale, and his film productions explore the middle ground in relation to sexuality, as well as many bodily states.

As much as he may play with audience members who try to read his own sexuality into his films, Fitzgerald's position in relation to homosexuality is key to his successes and failures in the process of becoming a filmmaker. In the early 1990s, Fitzgerald's NFSDC and Canada Council funding applications for a project about a young man hiding his gay identity, entitled "I'll Pour for the First Half Hour," were both rejected, the latter on the grounds that the Canada Council jury found Fitzgerald homophobic.[6] After two years working for Atlantic Independent Media, he quit his job and lived with his mother's financial support in order to finish the project. He split "I'll Pour" into a fringe stage play, *Bed and (Maybe) Breakfast*, that got mixed reviews (raves in Canada, rants in the US) and a film script that eventually became *The Hanging Garden*. Film production was plagued with long delays for funding and resistance from casting agencies who also suspected homophobia. Shot over a twenty-five-day period, the set enjoyed only one day of sunshine, offset by both a hurricane and a tropical storm.

After tremendous struggle and seemingly inauspicious signs, Fitzgerald's debut feature, *The Hanging Garden*, made when Fitzgerald was twenty-nine, was released in 1997 to immediate and widespread acclaim. In a year that also saw the release of such Canadian films as Atom Egoyan's *The Sweet*

Hereafter, François Girard's *The Red Violin*, and Louis Saia's *Les Boys*, *The Hanging Garden* was voted Most Popular Film at the Toronto International Film Festival, where it opened the *Perspectives Canada* series. It also won awards at Atlantic Film Festival, the Vancouver International Film Festival, and the Mar del Plata Film Festival in Argentina. In addition, the film won four 1997 Genie Awards from the Academy of Canadian Cinema and Television. For his impressive work on the film, Fitzgerald received the prestigious Claude Jutra Award for Best Direction of a First Feature.

The film focuses on an adolescent boy who is not only coming to terms with his own sexuality but also attempting to understand his family's fear and anxiety surrounding that sexuality. Similarly, Fitzgerald claims that his own mother begged him not to tell anybody about his sexuality when he was an adolescent, and just before the film was released, Fitzgerald's mother made him forewarn his estranged stepfather. As Fitzgerald explains, "She'd lived in mortal terror of his reaction, but he said it was fine so long as it's in the family. He just doesn't like other homos."[7] The script may well contain homophobia but only as a critique of the harm such attitudes can wreak. That is, there are homophobic characters in *The Hanging Garden*, but the film does not invite audience members to sympathize with their attitudes.

None of Fitzgerald's subsequent films have received the much-deserved attention lavished on his remarkable debut feature. Though prolific and successful in attracting considerable star-power cast to his films (including Olympia Dukakis, Kerry Fox, Lucy Liu, Sandra Oh, Sarah Polley, and Parker Posey), Fitzgerald has yet to attract sustained interest from the larger distribution companies. *Beefcake*, released in 1999 and accepted into the Sundance Film Festival, was generally met with disappointment in Canada from those hoping he would follow through on the edgy success of *The Hanging Garden* (in the US, however, this docu-comedy attracted large audiences drawn to its campy ode to 1950s fitness magazines). Because critics were so eager to read his own life story into his first feature film, Fitzgerald set out, in his second, to get as far away as possible from his own life experience. As a result, ironically, he found himself in semi-documentary mode, writing about homoerotic fitness photography celebrating the male physical form. He explains that the blend of fiction and fact was difficult: "It's much harder dealing with real people than made-up ones. People you make up co-operate without question."[8] The film is a "tongue-in-cheek" portrayal of Bob Mizer, a photographer who responds to the strength and health craze by launching the body-obsessed magazine, *Physique Pictoral*. The film plays up the ironic naïveté of newcomer Neil O'Hara (Josh Peace), who embraces his modelling job, unaware of what even his younger brother in Pugwash, Nova Scotia, understands about the subtext Mizer's photographs projects to audiences.

The made-for-television *Blood Moon* (2001, originally *Wolf Girl* on US cable), moves Fitzgerald's career from depictions of "real life," placing the director in the horror genre. Following Tod Browning's footsteps in employing disabled actors to play freaks in a travelling side show (*Freaks*, 1932), the film focusses on a hirsute girl and her search for love and a cure. The film invites unfavourable comparisons to the Canadian horror success *Gingersnaps*, released the same year, but does not measure up to the horror standards of that film. As do all Fitzgerald's works, *Blood Moon* explores the human quest for normalcy in conflict with the desire for acceptance of difference.

Fitzgerald's subsequent *The Wild Dogs* (2002) won four awards at the Atlantic Film Festival but received little popular attention. In the film, Fitzgerald plays the role of a pornographer, Geordie, sent by his boss to Bucharest to capture underage "Lolitas." *Wild Dogs* provides a somewhat heavy-handed critique of North American visitors who wish to rescue the city's most down-trodden inhabitants; at the same time, the film does not provide simple solutions or a neat conclusion to complicated topics. One Bucharest resident, Bogdan (Mihai Calota), risks losing his job as a dog-catcher by hiding the ownerless dogs he finds on the streets. A dog lover known for having his blind dog's name on his answering machine, Fitzgerald depicts a puppy euthanized on film, which does not win him a sympathetic audience despite its metaphorical overtones. Yet the film manages to convey both optimism and despair. Responding to Geordie's earnest plea that, "People don't just disappear," Radu (Marcel Catalin Ungureanu), a dancer/pimp/stripper/gambler/businessman, replies: "Yes, they disappear. The world is too big."

Fitzgerald's following film, *The Event* (2003), transfers the euthanasia theme to the human context. He continues to court controversy with his pro-assisted-suicide stance and the camera's sympathy for the characters who look to death as ultimate "mercy." Set in New York City, the film situates characters faced with the AIDS crisis in a "ground-zero" city. But the ritualized celebration of a life and the film's star-studded cast (Don McKellar, Parker Posey, Olympia Dukakis, Sarah Polley) fail to distinguish it from other mainstream films whose ideology suggests that the worst thing that can happen to a young, white male is that his body stops functioning perfectly. The subtlety that so distinctly marks Fitzgerald's feature-film debut is missing, and the narrative veers too frequently between the hard-hitting prosecutor and sympathetic pro-euthanasia characters. From his own description, it appears that Fitzgerald, in his next film 3 Needles (2005), risks a didacticism invoked by the subject matter. As he explains it:

> My thesis is that in a time when all of humanity has this common enemy, how rather than bring us together to fight it, it has actually served to be divisive and resulted in people accusing one another and making it someone else's problem. You know, in North America and Europe we had such a cognitive awareness of how not to spread it, but in China they're spreading it to millions through their blood collection practice. That ignorance is horrific.[9]

Despite being mostly ignored in the box-office, films such as *Beefcake* and *The Wild Dogs* continue to challenge normative filmic depictions of "freakish" bodies, and of characters whose lives rarely merit Hollywood moviedom. Though Fitzgerald continues to produce controversial, intellectual films such as *3 Needles* with impressive casts, to date his main influence on international and national cinema emerges from *The Hanging Garden*, a film that advances cinematic conceptions of physicality, identity, and family without overt didacticism. In its relation to a longstanding cinematic tradition of portraying physical difference on screen, *The Hanging Garden* brazenly challenges the critical limits of embodiment. Scholar Robert McRuer explains that:

> In queer studies it is at this point a well-established critical practice to remark on heterosexuality's supposed invisibility. As the heterosexual norm congealed during the twentieth century, it was the 'homosexual menace' that was specified and embodied; the subsequent policing and containment of that menace allowed the new heterosexual normalcy to remain unspecified and disembodied.[10]

Similarly, the emerging field of disability studies helps to explain how certain bodies figure more prominently as metaphorical and as destined for the sensational display required to assure supposedly "normal" viewers that their bodies belong within a category of normal or neutral. The Hanging Garden relies on the hyper-embodiment of a queer obese teenage boy who, though not represented as disabled (i.e., he does not use a wheelchair, walk with a white cane, or converse in American Sign Language), invites socializing reactions in his family members often meted out to disabled people, especially those of cure and normalization. The film simultaneously questions able-bodied and heterosexual norms, showing how homosexuality and other forms of difference share a currently pathologized, yet potentially liberating, social space. For this reason, we shall situate our reading of The Hanging Garden in a tradition of portraying disability on screen.

■ *The Hanging Garden* and Physical Difference

FILMS TOO FREQUENTLY portray disabled characters as either pathetic victims—for example, Tiny Tim in *Christmas Carol* (adapted for the screen at least fifty times between 1938 and now)—courageous heroes—Daniel Day-Lewis as Christy Brown in *My Left Foot* (1989)—avenging villains—Lon Chaney initiated the film role of Quasimodo in *Hunchback of Notre Dame* (repeatedly adapted for film between 1923 and 2002)—or as minor metaphorical glosses to a more important ableist central narrative—for example, Warren Jensen Matthews (W. Earl Brown) and Tucker (Lee Evans) in *There's Something About Mary* (1998), Virgil (Val Kilmer) in *At First Sight* (1998), and Nicholas Cage in *Moonstruck* (1987). However, the history of cinematic depiction of disability differs from that of literature and other representational arts in part because techniques such as lighting, framing, and editing control the gaze of the film audience. In addition, the film industry's domination by Hollywood renders film a unique example of visually imposed normativity (that is, the social demand that "we all" try to be normal, even though "normal" is an impossible state to define).

Film scholarship on disability representation has followed the patterns first named by film and disability scholar Martin Norden, in his book *The Cinema of Isolation: A History of Physical Disability in the Movies*, and is further delineated as stages by critics David Mitchell and Sharon Snyder in *Narrative Prosthesis: Disability and the Dependencies of Discourse*. Norden clarifies such disability critique by categorizing the disability stereotypes: the "Civilian Superstar," the "Comic Misadventurer," the "Elderly Dupe," the "High-Tech Guru," the "Noble Warrior," the "Obsessive Avenger," the "Saintly Sage," the "Sweet Innocent," the "Techno Marvel," and the "Tragic Victim."[11] He emphasizes the placement of these stereotypes in a number of films, especially those not predominantly focussing on disability. Mitchell and Snyder further enumerate stages of film criticism when they describe the stages as "Negative Imagery," "Social Realism," New Historicism," "Biographical Criticism," and "Transgressive Reappropriation."[12] Mitchell and Snyder's book participates in a stage of disability criticism that the co-authors have labelled "transgressive reappropriation," and it demonstrates that disability representation can work against dominant modes of understanding power and can undermine typical portrayals of social dynamics. For example, in Atom Egoyan's *The Sweet Hereafter*, released the same year as *The Hanging Garden*, the character of Nicole (played by Sarah Polley)—rather than metaphorically conveying her recently acquired disability as an outward signal of her father's sexual abuse—openly plays on the effects of her disability in order to emphasize her new-found power over her sexually abusive father.

Disability roles can be the focus of a movie—for example, Sam in *I am Sam* (2002), Mary Alice Culhane in *Passion Fish* (1992), or Susie Hendrix (Audrey Hepburn) in *Wait Until Dark* (1967)—or can be tangential to the main plot—for example, a character who happens to use a wheelchair or is deaf, such as the main character's brother, David (David Bower), in *Four Weddings and a Funeral* (1994). Frequently, filmmakers use disability to portray a character as essentially evil, the character's disability serving as bodily signifier to inherently "flawed" human characteristic—for example, the villains in *Unbreakable* (2000) or *Wild, Wild West* (1999). As Robert Bogdan says about the depiction of such characters (quoting his young son), in *Freak Show: Presenting Human Oddities for Amusement and Profit*, "If they look bad, then they are bad."[13] Almost as frequently, filmmakers portray the opposite; rather than presenting villains whose disabilities display their essential evil, many films depict "ordinary heroes" whose disabilities—in and of themselves—transform disabled characters into noble and dignified "better than average" characters. Examples of the dignified disabled character are Ben Affleck's blind and extremely physically adept do-gooder lawyer, Matt Murdoch, in *Daredevil* (2003), and the tormented yet dignified John Merrick (John Hurt) in *The Elephant Man* (1980).

In *The Hanging Garden*, Fitzgerald presents a challenge to pervasive patterns of film representation because he offers a fascinating, sophisticated, intriguing, engaging, and beautiful film about bodies and the choices characters make based on their own bodies and the bodies surrounding them. The film relies on a coming-of-age format, yet it disturbs this format with virtually every scene. The main character, Sweet William (Chris Leavins), is a young man who left his family when he was an unhappy teenager and has just returned, ten years later. But to simply summarize Fitzgerald's film is not to do justice to the complicated tale he weaves, to the family he presents his viewers, and to the unique characters that do—and do not—exist in this great Canadian film. The term the "problem body" as displayed in this film shows the many ways that bodily differences intersect in the film to create meaning.[14] In our reading of *The Hanging Garden*, we shift the "either/or" way of thinking about bodies to a "both/and" model, so that a person's physicality is bodily *and* social. Such analysis promises to create new space for the disabled figure on screen.

In *The Hanging Garden*, Sweet William returns to his familial home for his sister's wedding. William has been gone for ten years. Upon his arrival, he appears older, happier, thinner by 150 pounds, more beautiful, and now lives with his boyfriend in Toronto. The wedding—upon orders from his sister, Rosemary (Kerry Fox)—takes place in the garden where the teen-aged William hanged himself. The garden is not only the significant site of young William's attempted act of suicide but it also exemplifies the dynamics of William's family. It is the external domestic setting where his alcoholic father hides and spends his time nurturing everything in his beloved garden, rather than caring for his wife and children. The garden is the site of William's act of rebellion and escape, of joy as a son and heartbreak as a young adult.

When fifteen-year-old William (played by Troy Veinotte) hanged himself in the midst of his father's beloved flower garden, the film suggests that he both *did* and *did not* survive. Repeatedly, the audiences watches scenes of William's teenaged body swinging lifelessly from the tree where he hanged himself a decade before. Yet the twenty-five-year-old William has, indeed, returned for his sister's wedding, returned as a solid figure ready to face his horrific past. The film does not, moreover, propose a magic-realist ghost-returns scenario, despite what many reviewers claim.[15] William (along with his friends and family) lives inside two realities at once: he is the obese unhappy adolescent who killed himself ten years earlier *and* he is the slim, confident, attractive young man who returns home after running away to the big city.

The filmic "trick" of showing two bodily realities at once also appears in the infamous Farrelly brothers' production *Shallow Hal* (2001). But their film questions the social aspects of living with an obese body, rather than using it to highlight a Hollywood actress' already exaggerated thinness. As well, that film's dual-body suggests that "beauty" resides in other characters' perceptions, rather than presenting the possibility of a character who must exist socially within varying bodily realities. *The Hanging Garden* belongs better in a film category originated by a much earlier film, the German *Zuckerbaby* (Percy Adlon, 1985). In that narrative, Marianne (Marianne Sägebrecht), changes from a cheerless, celibate, middle-aged woman into a sexy seductress who literally steals her intended away from his world into hers. But though the film celebrates interconnections between fatness and sexuality, it focusses exclusively on heterosexual adults. William, a teenager confused by the sexual signals emanating from his own and others' bodies, chooses so desperate a way out that his dual-bodied solution—to the "problem" of attempts to reduce him to *either* fat *or* thin and *either* gay *or* cured—is impossible.

Despite the distributor's insistence that he clarify the impossible scenario, Fitzgerald refused to provide a definitive explanation for what reviewers at best refer to as a "point of view shift."[16] And, unlike the Farrelly brothers, Fitzgerald does not employ an obese figure for the purpose of humour. Conversely, we argue that to work as it does, *The Hanging Garden* requires *both* versions *at the same time*, with a very serious aim. William, a young man just becoming aware of his sexuality, feels compelled to commit suicide: a) because of his dysfunctional home situation; b) because his mother has arranged for him to have sex with a local trying-to-make-ends-meet single-mom-cum-prostitute; c) because his would-be lover rejects him over the phone after they've been caught together, and d) because the world around him refuses to accept his body as it is: obese and sexually nascent. But grown-up William escaped a confused mother, Iris (Seana McKenna), and an abusive father, Whisky Mac (Peter MacNeill), and he returns home because he wishes to celebrate with his sister.[17] Twenty-five-year-old William is a witty, sexually active waiter/actor who can speak freely of his new life and of his new love (of "Dick"), and he must now take responsibility for his own and other people's choices. One such "choice" is the "brother" he did not previously know about. When William arrives, he acts wryly surprised that his parents have produced another sibling, indicating that he regards this "boy" as a possible replacement for himself. The film challenges William's immediate assumptions, however, when audiences learn that the boy is in fact a girl. This depiction of William's new "sister" also challenges the conventional assumption of identity based on physical appearance and further pushes the boundaries of gendered readings in this film. Sweet William's "brother" is born after the hanging (after the move to Toronto), and throughout the film William must learn and unlearn his ongoing assumptions about this new sibling.

The two conflicting scenarios or alternate possibilities in *The Hanging Garden* must *both* unfold for the film to present successfully its complicated and unusual narrative.[18] Characters surrounding William simultaneously feel guilt at his suicide and mixed joy at his fortuitous homecoming. In a similar overlapping way, William's body reflects an intersection of "problems" that cannot be separated or isolated, or even narrowed to a single "cause." As a teenager, he is on the verge of retrieving a body not yet his own. For example, William avoids physical contact with girls, yet reacts slowly and awkwardly to sexual advances by the boy he is attracted to. His size and sexuality are closely tied together in ways that other characters in the film rarely acknowledge. Upon his return from the ten-year absence, he tells his mother that he never minded being overweight as a teenager because, as he puts it, "being fat meant that I didn't have to play any sports" and that "I didn't have to have a girlfriend." As well, his size attracts the boy with whom he has his first sexual experience. Just as the film hinges on his hanging body reappearing every night in his father's garden—even when an older William stands observing his teenaged body swinging beneath a tree—the "problem" with William's body is not his age or his weight or his sexuality. Rather, it is the intersection of all these, in combination with the social environment that rejects his body's role within these overlapping identities.

The Hanging Garden exploits its interconnecting narratives through a presentation of bodies that refuse to convey merely one physical manifestation or another. For example, just before cutting down his teenaged body, hanging in the garden, the older William experiences a violent and disturbing asthma attack. This attack, in the film, conjoins his double bodily reality by reminding viewers that William's strangulation continues. But acting as more than mere metaphorical double entendre, William's asthma also projects a visible contradiction to the twenty-five-year-old body-perfect projected on screen. The unique narrative structure offers this film a potent way to articulate how extreme identity categories refuse/fail to statically contain complicated characters. As a result, *The Hanging Garden* offers a narrative and visual example of a both/and narrative model. As Roger Ebert's Chicago *Sun-Times* review puts it, "Somehow we understand why a 300-pound body could be left hanging from a tree for 10 years. It isn't really there, although in another sense of course it is."[19] For the mainstream viewers to whom Ebert appeals, the physical representation of a disabled character on film is not the problem; in another sense, of course, it is.

In our interpretation, we wish to emphasize the very notion that "of course" William's body is/was a problem. William may be overweight, and he may be asthmatic, but our argument is not so much that his body could—at times—reside within the category of "disabled." Rather, we argue that within the shifting definitions of what constitutes "normal" and "abnormal" categories for bodies (especially those represented on screen), the characters in this film visually convey a shifting signifier, a concrete representation of a changing sense of self, one that we identify as the "problem body."

On-screen, William presents to viewers a physically different body, one which the film refuses to isolate as either "normal" or "not." William suffers from severe asthma; his grandmother, Grace, (Joan Orenstein) has been diagnosed with Alzheimer's since he last saw her; his surprise "brother" turns out to be, in the first of many surprises, a reluctant flower girl at the wedding; and his father is an alcoholic. In one scene, twenty-five-year-old William moves physically uninhibited but socially still contained by expectations regarding his younger self. His thin body invites comments just as his fat body did. His mother repeatedly attempts to feed him; he surreptitiously watches his younger self, both as a child and as a teenager; he witnesses his father relive the hanging each night; he binges with snacks when no one is looking; and he makes out on the dock with his sister's groom, Fletcher (Joel S. Keller).

A comfort to him, an attraction to some, and a challenge to most, his obesity signals ultimate weakness to most of the characters, although teenage William is more than satisfied with the body he carries. This obese body literally hangs over the ongoing narrative as a threat to the other characters of what succumbing to "weakness" could entail, physically and socially, but it does so without the film itself condemning obesity as undesirable. His family interprets his more mature, seemingly perfect body, in terms of "cure" for his former obese self. However, the film does not portray William's obesity as weakness, as illness, or even, predominantly, as disability; rather, it provides an example of how certain bodies more frequently invite the label "problem body" than do others, especially in relation to social, spatial, and temporal context. So, for teenaged William, when he is out on a double-date with his sister, his body is the furthest thing from a problem, it is his protection against attraction from the opposite sex. His mother's homophobia manifests itself when she considers the budding sexual desires she understands as coming from William's adolescent body as a severe problem that needs to be "cured" by initiating her son into the heterosexual act. So, too, William's grandmother's dementia only becomes a real problem when William's mother disappears, and the family flounders without its main care-giving character.

The Hanging Garden is a significant film because of its challenge to social expectations of normalcy, in part by showing how any sign of extreme difference can invite an extreme "cure." But to what extent does such a film challenge normative identity at the same time as the majority of its characters (especially in the present-tense narrative) project "normal" and even normative bodies? Although Sweet William is not a disabled character, the combination of his obesity with his homosexuality—exhibited in a world that wishes to deny or obliterate both—transforms his youth to such an extent that his body transforms into an extreme problem. For example, when his mother finds out he has been fooling around with a boy, she takes him to a female prostitute to be "fixed." The sexual pleasure that William desires turns his body into a "problem" his mother tries to solve, drawing on the rhetoric of cure. And the drastic nature of that cure leads William to the ultimate tragic choice of suicide in his father's beloved garden and also drives him to escape his geography, only to return as a physically changed and now-confident young gay man. In her attempt to "cure" his homosexuality, William's mother not only drives him away, but her actions contribute to the creation of an offspring—the daughter William soon discovers is his. His mother's act, then, leads to her repositioning herself as "mother" to a granddaughter she herself must take responsibility for until William's (impossible) return.

In analyzing film depictions in order to articulate disability as "problem body," we see Thom Fitzgerald's films as: a) revealing a pattern of representation that both mimics and affects social context, especially a Canadian social context, by depicting the ways in which physical difference is both socially and culturally embedded, so that a lived body exists in relation to its deliberate and accidental narration; and b) illuminating a gap in critical film studies that shies away from othered bodies (except, those bodies regularly portrayed within the realm of the horror film).

The Hanging Garden is most successful at achieving these two distinctions in a large part because of its filmic and narrative subtleties. In all his movies, Thom Fitzgerald disturbs what audiences can comfortably accept as "normal" or "abnormal" categories. Throughout his work, filmic attempts to represent a "problem body"—whether a hirsute girl in the circus, a Gypsy whose knees bend backwards, or a man dying of AIDS—persist throughout Fitzgerald's oeuvre.

Similar to director David Cronenberg's approach to his subject matter, Thom Fitzgerald pushes against the edges of social propriety when depicting physical difference. But whereas Cronenberg uncomfortably situates the female body as the unwitting object of "medical science" (*Dead Ringers*, 1988), the transgendered body as willing spectacle (*M. Butterfly*, 1993), the newly injured, disabled body as exclusively erotic (*Crash*, 1996)—in each case with gory violence as the end result—Fitzgerald resists such stereotyped bodily representations. Instead, Fitzgerald explores ambiguities of both sexual desire and disability through techniques analogous to those employed by director Atom Egoyan. Just as Egoyan's *Ararat* invents the putative border between Canada and the rest of the world as artificially situated at the airport, so, too, Fitzgerald keeps viewers in an uneasy borderline state, fluctuating between normalcy and difference and demanding a continuing dynamic between the two rather than the erasure of the spaces connecting them.

NOTES

1. Quoted in Susanne Hiller, "On the Verge," *Saturday Night*. June 1999, 59.

2. Matthew Hays. "Director Thom Fitzgerald's career flourishes as *The Hanging Garden* wins over audiences worldwide," *Mirror*, 15–22 January 1998, available online at: http://www.montrealmirror.com/ARCHIVES/1998/011598/cover.html (accessed 8 February 2007).

3. Hiller, "On the Verge," 58.

4. Shawna Dempsey and Lorri Millan, "Canada Uncut: The Roaring '90s," programme notes, Metro Cinema website: http://www.metrocinema.org/film_view?FILM_ID=703 (last accessed 3 June 2005).

5. Hays, "Thom Fitzgerald"; "Director Thom Fitzgerald's career flourishes as *The Hanging Garden* wins over audiences worldwide," *Mirror*, 15–22 January 1998. http://www.montrealmirror.com/ARCHIVES/1998/011598/cover.html (last accessed 5 June 2005).

6. Anthony Kaufman, "Poetics and Perseverance—Thom Fitzgerald of *The Hanging Garden*," *Indiewire*, http://www.indiewire.com/people/int_Fitzgerald_Thom_980514.html (last accessed 14 May 2005).

7. Hiller, "On the Verge," 59.

8. Ibid.

9. Walter Chaw, "The Fighting Fitzgerald," *Film Freak Central*, http://www.filmfreakcentral.net/notes/tfitzgeraldinterview.htm (last accessed 11 June 2005).

10. Robert McRuer "As Good As It Gets: Queer Theory and Critical Disability," *GLQ* 9, no. 1–2 (2003): 79.

11. Martin Norden, *The Cinema of Isolation: A History of Physical Disability in the Movies* (New Brunswick: Rudgers University Press, 1994).

12. David Mitchell and Sharon Snyder in their chapter, "Representation and Its Discontents: The Uneasy Home of Disability in Literature and Film," *Narrative*

Prosthesis: Disability and the Dependencies of Discourse (Ann Arbor: University of Michigan Press, 2000), 15–46.

13. Robert Bogdan, *Freak Show: Presenting Human Oddities for Amusement and Profit* (Chicago: University of Chicago Press, 1988), 6.

14. Nicole Markotić first used this term for critical analysis in an essay on the "coincidence" of body and texts, in *Tessera* 27 (Winter 1999): 6–15. We propose this term in alliance with—and juxtaposed to—other terms theorists have drawn on to investigate the role of the disabled body constructed within the framework of the normative body. Some examples include, Rosemarie Garland Thomson's the "extraordinary" body, Tom Couser's the "recovering" body, and Susan Wendell's the "rejected" body. Thanks to many writers and critics (especially Julia Gaunce) who helped us develop this term as a useful marker of physical and mental difference.

15. Even those mainstream Internet reviewers who do not attempt a magic realist reading come up with explanations for the impossible scenario. Widgett Walls reads William's first death as merely symbolic of change; Dennis Schwartz claims *Hanging Garden* must either be a ghost story or a figment of William's imagination; and Steve Rhodes tries to claim the first hanging as merely a failed attempt at suicide. The reviews are available at: http://www.needcoffee.com/html/reviews/hgarden.html; "Ozus' World Movie Reviews" http://www.sover.net/~ozus/hanginggarden.htm; and rec.arts.movie.reviews http://reviews.imdb.com/Reviews/127/12773 (accessed 8 February 2007).

16. Glenn Walton, "Thom Fitzgerald's *The Hanging Garden*," *Take 1* 6, no. 17 (1997): 34.

17. The character of the father is also known as "Poppy" throughout the film. Both McKenna and MacNeill won Genies for, respectively, Best Supporting Actress and Best Supporting Actor for their roles in this film.

18. In a similar way, a film released the next year, *Sliding Doors* (1998), invites audience members to contemplate the life difference its character experiences between the accidental choice of one life path over another. However, that film ultimately reveals the true protagonist through only *one* of the two alternatives.

19. Roger Ebert, "*The Hanging Garden*," review in the *Chicago Sun Times*, 29 May 1998. Available online at: http://rogerebert.suntimes.com/apps/pbcs.dll/article?AID=/19980529/REVIEWS/805290301/1023 (accessed 8 February 2007).

17

Zach Kunuk and Inuit Filmmaking

JERRY WHITE

ZACH KUNUK IS ONE OF THE STRANGEST, and therefore one of the most exciting, figures in contemporary Canadian cinema. As a new feature-film director, he fits into this section of the book about the future, and yet his work is explicitly concerned with the past. His videos are mostly set in the pre-collapse, pre-Second World War period, and the timeline in the companion book to *Atanarjuat: The Fast Runner* (2001) has the following entry: "500 to 1,500 years ago: Estimated date of events recounted in the legend of Atanarjuat."[1] Technically, his work is also an explicit rejection of the old chestnut that cinema involves only nineteenth-century technology, because *Atanarjuat*, which wound up on 35mm, originates on video. While it might be tempting to see Kunuk as a localist nostalgic because of his subject matter, it's more correct to see him as a harbinger of a future, globalized cinematic practice, most clearly, in terms of institutions and authorship.

■ Institutions

ONE OF THE FIRST THINGS that one needs to understand about Kunuk's work is that it springs from television not filmmaking. And while the televisual situation in the high Arctic is quite interesting, given the way that it has drawn upon satellite technology in order to create a community-oriented television that is spread over a territory roughly the size of Western Europe, Kunuk is both formed by it and opposed to it. Basic knowledge of the situation in the high Arctic really is useful when thinking about both the structure of Kunuk films, like *Nunavut*, and the look of the more narrative *Atanarjuat*.

Television came relatively late to the Arctic, and it came with controversy. Until the launch of the Anik communication satellite in 1972, it was almost impossible to receive television or radio signals in the Canadian Arctic, aside from occasional radio transmissions from Greenland. When television arrived that year, though, it arrived both without any consultation with the community and without any real local control over content. The Inuit Tapirisat of Canada, the association representing Inuit people, successfully advocated for the establishment of an Inuit Broadcasting Corporation (IBC), which was licensed by the CRTC in 1981 and went on the air shortly thereafter.[2] Although the IBC didn't broadcast with anything like the ambition of CBC or Radio-Canada, it did allow for the emergence of a network to exhibit locally produced work (especially difficult in the Arctic, where communities are very spread out) and for an environment where local people could be trained in media production and find some employment by working at one of four local stations.

One such person was Zack Kunuk. He began working for the IBC in 1983. He had been rejected from an NFB-sponsored program to train filmmakers, but he retained an interest in filmmaking. He also had a career as a soapstone carver and purchased his first video camera during a sculpture-related trip to Montreal in 1981. Grumbling slightly about the way in which Kunuk has been squeezed into a traditional version of auteurism, Laura Marks has written that "the story of his selling his soapstone carvings in Montreal, buying a video camera with the money, and teaching himself to use it, has become a story of the self-made artist that ignores the infrastructure of Inuit production that gave him able collaborators (like Paul Apak) and a place to broadcast the work."[3] Her point is well taken. It is clear that his experience working in Inuit television, with its concomitant need to produce work that was locally relevant and cost-effective, did a great deal to lay the groundwork for the independent artist that he would later become.

But it is understandable that this IBC narrative has receded to the background of the tale of Kunuk's development, for he did not have a very happy relationship with the station. He quit after a few years of working there, eventually telling Marks: "I saw the IBC as a dogteam: Inuit producers as dogs, the sled as the Ottawa office and people who sit in the sled as the board of governors. I didn't like what I saw, so I broke loose."[4] Although he produced a fair bit of work at the IBC, he is not able to access any of it. Indeed, during an interview that I conducted at the 2001 Telluride Film Festival for the magazine *Cinemascope*, Kunuk told me this:

SCOPE: *So you don't feel any personal connection to the tapes you made at the IBC?*

KUNUK: *I can't even touch them.*

SCOPE: *You just don't like to look at them at all?*

KUNUK: *No, I like them, but the system doesn't allow you to even take a hold of them, or use them for stock footage.*

SCOPE: *So you don't even have copies of the work you did for the IBC? Not even in your basement, that you can watch?*

KUNUK: *No. They called me a "disgruntled ex-employee."*[5]

While it is important to keep in mind that the IBC gave Kunuk his start and allowed him to develop, it was also an environment that showed Kunuk what he did *not* want to become. Indeed, the IBC remains a rather divisive group in Inuit communities, with a large number of activists (including Kunuk) feeling that too much power is invested in Ottawa-based administrators.

All that said, the institution that did form Kunuk's work, Igloolik Isuma Productions, certainly bears a televisual mark. Igloolik Isuma was established by Kunuk, Apak, Pauloosie Qulitalik, and Norm Cohn in 1985, largely as a means to produce Kunuk's projects. Isuma, however, gradually became a kind of magnet for local video makers. In 1991 they gave a home to Tarriaksuk Video Centre; the Women's Video Workshop of Igloolik; and Inuusiq Youth Drama.[6] What started out as an auteur forming his own production company—Clint-Eastwood-style, if you will—fairly quickly changed into something very different. A production company does not seem to me the correct approximation of what Isuma is; to my mind, it is closer to a studio and, perhaps, closest of all to being the kind of operation that Kunuk had wanted the IBC to be. Isuma is a place where artists are given a certain amount of autonomy but where work is created with the expectation that it will be relevant to the community. Various kinds of work have been made there: some projects are legends being retold using low-end computer graphics (*Piujuk and Angutautuk*, Women's Video Workshop, 1994); some are minimalist, semi-documentary recreations of traditional life (*Qulliq / Oil Lamp*, Women's Video Workshop, 1992). All projects are connected to the oral culture of the Igloolik region, but there is a fair degree of heterogeneity in these productions. Igloolik Isuma has, in short, become a hub, bringing together all sorts of people with different interests but a similar sense that media should have a place in the life of a community that goes beyond the passive-consumption model that defines commercial television. That sounds very close to what the IBC was supposed to be: a remedy for the invasion of southern TV signals and all the cultural values that went along with them.

■ Authorship

ONE PROBLEM that a redirected focus on institutions creates is authorship. Marks has explicitly drawn attention to the way that Kunuk complicates conventional notions of authorship. Other writers, such as Kathleen Fleming, who worked on some productions with Isuma, or Michael Robert Evans, who lived in Igloolik for nine months doing research on video production there,[7] have done so implicitly, by focussing on the way that the videos are received and used by communities as opposed to how they fit into one artist's overall body of work.[8] However, there is something to be gained by reading Kunuk's body of work along semi-auteurist lines; by doing so we can see a distinctive consciousness at work, a consciousness that is quite formally sophisticated. Marks seems to admit something close to this when, discussing how an auteurist sensibility isn't all bad, she writes:

> I think it is fine to discuss these works according to our own aesthetic and political interests, partly because they are now surrounded by a sort of protective layer of non-understanding. We have different agendas and interests in this work than its producers and primary artists do, and we must acknowledge that these interpretations matter more to us as southerners than they do to the people who produce them.
>
> And there may be good reasons why these aesthetic and political concerns matter to southerners like myself.[9]

One of these reasons is that Kunuk's work is, overall, an attempt to reconfigure ethnography; this is not true in the same way of work produced by Tarriaksuk Video Centre or Women's Video Workshop. It has become all to easy to compare Kunuk's early work to *Nanook of the North*, but that is not exactly what I mean. Rather, Kunuk's work, and especially his early work, is constituted as an attempt to recover the imperatives of ethnography and make an ethnographic practice relevant for the community that it documents. Ethnography, of course, has become something of an epithet, too often signifying either a *National Geographic*–style romanticism or a people-as-bugs scientism. Recently, though, scholars and filmmakers alike have begun to recover the imperatives of ethnography, particularly its interest in the hermeneutic circle of cultural detail and contexts. If Catherine Russell's 1999 book *Experimental Ethnography* is one of the signature scholarly texts of this redefinition, Kunuk's videos are among the signature media works.

Take a pair of early Kunuk productions like *Qaggiq* (1989) and *Saputi* (1993), two medium-length videos that document different aspects of traditional Inuit life. Both videos are set in the 1930s, the period just before the Canadian government made a concerted effort to settle the nomadic Inuit in order to shore up its Arctic sovereignty, which had taken something of a hit during the Second World War. Both videos visualize this period as a distinctly hybrid moment; technology is present (men hunt with rifles in *Saputi*, for instance), but so are traditional modes of nomadic life (carving ice bricks in *Qaggiq*, setting fish traps with large stones in a river in *Saputi*). Most of these pieces are given over to evocation of these sorts of details; there are minimalist narratives in both *Qaggiq* and *Saputi*, but the action, so to speak, is elsewhere. This detail-heavy and narrative-light structure reaches a kind of apotheosis with Kunuk's *Nunavut* (1995), a thirteen-part series running 6.5 hours altogether. It is not too southern to think of this work as a development of the structure of the previous two works. The narrative of *Nunavut* is entirely secondary; the series follows a group of families through an entire year of living on the land, and each episode focusses on a part of life on the land (building igloos, hunting, facing missionaries), not a narrative drive. When I asked Kunuk if *Nunavut* was mostly improvised, he responded: "Yeah, definitely. All we had to do was get the time right, the year, 1945, how people were clothed, what equipment they were using, and take it from there."[10] The most important concern throughout Kunuk's video work, then, has been detail, not story.

Knowing that Kunuk's work is detail-driven offers us a good way to re-frame *Atanarjuat*. It is quite easy to see the film as a purely narrative exercise, and that is certainly what a lot of critics have focussed on. Perhaps the most celebrated example of this kind of criticism of the film came from Margaret Atwood, who wrote of it as a "generational saga with many Homeric elements: love, jealousy, rivalry between young contenders, extraordinary feats of strength, resentments passed from fathers to sons, and crimes that beget consequences years later."[11] None of this is unreasonable, but it does strike me as a bit beside the point. Instead, it seems more useful to see *Atanarjuat* as a kind of expansion on the sorts of issues raised in Kunuk's video work. The large igloo that we see, not to mention the extraordinary feats of strength that unfold within them, are right out of *Qaqqiq*. Much of the lingering on details of hunting or house-building will be very familiar indeed to viewers of *Nunavut*. Given that there are hundreds of years between the period when the videos are set and *Atanarjuat* is set, this sense of familiarity makes it clear just how much continuity of culture existed in Inuit culture even following contact. But this sense of familiarity also makes it clear just how much *Atanarjuat* is part of an ongoing project of cultural preservation, of cultural activism. All of this work is of a piece with Igloolik videos generally. Kathleen

Fleming writes that "[t]he 'video movement' in Igloolik is not an anachronistic phenomenon arising inexplicably out of nowhere; it is the reasoned, organic response of a culturally strong community within a longer regional history of contact through telecommunications."[12] Part of understanding the degree to which this use of film and video is part of a sustained history of technologically informed cultural activism necessitates seeing Igloolik works within their institutional context. But placing them in the context of *Kunuk*'s past work is also a useful way of re-situating *Atanarjuat* away from the purely narrative work and toward the non-narrative, toward the auto-ethnographic.

Another part of Marks's complaint about an overly auteurist perspective on Kunuk's work is that it tends to ignore the role of Norm Cohn; this is a good point, for it is an auteur-style reading via Cohn that offers a means by which *Atanarjuat* can be moved out of the realm of the narrative and toward the impressionistic. Marks writes that "this auteurist discourse follows the conventional practice of crediting the director of a work, not the producer, cinematographer, or other contributors."[13] That may be true, but this is a convention, not a hard-and-fast rule. Indeed, there is no inherent reason why figures like Cohn can't be acknowledged by critics who are as interested in artistic (authorial?) contributions as they are in institutional or communitarian matters. Marks goes on to write that:

> Doubtless, the relative silence around figures like Cohn, Fleming, and [Marie-Hélène] Cousineau reflects southerners' reluctance to acknowledge the roles of white people in Inuit productions. The New Yorker Cohn, by moving permanently to Igloolik and apprenticing himself to his Inuit peers, and Cousineau, who moved to Igloolik from Montreal in order to facilitate local and women's media production [by running the Tariaksuk Video Centre] are probably more like "Inuit videomakers," certainly more Igloolik videomakers, than the southern, urban Inuit who hold administrative jobs in Ottawa.[14]

Focussing on both Cousineau and Cohn, then, helps us understand that in addition to being heavily determined by the influence of Arctic television, Kunuk's work is also highly influenced by southern video art, the communities from which both Cohn and Cousineau hail and which gave

Kunuk's videos their first exposure, as the list of screenings on Isuma's website clearly illustrates.[15] And just as it is important to understand how Arctic television's emphasis is on community and not consumption, it seems equally important to keep in mind that video art's emphasis is on imagery and not story. That helps us understand the opening shot of, say, the *Nunavut* episode "Qimuksik / Dog team," which opens with a *very* long take of a dog team in the distance that eventually arrives in the foreground (when its riders finally hop off they are basically in a medium shot); such a distinctly visual sensibility as that demonstrated in this shot—and one that relies on the distinct properties of video, such as the ease of shooting *extremely* long takes—is clearly connected to the aesthetic traditions of video art. Similarly, the virtuoso sequence of *Atanarjuat*, where the title character sprints naked across the sea ice, is a visceral, overlong scene whose visual power has very little to do with narrative and which is best understood as a kind of heightening of a video-art aesthetic. Seeing *Nunavut* and *Atanarjuat* via Cohn is an essentially auteurist move, albeit one that gets away from the traditional emphasis on directors, since Cohn is the cinematographer of these films. But this essentially auteurist reading is one that helps us see *Atanarjuat* as being more about image than narrative, and, ultimately, as less about narrative than cultural detail.

When you combine these two essentially auteurist readings, then, what I believe you wind up with is the insight that the relevant American comparison for Kunuk is not Flaherty but Newsreel. Contextualising radical 1960s film movements such as Newsreel in comparison to more mainstream representations, David James writes that:

> The most useful provisional schematization of the total field of political film clas-
> sifies together, on the one hand, the films made by the various minority and special
> interest groups on their own behalf and, on the other, the films made about them
> or for them by the establishment and industrial media.... In the student section, for
> example, Newsreel's Columbia Revolt and San Francisco State: On
> Strike confront The Strawberry Statement and Zabriskie Point; in the
> Black section Nothing But a Man and The Murder of Fred Hampton
> face Guess Who's Coming to Dinner and Shaft; in the Native American
> section Intrepid Shadows, A Navajo Weaver, and the other films made by
> the Navajo under the guidance of Sol Worth stand against A Man Called Horse

and Soldier Blue; *in the GI section* Winter Solider *and* Newsreel's *Army are matched with* The Green Berets, *and so on.*[16]

Similarly, *Atanarjuat* and *Nunavut* stand against works like *Nanook* or Claude Massot's 1995 making-of-*Nanook* docudrama *Kabloonak*, which featured Igloolik Isuma collaborator Pauloosie Qulitalik in a supporting role. In the radical films that James invokes, authorship is indeed more complicated than in Hollywood or auteur cinema, but it is not *absent*. One can understand *Nothing But a Man*, for instance, by examining it alongside other Michael Roemer films like 1963's *The Plot Against Harry* or alongside the films made by his collaborator Robert M. Young, like *Alambrista!* (1973), a portrait of illegal Mexican migrant workers starring a young Edward James Olmos. Such cross-examination of films would help give a very good general sense of the climate of American independent cinema of the 1960s and 70s, a cinema that also includes less auteurist-friendly works, such as the collectively produced material by Newsreel. This is not so different from acknowledging that auteurism can only take you so far in understanding Kunuk. To understand him you need a sense of Igloolik video art, a part of cinema that is similarly less auteurist-friendly and more dependent on the social value of art. But an author-centred approach can take you *somewhere*, even via an examination of his collaborator Norman Cohn, which would help give a very good general sense of the climate of Canadian video art of the 1980s and 90s.

■ Globalization

ON THE SURFACE, nothing could seem less connected to globalization than the detail-oriented, remote-landscape-set dramas that Kunuk has produced. Marks's analysis of Inuit video sees it in explicitly trans-national terms; her 1994 article, after all, is called "Reconfigured Nationhood" and makes a point of discussing how Inuit video connects not only with Inuit populations in Siberia, the USA, and Greenland, but also how the IBC has collaborated with the Japanese broadcaster NHK. In *100 Years of Canadian Cinema* George Melnyk includes the film in his chapter "A History of the Future" and argues that it is a crucial part of a Canadian national cinema less dependent on narrow notions of national identity. But Quíntin, the pen-name of Edgardo Antín, former director of the Buenos Aires Independent Film Festival and an important film critic, has written that *Atanarjuat* is symptomatic of the homogenising tendencies of globalization.[17] All of this seems counter-intuitive for a film based on a centuries-old legend but also points to the degree to which Kunuk's work first anticipated, and now is a crucial part of, debates about the relationship between the global and the local.

Melnyk reads *Atanarjuat* as a film that destabilizes Canadian culture by emphasizing its "foreign" elements. He writes that:

> When non-Inuit Canadians view the film, they experience it as "foreign" much in the same way, if not more so, as English Canadians view quintessentially Quebec films—with subtitles. Canadian cinema, when viewed from the perspective of Atanarjuat, *becomes a cinema of translation for its own inhabitants....* Embracing that internal foreignness prevents Canadians from accumulating a simplistic or exclusionary sense of self.[18]

Melnyk contrasts the film with more simplistic and comfortable visions of Canadian identity such as the popular comedy *Men with Brooms* (2002). The characterizing aspect of *Atanarjuat*, for Melnyk, is the sense of gentle confusion that it provokes in mainstream viewers; the film is quite specifically Canadian, and yet it is also in a language spoken by fewer than 50,000 people and set in a region that very few Canadians have any direct experience of. I agree with him here; this is not a film that is meant to fit easily into simplified heritage projects—there is no way in which the film links up with any received narratives of Canadian identity, other than its emphasis on frozen landscapes; it is thoroughly stationed in an Inuit world-view—and it also demands a fairly serious engagement on the part of the viewer because of its length and complex narrative.

It was, then, strange to see the film placed alongside *Amélie* by Quíntin. Comparing these films to the high-gloss, barely-French cinema of Luc Besson ("genre pieces spoken in English and difficult to separate from Hollywood fare"), he writes that:

> There is a place for films that convey a sense of exoticism and bring a touch of local atmosphere and language, providing, like ethnic food, that their tastes aren't too

weird for the consumer. Unlike Besson's cinema, Amélie *is one of these films, as are* Atanarjuat (The Fast Runner) *and* Crouching Tiger, Hidden Dragon. *The three are arguably modeled on Hollywood standards but look First Nations, Chinese and French.*[19]

Leaving aside for the moment the fact that First Nations people are distinct from the Inuit (to say that the film "looks First Nations" is like saying that Hollywood/Bollywood "looks Middle Eastern"), I can see how Quíntin is making an interesting provocation here. What is a crucial difference, though, is precisely the "look" of Crouching Tiger and Atanarjuat; these are films with very different visual schema. The images that form the centrepieces of these films provide fine explanations for their differences. The fight in the treetops in Crouching Tiger features highly choreographed camera movements, movements that synch up with the swaying of the bamboo trees and the acrobatic movements of the actors. Furthermore, the colour scheme is extremely vivid and accented even further by the relatively neutral white and brown garments of the main characters. There is a considerable gap between that sequence and the aforementioned sequence where Atanarjuat races naked across the sea ice. The moving camera that follows the titular fast runner adds a certain kinesis to the sequence, but the landscape is a kind of dirty-white (made even muddier-looking because of the video that this "film" is actually shot on); the surface on which he runs, far from being a lush bamboo forest, is semi-melted and puddle-strewn; the sequence also features images of Atanarjuat's bloody, shredded feet. Crouching Tiger, Hidden Dragon, and especially the bamboo forest sequence, certainly betrays its director's roots in slick, commercial projects such as Sense and Sensibility (1995), The Ice Storm (1997), or even Eat Drink Man Woman (1994). By the same token, Atanarjuat, and especially the sea-ice sequence, betrays Kunuk's roots in highly visual and semi-commercial video and TV productions such as Nunavut. Crouching Tiger, Hidden Dragon is a deeply conservative film not only because of the way that it draws upon shop-worn traditions of Chinese and Taiwanese cinema (it is most obviously influenced by King Hu's 1977 film A Touch of Zen) but also because it is so thoroughly stuck in a constricting, studio-bound mode of production. Atanarjuat, shot with low-cost digital video using non-professionals and on locations that global media had basically forgotten about, offers a model of cinema that, in its portability and flexibility, points the way for a revitalised, and potentially truly globalized, vision of moving image arts.

This kind of globalization could be said to have if not exactly a familial relationship with ethnography then at least a tight friendship. Ethnography, despite the ideological limitations that it has accrued over time, is a flexible form in terms of both technology and narrative form. Bill Nichols has quite a pithy definition of ethnography that is useful for understating its cinematic manifestations. He writes that such films "are extra-institutional,....address an audience larger than anthropologists per se...may be made by individuals more trained in filmmaking than in anthropology, and accept as a primary task the representation or self-representation of one culture for another"[20] The inter-cultural and extra-institutional elements are crucial here. Ethnographers have never been stuck in the capitalist, production-consumption oriented mode of filmmaking that so over-determines narrative cinema; ethnographers also take it as a given that more than one cultural context needs to figure into a film's voice. There is no doubt that ethnography has been influenced by other sorts of economies; there is also no doubt that despite the multicultural essence of ethnography it has a history of privileging one culture over others. But there is a possibility within this form of filmmaking that offers a good model for cinema to aspire to. Russell distinguishes this "ethnotopia" from Nichols's conception of the term, which she sees as more scopophilic. Playing out the tensions between them, she writes that:

> For [Nichols, ethnotopia] refers to an ideal of limitless observation, the desire behind the ideal of a limitless observation, the desire behind the fascination with the Other.... Such ethnotopian desires can be ascribed to a few generations of ethnographers whose faith in the principles of social sciences still takes them around the world. Another kind of ethnotopian desire informs the ethno-fictions of Jean Rouch and his advocation of "shared anthropology"—or participatory anthropology. What he described as science fiction was an ethnotopian form of filmmaking that freely deployed narrative and dramatic techniques, in conjunction with (scientific) anthropological material, to offset the apparatus of fascination and epistemological possession referred to by Nichols. It is not coinci-

dental that Jaguar, *the film that most overtly deployed this ethnotopian form, is a film about migration and travel.*[21]

These utopian aspirations—collaborative study of culture, free movement between narrative and documentary, nomadic internationalism—seem like a good set of aspirations for a globalized cinema. It is not coincidental that *Atanarjuat*, a film that overtly deploys a collaborative, ethnographic approach to filmmaking, is a film about a migrant community that has itself travelled all over the world, bringing a new internationalism to Canadian cinema.

ATANARJUAT is a film that makes the complexity of Canadian cinema clear, as Melnyk has pointed out, and one that can help usher Canadian cinema into the next century. Indeed, this notion of complexity synchs up nicely with John Ralston Saul's assessment of Canadian identity. Writing in *Reflections of a Siamese Twin*, he asserts Canada's "strength—you might even say what makes it interesting—is its complexity; its refusal of the conforming, monolithic nineteenth-century nation-state model."[22] That's also true of Canadian cinema. The work of Zack Kunuk helps to make that refusal clear and helps to show that Canada's cinema has refused a national cinema model. It is well-prepared to move right beyond a monolithic, conforming, twentieth-century model. With the help of Zack Kunuk, Canada's cinemas are comfortably moving into a bendable, internationalist future.

NOTES

1. Gillian Robinson, ed., *Atanarjuat: The Fast Runner* (Toronto: Coach House Books, 2002), p.7

2. Laura U. Marks, "Reconfigured Nationhood: A Partisan History of the Inuit Broadcasting Corporation," *Afterimage* 21, no. 8 (March 1994): 5–7.

3. Marks, "Inuit Auteurs and Arctic Airwaves," *Fuse Magazine* 21, no. 4 (Fall 1998): 16.

4. Marks, "Reconfigured Nationhood," 7.

5.   Jerry White, "Northern Exposure: Zacharias Kunuk on *Atanarjuat (The Fast Runner)*," *Cinemascope* 9 (December 2001): 32.

6.   This is all recounted on Isuma's website at http://www.isuma.ca/about_us/index.htmlMAKE, accessed 13 December 2006.

7.   See Kathleen Fleming, "Igloolik Video: An Organic Response from a Culturally Sound Community," *Inuit Art Quarterly* 11, no. 1 (Spring 1996): 26–34; and "Michael Robert Evans, Sometimes in Anger: The Struggles of Inuit Video," *Fuse Magazine* 22, no. 4 (January 2000): 13–17.

8.   Available at http://www.nunanet.com/~nunat/week/71024.html (accessed 13 December 2006).

9.   Marks, "Inuit Auteurs," 14.

10.   White, "Northern Exposure," 32.

11.   Margaret Atwood, "Of Myths and Men," *The Globe and Mail*, 13 April 2002, R10, quoted on the *Atanarjuat* website, http://www.atanarjuat.com/media_centre/ (accessed 13 December 2006).

12.   Fleming, "Igloolik Video," 28.

13.   Marks, "Inuit Auteurs," 15.

14.   Marks, "Inuit Auteurs," 16

15.   See the catalogue *Video By Igloolik Artists* (Igloolik: Igloolik Isuma, n.d.), p.4–5. On 13 December 2006, this was available at http://www.atanarjuat.com/media_centre/catalog_LR.pdf, accessed 13 December 2006.

16.   David James, *Allegories of Cinema: American Film in the Sixties* (Princeton: Princeton University Press, 1989), 173.

17.   Quíntin, "The Inmates of Montmartre," *Cinemascope* 9 (December 2001): 72–73.

18.   George Melnyk, *One Hundred Years of Canadian Cinema* (Toronto: University of Toronto Press, 2005), 263.

19.   Quíntin, "The Inmates of Montmartre," 73

20.   Bill Nichols, *Blurred Boundaries* (Bloomington: Indiana University Press, 1994), 66.

21.   Russell, *Experimental Ethnography*, 77–78.

22.   John Ralston Saul, *Reflections of a Siamese Twin: Canada at the End of the Twentieth Century* (Toronto: Penguin, 1999), 82.

18

Don McKellar
Artistic Polymath
PAUL SALMON

ARTISTIC POLYMATH Don McKellar is a figure whose work challenges a simplistic auteurist paradigm not only because he takes a very collaborative approach to filmmaking but also because the cinematic strand of his work is so entwined with his other artistic impulses. As an actor, McKellar has performed in plays, films, and television. As an author, he has written for the stage, screen, and television, and he has also penned witty cultural commentary for such publications as *The Village Voice*, *Cinemascope*, and *Shift* magazine. As a film director, he launched his career with the short film "Blue" (1992), which won awards at both the Toronto and Chicago International Film Festivals, and made an astonishing feature debut with *Last Night* (1998), winner of the Prix de la Jeunesse at Cannes among many other awards.

Even such an impressive catalogue of his artistic activities does not do full justice to McKellar's versatility, since he has often combined artistic roles in numerous projects. For example, for theatre he has both written and acted in numerous plays and has also taken on such a dual role in television, most notably with the tremendously popular situation comedy *Twitch City* (1998, 2000). He was involved as both a writer and actor in such seminal Canadian films as *Roadkill* (1989), *Highway 61* (1991), *Thirty-two Short Films about Glenn Gould* (1993), and *The Red Violin* (1998). For McKellar, the symbiotic interrelationship between his various artistic impulses is of crucial importance: "There is something unnatural about trying to distinguish between them. When I am writing, I am acting out all the parts; when acting I am directing and writing in my head; when directing, I am forcing people to act out little facets of myself."[1] Such creative multitasking has earned McKellar deserved accolades and has also made him refreshingly difficult to pigeonhole.

Don McKellar was born on 17 August 1963 in Toronto. He attended Lawrence Park Collegiate and later pursued a BA in English at the University of Toronto, but he left before taking a degree. McKellar started acting in high-school theatre and later performed in numerous university productions before becoming involved in the city's growing independent theatre scene in the mid-1980s. He was a founding member of both a touring company known as Child's Play Theatre and the Augusta Theatre Company, a collective he formed with Tracy Wright and Daniel Brooks. Working with these companies, he had a hand in inventive productions like *Drinking* (1990), *Red Tape* (1989), *The Book of Rejection* (1992), and the critically acclaimed Toronto Fringe Festival favourite, *Indulgence* (1989).

His beginnings in the theatre do not constitute a mere prelude to his work in film but are integral to an understanding of it on several levels. It is in his work in theatre that McKellar first established his interest in collective creations, often involving strong ensembles both in terms of acting and the production of texts. His theatrical background is also surely a source for his frequent utilization of scenic structures in such works as *Thirty-two Short Films About Glenn Gould*, *The Red Violin*, and, most obviously, in the episodic television series *Twitch City*.

■ The Writer as Actor/The Actor as Writer

IT WAS ALSO WHILE WORKING in theatre that McKellar met his first and arguably most important collaborator, Bruce McDonald. Mark Peranson opens his *Village Voice* article entitled "Histoire(s) du Canada" as follows:

A brief, revisionist history of Canadian cinematic hipness begins in the late '80s with an unshaven, hash-smokin' schlub, Bruce McDonald, persuading a theatre-trained aesthete, Don McKellar, to abandon his first love and co-author a rollicking road movie shot through a jaundiced, rock 'n' roll eye.[2]

McKellar wrote and acted in McDonald's first important features: as a director in *Roadkill* and *Highway 61*, and as an actor in a later McDonald film, *American Whiskey Bar* (1998). He was co-writer with McDonald and John Frizzell on another of McDonald's feature films, *Dance Me Outside* (1995), about relations between Natives and Anglo-Canadians, and he co-wrote the script for McDonald's short "Elimination Dance" (1998), based on a poem by Michael Ondaatje. On *Twitch City*, directed by McDonald, McKellar again did double duty by writing the series (with co-writer Bob Martin) and playing the central character, Curtis.

When McDonald and McKellar first met, McDonald was struggling to make a documentary on local Toronto indie band A Neon Rome. As troubles on the production mounted, McDonald enlisted McKellar's help, initially for salvage operations on the documentary. Though the idea of a non-fiction profile of the band was eventually scrapped, the genesis of *Roadkill* grew directly out of that doomed documentary project. In the film, Ramona (Valerie Buhagiar) is sent to northern Ontario by her enraged rock promoter boss to retrieve the members of Children of Paradise, a band whose northern tour has been a fiasco. Along the way, Ramona meets a string of strange male characters, all of whom try to get something from her. For example, there is aspiring filmmaker Bruce Shack, played by a perfectly cast Bruce McDonald. While Bruce is supposed to be filming a documentary on The Children of Paradise, he pines to make his own film, and clearly sees Ramona as his potential muse. There is also Russel the aspiring serial killer, hilariously played by Don McKellar. In one of the film's funniest moments, Russel argues that while places like California are more known for their serial killers, there is no reason that Canada should have to take a back seat in this regard to imperialist America. For a rock and roll road movie, the film is refreshingly feminist. Ramona manages not only to find her own way through the Oz-like strangeness of this world, but also discovers a new sense of self worth.[3]

For anyone fortunate enough to have seen *Roadkill* upon its original release, the film's vitality and raw exuberance are apt to remain a vivid memory. The spirit of guerrilla filmmaking that saturates the film is also vividly described in an article by Colin Brunton (a key member of the creative team on both *Roadkill* and *Highway 61*) and on the voice-over commentary by Brunton and McKellar for the DVD release of the film.[4] Truly a collaborative effort and shot on a budget that was miniscule even by the standards of Canadian independent film, the film was selected to open the *Perspective Canada* series at the Toronto International Film Festival and was voted most outstanding Canadian film.

The importance of *Roadkill* as McKellar's key apprentice work cannot be underestimated as it sets the pattern for how he has worked throughout much of his career. Already evident in *Roadkill* is the sheer diversity of his talents, some combination of which (writer, actor, director) is often on display within a given film. As a writer, some of his best work has been done for strong directors who he respects, as in the collaborations with McDonald and with François Girard. And while open to inspiration and ideas from others in the shaping of a screenplay, he is a painstaking wordsmith who clearly remains capable of putting his own stamp on the final version of a script. As an actor, he thrives as part of an ensemble, even though he may ostensibly be the central character of a given work. In *Last Night*, for example, McKellar as writer and director is attentive to the full ensemble of wonderful characters in the film, even though the film particularly focusses on the plight of Patrick, the character McKellar plays.

More particularly, Russel in *Roadkill* can be seen as the forerunner of *Highway 61*'s Pokey Jones, arguably the prototypical Don McKellar persona. In its various incarnations throughout his oeuvre, this character can be thought of as a kind of anglicized schlemiel. He is a character clearly baffled by the world but one whose perplexities we can definitely relate to. He tends to be hesitant about commitment, is prone to fear, anxiety, and guilt, yet ultimately is a character capable of chutzpah, a survivor. There is a deadpan slowness of delivery to his speech patterns that only serves to highlight the unexpected wit of what he says. The Jewish connection I am making here is not as far fetched as might at first appear. In a piece originally written for the *National Post*, McKellar describes his early infatuation with Woody Allen, claiming that "my identification [with Allen] led me into an intense period of Jewish identification."[5]

From another perspective, the passivity of the McKellar persona, and his status as an outsider lurking on the margins, can be seen as intensely Canadian traits. André Loiselle has argued that "much of McKellar's success in his collaborations with McDonald rests in his ability to construct personas and narratives that are aware of their own place in Canadian culture and do not simply reflect the Canadian imagination but make Canadianness the very core of their ironic commentary."[6] While steeped in Canadiana in terms of locations, attitudes, cultural references, and the like, the films are supremely self-aware. McKellar and McDonald are thereby able to situate themselves within a firmly Canadian context while at the same time mocking its more absurd eccentricities.

Highway 61's budget was larger than *Roadkill*'s, though still modest by the standards of mainstream commercial filmmaking. As the film's title suggests, *Highway 61* is a road movie about a journey along the legendary highway undertaken by an unlikely couple. As in *Roadkill*, McKellar and Buhagiar again team up as the oddball couple on the move. This time McKellar plays Pokey Jones, a small-town barber who finds himself in the spotlight when he discovers a corpse behind his barbershop. Enter Jackie Bangs, who claims the corpse is her dead brother. Her real intent, though, is to use the corpse to smuggle drugs across the border, a caper that Pokey is unwittingly drawn into. Writing in *Maclean's* at the time of the film's release, Brian Johnson aptly describes Pokey Jones as a "comically meek Canadian dreamer."[7] McKellar was not initially slated to take on the role of Pokey Jones but, in retrospect, seems born to play the part, especially since he is a character that McKellar will play variants of in a number of other works, particularly *Last Night*, *Twitch City*, and *waydowntown*.

The experience of collaborating on Bruce McDonald's first two important features paved the way for McKellar's own initial forays into filmmaking. While a student at the Canadian Film Institute, McKellar made two shorts, "Blue" and "The Bloody Nose," both released in 1992 and both now difficult to access. This seems particularly regrettable in the case of "Blue," which won the Best Canadian Short Film Award at the 1992 Toronto International Film Festival. "Blue" is about a porn-obsessed carpet manufacturer whose masturbatory activities are cleverly juxtaposed with old stag movie footage. Marc Glassman describes the film as "a cheeky look at skin mags, stag films and carpet manufacturing."[8] For the film, McKellar scored a wonderful casting coup by luring David Cronenberg to play the central role of the prurient businessman.

In the six-year period between making "Blue" and 1998 when his next directorial effort, *Last Night*, was released, McKellar continued his pattern of artistic hyperactivity. Most important, he wrote *Thirty-two Short Films about Glenn Gould*, his first collaboration with François Girard and the first of many projects involving a close association between McKellar and Rhombus Media, Canada's great producer of performing-arts films. As the title of this film suggests, the filmmakers undertook an innovative, non-linear approach in their attempts to capture the complex, often perplexing genius of its central character, played brilliantly by Colm Feore. The structure of the film was inspired by Bach's *Goldberg Variations*, the subject of Gould's most famous series of recordings. The "films" that comprise the work are of varying length, and dramatized sequences are intercut with documentary interviews with people who Gould knew. The result is a film that not only radically subverts the traditional narrative trajectory of the biopic but also challenges the viewer to actively engage in the process of trying to understand Gould's enigmatic character. To top off the considerable achievement of having written *Thirty-two Short Films about Glenn Gould*, McKellar took a small role in the film as a conductor.

In this same period of his career, McKellar cropped up frequently as an actor for hire. He took a small role as a security guard in Deepa Mehta's *Camilla* (1994) and also performed in Peter Lynch's short film *Arrowhead* (1994). According to Tom McSorley *Arrowhead* is a drama cum documentary in which "Ray Bud (Don Mckellar) plays our deadpan tour guide through his personal suburban Toronto history, imagining the long-buried histories of those—native tribes or mastodons—who once strode through the primeval swamps of Thorncliffe Park before him."[9] The film won the award for Best Short Film at the 1994 Genies. In Patricia Rozema's exquisite *When Night Is Falling* (1995), McKellar joins an extraordinary ensemble cast that includes Pascal Brussières, Rachael Crawford, Henry Czerny, David Fox, and Tracy Wright. In the film, he plays Timothy, the harassed leader of an experimental circus. Wright plays Tory, whose personal and professional relationship with Timothy is unravelling. In one of the film's many subtle conceits, Tory's exasperation rises to a boil, and she runs away *from* the circus.

McKellar could be seen in two films released in 1996, *Never Met Picasso* and *Joe's So Mean to Josephine*. The former, an American independent film directed by Stephen Kyak, concerns the tangled relationships among a number of members of the art world set, and it garnered mainly negative reviews (with one critic calling it "an excruciating mess of a movie"[10]). In the film Mckellar plays Jerry, the gay lover of Andy, the film's central character. The more successful *Joe's So Mean to Josephine*, directed by Canadian Peter Wellington, centres on the troubled romance of the title characters, with McKellar playing Joe's sidekick as a telephone wire-tapper for hire. In the following year, McKellar performed in Joan Micklin Silver's television film of *In the Presence of Mine Enemies* (1997) based on a play by Rod Serling that was first produced for television in 1960 as part of the critically acclaimed *Playhouse 90* series. In the film, McKellar plays Paul, the son of a rabbi who is the spiritual leader for a Jewish neighbourhood in the benighted Warsaw ghetto of 1942. Shot in Montreal within days of the fifty-third anniversary of the Warsaw Rising, the project gave McKellar the opportunity to work with a stellar cast, including Charles Dance and Armin Mueller-Stahl.

As if these projects weren't sufficient, McKellar also continued his close association with another key collaborator, Atom Egoyan. McKellar had already given a memorably creepy performance in Egoyan's *The Adjuster* (1991) as Tyler, a film-board censor, and followed this with a nuanced performance as Thomas Pinto in *Exotica* (1994), which earned him a Genie Award for Best Supporting Actor. McKellar also acted in Egoyan's *Bach Cello Suite #4: Sarabande* (1997), one of six films produced by Rhombus Media as part of their *Yo-Yo Ma: Inspired by Bach* series. McKellar even made his relationship with Egoyan the subject of one of his own short films, "A Portrait of Atom" (1995). Named after Egoyan's own 1995 short "A Portrait of Arshile," "A Portrait of Atom" features McKellar playing Egoyan and Egoyan himself playing an off-screen interviewer. The film doubles as a spoof on the fact that McKellar and Egoyan have sometimes been mistaken for one another and as a homage by McKellar to a cherished friend and creative associate. This association certainly continues into the new millennium, with McKellar taking a role in Egoyan's most recent film *Where The Truth Lies*, which premiered at Cannes in 2005.

■ The Writer/Actor as Director

MCKELLAR'S FEATURE FILM DEBUT, *Last Night* is one of a series of ten films commissioned by the French company, Arte, on the occasion of the encroaching new millennium. Other films in the series include Hal Hartley's *Book of Life*, Tsai Ming-liang's *The Hole*, Abderrahmane Sissako's *Life on Earth*, and Alain Berliner's *The Wall*, all released in 1998. With typical audacity, McKellar decided to make a film, not about the end of the millennium but about the end of the world itself. Besides writing and directing the film, McKellar plays the central character of Patrick, a brooding curmudgeon whose desire to spend his final hours alone conflicts with his family's attempts to behave as if it were the Christmas holidays and not the end of the world. Patrick's plans to confront the end in solitude go awry when he encounters Sandra (a brilliant characterization by Sandra Oh) who is struggling to make it across town to keep a death-pact appointment with her husband (a note-perfect David Cronenberg). Besides McKellar, Oh, and Cronenberg, the ensemble is finely rounded out by Tracy Wright, Callum Keith Rennie, Geneviève Bujold, and Jackie Burroughs. Appropriately, given the film's subject matter, its ending is particularly noteworthy. As Dennis Lim of *The Village Voice* notes, "The film builds to a pitch-perfect finale, an attack of desperate romanticism that sneaks up on you almost unnoticed."[11] *Last Night* also constitutes perhaps the most moving example of the debate between insecurity and courage that typifies the McKellar persona in so many films. Patrick is clearly guilty about resisting his parents' wishes for him as the end of the world draws near, and he consciously attempts to remain aloof from a relationship with the character played by Sandra Oh. But, like a character in a Saul Bellow novel, Patrick does learn to overcome his deep personal grief, to "seize the day" with Sandra, if only in the brief moment before the world's demise. With its deft handling of tonal shifts from humour to pathos and its insightful vision of both human frailty and the power of love, *Last Night* is a remarkable feature debut eminently worthy of the many prizes it received.

There is no doubt that 1998 has been has been the most remarkable single year of Don McKellar's career thus far. As mentioned, *Last Night* won the Priz de la Jeunesse at Cannes and opened the Toronto International Film Festival several months later. That year the Toronto Festival also featured a retrospective of past work by Canadian Film Institute students that included "Blue" and *Thirty-two Short Films about Glenn Gould*. McKellar acted in no less than four films released that year, *The Red Violin*, *Last Night*, *Elimination Dance*, and Peter Lynch's *The Herd*. The latter film is an intriguing docudrama about an actual, ill-conceived government project in 1929 that involved moving a herd of several thousand reindeer more than 3,000 kilometres to the starving Inuit of the Mackenzie Delta. In the film, Colm Feore and McKellar are again reunited, and this time they both play inept government bureaucrats eager to rationalize their profoundly limited understanding of the situation. Besides his triple duties as writer, director, and actor for *Last Night*, McKellar was co-writer of *Elimination Dance* and *The Red Violin*, besides taking acting duties in both films.

On its initial release, one of the most frequently cited aspects of *The Red Violin* was the sheer scale of its production. A truly international co-production (with major American, Canadian, British, and Italian sources of funding), the film charts the fortunes of a single violin across several centuries and several areas of the world, including seventeenth-century Italy where the violin has its origins, eighteenth-century Austria, nineteenth-century Oxford, China during the Cultural Revolution, and contemporary Montreal. The cast, too, is international, with Canadian stalwarts such as Colm Feore, Monique Mercure, Sandra Oh, Rémy Girard, and McKellar, joining such actors as Samuel L. Jackson, Carlo Cecchi, Greta Scacchi, Jason Flemyng, and the great Taiwanese actress Sylvia Chang. At first glance, nothing could seem more dissimilar than the earlier collaborations between McKellar and McDonald on *Roadkill* and *Highway 61* and McKellar's work with Girard on the Glenn Gould film and *The Red Violin*. Whereas it is the raw energy of rock 'n' roll that inspires the two earlier films, it is the realm of classical music that is central to the latter. Either way, music is not only a prominent element of the soundtrack but is also of key importance in defining the structural rhythm of the works.

These works also reflect the unwillingness of McKellar and many of his contemporaries to subscribe to rigid distinctions between "low" and "high" art or to be pigeon-holed artistically. Like his friend Atom Egoyan, who is a filmmaker, writer, opera director, sometime actor, and co-owner of Camera cinema in Toronto, McKellar, too, has pursued a multitude of artistic paths. Like McDonald, Rozema, and Egoyan, McKellar has sustained an interest in experimental short films, rather than merely seeing them as a calling card for work on features. Within the context of his film projects, McKellar also shares the Toronto New Wave tendency toward a kind of cultural sampling, whereby inspiration is found from a diverse range of subjects. Whether it is the ironic twist on the road movie in *Roadkill* and *Highway 61*, the exploration of Native experience in *Dance Me Outside*, the apocalyptic vision of *Last Night*, or the fresh approaches to traditionally highbrow subjects in his collaborations with François Girard, McKellar tackles each of his projects with the same intense curiosity and conviction. While it might be argued that such an approach precludes the development of a coherent artistic vision, it could be counter-argued that such an outlook perfectly suits the kaleidoscopic chaos of our postmodern world.

One of the more intriguing of the smaller projects completed during McKellar's *annus mirabilis* is the short film "Elimination Dance," written by McKellar and directed by Bruce McDonald. While the viewer would be well advised not to take this film too seriously, "Elimination Dance" packs more imaginative creativity into its twelve minutes than many Hollywood films of interminable length. The film begins in black and white, initially adopting a mock newsreel style to provide background on the phenomenon of the so-called elimination dance, a craze sweeping the world in which dance contestants are eliminated from the competition on the basis of whether they have had certain experiences as described by a master of ceremonies. The film then switches to colour and to a focus on one particular competition in which two partners (Don McKellar and Tracy Wright) successfully elude elimination. The film makes a nice use of comic counterpoint, playing off the serious tones of two BBC-style commentators on the dance and the absolute inanity of some of the questions posed by the mc (have you ever been penetrated by a Mountie? have you ever stapled yourself?). The inclusion of this work on the *Roadkill* DVD is a reminder of the value of judiciously selected "extras" in DVD packaging.

Astonishingly, 1998 also marked the debut on the CBC of *Twitch City*, the situation comedy written by McKellar (with Bob Martin) and featuring him as Curtis, a character one critic describes as "an agoraphobic weirdo with a TV fetish."[12] Set and shot on location in McKellar's beloved Kensington Market neighbourhood, the series is rife with witty pop-culture allusions, including a cameo by Al Waxman in homage to *The King of Kensington*, a popular CBC sitcom that flourished from 1975 to 1980. There were originally six, one-hour episodes of *Twitch City*, which competed with the CBC's coverage of the Olympics for airtime.[13] By popular demand, seven additional episodes were shot and aired in 2000. For *Village Voice* critic Dennis Lim, one of the most anxiously awaited aspects of a mini-retrospective of McKellar's work at the American Museum of the Moving Image in October of 1999 was the chance for American viewers to see episodes of *Twitch City*, which Lim claimed "plays like a strange new form of meta-television."[14] As is so often the case with McKellar's projects, the success of this one hinged primarily on razor-sharp writing and a fine ensemble of actors, including Molly Parker, Callum Keith Rennie, Daniel McIvor, and Bruce McCullough.

■ Feature Film Interregnum

AS IN THE PERIOD between his first short films and *Last Night*, McKellar kept up a frenzied pace of activity in the six-year period between the release of *Last Night* and his second feature *Childstar* (2004). Even a partial survey of his credits for this period underscores both the quantity of acting work he undertook and the variety of subjects the films tackle. In David Cronenberg's *eXistenZ* (1999), McKellar plays both Yvgeny Nourish, a character whose bad foreign accent perfectly suits his status as a character in the virtual reality game, eXistenZ, and a character who may be the brilliant designer of a rival game system. In Vic Sarin's *The Sea People* (1999), McKellar plays a school teacher in a whimsical fantasy about mermaids. He took a small role in the television film *The Passion of Ayn Rand* (1999), and in *Trudeau* (2002), the immensely popular television miniseries, McKellar plays the fictional character of Greenbaum, a communications consultant.

Assessing McKellar's career in 2002, Mark Parenson writes that "with McKellar retreating to supporting roles (including a supremely square office drone in Gary Burns's *waydowntown),* the Time of the Don has since partially eclipsed."[15] Yet, such an assessment is based on the arguable premise that Mckellar's artistic career must be seen within the limited context of traditional auteurism, whereby the role of film director is privileged. Alternately, McKellar's recent work as an actor for hire can be seen as his way of being supportive of emerging talents, as in the case of his work in Gary Burns's *waydowntown* (2000), Helen Lee's *The Art of Woo* (2001), and Soon Lyu's *Rub & Tug* (2002). Of the three films, *waydowntown* is the most important, both in terms of the overall calibre of the film and the quality of McKellar's performance. Winner of the Best Canadian Film Award at the Toronto International Film Festival, *waydowntown* is a darkly satiric comedy about the soul-numbing effects of downtown Calgary's intricate system of walkways and interconnected buildings. The film's plot centres on a wager among four office friends on who can last the longest without going outside their concrete office complex. McKellar plays the comically deranged Brad, an office drone who is not part of this group but whose actions (which include stapling inspirational slogans to his chest) typify the level of insanity that such urban claustrophobia can produce.

The Art of Woo is a romantic comedy about Alessa Woo (Sook-Yin Lee), an ambitious art dealer who meets her match in gifted painter Ben Crowchild (Adam Beach). McKellar has a cameo in the film as Nathan, one of Alessa's persistent suitors. In Soo Lyu's *Rub & Tug*, McKellar plays Conrad, the new manager of a massage parlour who has been hired to ensure that his three female employees don't overstep the legal bounds of what clients can be offered. According to *Eye Weekly*'s Ingrid Randoja:

> *McKellar's turn as the hapless manager with a greedy streak is the best thing about* Rub & Tug. *Like all great character actors, McKellar knows how to use his physical assets; in his case, his low-key, nervous energy, hesitating delivery and slightly Machiavellian charm. McKellar's performance keeps us guessing, and interested, in an otherwise dull comedy that teases but doesn't deliver.*[16]

It could be argued that as an actor McKellar has decided limitations, particularly with respect to his somewhat narrow emotional range and his tendency to play variants of a kind of hapless nerd probably most purely embodied in his Pokey Jones character. Yet, notwithstanding those limitations, McKellar remains much in demand as an actor, in part because of his ability to bring eloquence to the portrayal of quirky but recognizable characters, his capacity for hinting at the hidden depths of characters who are not outwardly emotive, and his deep devotion to words and their power to both articulate and obfuscate meaning.

■ *Childstar* (2004)

MCKELLAR'S SECOND FEATURE FILM·as director, *Childstar*, is about an American child star who comes up to Canada to shoot a big Hollywood film, called *First Son*, a silly Hollywood blockbuster about a president who is kidnapped by terrorists and must be rescued by his son. McKellar plays Rick, a failed experimental filmmaker who gets a job as the child star's driver but who is forced to become amateur sleuth when the young actor takes flight from the set. According to Wyndham Wise, McKellar's "latest is a character-driven comedy about the innate ridiculousness of child actors and their parents in a culture where the kids act too old and adults act too young."[17] For McKellar, the film is also "an exploration of the contrast between this giant spectacle and the hands on type of low-budget film-making my character represents."[18]

While the film is not without considerable interest, critical consensus would seem to suggest that it does not constitute a major step beyond *Last Night* in McKellar's artistic development. The film's plot seems pedestrian when compared to *Last Night*'s careful weaving of disparate narrative strands, and the film's performances feel tepid as compared to the stunning ensemble work at the heart of McKellar's first feature. While it is important not to make excuses for the film, it is interesting to note how challenging it is for filmmakers in this country to meet critical expectations on their second films, particularly if their feature debuts have been greeted with critical accolades. Consider, for example, the case of Patricia Rozema, who followed her Cannes prize-winning *I've Heard the Mermaids Singing* (1987), with *White Room* (1990), a film which divided critics, to say the least. And the curse of the second film assailed Mina Shum, as well. Whereas *Double Happiness* (1994) drew almost unanimous critical raves, critics were decidedly cool toward her sophomore film, *Drive, He Said* (1997). The filmmaker whose first film has been widely acclaimed is under extraordinary pressure to meet the extremely high expectations raised by his or her initial success. With such pressure surely comes the temptation to play it safe and repeat proven formulae at the risk of losing a precious opportunity for artistic growth. Although *Childstar* has divided critics, it is surely to McKellar's credit that he tackles a very different subject here as compared to *Last Night* and with a considerably different style and tone.

■ From the Toronto New Wave to Woody Allen

ALTHOUGH MCKELLAR is still precociously young, his career has now spanned a sufficient length of time and has been of such remarkable richness as to make at least a preliminary assessment of his position within the larger context of Canadian cinema possible. With the conspicuous exception of François Girard, most of McKellar's artistic collaborators, such as Bruce McDonald, Patricia Rozema, and Atom Egoyan, are members of what a number of critics have dubbed the Toronto New Wave.[19] Emerging in the mid-1980s, this group shares a number of basic characteristics, including: a rejection or at least deep questioning of the entrenched Canadian tradition of documentary realism, an openness to experiment in terms of narrative structures and subject matter, and a willingness to embrace collaboration and artistic versatility. While many New Wave filmmakers have been outspoken in their interest in remaining in Canada and in supporting an indigenous Canadian film industry, they often share an equally fierce desire to remain unfettered by any sense of obligation to focus on traditional Canadian subjects.[20] Though the output of such artists as McKellar, Atom Egoyan, Patricia Rozema, and Bruce McDonald varies widely, the fact that they all know each other both professionally and personally adds to the sense of cohesion among certain members of this group.

Yet the iconoclasm and independence of McKellar and other of the New Wavers shouldn't be seen as some kind of total disconnect from the cinematic past. For example, there are certainly strong links between road films like *Roadkill* and *Highway 61*, and the archetypal Canadian road film, Don Shebib's *Goin' Down the Road* (1970). Shebib's film takes its central (male) couple from Canada's Atlantic periphery to Toronto, its urban centre. McKellar and McDonald's *Roadkill* charts its couple's odyssey from northern Ontario to New Orleans, thereby reminding us of another key Canadian film trope, the engagement with America and American culture. And the kind of character that McKellar plays variants on throughout his career can be situated within the context of a long Canadian tradition of passive male figures. While a critic like Robert Fothergill has argued that this figure tends to be either a "coward, bully or clown"[21] that embodies a sense of Canadian inferiority, more recent feminist critics like Christine Ramsay and Lee Parapart have questioned the necessity of seeing such a conception of maleness as necessarily negative.[22] McKellar is also one of a number of the Toronto New Wave figures for whom David Cronenberg is an important mentor. McKellar has frequently mentioned Cronenberg in interviews and writes cogently about him in program notes for the 2004 Toronto International Film Festival catalogue on the occasion of a retrospective screening of Cronenberg's *The Brood* (1979):

> The Brood *got under my skin (to put it Cronenberg-ianly) not just because it exposed me to an illicit world of transgressive, exhilarating cinema, but because it taught me the secret of great horror—allegory. It showed me how someone could transform personal pain—and the subject was clearly autobiographical—into imaginative, grotesque, liberating metaphor...It was also the first film I recognized as undeniably Canadian.*[23]

On the most obvious level, the mutual admiration between the two film-makers can be seen in several professional interactions between them, including McKellar's ability to lure Cronenberg to play in "Blue" and *Last Night*, and McKellar returning the favour with his performance in *eXistenZ*.

Yet, the Cronenberg influence on members of the Toronto New Wave runs even deeper. For instance, he has exerted a strong influence on this group in terms of revealing how old artistic hierarchies can be usefully collapsed. Cronenberg has taken the horror genre, traditionally viewed as lowbrow, and used it to fashion highly personal, sophisticated works of art. At the same time, he has veered from the horror film to adaptations of challenging literary works like *M. Butterfly*, *Naked Lunch*, and *Spider*. While filmmakers like McKellar, Egoyan, Rozema, and McDonald have not tended to follow Cronenberg in terms of his specific interest in the horror genre, Cronenberg constitutes a potent pioneering figure, one who evidences little interest in the Hollywood mode of filmmaking, where big budgets usually come at the cost of artistic freedom.

At the same time, while having stayed based in Canada, Cronenberg has shown that this does not necessarily entail a slavish devotion to documentary realism or to being locked into a narrow conception of his subject matter or his self-perception as an artist. Also, as early as *Rabid* (1977, with porn star Marilyn Chambers) and *The Brood* (1979, with British-born performers Samantha Eggars and Oliver Reed) Cronenberg was utilizing creative casting choices that often involve the juxtaposition of Canadian talent with actors from elsewhere. One of the larger implications of such casting choices for Cronenberg, and those he has influenced, is that a Canadian filmmaker need not be straitjacketed by some preconception of "Canadian" experience. Projects of McKellar's that reflect this aspect of Cronenbergian influence include *The Red Violin* and, even more specifically, *Childstar,* where McKellar casts Jennifer Jason Leigh, who he had worked with in *eXistenZ.* Mckellar's most recent acting role in Olivier Assayas' *Clean,* where he plays opposite Maggie Chung and Nick Nolte, again reflects his rejection of a parochial career path. And, perhaps the most intriguing sign for McKellar's artistic growth is his current interest in writing the script for and directing a film based on Portuguese writer José Saramago's Nobel Prize-winning novel *Blindness,* about an epidemic of blindness that strikes the citizens of an unnamed country. "McKellar on Allen: A Director's Take" is a testimony to the fact that in addition to all of his other accomplishments, McKellar is also a perceptive analyst of other directors and their films. McKellar begins the piece by writing amusingly of being called "the Woodsman" as a kid, not for his sexual prowess, but for his resemblance to Woody Allen.[24] The comparison continued to dog him as he embarked on theatre work, especially after he capped a performance at Toronto's Theatre Passe Muraille with a clarinet solo and a headline in the next day's newspaper billed him as "Canada's Woody Allen." McKellar goes on in the piece to acknowledge his debt to Woody Allen, the impact of his early films and the allure of the Woody Allen persona. But McKellar is also astute about Allen's weaknesses:

> We've seen him recast and reshoot the same themes, the same scenes, shunt them
> from picture to picture. On one hand this sheer profligacy has afforded the artist
> some obvious benefits: the luxury he so obviously seeks, of an obsessively structured
> life, the freedom to flirt with genres and pastiches that more cautious direc-
> tors might dismiss as too slight- sometimes with surprisingly successful results
> (Zelig, Bullets Over Broadway), sometimes not (Midsummer Night's
> Sex Comedy). But at the same time the workaholic output would seem to create
> a dilemma for the ostensibly private Allen. Like no other celebrity I can think of we
> have watched him literally live his life on screen. Even on the rare occasions when
> the director himself is not in the picture, his personality is so familiar that it takes
> no stretch of auteurist analysis to see him in every frame.[25]

It is certainly tempting to pursue parallels between McKellar and Allen.
Both have written for film and theatre, and both are versatile, often combining the duties of writer, director, and actor on a given film. They are
comparable in their intense interest in music, with the Woody Allen clarinet echoed in McKellar's own clarinet playing and in Pokey Jones's trumpet.
Both have a darkly comic vision of the world, and both frequently play
characters in their own films that are tempting to read as autobiographical alter egos. Yet, such similarities remain superficial. Unlike Allen,
who has tended in recent years to focus almost exclusively on film directing
(with the exception of the occasional concert gig fronting a traditional
jazz ensemble), McKellar remains interested in following multiple artistic
paths, often simultaneously. And whereas Woody Allen is legitimately
open to the charge of having repeated himself in recent years, as he continues to make films about the same elite strata of New York society,
with a revolving door of characters, McKellar's work remains astonishingly diverse.

Perhaps one of the most fundamental differences between Allen and
McKellar has to do with the contrasting contexts within which the two
artists work. Woody Allen has worked for much of his career somewhat
on the fringes of the Hollywood mainstream and has pursued his craft
with a sometimes enviable degree of independence. But a comparison
between Allen and McKellar reminds us that "independence" is a relative term. Woody Allen is still American, and, as such, he is a bona fide

celebrity (perhaps notoriously so) with access to modes of distribution only rarely available to a Canadian filmmaker. As someone who has chosen, at least thus far, to remain within the Canadian scene, McKellar is a "star" only in the relative sense and must necessarily work at a level of independence that makes Allen seem like an established mainstream figure.

For McKellar such independence brings constraints, one obvious example of which involves the degree to which so much of his work remains poorly distributed regardless of quality. While any decent video store will have a sizable rack of Woody Allen DVDs available, most of McKellar's short films remain exceedingly difficult to access and much of his television work is now consigned to the vaults of the CBC and other networks. In this respect, McKellar's fate is no different than those other Canadian-based filmmakers such as Atom Egoyan and Patricia Rozema, whose early works and even some later short films are difficult to see. But such independence also brings the freedom to chart one's own course artistically. Will McKellar continue to embrace creative diversity by acting in a wide range of films by others while developing more personal projects in a range of media? Or, will he now take a more traditional auteurist stance by directing/writing his own films? And if the latter, will he continue to create vehicles to foreground the established McKellar persona, or will he follow Cronenberg's lead and just act in other people's films? What trajectory McKellar's artistic career will follow is anyone's guess. The only thing bound to be predictable about it is McKellar's capacity to surprise us. What more could an artistic polymath want?

NOTES

1. Veronica Cusak, "The Kink of Kensington," *Toronto Life* (January 1998): 76.
2. Mark Peranson, "Histoire(s) du Canada," *Village Voice* (23–29 January 2002): www.villagevoice.com/news/0204,peranson,31705,1.html, accessed 9 February 2007.
3. McKellar himself makes the connection to *Wizard of Oz* during the audio commentary of *Roadkill*.
4. Colin Brunton, "*Roadkill* and *Highway 61*: A Case Study, or how I got my job at the Canadian Film Centre," *Kulture Void Pictures: Journal of Independent Film*

3 (March 1996): www.kulture-void.com/visual/kvp/kvp3/index.html, accessed 9 February 2007.

5. Don McKellar, "Mckellar on Allen: A Director's Take," *National Post*, 16 September 1999, via *Don McKellar Online* at www.happypie.com/donmckellar/ print/, accessed 9 February 2007.

6. André Loiselle, "The Radically Moderate Canadian: Don McKellar's Cinematic Persona," in *North of Everything: English-Canadian Cinema Since 1980*, ed. William Beard and Jerry White (Edmonton: U of Alberta P, 2002), 260.

7. Brian Johnson, "*Roadkill*," *Maclean's* (17 February 1992): 64.

8. Marc Glassman, "*Last Night*: In the Year of the Don," *Take One* (Fall 1998): 12.

9. Tom McSorley, "*The Herd*: Peter Lynch and the Secret History of Canada," *Take One* (Fall 1998): 8.

10. Mick LaSalle, "*Picasso* a Jumbled Mess," *San Francisco Chronicle*, Friday, 2 January 1998, C6.

11. Shelly Lyons, "In the Presence (Still) of Rod Serling," *Rod Serling Memorial Foundation*, www.rodserling.com/presence.htm, accessed 9 February 2007.

12. Dennis Lim, "Flirting With Disaster: Director Don McKellar Begins with the End," *The Village Voice*, 10–16 November, 1999, www.villagevoice.com/film/ 9945,1im,9829,20.html, accessed 9 February 2007.

13. Malene Arpe, "Tuning in to *Twitch City*," *Eye Weekly* (15 January 1998): www. eye.net.eye.issue/issue_01.15.98/film/twitchcity.html, accessed 9 February 2007.

14. Dennis Lim, "Flirting With Disaster."

15. Mark Parenson, "Histoire(s) du Canada." *The Village Voice*, Jan. 23–29, 2003, www.villagevoice.com.

16. Ingrid Randoja, "Nothing Personal," *Eye Weekly* (31 October 2002). Available online at: www.eye.net/eye/issue_10.31.02/film/onscreen.html, accessed 9 February 2007.

17. Wyndham Wise, "Canadian Style: Don McKellar talks about *Childstar*, Hollywood and Fame," *Take One* (September–December 2004). Available online at: www.findarticles.com, accessed 9 February 2007.

18. Ibid.

19. See, for example, Cameron Bailey, "Standing in the Kitchen All Night: A Secret History of the Toronto New Wave," *Take One* (Summer 2000):6–11; Wyndham Wise, "The True Meaning of Toronto's (So-called) New Wave," in his introduction to a special edition of *Take One* (September–November 2004) devoted to such New Wave figures as Atom Egoyan, John Greyson, Bruce McDonald, Don McKellar, Peter Mettler, and Patricia Rozema; and Marc Glassman, "Ontario's New Wave," *Take One* (September 1996): 3–4.

20. See, for example, Gayle Macdonald, "Polley, McKellar blast Ottawa's Cultural Policy," *The Globe and Mail*, Thursday, 7 April 2005, R6.

21. Robert Fothergill, "Coward, Bully, or Clown: The Dream-Life of a Younger Brother," in *Canadian Film Reader,* ed. Seth Feldman and Joyce Nelson (Toronto: Peter Martin Associates and Take One Film Book Series, 1977): 235–56.

22. See, for example, Christine Ramsay, "Canadian Narrative Cinema from the Margins: 'The Nation' and Masculinity in *Goin' Down the Road*," *Journal Of Canadian Film Studies* 2, nos.2–3 (1993): 27–50; and Lee Parapart, "Cowards, Bullies, and Cadavers: Feminist Re-Mappings of the Passive Male Body in English-Canadian and Québécois Cinema," in *Gendering the Nation: Canadian Women's Cinema,* ed. Kay Armatage et al. (Toronto: University of Toronto Press, 1999), 253–73.

23. Don McKellar, "*The Brood*," *Toronto International Film Festival Catalogue* (2004): 385.

24. Don McKellar, "McKellar on Allen: A Director's Take," *National Post*, 16 September 1999, *Don McKellar Online* at www.happypie.com.donmckellar/print/, accessed 9 February 2007.

25. Ibid.

19

Lynne Stopkewich
Abject Sexualities

KALLI PAAKSPUU

WOMEN'S SEXUALITY has reached new levels of crossing over and performative space in Lynne Stopkewich's darkly feminist films. Influenced by the narrative experiments of Bergman, Lynch, and the Gothic novel, her films *Kissed* (working title was "Wide Awake") and *Suspicious River* feature complex and contradictory female characters in narratives of psychological realism. Stopkewich's storytelling pushes narrative structure and characterization into the unconscious of her characters and constructs a mirror for the viewing self: her ideal being two separate unconsciousnesses existing in the moment. Preferring to work with established relationships, her creative collaboration with actress Molly Parker, who played Leila in *Suspicious River* (2000) and Sandra Larson in *Kissed* (1996), has been outstanding. These roles stretch women's most twisted fantasies of sexual knowledge into encounters with the "other" within us. *Suspicious River* and *Kissed* are emancipatory narratives and allegories about women's empowerment through their bodies.

■ *Kissed* (1996)

STOPKEWICH WAS HAUNTED for years by an interview of Karen Greenlee, an embalmer-in-training convicted of necrophilia in Sacramento, California, in the late 1970s. Greenlee answered interview questions in a straightforward and unequivocal manner, but her extreme female sexuality was a subversion of societal mores and values. The discovery that necrophiles are generally single, have above-average IQs and unusual belief systems, and work in occupations that put them in close proximity to corpses became aspects of the Sandra Larson character in *Kissed*. When Stopkewich came across Barbara Gowdy's short story, "We So Seldom Look On Love," she found another strong female character:

> She delivers an unapologetic monologue describing the development of her "deviant" sexuality yet nonetheless retains my interest and sympathy through to the end when an obsessive relationship utterly challenges her personal philosophy.[1]

Sandra became a co-mingling of these two strong character sources and emerged as an id-driven, free spirit, in touch with her feelings and emotions—a loner with the sensitivity of a poet. She needed to be convincing in her ability to see the extended lives and spirits of the dead she dressed in the funeral home. These two influences, both disturbing, meshed together to produce a compelling character with surprising charm. The Gothic novel with a perverse union of passion, death, and vampirism figured poignantly in Barbara Gowdy's short story. Gowdy's attractive, well-spoken, sympathetic heroine and her poetic monologue became the foundation for Stopkewich's visual treatment of *Kissed*:

> When you die, and your earthly self begins turning into your disintegrated self, you radiate an intense current of energy. There is always energy given off when a thing turns into its opposite, when love, for instance, turns into hate. There are always sparks at those extreme of extreme points. But life turning into death is the most extreme of extreme points. So just after you die, the sparks are really stupendous. Really magical and explosive.[2]

The short story written entirely in the first person allows the reader to hear inner thoughts and observe the world completely through the character's eyes. Because of the strong female point of view, Matt, the medical student in *Kissed* became an important counterbalance. Stopkewich worked with male co-writer Angus Fraser to create a full-dimensional Matt, who is romantically and fatally attracted to Sandra in an oscillating love triangle where a live man cannot possibly compete with the dead. Matt's character is faced with an irreconcilable obstacle to his love: his mortal life. Stopkewich uses voice-over to poeticize the narrative as much as possible and to express Sandra's spirituality and worldview. Imaginatively crossing a taboo boundary from the opening sequences the monologue immediately draws us into Sandra's strange, forbidden and private world. Flashbacks of Sandra as a young girl of twelve and her early fascination with death create sympathy for her. Stopkewich felt that introducing Sandra as a girl through her adult voice would make the audience more accepting of her passion for dead men. To make the screenplay as "real" as possible, she included vivid details of her own childhood: burying dead animals in a Birk's blue box, keeping secret things under her bed, disco dancing, and the awkward moment between mother and daughter at the first menstruation. The biggest challenge in the screen adaptation was the softening of Sandra's character to create sympathy without sacrificing her strength of conviction.

The internal voice is used to draw us with gravitational force into a psychological realism that is deviant and which forces the audience to negotiate the subject matter carefully. Gowdy's monologue is translated and adapted to the film into a seduction:

> Streaks of light, magical and explosive. I've seen bodies shining. Like stars. I'm the only one I've ever heard of who has...[3]

Beautiful and ironic, Sandra's story spoke directly to Stopkewich: "It was a deeply personal journey, rich with insight, peppered by humour, and resonant with unforgettable emotion."[4] A marginalized woman addresses the "secret" world of the funeral industry, Western society's exclusion of death from the natural cycle of life, the many manifestations of desire, love and obsession, the relationship between Eros and death, and finally, the power and range of unrepressed female sexuality."[5]

As a theory of social action, the performative puts into circulation a representation that places subjects into a relation with one another like in a speech act. Judith Butler states:

> Gender cannot be understood as a role which either expresses or disguises an interior "self," whether that "self" is conceived as sexed or not. As performance which is performative, gender is an "act," broadly construed, which constructs the social fiction of its own psychological interiority.[6]

This dark love where sex and death meet figuratively and literally is naturalized through Sandra's emotional life, is made more knowable by a typical girlhood in a loving family. Spin the bottle and random first kisses are the local initiation rituals into teenage heterosexuality, yet Sandra's obsession with death is powerfully associated with her first menstrual blood.

The screenplay reads:

23. EXT. ANIMAL CEMETARY. DAY.
One large shrouded body and many little ones lie on the flat rock in the animal cemetery. Sandra and Carol stand by the open grave, heads bowed. It is the largest and most elaborately decorated of all the graves.

CAROL
Amen.

As she looks up, Sandra presses play on a portable cassette deck. A driving beat THUMPS out and Sandra begins to stomp.

CAROL *(Cont'd)*
What are you doing?

SANDRA
What does it look like?! Come on!

Carol loses her inhibitions, caught up by Sandra's enthusiasm. They chant to the beat, whooping and twirling. Sandra takes her shirt and swings it above her head. Carol follows suit, stripping down to her training bra. Sandra takes off her shorts and twirls both. So does Carol.

They dance and scream and Carol takes a handful of dirt and flings it up into the air.

Sandra takes her shirt and puts it on her head. Carol takes her blouse and starts whipping the trees with it.

Sandra takes the chipmunk and rubs it on her skin as she spins in circles.

The music stops.

Carol is standing by the cassette player, staring at Sandra, hands to mouth, horrified.

Sandra looks down at the chipmunk in her hand. It is bloody. There are streaks of blood on her arms and legs.

SANDRA (Cont'd)
Oh no. I hurt it.

She gently replaces the chipmunk on the rock.

SANDRA (Cont'd)
I must've squeezed it too hard.

Carol quickly grabs her things. She pulls on her shirt.

SANDRA (Cont'd)
Carol—

Carol runs off without a word.

Sandra stands, dazed.

SANDRA (Cont'd)
CAROL!

Sandra looks down. Blood trickles down her leg.

SANDRA (Cont'd)
Oh boy.

Treetops move in the wind.[7]

Stopkewich breaks the story into its main narrative beats, singling life's great moments. Carol plays fantasy games with Sandra but draws the line when she thinks the blood Sandra rubs on herself comes from the animal when it is actually menstrual blood. Carol's reaction makes us consider the moral belief systems of "good" blood (menstrual/life giving) and "bad" blood (from death and injury). The horror genre is subverted by a naturalization of deviance through the character's personal voice and its grounding in the typical and everyday. The performative is used to transgress the horror genre while it also positions Stopkewich's work within it. Where description was lacking in Gowdy's story, Stopkewich fills in details from her own girlhood and invents what had only been implied.

Like the Gothic classic *Dracula*, necrophilia is rife in *Kissed*. Stopkewich uses a visual shorthand for her necrophile "monster" who is presented as a light-drenched angel in an attempt to create a moral dichotomy. A symbolic colour palette in grey-blue is sparsely decorated, mirroring the cool, still, clarity of corpses. Matt's world is claustrophobic and distracting and associated with science and technology. Sandra's is pagan and ritualistic with affinities to nature. The contrast effectively pushes the audience's sympathies to Sandra. Though virginal and shy on the surface, her search for forbidden knowledge and deviant sexuality makes her a woman to fear. When she is courted by Matt, she is jubilantly in red, embodying the uncontained sensuality and sexuality of a noir vamp.

Stopkewich describes the dramatic use of lighting: "Darkness too plays a part if only to differentiate from the 'light' of Sandra's experience. Due to societal tendencies to view the subject as morbid, and to avoid heavy gothic overtones, we approached the character of Sandra as a child of light (and by association) of goodness."[8] Influenced by German filmmaker Rainer Werner Fassbinder whose burns to white in the film *Effi Briest* (1974) are a symbolic representation of the protagonist's desire to break free from the oppressive constraints of social status, Stopkewich also uses long, associative dissolves, slow-motion, overexposures, and "burns" to white.

Matt is connected with darkness of space (his basement apartment), of mind (Sandra finds him sitting in the dark in a black suit), and of body (Matt jumps out of the darkness at Sandra leaving the funeral home). Matt, a medical student, is interested in alternative realities and fills the void in his life by making Sandra's reality his own. He wants to make love to a corpse, dress like a corpse, and wear corpse make-up.

Sandra's encounters with death are rendered through a select use of bright white light that effectively "burns out" skin tones. Fog filters are used to create a spirit-filled glow or "aura" around the characters, which intensify the lyrical, dream-like quality of "crossing over" where Sandra contacts the dead. A midnight animal burial and a carwash kiss are equated with making love with a corpse in the prep room. The "direct link" to the inner monologue is translated musically to a simple instrumentation of sampled sound overlaid with electric violin, acoustic bass, and percussion with a female choral ritualistic wailing reminiscent of the rich lush choral movements of Estonian composer Arvo Part.

Stopkewich and the sound designers created separate soundscapes for Sandra and Matt. For Matt, it was culture: traffic, household appliances, and airplanes. For Sandra there were associations with nature: fire, water, wind, rain, volcanoes, insects, and animals.

The screenplay reads:

71. INT. FUNERAL HOME/PREP ROOM—NIGHT.
Sandra enters, breathing heavily. The room is SILENT. The light is cold.

SANDRA (V.O.)
It was like diving into a lake:
Sudden cold and silence.

There is a shrouded body on the prep table. Sandra locks the door behind her and switches on the work light over the table. It flickers, then illuminates the sheet.

Sandra slowly pulls back the sheet to the shoulders, revealing a MAN WITH BLONDE HAIR, mid 30s, dead to the world, and not embalmed. Sandra circles the table, briefly touching him here and there. She puts her head on his chest, listening.

Straightening, she begins to spin slowly, then faster and faster. Her clothes come off, piece by piece until she stops, catching her breath.

She is calm and almost entranced. She draws back the sheet, the white of his skin reflecting back like pure white light. She runs her hands over his skin.

Sandra climbs onto the table and straddles the Man. She buries her face in his shoulder.

SANDRA (V.O.)
The smell of danger and permission. My hands and thighs burn as though I were touching dry ice.

From the head of the Man, we look straight up as Sandra moves in sexual abandon. She closes her eyes.

SANDRA (V.O.)
All I could see was the white light.

BURN TO WHITE

Sandra is lying on the table embracing the Man. There is a trickle of blood from his mouth.

SANDRA (V.O.)
I looked right into the centre.

She pulls the sheet over their heads.[9]

Sound is dropped out at critical points, as when Sandra climbs on the dead man. We hear laboured breathing, her clothes falling, and the squeak of a steel gurney. When Matt hangs himself, all that is heard are ragged rhythmic breaths as she stares at him in shock and fascination.

A camera aesthetic of stationary static camera is quick to set up, simplifies blocking, and makes a reference for naturalism. The select use of camera movement— swooping, spinning, and soaring—in direct contrast to the humdrum, day-to-day activities—helps to underscore the heightened sense of euphoria felt by Sandra in those intense moments.

> By the time I get there (the prep room)...
> I'm almost out of myself![10]

As the story evolves, the camera-work becomes freer:

> The evolution of the static-to-moving-camera aesthetic provides an apt visual representation of the inner mind of the character through whose eyes we are experiencing the story: her early childhood thoughts, framed by time, are vignetted-like, static snapshots of important moments, whereas the closer we come to the end of the story and therefore her most recent memoires, the more the shots are fluid, moving, and intimate.[11]

■ Production Financing in *Kissed*

STOPKEWICH USED SAVINGS from production design fees from commercial films as seed money for *Kissed*. With a grant from UBC Film Department, producers Stopkewich and Dean English called up everyone they knew for financial support in the form of an evangelist's investment scheme, "You can be a five hundred dollar champion or a thousand dollar hero!"[12] Investors got a tail credit mention, as well as a signed, framed, limited-edition print interpreting the story, which Vancouver artist Jan Wade created and offered cocktail-hour notoriety: "I'm backing an X-rated feature film." Over a two-year period the production got the support of the actor's union, ACTRA, in the form of an across-the-board 50 per cent deferral of scale for performers as an ongoing agreement with the University (ACTRA has a special agreement with university film production programs). The NFB provided processing and printing the rushes. A specific window of opportunity based on access to equipment got the shoot into principal photography.

The picture edit was done on a Steenbeck in the basement of the executive producer's mother's home. Nettwerk Records offered the use of their library of music at deferred cost. Western Post Productions Ltd. gave a fantastic digital-sound editing suite at a deferred cost. Telefilm gave a one-time completion grant and BC Film provided an equity investment that allowed the project to get completed and blown up to 35mm. There were many moments of "interim" financing, where the project painfully overextended personal credit. Stopkewich in 1996 was $30,000 in debt over her $36,000 original investment. The company was $400,000 in deferrals and investment recoupment before seeing any profit. Stopkewich advises: "For the independent filmmaker, learning to live with debt is mandatory."[13] The shooting schedule was based on the availability of film equipment: three six-day weeks and two five-day weeks that became six-day weeks. Because there was no money for processing rushes, only select rushes from the first week of shooting were processed to ensure that the camera was working properly and the look was achieved.

Stopkewich felt that Gowdy's "We So Seldom Look On Love" was an ideal story to be realized on a low budget because of two main characters and a minimum of locations. Told in flashback, a 1970s look was required and achievable in a small town or suburb with frequent interiors. Sourcing thrift shops and garage sales, the 1970s look was cheaper to realize than a contemporary look. Her work associate-producing John Pozer's feature The Grocer's Wife (1991) gave the experience and connections to produce and direct a low-budget feature. Boneyard Film Company Inc. was incorporated with the principal partners of Stopkewich, John Pozer, and Dean English. An exclusive option agreement was sealed with Barbara Gowdy for the rights to the story. By the first day of production, Stopkewich's first feature had already been a seven-year process.

Necrophilia was one of the top three subjects guaranteeing an "X" rating, which possibly meant it might never achieve widespread theatrical distribution. In a genuine low-budget aesthetic, Stopkewich had a brilliant solution for reducing financial risk:

*While pacing through the production office I hit upon the idea of shooting all the
missing locations "in studio" in our office space. We decided to build our sets within
our production office, painting and set decorating to create all of the funeral home
interiors as well as Matt's basement apartment. If one looks carefully at the film,
one will notice that the prep room "set" and Matt's apartment are the very same
room.*[14]

Stopkewich's point-form list of advice based on experience includes:

- *Spend time on your script.*
- *Prepare yourself mentally and physically for the shoot.*
- *Come to set earlier than anyone else. Be the last to leave.*
- *Stay in touch with the art department during the shoot.*
- *Try to start the editing process while the shoot is happening.*
- *Don't wear too many hats at the same time—try and find a producer.*
- *Take every opportunity to work with actors before your shoot.*
- *Write backstories for each character and make them available to your actors.*
- *Try to minimize your locations or shoot in a set to avoid weather problems.*
- *Try to take some acting classes yourself to see how it feels being on the other side
  of the camera.*
- *If possible, keep your days short and the schedule long.*
- *Casting decisions are all-important.*
- *Trust your instincts.*
- *You only have one chance to make a first feature—take your time.*
- *Work with people you like rather than people who are experienced.*
- *Take risks.*[15]

■ *Suspicious River* (2000)

In *Suspicious River*, Stopkewich again uses internal monologue to draw us
into the psychological dimension. The screenplay reads:

1. EXT. MOTEL—SUNSET
*Golf Shirt Man exits Room 1 with a bag, gets into his car and drives away
revealing a pink neon sign: VACANCY. In the B.G. the Swan Motel looks wedding
cake clean with a glassed-in office, swing set and croquet set out front.*

SWANS *congregate on the motel lawn like rich old movie stars at a tea party,*
extending their necks, feigning nonchalance. A girl (10) concentrates, feeding a
swan bread from a bag.

1. INT. MOTEL OFFICE—SUNSET
LEILA (Lee-la) MURRAY (24) watches the swans through the window. She is
pretty and petite, like a shop-worn school girl in shiny shoes, cotton skirt and
lace-edged blouse.

LEILA (V.O.)
The first time I did it was late September. Afterwards I went straight
home, but the next day I did the same thing with someone else.

Turning away she checks the leather-bound guest register on the counter: seven
reservations.

LEILA (V.O.)
And the next with someone else.

The wall clock clicks 6 pm like the hammer on a toy gun. She grabs her cigarettes
and leaves.[16]

Leila in *Suspicious River* is in a dysfunctional marriage—a teenage coupling
through a pregnancy that resulted in infertility. Based on Laura Kasischke's
mesmerizing and unforgettable novel by the same name, Stopkewich's
film faithfully reproduces the psychic architecture of a young woman
traumatized by early family violence and an unbearable silence. The red-
headed Leila works as a clerk in a motel off an old highway nestled in a
coastal valley. In the first shots of the film a little red-haired girl played
by Mary Kate Welsly feeds swans and Leila mistakes her for one of the
motel guests. The little girl, established early as Leila's doppelganger, is
structured into the narrative as Leila's inside life re-enacting a life on
the outside. The symbolism of the swans, strongly sexual with the long
phallic necks, is a direct reference to the Greek myth of "Leda and the
Swan" in which Zeus, disguised as a swan, impregnates Leda. The mis-
recognition of the girl as a guest forebodes and parallels Leila's easy

sexual favours to the guests. The two red-haired females cross paths like shadows at various critical junctures of sexual encounters, where their personas merge.

Ingmar Bergman's influence is clearly evident in Stopkewich's creation of Leila's hybrid identity: two female characters create trajectories of self discovery around sexual encounters and eventually become one. In Kasischke's novel, the girl exists as Leila's inner monologue and as flashbacks of her child self. This is translated into the film with two characters having separate lives but co-existing in a temporal space. We only realize that the girl is a personality of Leila near the end of the film, when she dissociates from the immediate trauma of a gang rape and revisits her dead father's home to pick up mail. It is at this moment that we realize that the father and Leila's home are the very same place. Stopkewich intercuts moments of intensity in the emotional lives of her two female characters and creates mise-en-scene where just before or immediately after crises the two females physically inhabit the same space. The girl is the only person with whom Leila has real intimacy. They first meet at Suspicious River where the swans feed.

Stopkewich describes her connection with Kasischke's novel:

For me on a really basic level when I read that book it appealed to me not only because it is such an extreme story but because I could recognize myself and women around me in that character. I'm not someone who has prostituted myself or any of those things. However, I, myself, and my friends, who are educated, self-loving individuals, have all been in relationships that were not healthy ones, or made choices repeatedly that were probably not good ones and those kinds of things. Its always been interesting to me how women will internalize whatever is going on in their lives and turn it on themselves. Women, who will be the first to say, "Well, my life is screwed up because I'm not young enough or thin enough or pretty enough." It's never the guy. It's never the guy. It's never the man's fault and you can see that they are with guys that are complete losers and the tendency is always for them to take the blame. I can see this starting with women being mothers where everyone in the family will eat first and if there is no food left the mother will go hungry. I think it's part of how we've been socialized to take the back seat, to not ask for our needs to be met. It's a real extreme example, of course, but I just thought that there were things about her that I could understand somehow. Not in the literal narrative translation but somehow emotionally I could understand a little bit of what was going on for her.[17]

Leila cannot stop herself with the motel guests' advances and the girl is swept into a sexual precociousness vicariously through her mother's sexual encounters with a boyfriend that happens to be her husband's brother. She witnesses the exchanges between Leila and her men and tells her, "When I get older I will stay in a motel and have them pay me for it." They wait expectantly for the swans to suddenly fly off together and are psychically connected.

Life is so slow in the valley that watching the clock's minute hand is entertainment. It is easy for Leila to flirt with drifters and thrill-seeking tourists that stop at the motel. Similarities with Hitchcock's *Psycho*, its motel of a nostalgic past and the bored clerk bursting with a boundless sexuality, are unexpectedly framed. Stopkewich's Leila, however, resonates more with *Psycho*'s Marion, a character driven by such uncontainable desires that she steals from her company for a road trip to satisfy an illicit lust. Leila steals from the motel to intensify her desire for Gary Jensen, a two-faced bastard who forgets he has used his alias of Smith in making his reservation. If this is not enough to raise suspicions about Gary's character, the beating she soon gets should. Gary gives her sixty dollars when she visits his room, then smacks her across the face twice before raping her on the floor. Leila tells him it doesn't hurt because you can't hurt someone who doesn't feel. The money? She has no real purpose for it. It is a symbolic hoarding of experience needed to break out from the ever present traps of the town, herself, her mind, and her own history.

What's disturbing is that Leila does not conform to any stereotype of prostitute. Stopkewich negotiates our sympathies and identifications with Leila through first-person narration and an immersion into Leila's personal world and its painful recollections of sexual violence and denials. The wad of bills she earns from the men is concealed from her husband under a false bottom of her jewellery box—a relic of childhood with its once-prized ballet dancer and cheery wind-up melody. Stopkewich will not, however, allow us to marginalize her female characters in their sexual excess. Kasischke's poetics are translated into a mise-en-scene where the inside is turned out. Subverting the tradition of cinematic apparatus with masculine sexual specifications, Stopkewich draws us into the coupling game through a female scopic of masochism.[18] She describes the self-destruction in the film's climax where Leila throws her neck into the knife held by her captor:

> She basically says bring it on. I'm ready to die. I want to die. Kill me. I want to kill myself. In fact, I won't let you kill me. I want to kill myself before you can kill me. And that is her position of power.... What ends up happening is that she actually grabs it and cuts her own throat and then the guy who is there, Ron, a guy who is supposed to be taking care of her, starts freaking out and actually helps her to escape because he realizes nothing good is going to come from this.[19]

It is this difference and a psychological dimension that subverts and disidentifies her character's narrative from the Gothic genre, conjoining both *Kissed* and *Suspicious River* as psychological thrillers with physical and spiritual thematics of emancipation.

■ A Canadian Girlhood

WITH SANDRA in *Kissed* and Leila in *Suspicious River*, Stopkewich brings the material worlds of her Canadian girlhood to Sandra's burials of dead rodents and the little red-haired girl's solitary play on the swing sets and nature walks. The rich nostalgic enactments of past girlhood pleasures provide a normalcy to the instability of a world that seduces the female characters into a precocious sexuality and an alternate liminality. Leila, entrapped in a cycle of trauma, revisits the abusive relations of her girlhood in a twisted bid to finally claim some mastery over destiny. Stopkewich frames Leila's dissociation from the immediate and physical acts of violence by intercutting scenes of the little girl, creating a convention and strong linkage between them through suture. The scene is intercut with Leila returning home to pick up a letter from her mother's lover and murderer. Uncle Andy's voice reads the words, "I'm out of jail, Leila. If you need something just call." Leila then, with her neck slashed, is told to leap out of the second floor window and drop like garbage, her neck bleeding, in a living nightmare—the only physical escape she can have under the circumstances.

Like Sandra, a girl of a very normal and loving childhood in *Kissed*, Leila's experience of crossing over is addictive but complicated by the unresolved traumas that she must vindicate from memory. Both in *Kissed* and *Suspicious River*, character orbits are dependent on a twinning of pain and pleasure. A lonely little girl's tightly kept secrets echo and frame Leila's encounters with strangers. As they ride in Leila's car the little girl asks, "Do you ever want to run away?" She answers, "All the time." The two characters meld and reach out to each other from separate worlds that bleed together. After the initial brutal encounter with Leila, Gary apologizes and gives her an extra twenty dollars, which she accepts. Then Leila falls for his next affectionate advance and steps into a double life of the prostitute and the wife of an unsuspecting husband.

■ Contemporary Film Narratives

FILM NARRATIVES engage their audiences on several levels and audiences develop a critical and aesthetic appreciation for how they are engaged by emotion or intellect in an imaginary world through a number of different ways. First, representation—how a scene refers or signifies a world or body of ideas, i.e. the "semantics" of narrative. In *Kissed*, Sandra first appears as a bystander at a scene of an ambulance, watching as the person is taken away. The next scene introduces an early fascination with death in her childhood where she caretakes graveyards of dead animals and birds. She wraps these bodies carefully and ceremoniously in toilet paper keeping the rotting bodies in her room before giving them a proper burial. The pubescent Sandra then conducts a funeral ceremony for a rodent and chants, "Carry the body." A little later her friend Carol and her do a strip in the forest where she rubs her face in a dead chipmunk's body. The blood mark on her face, however, is not blood from a creature. It is her first menstruation. Stopkewich thus introduces a trope of death with a burgeoning sexuality early in the film.

Classical Hollywood narratives can be studied by their structure—the way their components combine to create a distinctive whole. Vladimir Propp's study of Russian fairy tales in *Morphology of the Folktale* (1929, translated 1958) argues that an elaborate pattern-sequence of thirty-one "functions" make up any hero story. Propp's "function" in a story is an event interpreted "according to its consequences" and is a plot motif in the story.[20] Stopkewich sees Kissed as a fairytale, and, according to Propp's framework, the hero is sent out to remedy a lack. In the first scenes, Stopkewich uses ambiguous sexual images of Sandra's hand on Matt's naked body, followed by his dead body being lifted into an ambulance and driven away. Sex and death thematics are thus associated together in the film's premise.

The Aristotelian three-act structure of the dramatic theatrical form is a dynamic process of story where source, function, and effect orchestrate a temporal progression of action and animate concepts like the "narrator." Kissed follows the classical three-act structure and uses the narrator to ground the super-ordinary into the everyday. A circular storytelling is effected by Stopkewich's use of a montage that conceptually builds on rituals, repeating motions, motifs, and symbols, so that by the end of the film we are at the beginning, visually and psychically—it is not unlike being present at birth and death simultaneously. The opening of the film is a sexual and loving display with Sandra exploring with her hands and mouth a man's body. The end of the film has Sandra drag her dead boyfriend onto the rug, kissing and caressing him for the final time:

> The very last image of the film, in which Sandra lies down next to Matt, stares into the camera, and slowly closes her eyes, was the very first image conceived of in the creation of the shooting script. Like Ingmar Bergman's merging faces in Persona, Matt and Sandra are joined at the eyes, nose and mouth, like a forced-dimension Picasso portrait, reiterating our profound connection to one another as well as death's ultimate necessity to life.[21]

■ **Feminism in a Regional and Globalized Context**

A STRONG SENSE of local culture make Kissed and Suspicious River rise above the American appropriation of Vancouver as a backdrop for American generic culture like in Jumanji (1995) and other North Hollywood films. The use of American currency in Suspicious River is ambiguous, appearing at first to situate the story in an American location. An against-the-grain reading and a recognizable mountain range make specific historical reference to the regional motel strip's north and south migration of American tourists, entrepreneurs, and workers—a thematic of colonization that Sandra Wilson, in her autobiographically inspired *My American Cousin* (1985) criticized a generation earlier. A regional consciousness is reinforced by Stopkewich's use of Country and Western music and actual vintage 1970s locations.

Though both Stopkewich's films explore the darker terrains of women's sexuality within a classical narrative form, her use of the per-formative de-familiarizes the cinematic conventions around women's bodies and sexuality and makes us reconsider what we think we know. In *Suspicious River*, she de-objectifies prostitution and controversially introduces it as a middle-class "problem" while presenting it as a multivariant and contra-dictory escapism. In *Kissed*, Sandra can only accept the love from a man after death: a denial of life altogether. Her actions exaggerate and self-consciously address the circumstances of a gendered world where generic conventions deliver entertainment value to both literal and ironic readings. Stopkewich's aesthetic of violence and masochism, however, raises pro-vocative questions about silences, morality, and a gendered world, which need articulation in the wake of serial and real violence toward women.

NOTES

1. Lynne Marie Stopkewich, *Wide Awake: That Necrophile Movie*, MFA Thesis, (Vancouver: Department of Film and Theatre, University of British Columbia, 1996), 4.

2. Barbara Gowdy, *We So Seldom Look on Love* (Toronto: Somerville House Publishing, 1992), 145.

3. Stopkewich, *Wide Awake: That Necrophile Movie*, 1.

4. Ibid., 5.

5. Ibid., 6.

6. Judith Butler, "Performative Acts and Gender Constitution: An Essay in Phenomenology and Feminist Theory," in Sue-Ellen Case, ed., *Performing Feminisms: Feminist Critical Theory and Theatre* (Baltimore: Johns Hopkins University Press, 1990), 279.

7. Angus Fraser and Lynne Marie Stopkewich, *Wide Awake* (Vancouver: Boneyard Film Company Inc., 1994), 14–15.

8. Stopkewich, *Wide Awake: That Necrophile Movie*, 12.

9.   Angus Fraser and Lynne Stopkewich, *Wide Awake*, 52–53.

10. Stopkewich, *Wide Awake: That Necrophile Movie*, 14.

11. Ibid.

12. Ibid., 18. They offered investors a 30 per cent tax deduction (on a declining balance basis) through a tax incentive offered to investors by the government through the Capital Cost Allowance under Provisions of Subsection #1104 (2) of the Income Tax Regulations (Interpretation Bulletin No. IT-441, 29 Nov. 1979).

13. Ibid., 20. The initial bottom line was $175,000. Crucial questions to prospective crew members were, "Do you still live at home with your parents?" "Can you survive for five weeks on $500?"

14. Ibid., 29.

15. Ibid., 41–42.

16. Lynne Stopkewich, *Suspicious River* (North Vancouver: Okulitch Pedersen Company/Metro Tartan, Suspicious Films Ltd., 1999), 1.

17. Interview with Lynne Stopkewich by the Author, Toronto, 19 September 2005.

18. Mary Ann Doane, "Film and the Masquerade: Theorizing the Female Spectator" in *Issues in Feminist Film Criticism*, ed. Patricia Erens (Bloomington: Indiana University Press, 1990), 43.

19. Interview with Lynne Stopkewich by the Author, Toronto, 19 September 2005.

20. Vladimir Propp, *Morphology of the Folktale*, Second ed. trans. Lawrence Scott. (Austin: University of Texas Press, 1968), 67.

21. Stopkewich, *Wide Awake: That Necrophile Movie*, 15.

Individual filmographies are listed chronologically.

Nell Shipman

The Grub Stake. Dir. Nell Shipman and Bert van Tuyle. Prod. Ernest Shipman and
   Nell Shipman. Nell Shipman Productions, 1923. Re-released as *The Golden Yukon*.
   Sierra Pictures, 1927.

Little Dramas of Big Places. Dir. Nell Shipman and Bert van Thuyle. Prod. Walter
   Greene and Nell Shipman. Nell Shipman Productions, 1926.

The Girl From God's Country. Dir. Nell Shipman and Bert van Tuyle. Prod. Nell
   Shipman. Nell Shipman Productions, 1921.

Something New. Dir. Nell Shipman and Bert van Tuyle. Prod. Nell Shipman. Nell
   Shipman Productions, 1920.

Joyce Weiland

The Far Shore. Dir. Joyce Wieland. Prod. Pierre Lamy, Judy Steed, and Joyce
   Wieland. Far Shore Inc./New Cinema, 1976.

Reason Over Passion. Dir. and Prod. Joyce Weiland. 1969.

Claude Jutra (Selected Filmography)

Short Films (Amateur)

Mouvement perpétuel. Dir. Claude Jutra. 16 mm, b&w, 15 min. 1949.

Le Dément du Lac Jean-Jeunes. Dir. Claude Jutra. 16 mm, b&w, 39 min. 1948.

Short Films

Marie-Christine. Dir. Claude Jutra. 35mm, colour, 10 min. Office du film du Québec, 1970.

Au cœur de la ville. Dir. Claude Jutra. 35mm, b&w, 5 min. Office du film du Québec, 1969.

Rouli-roulant. Dir. Claude Jutra. 16mm, b&w, 15 min. Les Films Cassiopée for NFB, 1966. English title: *The Devil's Toy*

Petit discours de la méthode. Dir. Claude Jutra and Pierre Patry. 16mm, b&w, 28 min. NFB, 1963.

Les Enfants du silence. Dir. Claude Jutra. 35mm, b&w, 24 min. NFB, 1962.

Québec-U.S.A. ou L'Invasion Pacifique. Dir. Claude Jutra and Michel Brault. 16mm, b&w, 28 min. NFB, 1962. English title: *Visit a Foreign Country*.

La Lutte. Dir. Claude Jutra, Michel Brault, Marcel Carrière, and Claude Fournier. 16mm, b&w, 28 min. NFB, 1961. English title: *Wrestling*.

Le Niger jeune république. Dir. Claude Jutra. 16mm, colour, 58 min. NFB, 1961. English title: *The Niger Young Republic*.

Anna la bonne. Dir. Claude Jutra. 35mm, b&w, 10 min. Les films du Carrosse, France, 1959.

Félix Leclerc troubadour. Dir. Claude Jutra. 35mm, b&w, 27 min. NFB, 1959.

Fred Barry, comédien. Dir. Claude Jutra. 16mm, b&w, 21 min. NFB, 1959.

A Chairy Tale. Dir. Claude Jutra and Norman McLaren. Prod. Tom Daly. 35mm, b&w, 10 min. NFB, 1957. French title: *Il était une chaise*.

Pierrot des bois. Dir. Claude Jutra. 16mm, b&w, 9 min. Les Films Cassiopée, 1956.

Chantons maintenant. Dir. Claude Jutra. 35mm, b&w, 29 min. NFB, 1956.

Jeunesses musicales. Dir. Claude Jutra. 35 mm, b&w, 43 min. NFB, 1956. English title: *Youth and Music*.

Feature Films

La Dame en couleurs. Dir. Claude Jutra. 35mm, colour, 111 min. Pierre Lamy/NFB, 1984. English title: *The Lady of Colours*.

Surfacing. Dir. Claude Jutra. Prod. Beryl Fox. 35mm, colour, 89 min. Pan-Canadian/Surfacing Film. 1981.

By Design. Dir. Claude Jutra. 35mm, colour, 91 min, 20s. B.D.F. Productions Ltd., 1981.

The Wordsmith. Dir. Claude Jutra. 16 mm, colour, 73 min. CBC, 1979.

Ada. Dir. Claude Jutra. 16mm, colour, 58 min. CBC, 1976.

Dreamspeaker. Dir. Claude Jutra. 16mm, colour, 75 min. CBC, 1976. French title: *Le conteur de rêves*.

Seer Was Here. Dir. Claude Jutra. 16mm, colour, 57 min. CBC, 1976.

Pour le meilleur et pour le pire. Dir. Claude Jutra. Prod. Pierre Lamy. 35mm, colour, 117 min. Carle-Lamy Productions/Cinepix, 1975. English title: *For Better For Worse*.

Kamouraska. Dir. Claude Jutra. Prod. Mag Bodard and Pierre Lamy. 35mm, colour, 124 min. Carle-Lamy Productions/Parc Film-UPF/SDICC, 1973.

Wow. Dir. Claude Jutra. 16mm, blown up to 35mm, colour, 95 min. Gendon Films/NFB, 1971.

Mon oncle Antoine. Dir. Claude Jutra. Prod. Marc Beaudet. 35mm, colour, 104 min. Gendon Films/NFB, 1971. English title: *My Uncle Antoine*.

Comment savoir... Dir. Claude Jutra. 16mm, b&w, 71 min. NFB, 1966. English title: *Knowing to Learn*.

À tout prendre. Dir. and Prod. Claude Jutra. 16mm, b&w, 99 min. Les Films Cassiopée/Orion Films, 1963. English titles: *Take It All*.

Les mains nettes. Dir. Claude Jutra. Prod. Gary Glover and Léonard Forest. 16mm, b&w, 73 min. NFB, 1958.

Jean-Claude Lauzon

Léolo. Dir. Jean-Claude Lauzon. Prod. Leon G. Arcand, Aimee Danis, and Lyse Lafontaine. Colour, 107 min. de Verseau-Flach Films/NFB/Telefilm Canada, 1993.

Un Zoo la nuit. Dir. Jean-Claude Lauzon. Prod. Roger Frappier and Pierre Gendron. Colour, 115 min. Franco London Films/NFB/Productions Oz, 1987. English title: *Night Zoo*.

Denys Arcand

Les invasions barbares. Dir. Denys Arcand. Prod. Denis Robert, Daniel Louis, and Fabienne Vonier. Colour, 112 min. Cinémaginaire/Pyramide Productions (France), 2003. English title: *The Barbarian Invasions*.

Stardom. Dir. Denys Arcand. Prod. Denise Robert, Robert Lantos, and Philippe Carcassonne. Colour, b&w, 100 min. Alliance Atlantis Communications/Serendipity Point Films/Cinémaginaire/Cine B Production (France), 2000.

Joyeux calvaire. Dir. Denys Arcand. Prod. Denise Robert. Colour, 90 min. Cinémaginaire/Société Radio-Canada, 1996. English title: *Poverty and Other Delights*.

Love and Human Remains. Dir. Denys Arcand. Prod. Roger Frappier and Peter Sussman. Colour, 100 min. Max Films/Atlantis Films/Ontario Film Development Corporation, 1993.

Jésus de Montréal. Dir. Denys Arcand. Prod. Roger Frappier, Pierre Gendron, Doris
Girard, and Jacques E. Strauss. Colour, 119 min. Max Films/Gérard Mital
Productions (France)/NFB, 1989. English title: *Jesus of Montreal*.

Le déclin de l'empire américain. Dir. Denys Arcand. Prod. Pierre Gendron, René Malo,
and Roger Frappier. Colour, 102 min. Corporation Image M&M/Office national
du film du Canada, 1986. English title: *The Decline of the American Empire*.

Le crime d'Ovide Plouffe. Dir. Denys Arcand and Gilles Carle. Prod. Jacques Bobet,
Gabriel Boustani, Justine Héroux, and John Kemeny. Colour, 120 min.
International Cinema Corporation/Société Radio-Canada/Office national du
film du Canada, 1984. English title: *The Crime of Ovide Plouffe*.

Le confort et l'indifférence. Dir. Denys Arcand. Prod. Roger Frappier and Jean
Dansereau. Colour, 108 min. Office national du film du Canada, 1981. English
title: *Comfort and Indifference*.

On est au coton. Dir. Denys Arcand. Prod. Marc Beaudet. Pierre Maheu Production
Company/ Office national du film du Canada, 1976.

Gina. Dir. Denys Arcand. Prod. Pierre Lamy. Les Productions Carle-Lamy, 1974.

Réjeanne Padovani. Dir. Denys Arcand. Prod. Marguerite Duparc. Colour, 90 min.
Cinak Productions/Cinepix, 1973.

La maudite galette. Dir. Denys Arcand. Prod. Pierre Lamy. Colour, 108 min. CINAK/
Marguerite Duparc Production Company, 1972. English title: *Darned Loot*.

Québec: Duplessis et après.... Dir. Denys Arcand. Prod. Paul Larose. Colour, 121 min.
Paul Larose Production Company/Office national du film du Canada, 1972.

Seul ou avec d'autres. Dir. Denys Arcand, Denis Héroux, and Stéphane Venne. Prod.
Denis Héroux. b&w, 65 min. Association générale des étudiants de l'Université
de Montréal, 1963. English title: *Alone or With Others*.

David Cronenberg

A History of Violence. Dir. David Cronenberg. Prod. Josh Braun, Justis Greene, and
Roger E. Kass. Colour, 96 min. New Line Cinema, 2005.

Spider. Dir. David Cronenberg. Prod. Catherine Bailey, et. al. Colour, 98 min.
Artists Independent Network/Capitol Films/Davis Films/Metropolitan Films,
2003.

eXistenZ. Dir. David Cronenberg. Prod. David Cronenberg, Andras Hamori, and
Robert Lantos. Colour, 97 min. Alliance Atlantis Communications/Natural
Nylon Entertainment/Serendipity Point Films, 1999.

Crash. Dir. David Cronenberg. Prod. David Cronenberg, et. all. Colour, 98 min.
Alliance Atlantis Communications/Fine Line Features, 1996.

M. Butterfly. Dir. David Cronenberg. Prod. Gabriella Martinelli and David Henry
Hwang. Colour, 100 min. Warner Brothers, 1993.

Naked Lunch. Dir. David Cronenberg. Prod. Jeremy Thomas. Colour, 117 min. 20th
Century Fox, 1991.

Dead Ringers. Dir. David Cronenberg. Prod. Carol Baum and Sylvio Tabet. Colour, 117 min. Mantle Clinic II, 1988.

The Fly. Dir. David Cronenberg. Prod. Marc Boyman and Kip Ohman. Colour, 96 min. 20th Century Fox/Brooks Films, 1986.

The Dead Zone. Dir. David Cronenberg. Prod. Debra Hill. Colour, 104 min. De Laurentis Entertainment Group/Paramount, 1983.

Videodrome. Dir. David Cronenberg. Prod. Pierre David and Victor Solnicki. Colour, 88 min. Filmplan International/Universal, 1982.

Scanners. Dir. David Cronenberg. Prod. Pierre David and Victor Solnicki. Colour, 120 min. Filmplan International, 1981.

The Brood. Dir. David Cronenberg. Prod. Pierre David and Victor Solnicki. Colour, 92 min. New World, 1979.

Fast Company. Dir. David Cronenberg. Prod. Michael Lebowitz and David Perlmutter. Colour, 90 min. Danton Films/Quadrant Films, 1978.

Rabid. Dir. David Cronenberg. Prod. Andre Link and Ivan Reitman. Colour, 91 min. Cinema Enterprises/New World, 1977.

Shivers. Dir. David Cronenberg. Prod. Alfred Pariser. Colour, 87 min. DAL Productions/Trans-American, 1975.

Crimes of the Future. Dir. and Prod. David Cronenberg. Colour, 65 min. Emergent Films, 1969.

Stereo. Dir. and Prod. David Cronenberg. B&w, 63 min. Emergent Films, 1969.

Atom Egoyan

Where the Truth Lies. Dir. Atom Egoyan. Prod. Robert Lantos, Chris Chrisasfis, and Sandra Cunningham. Colour, 108 min. Ego Film Arts/et. al., 2005.

Ararat. Dir. Atom Egoyan. Prod. Atom Egoyan, Robert Lantos, and Sandra Cunningham. Colour, 126 min. Alliance Atlantis Communications/et. al., 2002.

Felicia's Journey. Dir. Atom Egoyan. Prod. Bruce Davey and Robert Lantos. Colour, 116 min. Alliance Atlantis Communications/Icon Productions, 1999.

The Sweet Hereafter. Dir. Atom Egoyan. Prod. Atom Egoyan and Camelia Frieberg. Colour, 110 min. Alliance Atlantis Communications/Ego Film Arts/Fine Line Features, 1997.

Exotica. Dir. Atom Egoyan. Prod. Atom Egoyan and Camelia Frieberg. Colour, 104 min. ARP/Ego Film Arts, 1994.

Calendar. Dir. Atom Egoyan. Prod. Atom Egoyan, Arsinée Khanjian, and Robert Lantos. 16mm, colour, 75 min. Armenian National Cinema/Ego Film Arts/ Zweites Deutsches Fernsehen, 1993.

The Adjuster. Dir. Atom Egoyan. Prod. Atom Egoyan and Camelia Frieberg. Colour, 102 min. Alliance Atlantis Communications/Ego Film Arts/Orion Classics, 1991.

Speaking Parts. Dir. and Prod. Atom Egoyan. Colour, 92 min. Ego Film Arts, 1989.

Family Viewing. Dir. and Prod. Atom Egoyan. 16mm, colour, 92 min. Ego Film Arts/ Ontario Film Development Corporation, 1987.

Next of Kin. Dir. and Prod. Atom Egoyan. Colour, 72 min. Ego Film Arts, 1984.

John Greyson

Features

Cutthroat. Dir. John Greyson. In production. 2006.

Proteus. Dir. John Greyson and Jack Lewis. Prod. Anita Lee, Steven Markovitz, and Platon Trakoshis. Colour, 113 min. Big World Cinema/et. al., 2003.

The Law of Enclosures. Dir. John Greyson. Prod. John Greyson, Damon D'Oliveira, and Phyllis Laing. Colour, 111 min. Alliance Atlantis Communications/Buffalo Gal Pictures/Pluck, 2000.

Uncut. Dir. and Prod. John. Greyson. Colour, 92 min. Grey Zone, 1997.

Lilies. Dir. John Greyson. Prod. Robin Cass, Arnie Gelbart, and Anna Stratton. Colour, 92 min. Alliance Atlantis Communications/Galafilms Productions/ Triptych Media, 1996.

Zero Patience. Dir. John Greyson. Prod. Louise Garfield, Alexandra Raffe, and Anna Stratton. Colour, 100 min. Channel 4/et. al., 1993.

Urinal. Dir. and Prod. John Greyson. Colour, 100 min. 1988.

Selected Shorts

The Making of "Monsters." Dir. John Greyson. Prod. Laurie Lynd. Colour, 35 min. 1991.

A Moffie Called Simon. Dir. John Greyson. B&w, 15 min. 1987.

The AIDS Epidemic. Dir. John Greyson. 1987.

The Jungle Boy. Dir. John Greyson. Colour. 1985.

Kipling Meets the Cowboys. Dir. John Greyson. Colour. 1985.

The Perils of Pedagogy. Dir. John Greyson. Colour, 5 min. 1984.

Norman Jewison

The Statement. Dir. Norman Jewison. Prod. Norman Jewison and Robert Lantos. Colour, 119 min. BBC Films/et. al., 2003.

Dinner with Friends. Dir. Norman Jewison. Prod. Patrick Markey. Colour, 105 min. 2001.

The Hurricane. Dir. Norman Jewison. Prod. Armyan Bernstein, Norman Jewison, and John Ketcham. Colour, 146 min. Azoff Films/Beacon Pictures, 1999.

Bogus. Dir. Norman Jewison. Prod. Norman Jewison, Arnon Milchan, and Jeff Rothberg. Colour, 110 min. Warner Brothers, 1996.

Picture Windows. Dir. Norman Jewison/et. al. Colour, 95 min. 1994.

Only You. Dir. Norman Jewison. Prod. Robert Fried, Norman Jewison, Charles B. Mulvehill, and Cary Woods. Colour, 108 min. TriStar, 1994.

Other People's Money. Dir. Norman Jewison. Prod. Norman Jewison and Ric Kidney. Colour, 101 min. Warner Brothers/Yorktown Productions, 1991.

In Country. Dir. Norman Jewison. Prod. Norman Jewison, Michael Jewison, and Charles B. Mulvehill. Colour, 120 min. Warner Brothers, 1989.

Moonstruck. Dir. Norman Jewison. Prod. Norman Jewison, Patrick Palmer, and Lee Rich. Colour, 103 min. MGM, 1987.

Agnes of God. Dir. Norman Jewison. Prod. Norman Jewison, Bonnie Palef-Woolf, and Patrick Palmer. Colour, 94 min. Columbia Pictures/Delphi IV Productions, 1985.

A Soldier's Story. Dir. Norman Jewison. Prod. Norman Jewison, Patrick Palmer, and Ronald L. Schwary. Colour, 101 min. Caldix Films/Columbia Pictures, 1984.

Best Friends. Dir. Norman Jewison. Prod. Norman Jewison and Patrick Palmer. Colour, 116 min. Warner Brothers, 1982.

...And Justice for All. Dir. Norman Jewison. Prod. Norman Jewison, Patrick Palmer, and Joe Wizan. Colour, 120 min. Columbia Pictures, 1979.

F.I.S.T. Dir. Norman Jewison. Prod. Gene Corman, Norman Jewison, and Patrick Palmer. Colour, 145 min. United Artists, 1978.

Rollerball. Dir. Norman Jewison. Prod. Norman Jewison, Patrick Palmer, and Hal B. Wallis. 70mm, colour, 129 min. United Artists, 1975.

Jesus Christ Superstar. Dir. Norman Jewison. Prod. Norman Jewison, Patrick Palmer, and Robert Stigwood. Colour, 107 min. Universal, 1973.

Fiddler on the Roof. Dir. and Prod. Norman Jewison. Colour, 179 min. United Artists, 1971.

Gaily, Gaily. Dir. Norman Jewison. Prod. Hal Ashby and Norman Jewison. Colour, 106 min. Mirisch Company/United Artists, 1969.

The Thomas Crown Affair. Dir. and Prod. Norman Jewison. Colour, 102 min. Mirisch Company/United Artists, 1968.

In the Heat of the Night. Dir. Norman Jewison. Prod. Walter Mirisch. Colour, 109 min. Mirisch Company/United Artists, 1967.

The Russians are Coming, the Russians are Coming! Dir. Norman Jewison. Prod. Norman Jewison and Walter Mirisch. Colour, 126 min. Mirisch Corporation/United Artists, 1966.

The Cincinnati Kid. Dir. Norman Jewison. Prod. John Calley and Martin Ransohoff. Colour, 104 min. MGM, 1965.

The Art of Love. Dir. Norman Jewison. Prod. Ross Hunter. Colour, 99 min. Cherokee/Franco London Films/Ross Hunter/Universal, 1965.

Send Me No Flowers. Dir. Norman Jewison. Prod. Harry Keller and Martin Melcher. Colour, 100 min. Universal, 1964.

The Thrill of It All! Dir. Norman Jewison. Prod. Ross Hunter and Martin Melcher. Colour, 108 min. Ross Hunter Productions/Universal, 1963.

40 Pounds of Trouble. Dir. Norman Jewison. Prod. Stan Margulies. Colour, 106 min. Stan Margulies Company/Universal, 1963.

Robert Lepage

La Face cachée de la lune. Dir. Robert Lepage. Prod. Bob Krupinsk, Daniel Langlois, Robert Lepage, and Mario St. Laurent. Colour, 105 min. FCL Films/Media Principia, 2003. English title: *Far Side of the Moon*.

Possible Worlds. Dir. Robert Lepage. Prod. Sandra Cunningham and Bruno Jobin. Colour, 92 min. East Side Film Company/In Extremis, 2000.

Nô. Dir. Robert Lepage. Prod. Bruno Jobin. Colour, 85 min. In Extremis Images/ Sodec/Telfilm Canada, 1998. English title: *No*.

Le polygraphe. Dir. Robert Lepage. Prod. Philippe Carcassonne, Ulrich Felsberg, Bruno Jobin, and Jean-Pierre Saint Michael. Colour, 99 min. 1996. English title: *The Lie Detector*.

Le Confessionnal. Dir. Robert Lepage. Prod. Philippe Carcassonne, David Puttnam, and Denise Robert. Colour, 104 min. Cinea/Cinemaginaire/Enigma Productions, 1994. English title: *The Confessional*.

Bruce McDonald

Short Films

Fort Goof. Dir. Bruce McDonald. Prod. Fraser Robinson and Stacy DeWolfe. 6 min. Bravo!FACT, 1999.

Elimination Dance. Dir. Bruce McDonald. Prod. Sandy Kaplansky. 9 min. Bravo!FACT, 1998.

Let Me See... Dir. and Prod. Bruce McDonald. 30 min. 1982.

Merge. Dir. and Prod. Bruce McDonald. 30 min. 1980.

Features

The Tracey Fragments. Dir. Bruce McDonald. Prod. Sarah Timmins. 80 min. 2007.

The Love Crimes of Gillian Guess. Dir. Bruce McDonald. Prod. Debra Beard, Rob Bromley, and John Ritchie. Colour, 91 min. Canadian Television Fund/et. al., 2004.

Claire's Hat. Dir. Bruce McDonald. Prod. Julie Venerus. Colour, 103 min. Unreleased, 2002.

The Interview. Dir. Bruce McDonald. 2002.

Picture Claire. Dir. and Prod. Wendy Grean and Robert Lantos. Colour, 89 min. Alliance Atlantis Communications/First Look Home Entertainment, 2001.

Hard Core Logo. Dir. Bruce McDonald. Prod. Brian Dennis and Christine Haebler. Colour, 92 min. Shadow Shows/Terminal City Pictures, 1996.

Dance Me Outside. Dir. Bruce McDonald and David J. Webb. Prod. Brian Dennis, Bruce McDonald, and Norman Jewison. Colour, 84 min. Shadow Shows/Yorktown Productions, 1994.

Highway 61. Dir. Bruce McDonald. Prod. Colin Brunton and Bruce McDonald. Colour, 110 min. Film Four International/Shadow Shows/Skouras Pictures, 1991.

Knock! Knock! Dir. and Prod. Bruce McDonald. 62 min. Shadow Shows, 1985.

Roadkill. Dir. Bruce McDonald. Prod. Colin Brunton and Bruce McDonald. B&w, 85 min. Mr. Shack Motion Pictures, 1985.

For Television—Telefilms & Continuing Series

Killer Wave (miniseries). Dir. Bruce McDonald. Prod. Irene Litinsky. Colour, 170 min. RHI International Distribution Inc., 2007.

Road Songs: A Portrait of Robbie Robertson. Dir. Bruce McDonald. Prod. Marc Betsworth. 42 min. CBC, 2001.

American Whiskey Bar. Dir. Bruce McDonald. Prod. Carolynne Bell. 95 min. CITY-TV, 1998.

Twitch City. Dir. Bruce McDonald. Prod. Susan Cavan, Armand Leo, and Bruce McDonald. 30 min. CBC, 1998–2000 (series).

Scandalous Me: The Jacqueline Susann Story. Dir. Bruce McDonald. Prod. Jan Peter Meyboom. 120 min. Alliance Atlantis, 1998.

Platinum. Dir. Bruce McDonald. Prod. Claude Godbout and Madeleine Henrié. 92 min. CBC, 1997.

Train of Thought: The Life and Times of Norman Jewison. Dir. Bruce McDonald. 42 min. CBC, 1997.

For Television—Individual Episodes

ReGenesis. Episodes 2.2 "Escape Mutant" and 2.4 "Dim & Dimmer." Dir. Bruce Mcdonald. TMN, 2006.

Instant Star. Episodes 1.7 "I Wanna Be Your Boyfriend" and 1.8 "Unsweet Sixteen." Dir. Bruce McDonald. CTV, 2005.

The Collector. Episode 2.17 "The Pharmacist." Dir. Bruce McDonald. Chum Television, 2005.

The Tournament. Episodes 1.5 "Saturday at the Tournament" and 1.6 "The Final Game." Dir. Bruce McDonald. CBC, 2005.

Darcy's Wild Life. Episode. Dir. Bruce McDonald. NBC, 2005.

This is Wonderland. Episodes 1.1–1.3. Dir. Bruce McDonald. CBC, 2004.

Kevin Hill. Episode 1.3 "Making the Grade." Dir. Bruce McDonald. UPN, 2004.

Playmakers. Episode 1.4 "The Choice." Dir. Bruce McDonald. Buena Vista Television, 2003.

Radio Free Roscoe. Episodes 1.6 "I Am a Question Mark" and 1.8 "The Imposter." Dir. Bruce McDonald. Noggin, 2003.

Queer as Folk. Episodes 206, 209, 216, 302, 306, 308, 406. Dir. Bruce McDonald. Showtime Networks, 2002–2003.

Degrassi: The Next Generation. Episodes 101 "Mother and Daughter Reunion", 109 "Secrets and Lies", 212 "White Wedding", 216 "Message in a Bottle", and 301 "Father Figure". Dir. Bruce McDonald. Prod. Linda Schuyler and Stephen Stohn. Colour, 42 min. Alliance Atlantis/CBC, 2001–2005 (series).

Codename Eternity. Episode 1.14 "Deep Down." Dir. Bruce McDonald. Global, 2000.

Lexx. Episodes 3.31 "Tunnels" and 3.33 "Garden." Dir. Bruce McDonald. The Sci-Fi Channel, 2000.

The War Next Door. Episode 1.2 "Ménage-a-Kill." Dir. Bruce McDonald. USA Network Inc., 2000.

Emily of New Moon. Episodes 2.23 "Crown of Thorns" and 2.25 "Love Knots." Dir. Bruce McDonald. CBC, 1999.

Little Men. Dir. Bruce McDonald. Alliance Communications, 1998.

Welcome to Paradox. Episode 1.9 "All Our Sins Forgotten." Dir. Bruce McDonald. 1998.

Flash Forward. Episode 1.9 "Makeover." Dir. Bruce McDonald. Buena Vista Television, 1996.

Taking the Falls. Episode 1.10 "The Marrying Man." Dir. Bruce McDonald. Alliance Communications, 1996.

Lonesome Dove: The Outlaw Years. Episodes 1.16 "Betrayal" and 1.5 "The Alliance." Dir. Bruce McDonald. CTV, 1995.

Nancy Drew. Dir. Bruce McDonald. New Line/Nelvana, 1995.

Ready or Not. Episodes 5.53 "All or Nothing" and 5.55 "Cross My Heart." Dir. Bruce McDonald. Global, 1995.

The Hidden Room. Dir. Bruce McDonald. USA Network, 1991.

Liberty Street. Dir. Bruce McDonald. CBC, 1994.

Music Videos

"It's All Over." The Headstones. Dir. Bruce McDonald. 2000.

"Cemetery." The Headstones. Dir. Bruce McDonald. 1996.

"Lonesome." Vern Cheechoo. Dir. Bruce McDonald. 1996.

"Cigarette Dangles." The Pursuit of Happiness. Dir. Bruce McDonald. 1993.

"Dance." The Acid Test. Dir. Bruce McDonald. 1993.

"You and Me." Crash Vegas. Dir. Bruce McDonald. 1993.

Léa Pool

The Blue Butterfly. Dir. Léa Pool. Prod. Francine Allaire, Claude Bonin, and Arnie Gelbart. Colour, 100 min. Galafilm Productions, 2004.

Lost and Delirious. Dir. Léa Pool. Prod. Greg Dummett, Lorraine Richard, and Louis-Philippe Rochon. Colour, 102 min. Cite-Amerique/Greg Dummett Films, 2001.

Emporte-moi. Dir. Léa Pool. Prod. Louis Laverdière. Colour, 94 min. Catpics Co-
Producions/Cite-Amerique/Haut & Court, 1998. English title: *Set Me Free*.

Mouvements du désir. Dir. Léa Pool. Prod. Daniel Louis. Colour, 94 min. Catpics Co-
Productions, et. al., 1994. English title: *Desire in Motion*.

La demoiselle sauvage. Dir. Léa Pool. Prod. Denise Robert. Colour, 100 min. 1991.
English title: *The Savage Woman*.

Rispondetemi, segment in Montréal vu par. Dir. Léa Pool, et. al. Prod. Denise Robert,
Doris Girard, Michel Houle, Peter Sussman, and Yves Rivard. Colour, 127 min.
Atlantic/Cinémaginaire/NFBC, 1991. English title: *Montréal Sextet*.

Á corps perdu. Dir. Léa Pool. Prod. Denise Robert, Robin Spry. B&w, 92 min. Films
Telescene/et. al., 1988. English title: *Straight for the Heart*.

Anne Trister. Dir. Léa Pool. Prod. Roger Frappier, Claude Bonin. Colour, 115 min.
1986.

Femme de l'hotel. Dir. Léa Pool. Prod. Bernadette Payeur. Colour, 88 min. ACPAV/
J.A. LaPointe Films, 1984. English title: *A Woman in Transit*.

Strass Café. Dir and Prod. Léa Pool. 1980.

Patricia Rozema

Mansfield Park. Dir. Patricia Rozema. Prod. Sarah Curtis. Colour, 110 min. BBC/
Miramax, 1999.

When Night is Falling. Dir. Patricia Rozema. Prod. Barbara Tranter. Colour, 82 min.
Barbara Tranter Production Company/Crucial Pictures Inc., 1995.

White Room. Dir. Patricia Rozema. Prod. Alexandra Raffé and Patricia Rozema.
Colour, 93 min. VOS Productions Ltd., 1991.

I've Heard the Mermaids Singing. Dir. Patricia Rozema. Prod. Alexandra Raffé and
Patricia Rozema. Colour, 81 min. VOS Productions Ltd., 1987.

Mina Shum

Mob Princess. Dir. Mina Shum. Prod. Stephen Hegyes and Shawn Williamson.
Brightlight Pictures/The Nightingale Company, 2003.

Long Life, Happiness & Prosperity. Dir. Mina Shum. Prod. Scott Garvie,
Christina Jennings, Raymond Massey, and Mina Shum. Colour, 91 min.
Shaftesbury Films Inc./Massey Productions, 2002.

Drive, She Said. Dir. Mina Shum. Prod. Stephen Hegyes. Colour, 93 min. 47 Films/
Drive, She Said Productions/Malofilm Communications, 1997.

Thirsty. Dir. Mina Shum. 1997.

Double Happiness. Dir. Mina Shum. Prod. Stephen Hegyes and Rose Lam Waddell.
Colour, 92 min. First Generation Films Inc./New Views Films, 1994.

Me, Mom and Mona. Dir. Mina Shum. 1993.

Hunger. (Part of Cineworks Omnibus film, *Breaking up in Three Minutes*) Dir. Mina
Shum. 1993.

Love In. Dir. Mina Shum. 1991.

Shortchanged. Dir. Mina Shum. 1990.

Picture Perfect. Dir. and Prod. Mina Shum. 8 min. 1989.

Television Episodes

Noah's Arc. Episodes 12 " Desperado," 13 "Excuses for Bad Behavior," and 16 "Baby Can I Hold You." Dir. Mina Shum. CBC, 2006.

Romeo. Episode 13 "Rules of Engagement." Dir. Mina Shum. Nickelodeon, 2006.

Davinci's Inquest VII. Episode "That's Why They Call It a Conspiracy." Dir. Mina Shum. Prod. Chris Haddcock and Laszlo Barna. Super 16mm, colour, 46 min. Haddcock Entertainment, 2005.

Bliss III. Episode 19 "Tying up Gerald." Dir. Mina Shum. Showcase/Oxygen, 2004.

The Shields' Stories. Episode "Various Miracles." Dir. Mina Shum. Colour, 30 min. WNetwork, 2004.

These Arms of Mine II. Two episodes. Dir. Mina Shum. CBC, 2001.

Gary Burns

Beerland. Dir. and Prod. Gary Burns. Colour, 35 min. Burns Film Ltd., release date and place is n/a.

Radiant City (doc.). Dir. Gary Burns and Jim Brown. Prod. Graydon McCrea, Bonnie Thompson, and Shirley Vercruysse. Colour, 85 min. Burns Films Ltd./NFB, 2006.

Cool Money. Dir. Gary Burns. Prod. Aaron Barnett. Once Upon a Time Films/Darius Films/USA Network, 2005.

Northern Town (6-part miniseries). Dir. Gary Burns. Prod. Daniel Janke and Daniel Iron. Foundry Films, 2005.

A Problem with Fear. Dir. Gary Burns. Prod. George Baptist, Shirley Vercruysse, and Luc Déry. Colour, 92 min. Burns Films Ltd./Fear Alberta Ltd., 2003.

waydowntown. Dir. Gary Burns. Prod. Shirley Vercruysse. Colour, 87 min. Burns Films/Odeon Films (Canada), 2000.

Kitchen Party. Dir. Gary Burns. Prod. James Head and Scott Kennedy. Colour, 92 min. Highwire Entertainment (Cadence Entertainment)/Sub Urban Film Co. Ltd., 1997.

The Suburbanators. Dir. Gary Burns. Prod. Gary Burns and John Hazlett. Colour, 87 min. Burns Film Ltd./Red Devil Films Ltd., 1995.

Michael Dowse

It's All Gone Pete Tong. Dir. Michael Dowse. Prod. Rob Morgan, Rupert Preston, and Kim Roberts. Colour, 90 min. True West Films/Vertigo Films, 2005.

FUBAR. Dir. Michael Dowse. Prod. Michael Dowse, David Lawrence, Melanie Owen, Marguerite Pigott, Mark Slone, and Paul Spence. Colour, 77 min. Busted Tranny Productions, 2002.

Thom Fitzgerald

3 Needles. Dir. Thom Fitzgerald. Prod. Michael Gleissner, Thom Fitzgerald, and Bryan Hofbauer. Colour, 124 min. Bigfoot Entertainment/Courage Pictures/ Emotion Pictures, 2006.

The Event. Dir. Thom Fitzgerald. Prod. Robert Flutie, et. al. Colour, 110 min. Covington Intl./et. al., 2002.

The Wild Dogs. Dir. Thom Fitzgerald. Prod. William Ritchie, Christopher Zimmer, and Ann Bernier. Colour, 102 min. CHUM Television/IMX Communications, 2002.

Wolf Girl. Dir. Thom Fitzgerald. Prod. Donald Kushner, Peter Locke, and J. Miles Dale. Colour, 95 min. 2001 (made for television, also released as *Blood Moon*).

Beefcake. Dir. Thom Fitzgerald. Prod. Thom Fitzgerald and Shandi Mitchell. Colour, 93 min. Alliance Independent Films/et. al., 1999.

The Hanging Garden. Dir. Thom Fitzgerald. Prod. Thom Fitzgerald, Louise Garfield, and Arnie Gelbart. Colour, 91 min. Emotion Pictures/et. al., 1997.

Canada Uncut. Dir. and Prod. Thom Fitzgerald. 1995.

Cherries. Dir. and Prod. Thom Fitzgerald. 1995.

The Movie of the Week. Dir. and Prod. Thom Fitzgerald. 1990.

Zach Kunuk

The Journals of Knud Rasmussen. Dir. Norman Cohn and Zack Kunuk. Prod. Norman Cohn, et. al. 35mm, colour and b&w, 112 min, Inuktitut and Danish with English subtitles. Barok Film/Igloolik Isuma Productions/Kunuk Cohn Productions, 2006.

Kunuk Family Reunion. Dir. Zach Kunuk. Prod. Norman Cohn and Zach Kunuk. Colour, 48 min, Inuktitut with English or French subtitles. Nunavut Independent Television Network/History Television/Aboriginal Peoples Television Network, 2004.

Angakkuiit. Dir. Zach Kunuk. 48 min, Inuktitut with English or French subtitles. 2003. English title: *Shaman Stories*.

Arvik! Dir. Zach Kunuk and Paul Apak Angilirq. 52 min, Inuktitut with English subtitles. 2002. English title: *Bowhead!*

Atanarjuat: The Fast Runner. Dir. Zach Kunuk. Prod. Sally Bochner, Zach Kunuk, and Germaine Wong. 35mm, colour, 161 min, Inuktitut with English or French subtitles. Canadian Television Fund, et. all, 2001.

Nipi. Dir. Zach Kunuk. 52 min, Inuktitut with English subtitles. 1999. English title: *Voice*.

Sanaṅinguarti. Dir. Zach Kunuk. 26 min, Inuktitut with English subtitles. 1995. English title: *Carver.*

Angiraq. Dir. Zach Kunuk. Prod. Norman Cohn, Zach Kunuk, and Pauloosie Qulitalik. 29 min. Kunuk Cohn Productions, 1994. English title: *Home.*

Nunavut (TV series). Dir. Zach Kunuk. Video, 390m, Inuktitut with English or French subtitles. 1994–95.

Saputi. Dir. Zach Kunuk. Prod. Norman Cohn, Zack Kunuk, and Pauloosie Qulitalik. 30 min, Inuktitut with English or French subtitles. 1993. English title: *Fish Traps.*

Nunaqpa. Dir. Zach Kunuk. Prod. Norman Cohn and Zach Kunuk. 58 min, Inuktitut with English or French subtitles. 1991. English title: *Going Inland.*

Alert Bay. Dir. Zach Kunuk. 28 min, Inuktitut. 1989.

From Inuk Point of View. 9 min, Inuktitut with English subtitles. 1989.

Qaqqiq. Dir. Zach Kunuk. Prod. Norman Cohn and Zach Kunuk. 58 min, Inuktitut with English or French subtitles. 1989. English title: *The Gathering Place.*

Don McKellar (Selected Filmography)

Childstar. Dir. Don McKellar. Prod. Niv Fichman, Daniel Iron, and Jennifer Jonas. Colour, 98 min. Rhombus Media, 2004.

A Word from the Management. Dir. Don McKellar. Prod. Niv Fichman, Jody Shapiro, and Jennifer Weiss. Colour, 6 min. 2000.

Last Night. Dir. Don McKellar. Prod. Caroline Benjo, et. al. Colour, 94 min. ARTE/CBC/Rhombus Media, 1998.

A Portrait of Atom. Dir. Don McKellar. 1995.

Blue. Dir. Don McKellar. Prod. Bruce McDonald. 22 min. 1992.

The Bloody Nose. Dir. Don McKellar. Colour, 6 min. 1992.

Lynne Stopkewich

Features

Lilith on Top. Dir. Lynne Stopkewich. Prod. Dean English, Jessica Fraser, and Barbara Peterson. 35mm, colour, 100 min. Boneyard Films/Lilith Fair Productions/Telefilm Canada, 2001.

Suspicious River. Dir. Lynne Stopkewich. Prod. Raymond Massey. Colour, 95 min. Okulitch-Pederson Company/Suspicious Films, 2000.

Kissed. Dir. Lynne Stopkewich. Prod. Dean English, John Pozer, and Lynne Stopkewich. Colour, 94 min. Boneyard Films/British Columbia Films/Canada Council for the Arts, 1996.

Television Episodes

The L Word. Episodes 3 "Longing," and 12 "Locked Up." Dir. Lynne Stopkewich. Prod. Ilene Chaiken, et. al. Colour, 60 min. Anonymous Content/et. al., 2004.

Selected Bibliography

Abel, Marie-Christine, André Giguere, and Luc Perreault. *Le Cinéma québécois à l'heure internationale*. Montréal: Stanké, 1990.

Alemany-Galway, Mary. "'Family Viewing.'" In *A Postmodern Cinema: The Voice of the Other in Canadian Film*. Lanham, MD: Scarecrow Press, 2002. 165–90.

———. "I've Heard the Mermaids Singing." In *A Postmodern Cinema*, 140–63.

———. *A Postmodern Cinema: The Voice of the Other in Canadian Film*. Lanham, MD: Scarecrow Press, 2002.

Alioff, Maurie. "Haunted by Hitchcock." *Take One: Film & Television in Canada* 9 (1995): 8–15.

Anderson, Jason. "*Picture Claire*." *Eye Weekly* 10, no. 49 (13 September 2000): 18.

Armatage, Kay. *The Girl from God's Country: Nell Shipman and the Silent Cinema*. Toronto: University of Toronto Press, 2003.

Armatage, Kay, Kass Banning, Brenda Longfellow and Janine Marchessault, eds. *Gendering the Nation: Canadian Women's Cinema*. Toronto: University of Toronto Press, 1999.

Arroyo, José. "Howls from the Asphalt Jungle." *Cinema Canada* 141 (May 1987): 7–10.

Atwood, Margaret. *Second Words*. Toronto: Anansi, 1982.

———. *Survival: A Thematic Guide to Canadian Literature*. Toronto: Anansi, 1972.

Austin-Smith, Brenda. "'Gender is Irrelevant': *I've Heard the Mermaids Singing* as Women's Cinema." In *Canada's Best Features: Critical Essays on Fifteen Canadian Films*. Edited by Eugene P. Walz, 208–33. Amsterdam: Rodopi, 2002.

Babiuk, Todd. "Headbangers show heart." *Edmonton Journal*, 31 May 2002, E2.

———. "Wayne's World, Alberta–style." *Edmonton Journal*, 6 February 2002, C1.

Bailey, Cameron. "Standing in the Kitchen All Night: A Secret History of the Toronto New Wave." *Take One: Film & Television in Canada* 9, no. 28 (Summer 2000): 6–11.

Baker, Noel S. *Hard Core Roadshow: A Screenwriter's Diary*. Concord: Anansi, 1997.

Baldassarre, Angela. "Bruce McDonald." In *Reel Canadians: Interviews from the Canadian Film World*, 77–82. Toronto: Guernica, 2003.

Banning, Kass. "The Mummification of Mommy: Joyce Wieland as the AGO's First Living Other." *C Magazine* 13 (1987): 32–38. Reprinted in *Sightlines: Reading Contemporary Canadian Art*. Edited by J. Radley and L. Johnstone, 153–67. Montreal: Artextes, 1994; and in *The Films of Joyce Wieland*. Edited by Kathryn Elder, 29–44. Toronto: Cinematheque Ontario Monographs, 1999.

Beard, William. "The Canadianness of David Cronenberg." *Mosaic* 27 (June 1994): 113–33.

———. *The Artist as Monster: The Cinema of David Cronenberg*. rev. ed. Toronto: University of Toronto Press, 2005. First published in 2001.

Beard, William and Jerry White, eds. *North of Everything: English-Canadian Cinema Since 1980*. Edmonton: University of Alberta Press, 2002.

Beaty, Bart. "Imagining the Written Word: Adaptation in the Work of Bruce McDonald and Nick Craine." *Canadian Journal of Film Studies* 13, no. 2 (2004): 22–44.

Bell, Douglas. "Bruce McDonald Goes Platinum." *The Globe and Mail*, 11 October 1997, C6.

Berger, Sally. "Time Travellers." *Inuit Art Quarterly* 11, no. 2 (Summer 1996). 4–11. Originally published in *Felix* 2, no. 1 (1995).

Blount, Stephen. Review of DVD release of *Crash*. *Entertainment Weekly* #838/839 (9 September 2005): 131.

Bor, Aaron. "An Interview with Léa Pool." *Quebec Studies* 9 (Fall 1989/Winter 1990): 49–62.

Bordwell, David. *Narration in the Fiction Film*. Milwaukee: University of Wisconsin, 1985.

Brassell, R. Bruce. "The Making of Monsters: The queer as producer." *Jump Cut* 40 (1996): 47–54.

Brunton, Colin. "*Roadkill* and *Highway 61* or How I Got My Job at the Canadian Film Centre." Case Study for the Fall Lab, Canadian Film Centre, 13 October 1992, 1–11.

Burns, Gary. "Radiant City [Perfect]." Final draft manuscript, author's personal collection, 2005.

Burroughs, Alexandra. "Dowse's lean days All Gone." *Calgary Herald*, 10 June 2005, C1.

Buruiana, Michel. "Jean–Claude Lauzon." *Séquences* 158 (June 1992): 32–34; 41–44.

Butler, Judith. "Performative Acts and Gender Constitution: An Essay in Phenomenology and Feminist Theory." In *Performing Feminisms: Feminist Critical Theory and Theatre*, edited by Sue–Ellen Case. Baltimore: Johns Hopkins UP, 1990.

———. *Bodies that Matter: On the Discursive Limits of "Sex."* New York: Routledge, 1993.

Byford, Chris. "*Highway 61* Revisited." *CineACTION* 45 (1998): 11–17.

Caddell, Ian. "Mina Shum and the Pursuit of Happiness (Part 3)." *Reel West Magazine* 17, no. 2 (March–April 2002): 26–28.

Cagle, Robert L. "A Minority on Someone Else's Continent: Identity, Difference, and the Media in the Films of Patricia Rozema." In Armatage et. al., *Gendering the Nation: Canadian Women's Cinema*. 183–96.

Cagle, Robert. "'Tell the story of my life...': The Making of Meaning, 'Monsters,' and Music in John Greyson's *Zero Patience*." *The Velvet Light Trap* 35 (Spring 1995): 69–81.

Chabot, Jean, ed. *Claude Jutra*. Cinéastes du Québec 4. Montreal: Société pour la diffusion du cinéma au Québec, 1971.

Chaw, Walter, "The Fighting Fitzgerald." *Film Freak Central*. http://www.filmfreak-central.net/notes/tfitzgeraldinterview.htm. Accessed June 11, 2005.

Cinémathèque Québécoise. *Claude Jutra, filmographie et témoignages*. Numéro special de *Copie Zéro* 33 (September 1970).

Cineplex Odeon Films. *Kitchen Party* Press Kit. Toronto, 1997.

Clandfield, Peter. "Bridgespotting: Lepage, Hitchcock, and Landmarks in Canadian Film." *Canadian Journal of Film Studies* 12, no.1 (2003): 2–15.

Cloutier, Mario. "'Le film, c'est un outil de recherche et d'expression de soi': Entretien avec Léa Pool." *Cinebulles* 13, no.2 (Spring 1994): 32–34.

Coates, Paul. "Protecting the Exotic: Atom Egoyan and Fantasy." *Canadian Journal of Film Studies* 6, no.3 (1997): 21–33.

Cohan, Steve and Ina Rae Hark. "Introduction." In *The Road Movie Book*. Edited by Cohan and Hark, 1–14. London: Routledge, 1997.

Cook, David. *Lost Illusions: American Cinema in the Shadow of Watergate and Vietnam, 1970–1979*. Berkeley: University of California Press, 2000.

Cooper, Barry. "A *imperio ad imperium*: The Political Thought of George Grant." In *George Grant in Process*, edited by Larry Schmidt. Toronto: Anansi, 1978.

Corbeil, Carole. "The Indiscreet Charm of Jean-Claude Lauzon." *Saturday Night* 107 (December 1992): 58–61; 86–90.

Coulombe, Michel. "Entretien avec Robert Lepage." *Cinebulles* 17, no. 2 (1998): 6–10.

———. *Denys Arcand: La vraie nature du cinéaste*. Montréal: Boréal, 1993.

Couture, Claude. "La Censure: *Le Confessionnal* ou le stereotype d'une société tradi-
tionelle 'unique'." *Francaphonies d'Amérique* 8 (1998): 153–60.

Cuthbert, Pamela. "Drive on." *Take One: Film & Television in Canada* 19 (Spring 1998):
28–30.

Dault, Gary Michael. "Robert Lepage's 'Le confessionnal' & 'Le polygraphe'." *Take
One: Film & Television in Canada* 15 (1997): 17–21.

Del Rio, Elena. "The Body as Foundation of the Screen: Allegories of Technology in
Atom Egoyan's 'Speaking Parts'." *Camera Obscura* 38 (1998): 92–115.

Del Sorbo, Agata Smoluch. "The Polyphonic Nature of Patricia Rozema." *Take One:
Film & Television in Canada* 13, no. 48 (December 2004–March 2005): 14–21.

Desbarats, Carole, Daniele Riviere, Jacinto Lageira, and Paul Virilio. *Atom Egoyan*.
Translated by Brian Holmes. Paris: Editions Dis Voir, 1993.

Dickinson, Peter. "Space, Time, Auteurity, and the Queer Male Body: The Film
Adaptations of Robert Lepage." *Screen* 46, no. 2 (2005): 133–53.

———. *Screening Gender, Framing Genre: Canadian Literature into Film*. Toronto: U of
Toronto Press, 2007.

Dillon, Steven. "Lyricism and Accident in 'The Sweet Hereafter.'" *Literature/Film
Quarterly* 31, no. 3 (2003): 227–30.

Dix, Noel. "Flick Picks: A weekly roundup of the week's best bets." *Calgary Herald*, 5
August 2005, D2.

———. "Fubar." *Exclaim!* 10 December 2002. http://www.exclaim.ca/index.asp?la
yid=22&csid=5&csid1=1185. Accessed 9 February 2007.

Doane, Mary Ann. "Film and the Masquerade: Theorizing the Female Spectator."
In *Issues in Feminist Film Criticism*. Edited by Patricia Erens, 41–57. Bloomington:
Indiana University Press, 1990.

Dorland, Michael. "Jean-Claude Lauzon's *Un Zoo la nuit*." *Cinema Canada* 144
(September 1987): 37.

"Dossier Léa Pool." *24 Images* (Automne 1991): 56–57.

Dundjerovic, Aleksandar. *The Cinema of Robert Lepage: The Poetics of Memory*. London:
Wallflower Press, 2003.

Ebert Roger. Review: *The Hanging Garden*. *Chicago Sun Times*, 29 May 1998. http://
www.rogerebert.suntimes.com/apps/pbcs.d11/article.

Elder, Kathryn, ed. *The Films of Joyce Wieland*. Toronto: Cinematheque Ontario
Monographs, 1999.

Elia, Maurice. "*Un Zoo la nuit*." *Séquences* 130 (August 1987): 60–1.

Evans, Gary. *In the National Interest: A Chronicle of the National Film Board of Canada*.
Toronto: University of Toronto Press, 1991.

Evans, Michael Robert. "Sometimes in Anger: The Struggles of Inuit Video." *Fuse
Magazine* 22, no. 4 (January 2000): 13–17.

Feldman, Seth and Joyce Nelson, eds. *Canadian Film Reader*. Toronto: Peter Martin
Associates, 1977.

Fleming, Kathleen. "Igloolik Video: An Organic Response from a Culturally Sound Community." *Inuit Art Quarterly* 11, no. 1 (Spring 1996): 26–34.

Fothergill, Robert. "Coward, Bully, or Clown: The Dream-Life of a Younger Brother." In *Canadian Film Reader*. Edited by Seth Feldman and Joyce Nelson, 234–50.

Fourlanty, Eric. "Léa Pool: Director's Sheet." Pro Helvetia/Arts Council of Switzerland, 2002.

Fox, Angelica. "Storytime: Starting a New Tradition." *Canadian Forum* 67, no. 774 (December 1987): 36–38.

Fuller, Cam. "Good Good Good Vibrations: It's all gone right for locally grown director." *Calgary Herald*, 10 June 2005, SW09.

———. "Much-hyped Fubar doesn't quite deliver." *Saskatoon Star—Phoenix*, 13 September 2002, D7.

Gajan, Philippe, and Marie-Claude Loiselle. "Entretien avec André Forcier." *24 Images* 87 (Summer 1997): 8–13.

Garneau, Michèle and Pierre Véronneau. "Un cinéma 'de genre' révélateur d'une inquiétante américanité québécoise." In *L'aventure du cinéma québécois en France*. Edited by Michel Larouche, 181–207. Montréal: XYZ Éditeur, 1996.

Garrity, Henry A. "Robert Lepage's Cinema of Time and Space." In *Theater sans frontières: Essays on the Dramatic Universe of Robert Lepage*. Edited by Joseph I. Donohoe and Jane M.Koustas, 95–107. East Lansing, MI: Michigan State UP, 2000.

Gittings, Christopher E. "*Zero Patience*, Genre, Difference and Ideology: Singing and Dancing Queer Nation." *Cinema Journal*. 41, no.1 (2001): 28–40.

———. *Canadian National Cinema: Ideology, Difference and Representation*. London: Routledge, 2002.

Glassman, Marc. "*Last Night:* In the Year of the Don." *Take One: Film & Television in Canada* 7, no. 21 (Fall 1998): 10–14.

Glenn Walton. "Thom Fitzgerald's *The Hanging Garden*." *Take One: Film & Television in Canada* 6, no. 17 (1997): 34.

Goddard, Peter. "Bruce McDonald at the Crossroads with *Picture Claire*." *Take One: Film & Television in Canada* 10, no. 35 (December 2001–February 2002): 13–15.

Godwin, George. "Reclaiming the Subject: A Feminist Reading of *I've Heard the Mermaids Singing*." *Cinema Canada* 152, (May 1988): 23–24.

Golfman, Noreen. "The Spell of Carnal Beauty." *Canadian Forum* 74, no. 842 (Sept 1995): 28–29.

———. "Double Happiness." *Canadian Forum* 74, no. 843 (Oct 1995): 25–26.

Gordon, Daphne. "Hey, dude, where's my beer?: FUBAR mockumentary comes with buzz." *Toronto Star*, 23 May 2002, A26.

Gowdy, Barbara. *We So Seldom Look on Love*. Toronto: Somerville House Publishing, 1992.

Grant, George. *English-Speaking Justice*. New Brunswick: Mt. Allison University, 1974.

Gravestock, Steve. "Outlaw Insider: The Films of Bruce McDonald." In *North of Everything*, edited by Beard and White, 242–55.

Green, Mary Jean. "Léa Pool's *La Femme de l'hotel* and Women's Film in Quebec." *Quebec Studies* 9 (Fall 1989/Winter 1990): 49–62.

Greyson, John. "John Greyson on Bill C-12." *Fuse* 27, no. 2 (2004): 10.

———. "Security Blankets, Sex, Video and the Police." In *Queer Looks: Perspectives on Gay and Lesbian Film and Video*. Edited by Martha Grever, John Greyson, and Pratibha Parma, 383–984. London and New York: Routledge, 1993.

———. "The Coconut Strategy." *Essays on Canadian Writing* 76 (Spring 2002): 263–66.

———. *Fig Trees: A Video Opera*. Libretto: John Greyson; Music: David Wall; [essay by Bongani Ndodana]. Oakville, ON: Oakville Galleries, 2003.

———. *Urinal and Other Stories*. Toronto: Art Metropole, Power Plant, 1993.

Groen, Rick. "A good ol' boy from Rexdale." *The Globe and Mail*, 14 February 1992, C1 & C5.

Handling, Piers, ed. *The Shape of Rage: The Films of David Cronenberg*. Toronto: Academy of Canadian Cinema, 1983.

Harcourt, Peter. "Imaginary Images: An Examination of Atom Egoyan's Films." *Film Quarterly* 48, no.3 (1995): 2–14.

Hays Mathew, "Thom Fitzgerald." *Advocate* No. 753 (February 17 1998). http://www.montrealmirror.com/archives/1998/011598/cover/html

Hibon, Danièle, ed. *Atom Egoyan: Café des images*. Paris: Éditions du Jeu de paume, 1993.

Holden, Stephen, "Anomie's Insidious Grip on Suburban Affluence." *New York Times*, 10 April 1998.

Houle, Michel et Alain Julien: *Dictionnaire du cinéma québécois*. Montreal: Fides, 1978.

Hoven, Adrian Van Den. "The Decline of the American Empire in a North–American Perspective." In *Essays on Quebec Cinema*. Edited by Joseph I. Donohoe, Jr.,145–55. East Lansing: Michigan State UP, 1991.

Jameson, Frederic. *The Geopolitical Aesthetic*. London: BFI Publishing, 1992.

Jean, Marcel. "Jean–Claude–Lauzon." *24 Images* 90 (Winter 1998): 21.

———. *Le cinéma québécois*. Montreal: Boréal, 1991.

Johnson, Brian D. "A Bold and Blissful Leap of Faith." *Maclean's* 108, no. 31 (July 31, 1995), 42–44.

Johnson, Claudia L. "Introduction." In *Jane Austen's Mansfield Park: Final Shooting Script*, 1–10. New York: Hyperion Talk Miramax Books, 2000.

Jones, Kent. "Body and Soul: The Cinema of Atom Egoyan." *Film Comment* 34, no.1 (1998): 32–37, 39.

Jutras, Pierre, Réal La Rochelle and Pierre Véronneau, eds. "Denys Arcand: Entretien, points de vue et filmographie." *Copie Zéro* 34–35 (1988): 76.

Kasischke, Laura, *Suspicious River*. New York: Houghton Mifflin, 1996.

Kaufman, Anthony. "Poetics and Perseverance—Thom Fitzgerald of *The Hanging Garden*." *Indiewire*. http://www.indiewire.com/people/int_Fitzgerald_Thom_980514.html. Accessed 14 May 2005.

Killorn, Donnie, "FUBAR fine Canadian cinema." *Charlotteown Guardian*, 9 August 2002, C5.

Kunuk, Zacharias. "I want to show people who are not worrying about money" [Interview with Peter Steven]. In Peter Steven, *Brink of Reality: New Canadian Documentary Film and Video*, 155–65. Toronto: Between the Lines, 1993.

Kunuk, Zacharias and Puhipau [Joan Lander and Puhipau Nā Maka o ka 'Āina]. "Puhipau in Conversation with Zacharias Kunuk." In *Magnetic North: Canadian Experimental Video*. Edited by Jenny Lion, 218–25. Minneapolis and Winnipeg: University of Minnesota Press, Walker Art Center and Video Pool, 2000.

La Rochelle, Réal. *Denys Arcand: L'ange exterminateur*. Montréal: Leméac, 2004.

Laderman, David. *Driving Visions: Exploring the Road Movie*. Austin: University of Texas Press, 2002.

Lafon, Dominique. "Pour servir à la petite histoire d'un mélodrame québécois: la leçon d'un tapuscrit." *L'Annuaire théâtral* 17 (1995): 37–51.

Lafrance, André: *Cinéma d'ici*. Montreal: Leméac, 1973.

Leach, Jim. *Claude Jutra: Filmmaker*. Montréal: McGill-Queen's University Press, 1999.

Lefebvre, Martin. "A Sense of Time and Place: The Chronotope in *I Confess* and *Le Confessionnal*." *Quebec Studies* 26 (Fall 1998/Winter 1999): 88–98.

Lever, Yves. *Cinémas et société québécoise*. Montreal: Editions du Jour, 1972.

———. *Histoire générale du cinéma au Québec*. Montreal: Boréal, 1995.

Lewis, Jason, "Fearless Filmmaker." *FFWD Weekly* (Calgary), 25 September 2003, 2. Available online at: www.ffwdweekly.com. Accessed 8 February 2007.

Lind, Jane. *Joyce Wieland: Artist on Fire*. Toronto: James Lorimer & Co., 2001.

Lind, Laura. "Real Life: Cautionary Tale of Two Provinces." *Eye Weekly* (Toronto), 21 August 1997, 21.

Lippard, Lucy. *Joyce Wieland*. Toronto: Key Porter Books, 1987.

"Lorraine Chan in Conversation with Mina Shum." *Reverse Shot* no. 1–2 (Summer 1994): 34.

Loiselle, André. "The Radically Moderate Canadian: Don McKellar's Cinematic Persona." In *North of Everything*. Edited by Beard and White, 256–69.

———. *Stage-Bound: Feature Film Adaptations of Canadian and Québécois Drama*. Montreal: McGill-Queen's UP, 2003.

Loiselle, André and Brian McIlroy, eds. *Auteur/Provocateur: The Films of Denys Arcand*. Wiltshire: Flicks Books, 1995.

Longfellow, Brenda. "Gender, Landscape and Colonial Allegories in *The Far Shore*, *Loyalties*, and *Mouvements du désir*." In *Gendering the Nation: Canadian Women's Cinema*. Edited by Armatage, 165–82.

Magidson, Debbie and Judy Wright. "Making Films for Your Own People: An Interview with Denys Arcand." In *Canadian Film Reader*. Edited by Seth Feldman and Joyce Nelson, 217–34. Toronto: Peter Martin, 1977.

Major, Ginette. *Le cinéma québécois à la recherché d'un public*. Montreal: Les Presses de l'Université de Montréal, 1982.

Manning, Erin. "The Haunted Home: Colour Spectrums in Robert Lepage's *Le Confessionnal*." *Canadian Journal of Film Studies* 7, no. 2 (1998): 49–65.

Marchessault, Janine, "Feminist Avant-Garde Cinema: From Introspection to Retrospection." *Cineaction*, nos. 24/25 (1991): 30–37. Reprinted in *Gendering the Nation: Canadian Women's Cinema*. Edited by Armatage, 137–47.

Marks, Laura U. "Inuit Auteurs and Arctic Airwaves." *Fuse Magazine* 21, no. 4 (Fall 1998): 13–17.

———. "Nice Gun You Got There: John Greyson's Critique of Masculinity." *Parachute* 66 (1992): 27–32.

———. "Reconfigured Nationhood: A Partisan History of the Inuit Broadcasting Corporation." *Afterimage* 21, no. 8 (March 1994): 4–8.

Marshall, Bill. *Quebec National Cinema*. Montreal: McGill-Queen's UP, 2001.

Masterson, Donald. "Family Romances: Memory, Obsession, Loss, and Redemption in the Films of Atom Egoyan." *University of Toronto Quarterly* 71, no. 4 (2002): 881–91.

McCoy, Heath. "FUBAR: Pair wrestles with life's realities". *Calgary Herald*, 24 May 2002, E3.

McDonald, Bruce. "Scaling the Heights." *Cinema Canada* 141 (May 1987): 12–14.

———. "Dear Norman, What is to be done?" *Cinema Canada* 122 (Sept. 1985): 10–12.

———. "Listen, you screwheads." *Cinema Canada* 156 (October 1988): 4–5.

———. "Pictures." *The National Post*, 24 May 2004, D6.

McKay, John and Alexandra Burroughs, "Calgarian's film big winner." *Calgary Herald*, 20 September 2004, E1.

McRuer Robert. "As Good As It Gets: Queer Theory and Critical Disability." *GLQ* 9, no. 1–2 (2003): 79–105.

Melnyk, George. *One Hundred Years of Canadian Cinema*. Toronto: U of Toronto P, 2004.

Mendenhall, Marie. "Through the Lens of Robert Lepage: Special Effects in Theater and Film." *West Virginia University Philological Papers* 47 (2001): 96–102.

Monk, Katherine. "When the scene destroys its king." *The Vancouver Sun*, 10 June 2005, D1.

———. *Weird Sex & Snowshoes and other Canadian Film Phenomena*. Vancouver: Raincoast Books, 2001.

Morris, Peter. "In Our Own Eyes: The Canonizing of Canadian Film." In, *Responses in Honour of Peter Harcourt*. Edited by Blaine Allan, Michael Dorland, and Zuzana Pick. Toronto: The Responsibility Press, 1992.

Morris, Peter. *David Cronenberg: A Delicate Balance*. Toronto: ECW Press, 1994.

Naficy, Hamid. *An Accented Cinema: Exilic and Diasporic Filmmaking*. Pinceton, New Jersey: Princeton UP, 2001.

Noguez, Dominique. *Essais sur le cinéma québécois*. Montreal: Editions du Jour, 1970.

Nowell, Iris. *Joyce Wieland: A Life in Art*. Toronto: ECW Press, 2001.

Parpart, Lee. "Political Alignments and the Lure of 'More Existential Questions' in the Films of Patricia Rozema." In *North of Everything*. Edited by Beard and White, 294–311.

Pevere, Geoff. "Indie Route Runs Through Suburbs." *Globe & Mail*, 12 September 1997.

———. "In Others' Eyes: Four Canadian Films Come Home from Cannes." *Cineaction* 11 (Winter 1987–1988): 21–9.

———. "Letter from Canada." *Film Comment* 28, no. 2 (1992): 61, 63–65.

———. *Mondo Canuck*. Toronto: Prentice Hall, 1996.

———. "The Rites (and Wrongs) of the Elder *or* The Cinema We Got: The Critics We Need." In *Documents in Canadian Film*. Edited by Douglas Fetherling, 323–36. Peterborough: Broadview Press, 1988.

Pevere, Geoff, and Greig Dymond. *Mondo Canuck: A Canadian Pop Culture Odyssey*. Scarborough: Prentice Hall, 1996.

Pierson, John. *Spike, Mike, Slackers and Dykes: A Guided Tour Across A Decade of American Independent Cinema*. New York: Miramax Books, 1995

Poirier, Christian. *Le Cinéma québécois. À la recherche d'une identité? Tome 1. L'imaginaire filmique*. Montreal: Presses de l'Université du Québec, 2004.

———. *Le Cinéma québécois. À la recherche d'une identité? Tome 2. Les politiques cinématographiques*. Montreal: Presses de l'Université du Québec, 2004.

Propp, Vladimir. *Morphology of the Folktale*. 1928. 2 ed. Translated by Lawrence Scott. Austin: U of Texas P, 1968.

Rabinowitz, Lauren. *Points of Resistance: Women, Power, & Politics in the New York Avant-Garde Cinema, 1943–71*. Urbana: U of Illinois P, 1991.

Ramsay, Christine. "Canadian Narrative Cinema from the Margins: 'The Nation' and Mascuslinity in *Goin' Down the Road*." *Canadian Journal of Film Studies* 2, no.2 (1993): 27–50.

———. "Greyson, Grierson, Godard, God: Reflections on the Cinema of John Greyson." In *North of Everything*. Edited by Beard and White, 192–205.

Reid, Michael D. "Crude, rude and, admit it, a piece of our past." *Victoria Times-Colonist*, 13 June 2002, D6.

Robinson, Gillian, ed. *Atanarjuat: The Fast Runner*. Toronto: Coach House Books, 2002.

Rodley, Chris, ed. *Cronenberg on Cronenberg*. Toronto: Knopf, 1992.

Romney, Jonathan. *Atom Egoyan*. London: British Film Institute, 2003.

Russell, Catherine. "Role Playing and the White Male Imaginary in Atom Egoyan's 'Exotica'." *Canada's Best Features: Critical Essays on 15 Canadian Films*. Edited by Eugene Walz, 321–46. Amsterdam and New York: Rodopi, 2002.

Russell, David. "Two or Three Things We Know About Beineix." *Sight and Sound* 59, no. 1 (Winter 1989–1990): 42–47.

Sawhney, Pam. "A Success Story for Slackers: An Interview with *waydowntown* Writer/Director Gary Burns." *MovieMaker* 2, no. 20: 4. Available online at: http://www.moviemaker.com/hop/editorial.php?id=381. Accessed 9 February 2007.

Schwartz Dennis. "The ensemble acting is quite good." *Ozus World Movie Reviews*, 19 June 1999.

Schwartz, Nina. "Exotic Rituals and Family Values in 'Exotica'." In *Perversion and the Social Relation*. Edited by Molly Anne Rothberg, Dennis Foster, and Slavoj Žižek. Durham and London: Duke University Press, 2003.

Shary, Timothy. "Present Personal Truths: The Alternative Phenomenology of Video in *I've Heard the Mermaids Singing*." *Wide Angle* 15, no. 3 (July 1993): 37–55.

Shipman, Nell. *The Silent Screen and My Talking Heart*. Boise, Idaho: Hemingway Western Studies Series, 1987.

Simmons, Rochelle. "Border Crossings: Representations of North American Culture in Bruce McDonald's *Highway 61*." *Cineaction* 61 (2003): 58–61.

Sklar, Robert. "Of Warm and Sunny Tragedies: An Interview with Denys Arcand." *Cinéaste* 18, no. 1 (1990): 14–16.

Sperounes, Sandra, "Putting the proper spin on a DJ's disintegration." *Edmonton Journal*, 24 June 2005, G1.

Stone, Tammy. "Thom Fitzgerald." *The Canadian Film Encyclopedia (online)*. http://www.filmreferencelibrary.ca/index.asp?layid=46&csid1=19&navid=46. Accessed 10 April 2005.

Stone, Jay. "Dowse spins funny DJ tale." *The Kingston Whig-Standard*, 29 July 2002, 21.

———. "Quirky mockumentary fuelled by ale and f-word." *Ottawa Citizen*, 14 June 2002, D3.

———. "The headbangers next door." *Ottawa Citizen*, 11 June 2002, B7.

Stukator, Angela. "*Guide to the Cinemas of Canada*, *Take One's Essential Guide to Canadian Film*, and *Weird Sex & Snowshoes and Other Canadian Film Phenomena* (book reviews)." *Canadian Journal of Film Studies* 11, no.2 (Fall 2002): 101–05.

Schwartz, Nina. "Exotic rituals and Family Values in 'Exotica'." In Perversion and the Social Relation. Edited by Molly Anne Rothberg, Dennis Foster, and Slavoj Žižek, 93–111. Durham and London: Duke UP, 2003.

Tanner, Louise. "Chinese Girl Leaves Home." *Films in Review* 46 (November–December 1995): 112–13.

Telmissany, May. "La citation filmique comme anachronisme." *Essays on Canadian Writing* 76 (2002): 247–62.

Testa, Bart, "Technology's Body: Cronenberg, Genre, and the Canadian Ethos." *Post Script* 15, no. 1 (Fall 1995): 38–56.

———. 'The Decline of Frivolity and Denys Arcand's American Empire.' In *Canada's Best Features: Critical Essays on 15 Canadian Films*. Edited by Eugene P. Walz, 175–206. Amsterdam, Rodopi, 2002.

———. "Denys Arcand's sarcasm: a reading of *Gina*." In *Dialogue: cinéma canadien et québécois/Canadian and Quebec Cinéma*. Edited by Pierre Véronneau, Michael Dorland, and Seth Feldman, 203–22. Montréal: Mediatext Publications and La Cinémathèque québécoise, 1987.

Toronto Star. "Toronto Winner Is a Maverick," *GTA Today*, 27 September 2000, 32.

Tremblay, Odile. "Tourner en anglais au Québec," *Le Devoir*, 10 and 11 Juin 2000, B1.

Trusky, Tom, ed., *Letters From God's Country: Nell Shipman Selected Correspondence And Writings, 1912–1970*. Boise, Idaho: Hemingway Western Studies Series, 2003.

Tschofen, Monique. "Repetition, Compulsion, and Representation in Atom Egoyan's Films." In *North of Everything*, edited by Beard and White, 166–83.

Tschofen, Monique, and Jennifer Burwell, eds. *Imaginative Territories: New Essays on Atom Egoyan*. Waterloo, ON: Wilfrid Laurier UP, 2006.

Vaïs, Michael. "Robert Lepage: un homme de théâtre au cinéma." *Jeu* 88, no. 3 (1998): 123–30.

Vatnsdal, Caelum. *They Came From Within: A History of Canadian Horror Cinema*. Winnipeg: Arbiter Ring, 2004.

Vermee, Alison. "Identification Marks." *Take One: Film & Television in Canada*. No. 6 (Fall 1994): 46–49.

Véronneau, Pierre, and Piers Handling, eds. *Self Portrait: Essays on the Canadian and Quebec Cinemas*. Ottawa: Canadian Film Institute, 1980.

Walls Widgett. "*The Hanging Garden*." www.Needcoffee.com. Accessed May 26, 2005.

waydowntown press kit. Odeon Films, Toronto, 2000.

Weinmann, Heinz. "*Un Zoo la nuit*: Le Québec amnésique." In *Cinéma de l'imaginaire québécoise: De La Petite Aurore à Jésus de Montréal*, 107–20. Montreal: L'Hexagone, 1990.

———. *Cinéma de l'imaginaire québécois: De La Petite Aurore à Jésus de Montréal*. Montreal: L'Hexagone, 1990.

WestEnder. "'Mock biopic' of deaf DJ fools, inspires, and garners Leos," 9 June 2005, 17.

White, Murray. "Where Films Made in English Can Seem a Cultural Betrayal." *The New York Times*, 17 September 2000, Sec. 2, 11.

Wyndham Wise, ed. *Take One: Special Edition*. September–November 1994.

Yoram, Allan, ed. *Contemporray North American Film Directors—A Wallflower Critical Guide*. London: Wallflower Press, 2002.

Žižek, Slavoj. *For They Know Not What They Do: Enjoyment as a Political Factor*. London: Verso, 1991.

———. *The Fragile Absolute—or, Why is the Christian Legacy Worth Fighting For?* London: Verso, 2000.

Contributors

Kay Armatage is Professor at the University of Toronto, where she holds a cross-appointment to the Cinema Studies Institute and the Women's and Gender Studies Institute. She is the author of *The Girl from God's Country: Nell Shipman and the Silent Cinema* (U of Toronto Press, 2003) and co-editor of *Gendering the Nation: Canadian Women's Cinema* (U of Toronto Press, 1999). She has also produced and directed documentary and experimental films including *Artist on Fire: The Work of Joyce Wieland* (1987).

Brenda Austin-Smith is Associate Professor of Film and English at the University of Manitoba. She has published essays on Particia Rozema, Henry James, Lars von Trier, film adaptation, prairie filmmaking, Bette Davis and personal modernity, and women's emotional responses to film melodrama. She served as President of the Film Studies Association of Canada in 2004–05.

William Beard is Professor of Film Studies at the University of Alberta. He is co- editor of *North of Everything: English-Canadian Cinema since* 1980 (U of Alberta Press, 2002) and the author of *Artist as Monster: The Cinema of David Cronenberg* (U of Toronto Press, 2001 and second edition 2005), and *Persistence of Double Vision: Essays on Clint Eastwood* (2000). Besides work on New German Cinema, Hollywood modernism and Guy Maddin, he has published articles on Atom

Egoyan in *Imaginative Territories: New Essays on Atom Egoyan* (eds.Monique Tschofen and Jennifer Burwell) and *24 Frames: Canada* (ed. Jerry White).

Bart Beaty is Associate Professor, Faculty of Communication and Culture at the University of Calgary. He is the author of *Fredric Wertham and the Critique of Mass Culture* (University Press of Mississippi, 2005), *Unpopular Culture: Transforming the European Comic Book in the 1990s* (University of Toronto Press, 2007) and, with Rebecca Sullivan, *Canadian Television Today* (University of Calgary Press, 2006). With Will Straw, he is the co-editor of the University of Toronto Press's Canadian Cinema book series.

Sally Chivers is Assistant Professor in Canadian Studies and English at Trent University. She is the author of *From Old Woman to Older Women: Contemporary Culture and Women's Narratives* (Ohio State University Press, 2003), and her current research is in the area of Canadian Disability Studies. She is editing an anthology of film and disability with Nicole Markotić.

David Clandfield is Professor of French and Cinema Studies at New College in the University of Toronto. His writings on Canadian and Québécois cinema have appeared in English and other languages. His most recent book is *Pierre Perrault and the Poetic Documentary* (TIFF and Indiana University Press, 2004). He is currently working on a history of sensuality in French culture.

Peter Dickinson is Assistant Professor in the Department of English at Simon Fraser University. He is the author of *Here is Queer: Nationalisms, Sexualities, and the Literatures of Canada* (U of Toronto Press, 1999) and *Screening Gender, Framing Genre: Canadian Literature into Film* (U of Toronto Press, 2007), and co-editor, with Richard Cavell, of *Sexing the Maple: A Canadian Sourcebook* (Broadview Press, 2006).

Jennifer L. Gauthier is Assistant Professor of Communications Studies at Randolph College (founded as Randolph-Macon Woman's College in 1891) in Virginia, where she teaches courses in rhetoric, film studies, and cultural studies. She has published in *TOPIA: The Canadian Journal of Cultural Studies*, *Cineaction*, and *The Canadian Journal of Film Studies*. She has presented her work on national cinema, cultural policy and indigenous film at both national and international conferences.

Christopher Gittings is Associate Professor in and Chair of the Department of Film Studies at the University of Western Ontario. He has taught film studies at the University of Birmingham, UK and the University of Alberta. His publications include *Canadian National Cinema* (Routledge, 2002) and *Imperialism and Gender: Constructions of Masculinity* (Dangaroo, 1996).

Patricia Gruben is a filmmaker, who has made experimental narratives, documentaries and dramatic features. She is Associate Professor of Film in the School for the Contemporary Arts at Simon Fraser University. She has contributed to a book on Atom Egoyan titled *New Essays on Atom Egoyan* (Wilfrid Laurier University Press, 2005), as well as articles on important Hollywood films. She is currently developing a historical drama set in the nineteenth century.

Jim Leach is Professor of Communications, Popular Culture, and Film at Brock University. His publications include *British Film* (Cambridge University Press, 2004), co-editor, *Candid Eyes: Essays on Canadian Documentaries* (University of Toronto Press, 2003), and *Claude Jutra: Filmmaker* (McGill-Queens University Press, 1999). His most recent book is *Film in Canada* (Oxford University Press, 2006).

Jacqueline Levitin is a filmmaker and a film historian-critic. She has written, produced and directed a number of films and videos. Her special focus is women filmmakers and national schools of filmmaking. She is co-editor of *Women Filmmakers: Refocusing* (2003). She teaches in both the School for Contemporary Arts and Women's Studies at Simon Fraser University.

Nicole Markotić is Associate Professor in Creative Writing, Canadian Literature and Disability Studies at the University of Windsor. She has published a novella, two poetry books, edited *By Word of Mouth: The Poetry of Dennis Cooley* (2007), and has published widely on contemporary film, literature, and disability theory.

George Melnyk is Associate Professor, Faculty of Communication and Culture, University of Calgary. His specialty is the history of Canadian cinema. He has published *One Hundred Years of Canadian Cinema* (University of Toronto Press, 2004) and is the editor of *Great Canadian Film Directors* (University of Alberta Press, 2007). He is currently co-editing a book on Canadian women filmmakers.

Kalli Paakspuu is an award-winning filmmaker, theatre, and new media artist completing a dissertation, "Colonial Rhetorics of Visual Documentation" at the University of Toronto. She has published on cross-cultural photography, developed new media games at the Canadian Film Centre and is working on a feature-film adaptation of Liliane Atlan's "Les Mers Rouges. "

Paul Salmon teaches English and Film Studies in the School of English and Theatre Studies at the University of Guelph. He has published widely on Canadian and international cinema and runs the "Beyond Hollywood" film series at the University of Guelph. He has served as secretary-treasurer of the Film Studies Association of Canada.

Aaron Taylor is a Limited Term Assistant Professor in the Department of Communications, Popular Culture and Film at Brock University. His doctoral dissertation (University of Kent, UK) is a study of villainy and "perverse allegiance" in American cinema. He has published on both Canadian and American cinema in *The Journal of Film and Video*, *The Journal of Popular Culture*, *The Canadian Journal of Film Studies* and *Cineaction*.

Bart Testa teaches cinema studies at Innis College, University of Toronto. He is the author of *Back and Forth: Early Cinema and the Avant-garde* (1992). He has published extensively on a variety of cinema subjects and lectured frequently in the US, Mexico, Italy, Austria and Germany on experimental film and Canadian cinema.

Pierre Véronneau is a widely known and respected member of the Canadian film studies community. He is curator of Quebec and Canadian film at the Cinémathèque québécoise in Montreal, with which he has been associated since 1973. He is Adjunct Professor of Film at the Université de Montréal and the Université du Québec à Montréal. Most recently, he has published on David Cronenberg (*La beauté du chaos*, Cert-Corlet, 2003).

Jerry White is Associate Professor of Film Studies at the University of Alberta and a member of the education staff of the Telluride Film Festival. He publishes in scholarly journals, writes for film magazines such as *Cinemascope* (Toronto) and *Dox* (Copenhagen), and contributes regularly to *Books in Canada*. He is co-editor of *North of Everything: English-Canadian Cinema Since 1980* (University of Alberta Press, 2002), editor of *The Cinema of Canada* (Wallflower Press, 2006), and author of *Of This Place and Elsewhere: The Films and Photography of Peter Mettler* (Toronto Film Festival/Indiana University Press, 2006).

Photo Credits

Mina Shum, p. 270. Photo courtesy of Shaftesbury Film Inc.

Gary Burns, p. 294. Photo courtesy of Burns Film Ltd.

Michael Dowse, p. 312. Photo courtesy of Esther Choi.

Thom Fitzgerald, p. 328. Photo courtesy of Thom Fitzgerald and Emotion Pictures.

Zach Kunuk, p. 346. Photo by Oana Spinu, courtesy of Lucius Barre.

Don McKellar, p. 362. Photo courtesy of Camilla Pucholt Photography.

Lynne Stopkewich, p. 384. Photo courtesy of Lynne Stopkewich.

Index

shorts
"Beerland," 295; "Happy
Valley," 295, 300
Sundance Film Festival, 302
television
Cool Money, 308; Northern Town
(mini-series), 308
Toronto International Film
Festival, 295, 302, 304, 306,
308, 309
Burrage, Ron, 181
Burroughs, Jackie, 370
Burroughs, William S., 81, 88, 203
Burton, Richard Francis, 136
Bussières, Pascale, 255, 262
Butler, Judith, 388

Cadieux, Anne-Marie, 187, 192
Cage, John, 203
Cage, Nicholas, 156, 335
Cagle, Robert, 136, 257, 260
Calendar, 103, 112, 114, 123n7
ethnicity and ethnic identity,
117–19
narrative structure in, 101, 122n2
themes in, 104–5, 106–7, 111
Calgary, 299, 304, 309, 314
Calgary Herald, 321, 324–25
Calota, Mihai, 333
Calvin College, 255
Camera cinema, 372
Cameron, James, Aliens, 87
Camilla, 368
Canada Council for the Arts, 209,
224n22, 295, 331
Canada First movement, 11
"Canada Uncut," 330–31
Canada Uncut: the Roaring 90s
(festival), 330–31
Canadian cinema, xviiin2, 170n24
audience for, x, xviiin1, 92

Canadian archetypes, 323–25
Canadian identity and, 309–10,
367
diversity in, xvii
Fothergill on, 313–14, 315, 316, 317,
323, 324, 325–26, 377
globalization and, 355–59
growth of, ix
nationalist concept of, 325–26
queer nationalism and, 130–31
stereotypes of, 6, 7, 8, 9, 10, 12–13,
314
Canadian Film Awards
The Far Shore, 5, 24n5
Mouvement Perpétuel, 36
Canadian Film Centre, 133, 138,
146n40, 151, 205, 288n3
Canadian Film Development
Corporation (CFDC), 82–83,
84, 92
Canadian Film Encyclopaedia, 211
Canadian Film Institute, 367, 371
Canadian Filmmakers Distribution
Cooperative, 17
Canadian liberalism, 156–58, 161–63
Canadian National Cinema (Gittings), 7
Canadian Perspective program, 308
Canadian Wildlife Service, 207
Canby, Vincent, 129
Cannes Film Festival
Atanarjuat: The Fast Runner, xi
Le Confessionnal, 180
Crash, 89
Le Déclin de l'empire américain, 73
A History of Violence, 91
Les Invasions barbares (The Barbarian
Invasions), 75–76
I've Heard the Mermaids Singing, 255,
258
Jésus de Montréal, 74
Last Night, 363, 371

French-Canadian culture, 261–62
independence movement, 41–42,
    43, 44n6
October Crisis, 33, 42, 44n7, 69,
    187, 188
Office National du Film (ONF),
    68, 69, 72
Parti Québécois, 31, 42
Quiet Revolution, 37–38, 68
and sovereignty association, 50,
    187–89
Quebec cinema
  audience for, x, xviiin1, 73, 92
  child motif in, 60
  English-Canadian cinema and, 49
  government funding, 247
  questioning of, 71–72
  role of ONF in, 68, 69
  and sovereignty association, 50
  tensions in, 61
  women's issues, 245–49
Québec: Duplessis et après..., 69–70, 72
Québécois *automatistes*, 33–34
Queer as Folk, 201
queer cinema, 125–47, 272
  AIDS activism and, 132
  gay and lesbian film festivals, 130
  government funding, 131
  homophobia, 134, 145n28, 331, 341
  "Homo Pomo," 131–32
  Le Dément du Lac Jean-Jeunes, 36
  New Queer Cinema, 131–32
  Toronto New Wave, 202
Queer Looks: Perspectives on Lesbian and Gay
    Film and Video, 129
queer theory
  and heterosexual normalcy, 334
  homographesis, 126
  queer activism, 132–33
Quiet Revolution, 33, 37–38
Quíntin (Edgardo Antín), 355–56

Amélie, 356–57
Qulitalik, Pauloosie, 349, 355
Qulliq/Oil Lamp, 350

Rabid, 83, 84, 89, 378
Rabinowitz, Lauren, 6, 18–19
race and racism, 211
Rached, Tahani, 73
Radiant City, 308–9
Radio-Canada, 247, 348
Rafelson, Bob, 154
Ramone, Joey, 205, 206
Ramsay, Christine, 51, 55, 137, 138,
    377
Randoja, Ingrid, 374
Rat Life and Diet in North America, 7, 10,
    20
Rayn, Tony, 129
Reagan, Ronald, 204, 224n32
realist style, 296–99, 318–19
Reason Over Passion, 4, 7, 10, 11–12
Red River, 127
Red Tape (stage play), 364
Red Violin, The, 332, 364, 371, 378
Reed, Oliver, 378
Reflections of a Siamese Twin (Saul), 359
Refus Global, 34
Reid, Michael, 322
Reiner, Carl, 152, 168n10
Reitman, Ivan, *Meatballs*, 313
Réjeanne Padovani, 70–71
Renaud, Gilles, 34
Rennie, Callum Keith, 370, 373
Rennie, Michael, 192
Reno, Ginette, 55
Renoir, Jean, 76
Resnais, Alain, 177
revisionist cinema, 253–69
Rhombus Media, 368, 369
Rich, Adrienne, 232, 235
Rich, B. Ruby, 131